GLOBAL ISSUES

TERRORISM AND GLOBAL SECURITY

Ann E. Robertson

Foreword by James O Ellis III

Memorial Institute for the Prevention of Terrorism

Viva Books

New Delhi | Mumbai | Chennai | Kolkata | Bangalore | Hyderabad | Kochi | Guwahati

First Indian Edition 2010

VIVA BOOKS PRIVATE LIMITED

- 4737/23 Ansari Road, Daryaganj, New Delhi 110 002
  E-mail: vivadelhi@vivagroupindia.net, Tel. 42242200
- 76, Service Industries, Shirvane, Sector 1, Nerul, Navi Mumbai 400 706
  E-mail: vivamumbai@vivagroupindia.net, Tel. 27721273, 27721274
- Jamals Fazal Chambers, 26 Greams Road, Chennai 600 006
  E-mail: vivachennai@vivagroupindia.net, Tel. 28290304, 28294241
- B-103, Jindal Towers, 21/1A/3 Darga Road, Kolkata 700 017
  E-mail: vivakolkata@vivagroupindia.net, Tel. 22836381, 22816713
- 7, Sovereign Park Apartments, 56-58, K. R. Road, Basavanagudi, Bangalore 560 004
  E-mail: vivabangalore@vivagroupindia.net, Tel. 26607409, 26607410
- 101-102 Mughal Marc Apartments, 3-4-637 to 641, Narayanguda, Hyderabad 500 029
  E-mail: vivahyderabad@vivagroupindia.net, Tel. 27564481, 27564482
- First Floor, Beevi Towers, SRM Road, Kaloor, Kochi 682 018, Kerala
  E-mail: vivakochi@vivagroupindia.net, Tel: 0484-2403055, 2403056
- 232, GNB Road, Beside UCO Bank, Silpukhuri, Guwahati 781 003
  E-mail: vivaguwahati@vivagroupindia.net, Tel: 0361-2666386

www.vivagroupindia.com

Published by arrangement with

Facts on File, Inc.
132 West 31st Street
New York 10001
USA

ISBN 978-81-309-1425-1

Published by Vinod Vasishtha for Viva Books Private Limited, 4737/23, Ansari Road, Daryaganj, New Delhi-110 002. Printed and bound by Anand Sons, Delhi - 110 092.

CONTENTS

Foreword

Though Edmund Burke coined the term *terrorism* in the 18th century to describe Robespierre's Reign of Terror during the French Revolution, acts of terrorism have been documented as early as 66 C.E. between the Zealots and the Romans. Throughout time, it has reappeared as an instrument of manipulation and desperation for those who think they require fear to further their cause. At its heart, terrorism is a method to gain social, economic, and political concessions and to provoke change, often through the appearance of government overreaction or underreaction to violence against civilians.

Despite its ancient roots, terrorism has only received formal study for a few decades. Much of the scholarship on terrorism has focused almost exclusively on international terrorism—terrorism involving the citizens of more than one country. As this book helps to make clear, however, terrorism is usually a domestic phenomenon. Within the United States, groups such as the Ku Klux Klan have long sown violence and hate, and terrorism has been a part of this country's story since its founding.

For most of the 19th and early 20th centuries, the major form of terrorism confronting the United States came from within the country rather than without. Anarchists, anti-alienists, and violent labor movements perpetrated the majority of terrorist acts during this time period. Radicals called for "propaganda by the deed" and depended upon the "philosophy of the bomb." Unabashedly proclaiming themselves to be terrorists, some anarchists sought to inspire the masses to revolution through spectacular acts of terrorism meant to show that the powerful could be made vulnerable. This violence spread into parts of the labor movement, sparking explosions at bridges and factories across the country. Prominent government and business figures, including John D. Rockefeller, J. P. Morgan, and Supreme Court Justice Oliver Wendell Holmes were also targeted. In September 1919, a huge bomb exploded on Wall Street, damaging the headquarters of J. P. Morgan and the stock exchange, killing 29 people.

Following the end of World War II, terrorism in the United States increasingly came from extreme left, right, and nationalist-separatist groups. Domestic unrest emerged from the Civil Rights movement and the anti–Vietnam War movement. Though both of these movements had admirable aims and ultimately changed the character of our society, elements associated with them perpetrated considerable violence and terrorism. Left-wing radical terrorists pursued open class warfare and revolution against what they perceived to be an oppressive and racist capitalist system. Groups such as the Symbionese Liberation Army, the New World Liberation Front, and the Weather Underground used violence in the name of the poor or for social justice. These organizations were often fellow travelers with African-American separatist groups that occasionally resorted to terrorist activity, such as the Black Liberation Army or the Black Panther Party, whose members conducted two hijackings. Other notable nationalist or separatist groups during this period have included the Cuban Omega-7, the Croatian Freedom Fighters, and the Puerto Rican Armed Forces of National Liberation (FALN). As you will read, Puerto Rican nationalists have carried out hundreds of attacks, including an attempt to assassinate President Harry S. Truman and an assault in the gallery of the U.S. House of Representatives.

American right-wing extremists, on the other hand, have often employed terrorism to preserve the status quo or restore previously existing circumstances. These groups often embrace some form of racism, anti-Semitism, and anti-government rhetoric as part of their ideology. Organizations such as Posse Comitatus and The Order oppose taxes and gun control, while others focus on white supremacy and survivalism. Many within this movement have been inspired by William Pierce's book, *The Turner Diaries,* which provided a blueprint for the violent overthrow of the U.S. government and helped inspire Timothy McVeigh to commit the Oklahoma city bombing on April 19, 1995. Some right-wing groups include an element of separatism as well, such as the Aryan Nations, which has sought the creation of an independent, whites-only homeland. In discussing right-wing terrorists, however, it is important to remember that militia members and survivalists are not always terrorists. Militias, however, often provide an environment where terrorist groups and lone wolves can grow and flourish. In recent times, secular terrorists have lost momentum when compared to religious fanatics.

Much has been written about the current wave of Islamic fundamentalist terrorism targeting western countries in general and the United States in particular. However, many fail to appreciate the significant history of other types of religious extremist terrorism. For example, members or groups such as the Jewish Defense League and Kach have been responsible for bombings, shootings, arson, and kidnapping. Members of the Sikh faith have also used terrorism in America including several murders and bombings. Cults and religious sects have even resorted to bioterrorism, as was the case with the mass poisoning by the Bhagwan Shree Rajneeshees in Oregon. This volume also describes the acts of the Covenant, Sword and Arm of the Lord—a Christian fundamentalist terrorist group. Some of these Christian Identity followers assert that the white Aryan race is God's chosen race, that whites comprise the lost tribes of Israel, and that a cleansing process must occur before Christ's kingdom can be established on earth. This cleansing may only be brought about by a violent and bloody struggle—a war between God's forces and the forces of evil. They use violence to punish violators of God's law, killing interracial couples, abortionists, prostitutes, and homosexuals, burning pornography stores, robbing banks, and perpetrating frauds to undermine the "usury system."

Since the attacks of September 11, 2001, attention to terrorism has increased dramatically, though it has been a feature of the political and cultural landscape of America throughout its history. No one category of people has monopolized the use of terrorism in the United States. Groups from many political ideologies, religious persuasions, nationalities, and ethnicities have been associated with extremist violence at one time or another in the United States. Indeed, the groups, causes, and incidents are so vast and varied that it is very difficult to give a comprehensive overview, but Dr. Robertson is to be commended for the thorough survey that follows. It is important to remember that it is not the political or religious view that makes one a terrorist, nor is there anything inherently suspect about holding unconventional or even radical views. The advocacy and use of these ideas as the basis for violence, however, moves beyond the acceptable dialogue, debate, and protest enshrined in the American system. In a democratic society, taking up arms in furtherance of a cause is a sign of weakness, not strength, and those who do so admit their own inability to convince others through a reasonable exchange of ideas.

In the modern age, terrorism often takes the form of assassinations, bombings, kidnappings, hostage situations, hijackings, arson, and armed assaults. Though many of today's terrorist groups use the same time-tested tactics, they increasingly operate in new and unconventional ways. Terrorists typically do not control territory, wear uniforms, carry their weapons openly, or maintain permanent bases. Many groups have evolved into networks and movements with fluid organization and infrastructure and little formal leadership. This change requires less frequent communication, making them much more difficult to spot, track, and intercept. Most experts believe terrorism is becoming more sporadic, more difficult to predict, and more difficult to trace. Terrorism is increasingly perpetrated by amateurs and splinter groups with hazy objectives and short life spans. The ease of international travel, Internet communication, and free-flowing finance means that terrorism cannot be contained within particular countries or regions. Radical ideologies inspire individuals across the globe, making international cooperation a must in dealing with terrorism in the 21st century.

Researching and understanding such a complex mix of acts, actors, and countries is no easy task. This volume, however, offers a compelling summary of the history of terrorism, its key players, and recent developments in world events. Combining facts and figures, important source documents, and useful tools, this book should help you make sense of the current terrorist threat and the political reactions to it. It is a valuable starting point for further research on this subject, and it provides ample avenues for additional resources and reference. The threat of global terrorism will undoubtedly persist, and it is incumbent upon this generation to meet this challenge to our national security and way of life. Through shared knowledge, we are better prepared to deal with the forces that shape our world and to lead in trying times.

— James O Ellis III
Research and Program Director
Memorial Institute for the Prevention of Terrorism

PART I

At Issue

1

Introduction

Most political and academic experts would agree that terrorism is the greatest threat to global security in the 21st century. Few of those experts, however, would agree about a definition of what exactly constitutes terrorism. Books on terrorism usually include a chapter on the fact that there is no prevailing definition. There is no standard international definition of terrorism nor is there even one single definition used by the U.S. government. Almost none of the proponents of this form of political expression would admit to being a terrorist, preferring to call themselves more glamorous terms such as *freedom fighters, guerrillas,* or *mujahideen.* Yet the images of violence, hatred, and death that appear in the daily newspaper are posted on Internet chat rooms and blogs and are shown on the evening news help perpetuate the main purpose of terrorism: to create an atmosphere of fear—of terror.

For most Americans the terrorist attacks of September 11, 2001, are a watershed event. Before that date the United States had suffered occasional attacks on its citizens abroad, but the homeland remained secure, and public safety focused on ordinary dangers such as crime, fire, flood, and influenza. After 9/11, new fears intruded on daily life: al-Qaeda, anthrax, unclaimed packages left in public areas, young men who "appear" to be Muslim. Americans were now forced to face a clever enemy that could seemingly attack any time, any place. In short, Americans now had to face the same security threats with which other countries had lived for decades.

The terrorist attacks of September 11 will be a defining event for Americans. Just as earlier generations remember exactly where they were when they learned of John F. Kennedy's assassination, the explosion of the *Challenger* space shuttle, or the death of Princess Diana, 9/11 marks the moment many American adolescents became aware of how international events and the broader outlines of global security issues can have a personal impact. The subsequent U.S. "War on Terrorism" also dramatically changed the terms of a possible career in the military. While some high school students may choose to enlist, learn Arabic, and serve in Afghanistan or Iraq, others remain at home while their parents fight overseas, mourn the death of brothers, sisters, and friends, or protest military recruitment drives on campus.

This book offers a broader survey of terrorism than the brief sound bites heard on television or talk radio and provides more background than the typical newspaper or magazine article. Specifically, this book makes three key points about terrorism and global security.

First, the perpetrators of 9/11 did not invent terrorism. It is a form of political drama that is 2,000 years old. The vocabulary of modern terrorism is largely taken from the name of historical terrorist groups. *Thugs,* for example, were a terrorist group active from the seventh through at least the 13th century, which sought to appease the Hindu goddess Kali through violence. Similarly, *Assassins* were a group that sought to purify Islam by stabbing infidels from 1090 to 1275. Perhaps the oldest recorded terrorist group is the *Zealots,* Jewish terrorists who sought to drive Roman rulers and Greek settlers out of the Holy Land in the period 66–73.[1] With the French Revolution of 1789 terrorism was used to pursue nonreligious goals, and Russian anarchists, nihilists, and populists of the 19th century refined it as a tool for political, economic, and social change. Terrorism can be sponsored by a country, such as in revolutionary France, Libya in the 1980s, or Syria, Cuba, and Iran; they use individuals or groups to carry out the actual attack.[2] Terrorism can be conducted by structured groups against specific targets, such as the Palestine Liberation Organization against Israel in the 1970s or the Tupac Amaru movement against the government of Peru in the 1980s. Some terrorist operations are carried out by small groups formed for a specific attack, such as the 1993 World Trade Center bombing. Terrorism can also be conducted by the solitary terrorist, such as Timothy McVeigh in Oklahoma City in 1995 and Eric Rudolph at the Atlanta Olympic Games in 1996. Prior to 2001, the United States had largely been insulated from international terrorism, as Europe and the Middle East were the main focus of terrorist organizations. While there were few foreign-triggered terrorist attacks in the United States, there were cases of homegrown terrorists, such as the Weather Underground (usually called "Weathermen") and the Symbionese Liberation Army, both active in the early 1970s.

Acts by these groups differ significantly from other bloody assaults attributed to extremists, such as the Unabomber, Theodore Kaczynski, or the homicidal students at Columbine High School near Denver, Colorado, in 1999. While these actors were certainly violent, they do not qualify as "terrorists." They were motivated by revenge; they were not trying to force a government to adopt a different course of action. Similarly, states may themselves use terror to control their populations, such as Stalin's Soviet Union of the 1930s, Nazi Germany, fascist Italy, or Argentina, Chile, and other Latin-American authoritarian regimes of the 1970s and 1980s. This type of political violence is a separate phenomenon and will not be covered in this text. As terrorism expert Bruce Hoffman explains, "These state-sanctioned or explicitly ordered acts of *internal* political violence directed mostly against domestic populations . . . are generally termed 'terror' in order to distinguish that phenomenon from 'terrorism,' which is understood to be violence committed by non-state entities."[3] Acts committed directly by states against another country's citizens are acts of war, not terrorism.

Second, not all terrorists are Muslims and not all Muslims are terrorists. Due to the background of the 9/11 attackers and the forces the United States subsequently fought in Iraq and Afghanistan some people think of terrorists as Muslim, but this profile only applies to the most visible group of terrorists active today. The majority of terrorist groups currently operating in the United States actually are populated by white male Christians seeking to curtail federal authority or college-educated environmental activists, and terrorist factions are found far from the Middle East in places such as the Philippines, Colombia, Northern Ireland, Nepal, Sri Lanka, and Spain. These groups may be pursuing an independent state for their ethnic group (Irish Republican Army, the Tamil Tigers of Sri Lanka, or the Basque people of Spain) or to implement a communist-style political system in an existing country (the New People's Army of the Philippines, Colombia's Revolutionary Armed Forces, Shining Path in Peru, and Nepal's People's Liberation Army).

Finally, terrorism is typically a battle fought by young, often well-educated individuals, demographic characteristics that are not always discussed in the media. What would motivate a teenager or 20-something to become a suicide bomber? Too often the backgrounds of terrorists are glossed over, quickly dismissed as religious zealotry. But since at least the 19th century, perceived socioeconomic and political injustices have caused the sons and daughters of the middle and upper classes to take up arms on behalf of the poor to change government policies.

WHAT IS TERRORISM?

Terrorism is a political strategy whereby groups or individuals use violence against civilian or symbolic targets to persuade a government to change a specific policy. It is a strategy particularly useful in democracies, retired foreign service officer Marc Nicholson writes, whereby "terrorists seek to wear down the voting majority until it is so sick of strife and uncertainty as to consent to a political solution by meeting the minority's demands."[4] Terrorism is not an ideology, a political party, or a goal, but a *method* of achieving a particular goal. Terrorists seek to disrupt daily life to effect change. They draw their power both from the violence of their activities and from the unpredictability of who a group chooses to target. If anyone anywhere could become a victim of terrorism at any time, frightened citizens might pressure their government to take action. However, governments rarely give in to terrorist demands, preferring instead to eliminate terrorist groups. Even more rarely do governments work to alleviate the causes of terrorism, such as poverty, alienation, and perceived discrimination.

Terrorist and *terrorism* are negative words applied to people who commit appalling crimes. However, most terrorists reject those terms for themselves. They see themselves as *freedom fighters, guerrillas,* holy warriors, or martyrs rather than terrorists. Therefore, writes terrorism expert Bruce Hoffman,

> *The decision to call somebody or label some organization "terrorist" becomes almost unavoidably subjective, depending largely on whether one sympathizes with or opposes the person/group/cause concerned.*[5]

Watching television news or reading newspapers offers students a fairly good impression of what terrorism entails. But when it comes to writing a precise definition, one to be used for criminal prosecutions, for example, no one can quite agree on the wording. Therefore countries and international organizations have taken a piecemeal approach, focusing on specific actions, such as hijacking, hostage taking, or financing such illicit activities. In the United States terrorists are more apt to be arrested for possession of illegal firearms, failure to observe local laws, or tax evasion than for terrorism.

Use of Violence

Although the many definitions use different terminology, they all usually focus on three characteristics. First, terrorists use violence to draw attention to their cause. They seek to frighten populations and governments by damaging people, property, or both. If they provoke enough fear, according to this logic, then governments will agree to meet their demands in order to stop the violence.

Historically, their weapons have been low-tech: the knife, the gun, and the bomb. They stab leaders, shoot tourists, plant bombs aboard airplanes, and crash trucks loaded with explosives into buildings. The terrorists of the 1960s and 1970s frequently sought to minimize the loss of life, killing only one or two highly visible individuals, in order to attract attention to their cause. That self-imposed boundary against slaughter began to erode in the 1980s, and in the 1990s terrorist attacks became markedly more lethal. For example, in the 1980s, the FBI recorded 267 terrorist events in the United States, causing a death toll of 23 people. In the 1990s those numbers changed to 60 attacks and 182 lives lost.[6]

Innocent Targets

Second, terrorists attack innocent targets. On occasion terrorists have successfully attacked the individuals they hold responsible for a particular grievance. Terrorists assassinated Russia's Czar Alexander II in 1881, Egyptian president Anwar Sadat in 1981, and Israeli prime minister Yitzhak Rabin in 1995. In each case the victim was blamed for a particular policy: Czar Alexander II by radicals dissatisfied with the scope of his political reforms, Sadat by Egyptian soldiers for signing a peace accord with Israel, and Rabin by a Jewish extremist angry that Israel had negotiated a peace agreement with the Palestinians. But more often the victims of terrorists are casual bystanders. They are the people who happen to be shopping when a bomb explodes in a market, the passengers aboard a hijacked airplane, the parents and children trapped inside a school or theater overrun by terrorists.

Some terrorists choose their targets for symbolic reasons. Although they have no direct grudge against a particular businessman, a chief executive officer might be kidnapped as a symbol of "capitalist domination." For example, West Germany's Red Army Faction (aka the Baader-Meinhof Gang) kidnapped and executed the president of the German Employers' Association, Hanns Martin Schleyer, in 1977 and killed the head of Deutsche Bank, Alfred Herrhausen, with a car bomb in 1989. More recently, Africa's Movement for the Emancipation of the Niger Delta (MEND) has kidnapped foreign oil workers in Nigeria, demanding that Shell and other foreign oil companies go home and allow locals to benefits from the Delta region's vast oil holdings.

Terrorists who oppose policies of the United States government may detonate bombs at U.S. facilities abroad, such as embassies or military barracks. For example, the Red Army Faction bombed U.S. and NATO military bases in West Germany as well as the U.S. Embassy in Bonn. In El Salvador, the Central American Revolutionary Workers Party killed four U.S. Marines and two U.S. businessmen dining at an outdoor café in the Salvadoran capital in 1985. Al-Qaeda sponsored near-simultaneous attacks on the U.S. embassies in Kenya and Tanzania in August 1998.

Radicals might attack popular tourist sites hoping to damage the economy in the process. In October 2002 Jemaah Islamiah, a militant Islamic group, attacked a nightclub in Kuta on the Indonesian island of Bali, killing

202 people, primarily foreign tourists. The following year foreign tourism to Indonesia dropped by 48 percent.[7] New York City's office of tourism marketing reported that the 9/11 attacks resulted in a $1 billion loss in tourism revenue in the last three months of 2001.[8] In Washington, federal buildings shut down and Reagan National Airport was closed for three weeks following the attacks. Tourism experts in the District of Columbia estimated that the city lost $10 million in revenue each day the airport was dark. Museum attendance plummeted 70 percent, hotel occupancy rates halved, and 25,000 hospitality employees lost their jobs.[9]

The U.S. tourism industry has yet to recover fully from the 9/11 attacks, the subsequent anthrax scare, and tightened visa regulations. In 2005 foreign visitors to the United States were down 9 percent from the level seen in 2000. This drop occurred despite a 17 percent global increase in foreign travel. "Had the USA kept pace with the increase of foreign travel around the world," *USA Today* estimated, "an additional 9 million foreigners would have visited [in 2005]. The USA's lost opportunity: more than $12 billion in spending and 150,000 new jobs."[10]

Attacks may be scheduled to coincide with an important date. The suicide bombing in Bali took place exactly two years after the 2000 suicide bombing of the USS *Cole* while docked in Yemen; both incidents were attributed to groups linked to al-Qaeda. Nearly a decade earlier Timothy McVeigh chose to blow up a U.S. government office building on April 19, 1995, the second anniversary of U.S. government actions against the Branch Davidian religious sect in Waco, Texas; exactly 10 years earlier federal agents had raided a compound belonging to the Covenant, the Sword, and the Arm of the Lord, a Christian separatist group in Arkansas.[11] Although investigations suggest that the 9/11 attackers had several possible dates in mind, it remains an eerie coincidence that the operation was executed on a date—September 11—that matches the familiar U.S. telephone number for emergencies: 9-1-1.

Drawing Attention to a Cause

Third, terrorists want to draw attention to their cause. They seek to create an unforgettable image that announces their presence and conveys their grievance to a larger audience. More important, "Terrorists do not want to win the hearts of ... the people they target and even not those who look on in the international realm," argues terrorism and media expert Brigitte Nacos. "They want the attention. And they want people to know what are their causes, what are their grievances."[12] Similarly, psychiatrist Fredrick Hacker wrote 30 years earlier: Terrorists want "to frighten and, by frightening to dominate and control. They want to impress. They play for an audience and solicit audience participation. Their appearances and disappearances are carefully staged and choreographed to get maximum attention."[13] British prime minister Margaret Thatcher famously said, "We must try to find ways to starve the terrorist and the hijacker of the oxygen of publicity on which they depend," but she also noted the almost irreconcilable dilemma of limiting media coverage in a democratic society.[14]

The point is to gain publicity for a cause, and terrorists seem to subscribe to the old Hollywood saying, "There is no such thing as bad publicity." Jamil Al Gashey, the last surviving member of the Palestinian team that assassinated Israeli athletes at the 1972 Munich Olympics, proudly recalled, "Before Munich, the world had no idea about our struggle, but on that day, the name of 'Palestine' was repeated all over the world."[15] A statistical study of U.S. newspaper coverage of Muslim and Palestinian issues before and after 9/11 found a 10-fold jump in the number of paragraphs devoted to these topics. When Osama bin Laden explained that his goals included peace in Palestine and gaining respect for Muslims, reporters frequently turned to Palestinians and Muslims for their reaction, providing them greater visibility and higher status, possibly creating a greater level of respect for their viewpoint. In this aspect, at least, the 9/11 attacks were a success for bin Laden.[16]

That need for publicity creates ethical issues for journalists covering terrorist events. If they attempt to explain the motives behind the event they can be accused of aiding an outlaw group. If they give too much attention to the victims of an attack they may create extreme pressure on a government to give in to terrorist demands. "Public opinion polls reveal that a majority of Americans agree that we should never negotiate with terrorists," Nacos commented, "but in a time of crisis public opinion flip-flops. The media's efforts usually enhance the public siding with victims. As this shows, terrorists have achieved their objective. They've coerced government officials indirectly through the media."[17] The media tend to report only the bloodiest, most sensational cases or unfolding dramas such as hostage crises, ultimately providing the public with a distorted view of the situation. "Most people may think that Italy is constantly convulsed by terrorist battles," wrote Brian Jenkins in 1981, "but visitors to that country see no trace of it. The media exaggerates the strength of the terrorists, creating the illusion of their omnipresence."[18] Few terrorist groups have more than 20 to 25 members, but the media attention can inflate the group's influence. Adding the word *army* to the name of a terrorist group also helps exaggerate the group's size and significance.

At times, journalists may go to extreme measures to appear unbiased. Nearly 20 years after the tragedy, ABC newsman Peter Jennings still faced biting criticism for his stilted reporting of the Israeli hostage crisis at the 1972 Munich Olympics, in which members of the Palestinian Black September movement held 11 Israeli athletes hostage on live television. In reviewing a 2000 documentary on the incident, *Washington Post* television critic Tom Shales pointed out, "Not once in the footage used in the documentary do we hear the reputedly pro-Palestinian Jennings refer to the terrorists as 'terrorists.' He will only go so far as to use the much more benign word 'guerrillas.' Once he even uses the rather glamorizing term 'commando.' What was going through this strange and stupid man's mind?"[19]

The June 1985 hijacking of TWA Flight 847 is considered a prime example of media-encouraged terrorism at its worst. For 17 days Hezbollah terrorists held 40 crew members and passengers hostage. They killed a U.S. Navy diver, Robert Stethem, who happened to be on the flight and dramatically pushed his body out of the plane onto the tarmac. The U.S. media gave near constant coverage to the incident, repeatedly interviewing frantic relatives. NBC's *Today* show flew hostage families to Germany, housing them in luxury hotels in return for "exclusive" comments.[20] The terrorists gladly obliged by arranging press conferences with the hostages and daily briefings for the press corps. An Australian correspondent even apologized to the terrorists for the confusion caused by their rush for prime positions at the news conferences.[21] Perhaps the most embarrassing media intrusion came when David Hartman, anchor of ABC television's *Good Morning America,* helpfully asked the terrorists, "Any final words for President Reagan this morning?" Another ABC reporter had the opportunity to interview the pilot, John Testrake, and, while a hijacker held a gun to the pilot's head, asked, "Captain, many people in America are calling for some kind of a rescue operation or some kind of retaliation. Do you have any thoughts on that?"[22] What answer did the reporter really believe he would receive? U.S. reporters competed for the best coverage, accusing rivals of questionable ethics. According to *Newsweek,* "When ABC won an exclusive interview with [Testrake], NBC and CBS refused to relinquish previously booked satellite time so that ABC could transmit its tape right away."[23] The networks sniped at each other, with ABC and CBS accusing NBC of locking hostage families into "exclusive" deals[24] and CBS anchor Dan Rather looking down his nose at networks that aired live interviews. "We believe, that is CBS believes," Rather explained, "that there is some danger in putting the hostages on with an interview like this. . . . We just think we have to keep control of the air."[25] The print media, trying to scoop the live television coverage, tipped off the terrorists to a possible rescue attempt by reporting movements of the U.S. military's elite Delta Force. As one exasperated Pentagon spokesperson complained, "There seem to be more respect for the next fall's scripts for 'Dynasty' and 'Dallas' than there is for U.S. contingency plans."[26]

Great Britain went to the opposite extreme to keep members of the Irish Republican Army and Sinn Féin, the IRA's political wing, out of the public eye. From 1988 to 1994 British television and radio outlets were banned from broadcasting the voice of Sinn Féin president Gerry Adams. Instead broadcasts would show video of Adams mutely moving his mouth while his words either appeared in subtitles or with his comments dubbed in by actors.[27] These efforts to censor provocative statements wound up as fodder for satirists.

After the attacks of 9/11 several media outlets, including Reuters news agency and the British Broadcasting Corporation, deliberately chose not to use the "t-word," because it was a "politically loaded" term. Even after the July 7, 2005, London attacks, the BBC advised using the term *bomber,* rather than *terrorist.*[28] The *Chicago Tribune* opted only to label as *terrorism* incidents that affected Americans, therefore 9/11 was committed by terrorists, but the suicide bombers attacking Israel or Sri Lanka were a different species altogether.[29] When Osama bin Laden began to release videotaped messages after 9/11, the five leading American television networks agreed to edit the tapes before broadcast, because the statements might contain coded messages for his followers.[30]

Deliberate Planning

Terrorist attacks may appear to be random, but their target, method, and purpose are usually very carefully researched, selected, and carried out. According to Bruce Hoffman, "The terrorist act is specifically designed to communicate a message.... it is also conceived and executed in a manner that simultaneously reflected the terrorist group's particular aims and motivations, fits its resources and capabilities, and takes into account the 'target audience' at which the act is directed."[31]

Terrorist acts are rarely impulsive. In fact, they normally require a considerable level of technical training and a large dose of ideological instruction—or brainwashing, depending on one's perspective. Famed Palestinian hijacker Leila Khaled described her preparation to *Aviation Security* magazine: "I had to read about the aircraft, how it works. I don't know everything about the aircraft, but ... just [enough] to make the captain understand that we know everything about the aircraft and we can do the same thing [fly the plane] he is doing if he didn't obey."[32] Similarly, the 9/11 hijackers underwent extensive flight school training in the United States. (The oft-repeated story that rejected hijacker Zacarias Moussaoui told his flight instructors that he only needed to know how to fly—not take off or land—an airplane is an urban legend.)

The increasing use of suicide bombers reveals the deep commitment many terrorists hold for their cause. They are so confident of their purpose that they are willing to die. This fatal belief is most often found in religious-based terrorist groups, where members believe they are carrying out their god's orders and will be rewarded in the afterlife. The last words on the cockpit voice recorder of United Flight 93, the 9/11 plane that crashed short of its target, were "Allah is the greatest!" repeated nine times.[33]

But while suicide bombings are becoming more popular among Islamist terrorist groups, they are following the example set by the Liberation Tigers of Tamil Eelam (LTTE), a secular group seeking a homeland for the Tamil people. Since launching their guerrilla war against the government of Sri Lanka in 1976, LTTE members have carried out more than 200 suicide bombings, often seeing it as a last recourse when negotiations fail. Tamil suicide bombers tend to be young people with few job prospects and many grievances against the Sri Lankan government. They see extreme violence through suicide as their only way to strike back at the authorities, a view encouraged by Villupilai Prabhakaran, the LTTE's charismatic leader.[34]

Suicide bombers typically leave "martyr statements"—letters or videotaped statements expressing the reasons for their sacrifice, so that their message does not get lost in the tragedy. Suicide attacks are also cheap: about $150 for supplies and training. Families of successful suicide bombers usually are given $3,000–5,000 by the organizers.[35] The preparation cost for 9/11 is estimated at $400,000–500,000,[36] while the economic damage has been estimated at $54 billion for New York alone.[37] The July 7, 2005, London bombings cost less than $2,000.[38] Suicide bombers are typically more accurate than conventional bombs, they can make last-minute target adjustments, and they are often more deadly because they can penetrate deeper into target zones. According to one major study of the phenomenon, "the average suicide attack [is] twelve times deadlier than other forms of terrorism."[39]

Unlike their predecessors, terrorists of the 21st century are starting to take a more random approach to selecting their targets. The aim of terrorism, according to Walter Laqueur, "is no longer to conduct propaganda but to effect maximum destruction."[40] But who are these people? What makes them so angry—or hopeless—that they turn to murder or even suicide?

WHO ARE THE TERRORISTS?

Before looking at the characteristics of individuals who choose to become terrorists, it is important to remember that terrorism is heavily influenced by local conditions. Social problems, ethnic conflict, or religious differences may encourage terrorism in one setting but not in others. It is also extremely difficult to gather data about terrorists; individuals planning to commit massive crimes are not likely to give interviews, and the families of suicide bombers and other terrorists killed in action may stretch the truth to influence how their loved ones are remembered. Psychology also plays a role; some personality types are more prone to manipulation, hopelessness, or delusions of grandeur. But despite these numerous differences, a few characteristics are seen more often than others.

Terrorists rarely act alone. They usually band together with like-minded individuals to formulate their strategies. The groups may be very small and isolated into cells—small groups that operate independently so that if one cell is exposed to the authorities, the entire group's membership and plans are not revealed. Movements usually have a supreme, often very charismatic leader and may have specialized divisions for finance, recruitment, training, and even public relations. The Communist Party of Nepal (Maoist) even has a song-and-dance troupe.[41] If the group is religious-based, it will typically have some sort of cleric or minister to justify the cause and sanction any potentially criminal activities.

Terrorists may claim to be acting on behalf of the poor or another repressed group, but their own backgrounds rarely include poverty or hardship. More often terrorists are from middle-class families and have university degrees. The Japanese doomsday cult Aum Shinrikyo, observed the *New York Times,* "was remarkable in several respects. It attracted brilliant young university graduates, particularly scientists, and put them to work developing biological and chemical weapons."[42] The four men behind the July 7, 2005, bombings in London had been born in England, and their high school friends regarded them as remarkably assimilated. A classmate of Mohammad Sidique Khan, the ringleader, remembers him avoiding Asians, avoiding mosques, and wearing cowboy boots and a leather jacket.[43] Three, including Khan, were children of Pakistani immigrants, and at least two had recently visited Pakistan where they attended radical Islamic schools. They returned with a deeper focus on religion and began to withdraw from secular activities before they traveled from the town of Leeds to London.[44]

In a landmark study, Nasra Hassan, an international relief worker, interviewed some 250 militant Palestinians who either recruited, trained, or aspired to be suicide bombers. Many had staged unsuccessful attacks and thus lived to describe their motivations. Hassan found that "none of them were uneducated, desperately poor, simple-minded, or depressed ... two were the sons of millionaires."[45] Though female, an anomaly discussed below, Uzbek suicide terrorist Dilnoza Holmuradova also fits this character profile quite well. At age 19, Holmuradova spoke five languages, was independent enough to hold a driver's license, and had even attended the local police academy before she killed herself in a March 2003 attack on a market in Tashkent, the capital of Uzbekistan.[46]

Walter Laqueur of the Center for International and Strategic Studies notes that terrorism long has been attractive to educated youth, as demonstrated by the leftist terrorist groups in the United States, Latin America, and Western Europe in the 1970s. He suggests several explanations for this pattern of middle- and upper-class attraction to terrorism. First, an operative in a foreign country would need knowledge of a separate culture and language in order to assimilate, and this demographic group often has been exposed to different cultures and traveled extensively. Second, their "advanced" education may, in fact, not be secular or broad-minded. As governments have slashed spending for education, religious groups have stepped in to fill the void. As a result, some young men and boys considered to be "well-educated" have only experienced a curriculum with religious overtones. Individuals may also choose to travel abroad to study at a madrassa, an Islamic religious school. Pakistan alone has some 30,000 madrassas, many with a reputation for spreading radical Islam.[47] Two of the London 7/7 bombers had studied in such schools in the two years prior to the 2005 attack. One, Hasib Hussein, "came back a changed young man, dressing in the robes of the devout and devoting to religion the energy he had once reserved for schoolyard fights."[48] Third, they may be frustrated by a lack of opportunity to use their training. In many less-developed countries there are high birth rates and too few jobs for college-educated citizens, leading to restlessness, resentment, and anger.[49]

Typically, terrorists are young people who have identified social inequalities and injustices in their country and are seeking ways to correct this imbalance. Alan Krueger of Princeton University and Jitka Maleckova of Charles University in Prague have suggested that higher education might in fact make potential terrorists more aware of and sensitive to discrimination and inequality.[50] Unfortunately their strategies are often misplaced. As the 19th-century Russian anarchists and populists discovered, assassinating top government officials did not improve the plight of the peasantry. In fact, by going for the most visible targets, such as Czar Alexander II and Prime Minister Pyotr Stolypin, they often killed the most reform-minded among the leadership, ensuring a repressive backlash. Believing that reforms had led to his father's murder, for example, Alexander III instituted one of the harshest regimes in Russian history.

Terrorism is an occupation for the young, the idealistic, and the naïve. Most terrorists, either recruits or volunteers, tend to be in their 20s. One study of Palestinian suicide bombers found that the majority were unmarried men between 17 and 28 years old.[51] They may be disillusioned or angry that jobs are not available for them due to their local economies. By and large, terrorism is a phase of political development. If they are not themselves killed in suicide attacks, in time young operatives tend to turn to other methods to pursue their goals.

While communist-oriented terrorist groups often have influential female members, female terrorists are still a novelty in the eyes of the media. In Muslim regions they are even rarer, as the strictest interpretations of Islam—such as those favored by Osama bin Laden—segregate the sexes. The media find female terrorists particularly fascinating and may play up their roles. *Newsweek,* for example, ran a feature story on women Muslim terrorists in its December 12, 2005, issue, with a cover photo of a veiled woman staring intently into the camera. Possibly the most famous female terrorist has been Palestinian activist Leila Khaled, who became known for successfully hijacking a TWA flight departing Rome for Athens in August 1969, forcing the pilot to land in Damascus, Syria. She became even more famous when the Popular Front for the Liberation of Palestine (PFLP) attempted to hijack four aircraft simultaneously on September 6, 1970. While the other three attacks were successful, Khaled was recognized, arrested, and jailed in London.

In retrospect, Khaled has no regrets about her actions, claiming that she brought much-needed attention to the Palestinian issue. "We hijacked planes," she recalls, "because the whole world was deaf when we were screaming from our tents, and nobody heard our suffering. Until the beginning of the revolution in 1967, Palestinians were only dealt with as people needing humanitarian aid, not as people with a cause."[52] The PFLP was also encouraged when the British government agreed to swap Khaled for Westerners held hostage from the other three hijackings. "The success in the tactics of the hijacking and imposing our demands and succeeding in having our demands implemented gave us the courage and the confidence to go ahead with our struggle."[53] Despite the similarities between the four 1970 PFLP hijackings and the four hijackings on September 11, 2001, Khaled refuses to see any connection. "That [9/11] was an act of terror and did not serve a humanitarian cause," she says. "What we did was a means of struggle," she recalled. "We said why we were doing the operation. Those who killed themselves and others in New York had no cause. We didn't kill anybody."[54] Similarly, she denounced the July 2005 London bombings, "Those who did it, they are the real terrorists, because they are aiming at innocent people, and nobody knows what they want."[55]

For all of Leila Khaled's notoriety, female terrorists are not a completely rare breed. One contemporary estimate believes that almost one-third of terrorists active today are female.[56] Khaled herself noted that there were many active Palestinian women when she joined the movement after the 1967

Six-Day War.[57] Women were particularly prominent in the left-wing terrorist groups of the 1970s, such as the Baader-Meinhof Gang in West Germany, the Italian Red Brigades, and the Weather Underground and the Symbionese Liberation Army based in the United States. Media coverage of female terrorists tends to be narrow-minded and somewhat romanticized, focusing on what could have led these women astray (boyfriends, broken hearts, boredom, feminism, and so on) rather than accepting that they might truly have political convictions. Journalists often write more about the women's clothing and physical demeanor than their politics. "If one takes the news at face value," writes media analyst Nacos, "female terrorists are almost always good-looking, trim, and pleasant."[58] However, the tendency to dismiss the possibility of female terrorists may actually give them an edge. There are reports from Ireland to Iraq, for example, of "pregnant" women who are actually concealing bombs under their clothing. They might approach a police offficer or security checkpoint, cry for help, and then detonate the explosives.[59] Furthermore, acts committed by female terrorists often receive additional publicity due to their higher shock-value.

What is a recent development among female terrorists is their increasing participation in suicide terrorism. The first female suicide bomber in the contemporary Middle Eastern conflict was Wafa Idriss, a 28-year old Palestinian woman who blew up a shopping area in Jerusalem in 2002. She quickly acquired a cultlike status, with press accounts describing "dreamy eyes and a mysterious smile on her lips," much like the Mona Lisa.[60] The most notorious group of female suicide bombers is known as the "Black Widows." These are women from Chechnya who have reportedly lost their husbands, brothers, and fathers to the decade-long Chechen campaign for independence from Russia. The phenomenon was first seen when a group of Chechens seized a theater in Moscow in 2002; half of the group were women dressed head to toe in black with bombs strapped to their bodies. The Black Widows were blamed for a series of explosions around Moscow subway stations as well as two simultaneous midair explosions of Russian passenger jets in August 2004. But as with the female terrorists of the 1970s, the women are assumed to be motivated solely by personal revenge, not political principles.[61] Reports frequently describe the women as desperate and hopeless because their families somehow consider them to be "damaged goods" (perhaps from rape, divorce, or infertility) and they believe that suicide is their only escape.[62]

WHAT DO THE TERRORISTS WANT?

Terrorists can be categorized by their motives and their methods. Based on their ultimate goals, terrorists, like any political group, can be classified along a spectrum of beliefs. Groups classified as "left-wing" or "leftist" oppose capitalism and plan to institute a communist (far left) or socialist system that would eliminate most or all forms of private property. Left-wing groups promote social equality and equal access to economic, educational, social, and political resources for all, and they want to change the political system to achieve this goal. At the opposite end, right-wing groups tend to resist change, hail the importance of tradition for society, and favor a hierarchical society in which some groups have more privileges than others. Religious-based groups tend to fall into this category, as do racist movements such as the Nazi party or the Ku Klux Klan.

Most of the earliest known terrorist groups were based on religion, and much of the terminology of terrorism comes from groups that were active centuries ago, namely the Zealots, Thugs, and Assassins mentioned above[63]

Religious-based terrorism tends to be the most brutal because the actors believe that even their most heinous crimes have the endorsement of their supreme being. Only 25 percent of the 278 recorded terrorist attacks in 1995 were committed by religious-oriented groups, but they counted for 58 percent of the fatalities for that year.[64] Plots often require the blessing of a religious scholar before they are enacted. Furthermore, while social-activist terrorism is often trying to win an audience over to its cause, religious terrorists have a more violent aim—eliminating the "wicked non-believers," whether men, women, or children.[65] James Ellison, founder of the militant Christian movement the Covenant, the Sword, and the Arm of the Lord, made his views clear to CSA members:

> *The ZOG, this Zionist Occupied Government, is killing our white babies through abortion! It is destroying white minds with its humanistic teachings of evolution! I tell you this—n****** may be descended from apes, but my ancestors never swung from trees by their tails. In order to preserve our Christian heritage and race, it is our right, our patriotic duty, to overthrow the Antichrist government!*[66]

Terrorism also goes in cycles. After centuries of religious-based terrorism, many movements of the 19th and 20th centuries were based on rectifying social wrongs such as demanding a political voice for a particular repressed population, such as the Tamils, Algerians, or Palestinians. Bruce Hoffman notes that beginning about 1990, "as the number of religious terrorist groups was increasing, the number of ethno-nationalist/separatist terrorist groups declined appreciably."[67]

As terrorism began to swing back toward religious justifications in the 1990s, the number of victims increased correspondingly. Groups were no longer satisfied with drawing attention; now they wanted to eliminate the enemy. Their "aim is to convey rage or to exact revenge with little thought to long-term consequences."[68] The simultaneous collapse of communism in Eastern Europe and the Soviet Union meant that political ideologies—especially ones based on Marxism—lost their popularity. As a consequence, the next generation of disaffected young people often turned to older codes of morality, ones based on religion. Internationally, the most prominent religious-based groups are Islamic fundamentalists, devotees who advocate strict adherence to the Koran, including governance based on Islamic law (sharia). "With the resurgence of fundamentalism came a recurrence of fanaticism," writes former National Security Council staffer Jessica Stern. "The idea of saving the souls of their victims is certainly alien to the present-day terrorists," writes Laqueur. "On the contrary, victims should be annihilated so that there should be no remembrance of them."[69] In the United States home-grown terrorists tend to be white Christian supremacists, who believe that the federal government has been corrupted by Jews, African Americans, and Hispanics.

The structure of terrorist groups also began to change in the 1990s. Instead of hierarchically organized groups with clearly identified goals and leaders, 21st-century terrorists tend to be loose groups of like-minded individuals whose main goal is less political reform than creating havoc or simply exterminating the enemy. While the leftist terrorists of the 1970s such as the Baader-Meinhof Gang, the Weathermen, and the Symbionese Liberation Army were co-ed groups that tended to live together in communal housing and often have romantic entanglements, the 9/11 attackers were a disparate group of men who were assigned to work together for a single purpose. Terrorist groups are now more diverse, drawing individuals from multiple countries and funding from multiple sources. According to Rear Admiral Hamlin Tallent, the director of the U.S. European Command's European Plans and Operations Center,

> *Originally, back in 2000 and before, for instance, al-Qaeda had somewhat of a hierarchical structure, a leadership-to-operations-to-tactics kind of structure that you see at IBM or any large organization. What we see now is a change in this. We see the enemy changing into something that has less symmetric lines of understanding, less symmetric lines of power. So instead of having an IBM-type of organization, now you have a franchising situation. It's like McDonald's. There are all different kinds of these things all over the world. They generally have their own way of doing things, they just use a kind of a common menu. And this is all supported by the Internet.*[70]

The Internet in particular has facilitated a decentralized structure by allowing rapid communications across long distances. Terrorist groups can distribute encrypted messages, maps, and diagrams across the World Wide Web.[71] They also use the Internet to recruit, raise funds, and research potential targets.

TERRORIST TACTICS

In the earliest recorded terrorist instances, attackers used simple weapons to kill their victims. The Zealots slit throats with daggers, the Assassins used swords, while the Thugs strangled their targets. In the 19th and 20th centuries guns and bombs were popular weapons. Terrorists can plant bombs and detonate them remotely or strap explosives to their body and detonate themselves when they are near the target. Attackers can also ram explosive-laden cars, trucks, or airplanes into targets. But as technology advanced in the 20th and 21st century, new methods became available.

Hijacking

Aviation and communications evolved at a similar pace in the 1960s and 1970s, providing opportunities for terrorists to seize large groups of people in a controlled, self-contained environment and to broadcast their demands to worldwide audiences. Security was also fairly lax in the early days of commercial aviation, with few baggage inspections, metal detectors, or transit police. Would-be hijackers, such as the Palestinian operatives in 1969 and 1970, were able to smuggle guns and hand grenades easily on board their flights. Minimal computerization also made it difficult to profile passengers or prescreen passenger lists. One key characteristic of hijackings, at least prior to September 11, 2001, was that the passengers were considered hostages to be traded for specific demands; the hijackers did not necessarily plan to kill anyone. As Palestinian hijacker Leila Khaled recalled, "We were given very strict instructions that we shouldn't hurt anybody, and we had to make the pilot and the crew comfortable."[72]

Hijacking proved to be a short-lived technique, as airlines and national security agencies rapidly enacted precautions and closed security gaps. In the 1970s and 1980s terrorists kidnapped victims in hopes of negotiating—or extorting—lucrative ransoms from the families or employers of the hostages, said Nacos. "Up to Munich basically when we talked about international terrorism we talked about hijackings and bombings. Afterwards . . . you moved towards more hostage situations, and of course then when you had the Iranian hostage situation that fueled even more of those."[73]

Kidnapping

Kidnappers have specific targets in mind and do not capture random individuals to carry out their plans. They snatch their targets in violent raids and then announce who they have and what they want.

Some of the more notorious U.S.-related cases of the 1970s involved employees of the U.S. Embassy in Tehran and U.S. newspaper heiress Patricia Hearst. During the 1979 revolution in Iran, religious leader Ayatollah Ruhollah Khomeini encouraged anti-American protests. Iranians were angry that Washington had allowed their deposed ruler, Shah Mohammad Reza Pahlavi, to enter the United States for medical treatment. As the demonstrations swelled, a crowd of hundreds surged forward and seized the U.S. Embassy and 66 American employees. Although a few hostages were initially released, 53 were held until January 20, 1981—a total of 444 days. A number of factors contributed to the ultimate resolution of the crisis, including Iran's war with Iraq that began in 1980, the death of the shah in July 1980, and Jimmy Carter's defeat in the U.S. presidential election. The hostages were released 30 minutes after Ronald Reagan was inaugurated on January 20, 1981. The hostage crisis created a dramatic, ongoing story for the media. ABC news began a nightly update on "The Iran Crisis: America Held Hostage." The regular segment, hosted by Ted Koppel, counted the days the hostages had been held and re-aired images of blindfolded hostages and burning American flags. The updates eventually became the long-running series *Nightline.*[74]

Before the Iran hostage crisis, the United State was transfixed by the kidnapping of Patty Hearst. The Symbionese Liberation Army (SLA) kidnapped newspaper heiress Patricia (Patty) Hearst on February 4, 1974, from her apartment in Berkeley, California. The SLA consisted of about a dozen people in their 20s seeking to mobilize students and African-American prisoners. They wanted to improve the lives of African Americans who were impoverished by capitalism in the United States and to promote racial harmony. They robbed at least two banks, planted a few small bombs, murdered a public school superintendent, and mainly spent their time plotting and honing their firearms skills. Their goal in kidnapping Hearst was twofold: to attract publicity to their cause and to swap her for two jailed SLA members. When their scheme did attract enormous publicity, particularly from audiotapes released to the media of Hearst explaining their ideology, they changed their demands to a $6 million ransom. The ransom was ultimately paid in food donated to the poor, but Hearst was not released. She remained with the group until she was arrested by the police in September 1975, and at trial claimed she had been brainwashed into sympathizing with her captors.[75]

Terrorist groups linked to the Tehran regime also adopted the hostage technique. Americans have been kidnapped and held hostage in the Middle East in Lebanon in the 1980s and in Iraq beginning in 2004. Hezbollah militants captured nearly a dozen Americans living in Beirut in the 1980s and held them to protest U.S. policy in the Middle East, particularly Washington's support for Israel. The hostages were kept virtually incommunicado for years. The longest-serving captive, journalist Terry Anderson, was held for nearly seven years. Hezbollah operatives also seized Terry Waite, an envoy from the Church of England who was trying to negotiate for the captives' release. They were eventually released when interest in the story began to wane. Beginning in 2004 Abu Musab al-Zarqawi's al-Qaeda faction in Iraq began to kidnap foreign nationals to protest the presence of the United States and its allies in Iraq. At least eight foreigners (U.S., Japanese, Korean, and Bulgarian citizens) were beheaded when demands were not met. The executions were carefully staged and videotaped by uniformed militants in front of banners identifying the responsible group, and the gruesome footage was then posted on the Internet.[76]

Kidnapping has also become a major industry in Latin America, with Colombia in the lead. With three paramilitary groups competing for supporters and a share of the lucrative illegal narcotics industry, Colombia has become the kidnapping capital of the world. Year after year Colombia records more cases of kidnapping than any other country: in 2003 there were 2,200 reported cases, down from a high of 3,706 in 2000.[77] The U.S. Department of State noted in 2002, "The financial transfer from victims to terrorists by way of ransom payments and extortion fees continued to cripple the Colombian economy."[78] Private companies now even offer "kidnap and ransom" insurance policies; some agencies collect $150 million in annual premiums.[79]

Kidnapping remains a relatively safe (for the kidnapper) and lucrative industry. "Few suspects ever get caught," according to Kroll Associates, a private security firm based in New York City. "Seventy-nine percent of all hostages are killed during rescue attempts in Latin America,"[80] possibly because rescues do not bring ransom money; the police are widely believed to "earn" a share of any ransom money by looking the other way.

Weapons of Mass Destruction

Many analysts fear that terrorists will try to use weapons of mass destruction (WMD). WMD come in four varieties: nuclear, radiological, biological, and chemical. Nuclear weapons are bombs that could wipe out entire cities, as in Hiroshima and Nagasaki, Japan, in 1945, while radiological devices ("dirty bombs") are ordinary explosives laced with radioactive materials. Dirty bombs would kill fewer people than nuclear bombs, but the radiation release could create mass panic, and the affected area would need to be quarantined for an extended period—possibly decades.[81] Biological weapons spread disease-causing agents, such as anthrax, plague, Ebola, salmonella, botulinum, and smallpox, while chemical weapons are manufactured poisons, such as sarin and ricin. In March 1988 Iraqi dictator Saddam Hussein ordered poison gas used against ethnic Kurds living in northern Iraq; some casualty estimates run as high as 7,000 dead.

No individual terrorist group has acquired or deployed nuclear weapons, but there is concern that several states believed to sponsor terrorism (such as Iran and North Korea) are working to acquire nuclear technology. Immediately following the collapse of the Soviet Union there was international concern that unguarded Soviet nuclear or biological weapons might be sold on the black market, but these fears have not materialized. The U.S. government provided $3 billion in aid as part of the Nunn-Lugar Cooperative Threat Reduction Act to be used to secure and properly decommission more than 6,000 Soviet weapons of mass destruction,[82] but stockpiles of conventional weapons remain unprotected and potentially dangerous.[83] Soviet-era bioweapons labs remain understaffed, underfunded, and vulnerable to theft. Some labs could not even report a break-in because they cannot afford telephone service.[84]

While the prospects are frightening, there are two obstacles to using WMD for terrorist acts. First, few terrorist groups possess the skills needed to create, deploy, and activate such weapons. Even with such skills, the attacks can be difficult to pull off, as was demonstrated on March 20, 1995, when members of a religious cult in Japan, Aum Shinrikyo, released sarin, a highly toxic nerve gas, into the Tokyo subway system. Sarin paralyzes the respiratory system, leaving victims unable to breathe, and can be particularly lethal when released in a closed environment, such as a subway car or an underground station. Twelve people died, and another 5,000 were injured in Tokyo. Shoko Asahara, the charismatic leader of this doomsday cult, was arrested for the attack. Cult members who directly participated in the attack were alternately murdered by other group members, given life sentences in prison, or executed by the government.[85] The group had greater ambitions, but even with "more than a billion dollars in assets and 50,000 members, several of whom were skilled biologists," notes Stern, ". . . the cult was unable to mount a successful biological attack despite numerous attempts."[86] The attack did cause extensive psychological consequences in Japan. For weeks after the attack, each day hundreds of people sought health care, convinced that they also had been poisoned.[87]

Second, even groups that might have such skills have hesitated to make widespread lethal attacks for fear that such brutality would harm their cause more than advance it. However, the 9/11 attacks suggest that some Islamic fundamentalist terrorists have lost that restraint, and there are continuing fears that al-Qaeda or a similar group might acquire nuclear or biological weapons.[88]

Extremist groups in the United States have stockpiled various toxins but have not been able to deploy them successfully. For example, in 1972 police arrested college student Stephen J. Perra, coleader of the ecoterrorist group R.I.S.E. They discovered that Perra had five biological cultures in his possession: typhoid, bacterial meningitis, diptheria, botulinum, and dysentery. The 1985 raid on the Covenant, the Sword, and the Arm of the Lord, a Christian cult based in Arkansas, yielded 30 gallons of cyanide. Both groups planned to poison the U.S. water supply.[89] Before 2001, the only successful bioweapons attack in the United States came in The Dalles, Oregon, in 1984. Devotees of the Bhagwan Shree Rajneesh poisoned salad bars in 10 local restaurants with salmonella, hoping to keep voters away from a local election to ensure victory for their own candidate. Some 751 people became ill as a result.[90]

Many insurgent groups have falsely claimed to have anthrax while boasting to other groups and trying to stir up public fear. The Anti-Defamation League reports that anthrax was the "hoax of choice" among domestic terrorists in the 1980s and 1990s. Iraq's suspected use of anthrax in the 1991 Gulf War followed by the Aum Shinrikyo attack in 1995 raised public awareness of the potential threat. "By the beginning of the 21st century it had become abundantly clear that the U.S. had developed an almost primal fear of anthrax—and anybody who wanted to throw the country into a panic need look no further for an instrument to do so."[91] The popular fear of anthrax was soon justified.

Barely 10 days after the 9/11 attacks, the United States witnessed an assault using the deadly bacteria. Envelopes containing anthrax powder were mailed to the *New York Post,* NBC News, American Media, Inc., Senator Tom Daschle (D-S.D.), and Senator Patrick Leahy (D-Vt.). Twenty-one people were infected with anthrax from handling these envelopes or other letters and packages that had gone through the same postal sorting facilities as the contaminated letters, including post offices in Trenton, New Jersey; Hamilton Township, New Jersey; Washington, D.C.; and Sterling, Virginia. People who only had touched the powder contracted cutaneous (skin) anthrax, which is easily treated with antibiotics. But people who had breathed in the power developed a more life-threatening form, pulmonary anthrax. Five people died. Testing proved that all of the samples were from the same strain of anthrax, but the source has not been identified. Investigators focused their attention on Steven J. Hatfill, a government scientist trained to work with biological weapons, but they never charged him with the crime. (Hatfill later sued the FBI for harassment.)[92]

Cyberterrorism

The newest form of terrorism is cyberterrorism—attacks involving computer systems. Cyberterrorism differs from more routine cyber crimes such as identity theft, viruses, and bogus business deals because it is meant to disable systems, disrupt daily life, and cause panic. Cyberterror attacks might disrupt air traffic control systems, scramble emergency communications networks, or shut down power generation grids. For example, in a 2002 speech U.S. Director of Homeland Security Tom Ridge declared, "Terrorists can sit at one computer connected to one network and can create worldwide havoc—[they] don't necessarily need bombs or explosives to cripple a sector of the economy, or shut down a power grid."[93] Computer experts, however, downplay the threat, pointing out that critical computer systems are "air-gapped" (not physically connected to the Internet), so hackers cannot interfere with them. "There is no such thing as cyberterrorism—no instance of anyone ever having been killed by a terrorist (or any one else) using a computer."[94] Even Richard Clarke, President George W. Bush's adviser for cyberterrorism, had to admit, "To date we've never seen any of the officially designated terrorist groups engage in a cyberattack against us."[95]

Instead, terrorists use computer technology more as an organizing tool than a mode of attack. The Internet makes it easier to recruit members, raise funds, communicate with other groups, spread propaganda, and collect vital data. For example, computer hackers provided Irish terrorists with the names and addresses of British law-enforcement personnel who were then targeted for attack. Aum Shinrikyo, using several front organizations, developed vehicle-tracking software, later even selling it to several Japanese police forces.[96] Iraqi militants have been careful to record each time they behead a Western hostage, promptly posting it on the Internet for all to see.[97] The al-Qaeda laptops that were found in Afghanistan in late 2001 had schematic diagrams of potential targets, but, Clarke admitted, "Osama bin Laden is not going to come for you on the Internet."[98]

Narcoterrorism

Criminals may turn to terrorist tactics to influence governments to turn a blind eye to their activities, particularly in the lucrative narcotics trade. In

1983 Peruvian president Belaunde Terry coined the term *narcoterrorism* to describe this phenomenon. The U.S. Drug Enforcement Agency works with the following definition: "a narcoterrorist organization is an organized group that is complicit in the activities of drug trafficking to further or fund premeditated, politically motivated violence to influence a government or group of people." Put simply, government officials are given a choice: Accept a bribe or prepare for eventual assassination. Terrorist groups may also use the illegal drug trade to finance their operations.

Narcoterrorism has been especially prevalent in Colombia (cocaine) and Afghanistan under Taliban rule (heroin), but terrorist groups such as Shining Path (Peru), Liberation Tigers of Tamil Eelam (Sri Lanka), Hezbollah (Lebanon), Kurdistan Worker's Party (Turkey), and Basque Fatherland and Liberty (Spain) are also believed to be involved in narcotics trafficking.

The Taliban, the austere Islamist fundamentalist regime that controlled Afghanistan in the 1990s, allowed the opium poppy trade to thrive, although consumption was prohibited by the Koran. Much of the domestic conflict in Afghanistan in recent years is actually a war over control of poppy fields. According to the Afghan Counter Narcotics Directorate, the Taliban earned more than $150 million from drugs in 2003.[99] The Taliban outlawed poppy production in 2001, but drug enforcement officials believe it to have been more of an effort to drive up the international price of heroin than to curb abuse.[100] The post-Taliban government of President Hamid Karzai outlawed poppy production at international request, but the law has been generally ignored.

Paper Terrorism

Paper terrorism is more of a nuisance than a threat to public safety, but it does disrupt daily life. Groups such as the Militia of Montana/Freemen file numerous frivolous lawsuits to try to clog the court system or to challenge the title to various real estate parcels, usually belonging to government officials. By clogging the judicial system with frivolous lawsuits, paper terrorism can impede the prosecution of more legitimate cases. The procedure is highly contradictory, as the antigovernment groups are participating in a system to which they strenuously object. It is also highly effective, as demonstrated by Rodney Skurdal of Roundup, Montana. According to Musselshell/Golden Valley County attorney Vicki Knudsen, "We wasted 40 or 50 hours every month dealing with these cases." Skurdal appealed to the Montana Supreme Court three times, and his filings were so voluminous they were measured in pounds rather than by pages. The offense that triggered the paper deluge? Failure to have a driver's license.[101] The Freemen also engaged in bank fraud and several forms of counterfeiting.[102]

LEGAL DEFINITIONS OF TERRORISM

Although terrorism is easy to describe in general terms, it is difficult to define in legal terms and therefore difficult to prosecute. There is no internationally accepted definition of terrorism, although there are provisions for punishing terrorists and terrorist activities. Instead, individual countries and international organizations have been left to formulate their own laws on terrorism. As a result, there is no one law applicable to everyone on the planet, and potential terrorists can base themselves in countries that do not proscribe the activities they plan to carry out. Because of the diverse motives behind terrorism, law-enforcement efforts have focused on specific acts of terrorism or activities that facilitate terrorism, such as weapons sales or money laundering.

Western Europe, the locus of numerous terrorist groups and incidents in the 1970s and 1980s, has been at the forefront of a rather ill-equipped movement to address criminal aspects of terrorism. The Council of Europe adopted a landmark convention in 1977 that addresses terrorism as a phenomenon distinct from activities such as bombing or hijacking, but, in an apparent contradiction of most definitions, specifically says that terrorist actions should *not* be regarded as politically motivated attacks.[103] The United Nations is currently working toward a common international definition of what constitutes terrorism.

United States

Even after 9/11, the United States does only slightly better in terms of providing a legal framework for prosecution. The U.S. Code is the collection of fundamental, permanent laws made by the U.S. Congress to guide the U.S. government. The State Department and Central Intelligence Agency—both governed by Title 22, Section 2656f(d), which requires annual reports on terrorism to the Congress—focus on identifying terrorists and preventing terrorist acts. According to this regulation:

> *(1) The term "terrorism" means premeditated, politically motivated violence perpetrated against noncombatant targets by subnational groups or clandestine agents, usually intended to influence an audience.*
>
> *(2) The term "international terrorism" means terrorism involving the territory or the citizens of more than one country.*
>
> *(3) The term "terrorist group" means any group that practices, or has significant subgroups that practice, international terrorism.*[104]

In addition to the U.S. Code, the separate Code of Federal Regulations provides interpretations of the law. These interpretations clarify the U.S. government's definitions of terrorism in terms of functional responsibility. While the Department of State and the Central Intelligence Agency are tasked with preventing international terrorism, the Federal Bureau of Investigation has been designated as the lead agency for any terrorist-related act that occurs within the jurisdiction of the United States. Specifically, the Judicial Administration section of the U.S. Code of Federal Regulations (28 CFR Section 0.85) defines terrorism as "a violent act or an act dangerous to human life, in violation of the criminal laws of the United States or of any state, to intimidate or coerce a government, the civilian population, or any segment thereof, in furtherance of political or social objectives."

European Union

The European Union (EU) had no common definition of terrorism before 2002, but in 1995 members agreed that "terrorism constitutes a threat to democracy, to the free exercise of human rights, and to economic and social development."[105] Seven of the (then) 15 EU member states had their own national definitions of terrorism (France, Germany, Italy, Portugal, Greece, Spain, and the United Kingdom), while the other eight did not. In June 2002 the EU membership adopted the Framework Decision on Combating Terrorism that describes types of terrorist acts and instructs member states to outlaw the activities described, including attacking people or property, kidnapping, seizing aircraft, manufacturing nuclear, biological, or chemical weapons, releasing explosions, and tainting water supplies. The document recognizes that terrorists often have political motivations and summarizes the most common goals of terrorists, namely:

- seriously intimidating a population, or
- unduly compelling a government or international organizations to perform or abstain from performing any act, or
- seriously destabilizing or destroying the fundamental political, constitutional, economic, or social structures of a country or an international organization.[106]

Instead of offering specific law-enforcement steps, the 2002 framework decision called upon member states to harmonize their laws related to terrorism. In 2004 the EU appointed its first counterterrorism coordinator, Gijs de Vries, who is tasked with improving information sharing among national intelligence agencies, but prosecutions are to be handled by individual countries. The EU member states are hesitant to create pan-European laws because they want to maintain maximum flexibility in dealing with local problems.

NATO

Within hours of the September 11, 2001, terrorist attacks in the United States, NATO invoked Article 5 of the Washington Treaty. According to this provision, "an armed attack against one or more of the Allies in Europe or North America shall be considered an attack against them all." This decision was the first time in NATO's history that Article 5 had been put in force. Under that provision, all members of NATO are required to act to restore international security.[107] NATO members agreed to send troops to Afghanistan to destroy al-Qaeda, but Germany and France refused to participate when Washington expanded the War on Terrorism to Iraq.

NATO was already in the process of redefining its mission in the post–cold war era, and terrorism is certainly a point of interest. While European institutions such as the EU and the Council of Europe continue to expand membership and to evolve policy, NATO provides a key link between Europe and North America and eventually could become a channel for harmonization of laws between Europe and North America.

United Nations

Prior to the terrorist attacks of September 11, 2001, the United Nations largely tried to ignore the issue of terrorism as a distinct action. Because UN Resolution 1514 legitimizes actions to achieve national self-determination (to become a self-ruled independent state), it was exceedingly difficult to condemn nationalist-based terrorism, which was the dominant form for the first 50 years of the United Nations. Another complicating factor was the cold war. Many of the state sponsors of terrorism were neither exactly in the Soviet camp or the U.S. camp, and neither superpower wanted to alienate a potential ally.

Rather than outlawing terrorism per se, the United Nations adopted a series of conventions to address specific acts or forms of terrorism. These are listed in Table 1 and described in the Documents section of this book.

In 1985 the United Nations General Assembly issued its first concrete definition of terrorism, namely "acts ... which endanger or take innocent human lives, jeopardize fundamental freedoms, and seriously impair the dignity of human beings."[108] The phrasing dodges several fundamental aspects of terrorism discussed here: Who are the terrorists (individuals, groups, or countries) and what do terrorists want (what motives underlie terrorist incidents). The definition also does not specify what acts constitute terrorism,

Table 1
United Nations Conventions against Terrorism

DESCRIPTION	YEAR
Acts Committed on Board Aircraft	1963
Unlawful Seizure of Aircraft	1970
Unlawful Acts against the Safety of Civil Aviation	1971
Crimes against Internationally Protected Persons	1973
Taking of Hostages	1979
Physical Protection of Nuclear Material	1980
Unlawful Acts of Violence at Airports Serving International Civil Aviation	1988
Unlawful Acts against the Safety of Maritime Navigation	1988
Unlawful Acts against the Safety of Fixed Platforms on the Continental Shelf	1988
Marking of Plastic Explosives for the Purpose of Detection	1991
Suppression of Terrorist Bombing	1997
Suppression of the Financing of Terrorism	1999
Suppression of Acts of Nuclear Terrorism	2005

Source: United Nations Office on Drugs and Crime, "Conventions against Terrorism," at www.unodc.org/unodc/terrorism_conventions.html

but the accompanying text does refer to the various conventions mentioned in Table 1. Following the 2001 terrorist attacks against the United States, the United Nations Security Council adopted Resolution 1373, which requires states to suppress terrorist financing, refrain from supporting terrorist groups, deny safe haven to terrorist groups, better enforce border controls, share information about terrorist activities, and cooperate in the prosecution of terrorist crimes. The resolution created a Counter-Terrorism Committee (CTC) to monitor individual countries' compliance with the resolution. However, 1373 does not enumerate what groups are considered terrorists nor does it even clearly define *terrorism*; individual states are left to make their own judgments. Russia's list of terrorist organizations, released in July 2006, does not include Hamas or Hezbollah, both defined as terrorist groups by the United States.[109] CTC Chairman Sir Jeremy Greenstock was blunt on this issue, saying that the committee "is not going to define terrorism in a legal sense, although we will have a fair idea of what is blatant terrorism; where necessary, we will decide by consensus whether an act is terrorism."[110]

In 2004 UN Secretary General Kofi Annan assembled a high-level panel to investigate terrorism, and the panel provided a concise, human-rights–based definition of terrorism as any act that is "intended to cause death or serious bodily harm to civilians or non-combatants with the purpose of intimidating a population or compelling a government or an international organization to do or abstain from doing any act." Annan has called for global adoption of this concept as the standard definition of terrorism.[111] However, objections have been raised, particularly by the Arab League in reference to the Palestinian issue, that a definition must recognize that violence is legitimate when used to resist occupation.[112] As with previous efforts at definition, Annan's proposal remained mired in debate and was not resolved when he stepped down in late 2006.

COUNTERTERRORISM

Terrorism's power is its unpredictability. It is extremely difficult to anticipate where the next attack will take place, who will carry it out, and what method they will use. This makes it difficult for governments to fight terrorism. Three strategies are possible: prepare, prevent, and prosecute.

Prepare

Countries cannot simply pull the covers over their heads and hope nothing bad happens. While trying to prevent terrorist activities from occurring, governments must simultaneously maximize their response and relief resources in the event that a tragedy occurs. Such preparations are prudent and can be cost effective, as the same strategies and resources can be used to alleviate damage from natural disasters, such as hurricanes and tsunamis. National, state, and local governments must prepare evacuation plans, determine optimal deployment of rescue personnel and equipment, ranging from blood, to blankets, to bathroom provisions. Such simple steps as coordinating communications equipment to maximize interoperability should be determined before a crisis occurs.

The advance preparation approach is called *antiterrorism.* While some analysts would argue that *antiterrorism* and *counterterrorism* are redundant, the U.S. Federal Emergency Management Agency (FEMA) describes the difference as follows:

> *Antiterrorism refers to defensive measures used to reduce the vulnerability of people and property to terrorist acts, while counterterrorism includes offensive measures taken to prevent, deter, and respond to terrorism. Thus, antiterrorism is an element of hazard mitigation, while counterterrorism falls within the scope of preparedness, response, and recovery.*[113]

Thus counterterrorism efforts seek to prevent terrorist attacks from occurring, while antiterrorism efforts work to lessen the damage if an attack should occur despite the counterterrorism measures.

The 9/11 attacks graphically revealed holes in U.S. antiterrorism preparations, notably communications. Chapter 9, "Heroism and Horror," of the official 9/11 report details repeated communication breakdowns among first responders, including 911 emergency operators and fire-dispatch personnel. Excerpts are reproduced below:

> **Lack of Coordination among First Responder Agencies.** *Any attempt to establish a unified command on 9/11 would have been further frustrated by the lack of communication and coordination among responding agencies. Certainly, the FDNY [Fire Department of New York] was not "responsible for the management of the City's response to the emergency," as the Mayor's directive would have required. The command posts were in different locations, and OEM [Office of Emergency Management] headquarters, which could have served as a focal point for information sharing, did not play an integrating role in ensuring that information was shared among agencies on 9/11, even prior to its evacuation. There was a lack of comprehensive coordination between FDNY, NYPD [New York Police Department], and PAPD [Port Authority Police Department] personnel climbing above the ground floors in the Twin Towers. . . .*
>
> *The FDNY, PAPD, and NYPD did not coordinate their units that were searching the WTC [World Trade Center] complex for civilians. In many cases, redundant searches of specific floors and areas were conducted. It is unclear whether fewer first responders in the aggregate would have been in the Twin Towers if there had been an integrated response, or what impact, if any, redundant searches had on the total number of first responder fatalities.*
>
> *Whether the lack of coordination between the FDNY and NYPD on September 11 had a catastrophic effect has been the subject of controversy. We believe that there are too many variables for us to responsibly quantify those consequences. It is clear that the lack of coordination did not affect adversely the evacuation of civilians. It is equally clear, however, that the Incident Command System did not function to integrate awareness among agencies or to facilitate interagency response.*[114]

In contrast, Washington, D.C., area personnel were more experienced at coordination:

> *While no emergency response is flawless, the response to the 9/11 terrorist attack on the Pentagon was mainly a success for three reasons: first, the*

strong professional relationships and trust established among emergency responders; second, the adoption of the Incident Command System; and third, the pursuit of a regional approach to response. Many fire and police agencies that responded had extensive prior experience working together on regional events and training exercises. Indeed, at the time preparations were under way at many of these agencies to ensure public safety at the annual meetings of the International Monetary Fund and the World Bank scheduled to be held later that month in Washington, D.C.

Local, regional, state, and federal agencies immediately responded to the Pentagon attack. In addition to county fire, police, and sheriff's departments, the response was assisted by the Metropolitan Washington Airports Authority, Ronald Reagan Washington National Airport Fire Department, Fort Myer Fire Department, the Virginia State Police, the Virginia Department of Emergency Management, the FBI, FEMA, a National Medical Response Team, the Bureau of Alcohol, Tobacco, and Firearms, and numerous military personnel within the Military District of Washington. . . .

Several factors facilitated the response to this incident, and distinguish it from the far more difficult task in New York. There was a single incident, and it was not 1,000 feet above ground. The incident site was relatively easy to secure and contain, and there were no other buildings in the immediate area. There was no collateral damage beyond the Pentagon.

Yet the Pentagon response encountered difficulties that echo those experienced in New York. As the "Arlington County: After-Action Report" notes, there were significant problems with both self-dispatching and communications: "Organizations, response units, and individuals proceeding on their own initiative directly to an incident site, without the knowledge and permission of the host jurisdiction and the Incident Commander, complicate the exercise of command, increase the risks faced by bonafide responders, and exacerbate the challenge of accountability." With respect to communications, the report concludes: "Almost all aspects of communications continue to be problematic, from initial notification to tactical operations. Cellular telephones were of little value. . . . Radio channels were initially oversaturated. . . . Pagers seemed to be the most reliable means of notification when available and used, but most firefighters are not issued pagers.[115]

Israel offers another approach to antiterrorism efforts. It too experienced communications breakdowns during the 1990–91 war with Iraq, and to remedy the situation, the government implemented a new form of civil defense, the Home Front Command. By law, each home, school, office building, and other public facility in the country is required to have a "protected space" to serve as a bomb shelter in case of attack. The government also provides each resident with protective kits that include gas masks for use in case of a chemical attack. The media broadcast regular updates on security information and training instructions on what to do in case of an attack.[116]

Prevent

The second approach calls for stopping terrorist attacks before they happen. A mixture of law-enforcement, intelligence, and sometimes military techniques is used to monitor suspects, including stakeouts, monitoring weapons purchases and financial transactions, and wiretaps on telephone and computer equipment. While it can be difficult to identify appropriate suspects for surveillance, securing legal permission to monitor people can be particularly difficult in democracies in which freedom of expression, personal privacy, and the right to due process of law are fundamental rights enshrined in the constitution.

If criminal activity is suspected or detected, law-enforcement agents can apprehend the suspects before they commit a terrorist act. If the terrorist attack is already underway, military resources can be deployed to intercept the perpetrators. Unfortunately, it can be exceedingly difficult to connect the dots among potential terrorists *before* an attack. The 9/11 investigation commission discovered that while the FBI was overseeing extensive wiretaps of suspected terrorists, it lacked Arabic-language staff to translate—much less analyze—hours of recordings. And even if the data had been translated, FBI agents had few ways to share the information—many agents did not even have e-mail access.[117]

The moral and legal dilemma facing governments is what steps to take *after* a terrorist attack. When is retaliation justified—or is it ever? Will it create an endless spiral of subsequent revenge attacks? Following the massacre of its athletes at the 1972 Olympics, Israel launched a campaign to assassinate every member of the terrorist team responsible and succeeded in killing all but one suspect.[118] But, as Steven Spielberg asks in his 2005 movie *Munich,* was targeted killing a correct response, or did it merely provoke more attacks?

Prosecute

Once a terrorist, potential or active, has been identified and apprehended, the next step is prosecution, that is, determining guilt and applying appropriate punishment. A rift is emerging between the United States and Europe regarding the proper scope of prevention and prosecution techniques. Following the terrorist attacks of September 11, 2001, the U.S. government proclaimed a "War on Terrorism." Consequently it is conducting terrorist-related investigations under military rules rather than in civilian venues. Many U.S. allies object to this change of venue, seeing it as depriving individuals of due process. A second area of contention is the death penalty. The United States is one of only a handful of countries that allow criminals to be sentenced to death. Because they find the death penalty so abhorrent, other countries may be hesitant—or even barred by their domestic laws—from extraditing terror suspects to the United States where they may face the death penalty.

Many governments believe that crimes that cross borders and involve multiple jurisdictions would best be considered by an international court. A World Court (International Court of Justice) has existed since the creation of the United Nations in 1948 and is designed to adjudicate disputes between countries. However, the World Court has few powers to sanction countries that refuse to obey its rulings. For example, the government of Nicaragua brought the United States before the court in the 1980s for interfering in the affairs of another country by supporting the contra (anticommunist) insurgency. The court ruled in Nicaragua's favor, finding the United States guilty of violating customary international law. But in a highly controversial move, the Reagan administration declared that it would not recognize the jurisdiction of the World Court on the contra matter—and the court had no recourse to enforce its ruling.

The United Nations created a separate International Criminal Court (ICC) in 2002 to prosecute *individuals* charged with crimes against humanity, such as genocide, and war crimes. In the previous decade the United Nations had established special bodies to investigate criminal acts by the former government officials of Yugoslavia and Rwanda, and there was a desire to create a permanent forum for such crimes.[119] However, the United States has refused to ratify the document that formally creates the ICC, known as the Rome Charter, for at least three reasons: its mandate is vague; it allows the United Nations to make decisions that could override U.S. government laws; and it would make U.S. military personnel vulnerable to prosecution for war crimes.[120] Instead, Washington has pressed individual countries to sign the American Service Members' Protection Act, U.S. legislation that gives U.S. soldiers immunity from prosecution. This decision has been widely criticized, especially as the only other countries to refuse to sign are China, Iraq, Qatar, Libya, and Yemen—hardly bastions of liberal democracy—as well as Israel.

[1] David C. Rapoport. "Fear and Trembling: Terrorism in Three Religious Traditions." *American Political Science Review* 78, no. 3 (September 1984), pp. 658–677.

[2] The U.S. Department of State maintains a list of countries designated as sponsors of terrorism. As of mid-2006 the list includes Cuba, Iran, Libya, North Korea, Sudan, and Syria. The list changes over time; a country mentioned in this book as a state-sponsor at a particular point in time may have since been removed from the list. See U.S. Department of State. "State Sponsors of Terrorism." Available online. URL: http://www.state.gov/s/ct/c14151.htm. Accessed July 15, 2006.

[3] Bruce Hoffman. *Inside Terrorism.* New York: Columbia University Press, 1998, p. 25. Emphasis in original.

[4] Marc E. Nicholson. "An Essay on Terrorism." *American Diplomacy* 8, no. 3 (2003).

[5] Bruce Hoffman. *Inside Terrorism.* New York: Columbia University Press, 1998.

[6] Federal Bureau of Investigation. *Terrorism in the United States, 1999.* Washington, D.C.: GPO, 2000, p. 16.

[7] "Bombings Hit Bali Tourist Numbers." *BBC News,* December 2, 2005. Available online. URL: http://news.bbc.co.uk/2/hi/business/4491356.stm. Accessed July 10, 2006; Charles Levinson, "Terror Threat Not Halting Tourism." *Christian Science Monitor,* August 2, 2005; Karl Vick. "Blast in Turkish Resort Town Kills 5." *Washington Post,* July 17, 2005.

[8] "New York City's Tourism Industry: One Year after September 11." NYC and Company press release, September 4, 2002. Available online. URL: http://www.nycvisit.com/content/index.cfm?pagePkey=786. Accessed July 10, 2006.

[9] Earle Eldridge. "Cities Suffer as Travelers Stay Home." *USA Today,* October 3, 2001, p. B3.

[10] Barbara De Lollis. "USA Tries to Be Less Daunting to Foreign Visitors." *USA Today,* February 17, 2006, p. B1.

[11] Jessica Stern. *Terror in the Name of God: Why Religious Militants Kill.* New York: HarperCollins, 2003, p. 10.

[12] Brigitte Nacos, adjunct professor of Political Science, Columbia University. Interviewed on "Black September" edition of NPR's *On the Media,* August 30, 2002. Available online. URL: http://www.onthemedia.org/yore/transcripts/transcripts_083002_september.html. Accessed November 18, 2005.

[13] Frederick J. Hacker. *Crusaders, Criminals, Crazies: Terror and Terrorism in Our Time.* New York: W. W. Norton, 1976.

[14] Margaret Thatcher. "Speech to American Bar Association." London, July 15, 1985. Available online. URL: www.margaretthatcher.org/speeches/displaydocument.asp?docid=106090. Accessed January 11, 2006.

[15] Quoted in Richard Sandomir. "When Innocence Died at the Olympics." *New York Times,* September 3, 2000, p. B25.

[16] Jensen Moore et al. "Effects of the September 11, 2001 Terrorist Attack on U.S. Press Coverage." In Association for Education in Journalism and Mass Communications Annual Convention, Miami Beach, Fla.: 2002. Available online. URL: list.msu.edu/cgi-bin/wa?A2=ind0209b&L=aejmc&D=0&P=9376&F=P. Accessed November 16, 2005.

[17] "Media 'Crucial' to Terrorists, Author Finds." *Columbia University Record* 20, no. 18 (February 25, 1995). Available online. URL: www.Columbia.edu/cu/record/rchives/vol20/vol20_iss18/record2018.16.html. Accessed November 18, 2005.

[18] Brian Michael Jenkins. "The Psychological Implications of Media-Covered Terrorism." RAND, 1981. Available online. URL: http://www.rand.org/pubs/papers/p6627/p6627.pdf. Accessed November 16, 2005.

[19] Tom Shales. "On HBO, a Searingly Tragic 'September'; Terrorist Attack at '72 Olympics Recalled." *Washington Post,* September 11, 2000, p. C1.

[20] Major U.S. television networks provided first-class airfare and luxury hotel accommodations to hostage families in return for exclusive interviews. See Tom Shales. "Unanswered Questions: Television's Excesses, on Screen and Off." *Washington Post,* July 1, 1985, p. D1; Tom Shales. "America's Ordeal by Television: With the Beirut Hostages Free, Videoland Forgets Oh So Quickly." *Washington Post,* July 2, 1985, p. C1.

[21] Jonathan Alter. "Does TV Help or Hurt." *Newsweek,* July 1, 1985, pp. 32–33.

[22] Garry Hamilton. "Under the Gun." *Ryerson Review of Journalism* (1986). Available online. URL: http://www.rjj.ca/print/575. Accessed January 11, 2006.

[23] Jonathan Alter. "Does TV Help or Hurt?"

[24] Shales. "Unanswered Questions."

[25] Eleanor Randolph. "Networks Turn Eye on Themselves." *Washington Post,* June 30, 1985, p. A25.

[26] Quoted in Raphael Cohen-Almagor, "Media Coverage of Acts of Terrorism: Troubling Episodes and Suggested Guidelines." *Canadian Journal of Communication* 38, no. 3 (2005), pp. 383–409.

[27] Michael Foley. "Dubbing SF Voices Becomes the Stuff of History." *Irish Times,* September 17, 1994, p. 5.

[28] BBC Editorial Guidelines, Section 11, War, Terror and Emergencies. Available online. URL: http://bbc.co.uk/guidelines/editorialguidelines/edguide/war/mandatoryreferr.shtml. Accessed July 10, 2006.

[29] Don Wycliff. "Sorting out Usage of the T-Word." *Chicago Tribune,* March 21 2002, p. A25.

[30] Democracy Now. "Major TV Networks Crack Down—on Themselves—to Restrict Their News Coverage of Osama Bin Laden and Afghanistan." Available online. URL: http://www.democracynow.org/print.pl?sid=03/04/07/0213247. Posted on October 11, 2001. Accessed January 12, 2006.

[31] Hoffman, *Inside Terrorism.* p. 157.

[32] Philip Baum. "Leila Khaled: In Her Own Words." *Aviation Safety International,* October 2000. Available online. URL: www.asi-mag.com/editorials/leila_khaled.htm. Accessed November 23, 2005.

[33] Jerry Markon and Timothy Dwyer. "At Trial, Flight 93 Myth Finally Becomes Reality." *Washington Post,* April 13, 2006, p. A1.

[34] Mia Bloom. *Dying to Kill: The Allure of Suicide Terror.* New York: Columbia University Press, 2005, pp. 63–64.

[35] Nasra Hassan. "An Arsenal of Believers: Talking to the 'Human Bombs." *New Yorker,* November 19, 2001, pp. 36–41.

[36] National Commission on Terrorist Attacks upon the United States. *The 9/11 Commission Report: Final Report of the National Commission on Terrorist Attacks upon the United States,* authorized edition. New York: W. W. Norton, 2004, section 5.4.

[37] General Accounting Office Report GAO-02-700R. "Impact of Terrorist Attacks on the World Trade Center." Posted May 29, 2002. Available online. URL: http://www.gao.gov/new.items/d02700r.pdf.

[38] Tariq Panja. "Analysts Say London Bombings Inexpensive." Associated Press. Available online. URL: http://abcnews.go.com/international/print?id=1466463. Accessed January 3, 2006.

[39] Robert A. Pape. *Dying to Win: The Strategic Logic of Suicide Terrorism.* New York: Random House, 2005.

[40] Walter Laqueur. *No End to War: Terrorism in the 21st Century.* New York: Continuum, 2004.

[41] Somini Sengupta. "Where Maoists Still Matter." *New York Times Magazine,* October 30, 2005, p. 64.

[42] Nicholas D. Kristof. "At Trial in Tokyo, Guru Says Aim Was to Give 'Ultimate Joy.'" *New York Times,* April 25, 1996, p. A11.

[43] Tom Hundley. "Attacks Spur Identity Crisis for Britain." *Chicago Tribune.* December 16, 2005, p. 6.

[44] Charles M. Sennott and Kevin Cul. "Video Shows Bomb Suspects' Final Steps." *Boston Globe,* July 17, 2005, p. A1.

[45] Hassan. "An Arsenal of Believers: Talking to the 'Human Bombs.'"

[46] Farhana Ali. "Muslim Female Fighters: An Emerging Trend." *Terrorism Monitor.* Posted November 3, 2005. Available online. URL: http://www.jamestown.org/terrorism/news/article.php?articleid=2369824. Accessed January 3, 2006.

[47] Charles M. Sennott and Kevin Cul. "Video Shows Bomb Suspects' Final Steps." *Boston Globe,* July 17, 2005, p. A1.

[48] Charles M. Sennott and Kevin Cul. "Video Shows Bomb Suspects' Final Steps." *Boston Globe,* July 17, 2005, p. A1.

[49] Laqueur. *No End to War: Terrorism in the 21st Century,* p. 17.

[50] Alan B. Krueger and Jitka Maleckova. "Does Poverty Cause Terrorism? The Economics and Education of Suicide Bombers." *New Republic,* June 24, 2002, p. 32.

[51] Avishai Margalit. "The Suicide Bombers." *New York Review of Books.* Posted January 16, 2003. Available online. URL: http://www.nybooks.com/articles/15979. Accessed December 31, 2005.

[52] Timur Moon. "Leila Khaled: Hijacked by Destiny." *Al-Jazeerah.* Posted October 17, 2002. Available online. URL: http://www.aljazeerah.info/Opinion%20editorials/2002%20Opinion%20editorials/Oct%2020 02%20op%20eds/Oct%2017,%202002%20op%20eds.htm. Accessed November 28, 2005.

[53] BBC News UK Confidential. "Black September: Tough Negotiations." Posted on January 1, 2001. Available online. URL: http://news.bbc.co.uk/2/hi/in_depth/uk/2000/uk_confidential/1089694.stm. Accessed November 23, 2005.

[54] Moon. "Leila Khaled: Hijacked by Destiny."

[55] Deaglan de Breadun. "Plane Hijacker Turned Politician Disapproves of Today's 'Terrorism.'" *Irish Times.* Posted on August 4, 2005. Available online. URL: http://www.ireland.com/newspaper/world/2005/0804/2293435572FR04KHALED.html. Accessed November 28, 2005.

56 Christopher C. Harmon. *Terrorism Today.* Portland, Oreg.: Frank Cass, 2000, p. 212.

57 Baum. "Leila Khaled: In Her Own Words."

58 Brigitte L. Nacos. "The Portrayal of Female Terrorists in the Media: Similar Framing Patterns in the News Coverage of Women in Politics and in Terrorism." *Studies in Conflict and Terrorism* 28, no. 5 (2005): 435–451.

59 Laurie Kassman. "Women Terrorists Force Changed Thinking by Security Officials." *Voice of America.* Posted on September 2, 2004. Available online. URL: www.iwar.org.uk/news-archive/2004/09-02.htm. Accessed November 29, 2005.

60 Quoted in Libby Copeland. "Female Suicide Bombers: The New Factor in Mideast's Deadly Equation." *Washington Post,* April 27, 2002, p. C1.

61 Nacos. "The Portrayal of Female Terrorists in the Media: Similar Framing Patterns in the News Coverage of Women in Politics and in Terrorism."

62 Dickey. "Women of Al Qaeda."

63 Hoffman, *Inside Terrorism,* pp. 88–89.

64 Ibid.p. 93.

65 Laqueur. *No End to War: Terrorism in the 21st Century,* pp. 24–29.

66 Quoted in Jessica Stern, *Terror in the Name of God: Why Religious Militants Kill.* New York: HarperCollins, 2003, p. 18.

67 Hoffman, *Inside Terrorism.* p. 90.

68 Stern, *Terror in the Name of God,* p. 7.

69 Laqueur, *No End to War: Terrorism in the 21st Century,* p. 27.

70 George C. Marshall European Center for Security Studies. News Brief "Conference Focuses on NATO and EU's Strategies against Terrorism." Posted on July 20, 2005 at www.marshallcenter.org. Available online. URL: http://homelandsecurity.osu.edu/NACHS/nachsfeatures/terrorismconference.html. Accessed December 14, 2005.

71 Michael Mates. "Report: Technology and Terrorism." NATO Parliamentary Assembly, 2001. Available online. URL: http://www.naa.be/archivedpub/comrep/2001/au-221-e.asp. Accessed December 14, 2005.

72 Baum, "Leila Khaled: In Her Own Words."

73 Brigitte Nacos, Columbia University, interview from *On the Media.* WNYC Radio, August 30, 2002.

74 John Giuffo. "*Nightline* Is Spawned out of the Hostage Crisis." *Columbia Journalism Review* 40, no. 4. November/December 2001, pp. 86–87.

75 PBS American Experience. "Guerrilla: The Taking of Patty Hearst." 2004. Transcript and background materials available online. URL: www.pbs.org/wgbh/amex/guerrilla/index.html. Accessed December 6, 2005.

76 Mary Anne Weaver. "Inventing Al-Zarqawi." *Atlantic Monthly,* July/August 2006, pp. 87–100.

77 International Crisis Group. "Hostages for Prisoners: A Way to Peace in Colombia?" *ICG Latin American Briefing.* March 8, 2004.

[78] U.S. Department of State. "Latin America Overview." *Patterns of Global Terrorism, 2001.* Washington, D.C.: GPO, 2002. Available online. URL: www.state.gov/ct/rls/pgtrpt/2001/html/10246.htm. Accessed October 3, 2005.

[79] Seth Mydans. "How to Succeed in the Kidnapping Business." *New York Times,* October 8, 2000; "Kidnapping: Not Just for Kids." *Insurance Buyers' News* 15, no. D4 (July/August 2004): 1, 3.

[80] Steve Macko. "Kidnapping: A Latin American Growth Industry." *ENN Daily Intelligence Report* 3, no. 120 (1997). Available online. URL: http://www.emergency.com/latnkdnp.htm. Accessed December 19, 2006.

[81] CNN.com In-Depth. Council on Foreign Relations Terrorism Q&A "Dirty Bombs," January 7, 2005. Available online. URL: www.cnn.com/SPECIALS/2002/cfr/stories/dirty.bomb/index.html.

[82] Jessica Reaves. "The Nunn-Lugar Act: Old Fears, New Era." *Time.* Posted on October 1, 2001. Available online. URL: http://www.time.com/time/nation/article/0,8599,177183,00.html. Accessed December 19, 2006. See also www.nunn-lugar.com.

[83] C. J. Chivers. "Ill-Secured Soviet Arms Depots Tempting Rebels and Terrorists." *New York Times,* July 16, 2005, p. A1.

[84] Joby Warrick. "Soviet Germ Factories Pose New Threat; Once Mined for Pathogens in Bioweapons Program, Labs Lack Security." *Washington Post,* August 20, 2005, p. A1; David S. Cloud, Marilyn Chase, and John J. Fialka. "Cold War Echo: The Soviet Germ Program Is a Worry Once Again Amid Anthrax Scare." *Wall Street Journal,* October 15, 2001, p. A1.

[85] J. Poolos. *The Nerve Gas Attack on the Tokyo Subway.* Terrorist Attacks. New York: Rosen, 2003; Patrick Bellamy. "False Prophet: The Aum Cult of Terror." Court TV Crime Library. Available at: www.crimelibrary.com/terrorists_spies/terrorists/prophet. Accessed December 1, 2005.

[86] Jessica Stern. "Taking the Terror out of Bioterrorism." *New York Times.* Posted on April 8, 1998. Available online. URL: http://www.mtholyoke.edu/acad/intrel/stern.htm. Accessed January 1, 2006.

[87] David Van Biema. "Prophet of Poison." *Time,* April 3, 1995, pp. 27–32.

[88] Michael R. Gordon. "U.S. Says It Found Qaeda Lab Being Built to Produce Anthrax." *New York Times,* March 23, 2002, p. A1. David Johnston and James Risen, "U.S. Concludes Al Qaeda Lacked a Chemical or Biological Stockpile." *New York Times,* March 20, 2002, p. A14.

[89] Barry Hillenbrand, J. F. O. McAllister, Mark Thompson. "The Price of Fanaticism." *Time* (April 3, 1995), pp. 38–41. Stern, *Terror in the Name of God,* pp. 10–11.

[90] John Cramer. "Oregon Suffered Largest Bioterrorist Attack in U.S. History 20 Years Ago." *Bend (Oreg.) Bulletin,* October 14, 2001. Available online. URL: http://home.att.net/~meditation/bioterrorist.html. Accessed July 15, 2006.

[91] Anti-Defamation League. *Beyond Anthrax: Extremism and the Bioterrorism Threat.* New York: Anti-Defamation League, 2001, p. 9.

[92] Rachael Bell. "Amerithrax 2001." Court TV Crime Library Available at: www.crimelibrary.com/terrorists_spies/terrorists/anthrax. Accessed December 19, 2006.

[93] "Remarks by Homeland Security Director Tom Ridge to the Electronics Industries Alliance." Washington, D.C., April 23, 2002. Text from White House press release. Available

online. URL: http://www.whitehouse.gov/news/releases/2002/04/print/20020423-15.html. Accessed July 15, 2006.

[94] Joshua Green. "The Myth of Cyberterrorism." ***Washington Monthly*** (November 2002), pp. 8–13.

[95] Quoted in Green. "The Myth of Cyberterrorism."

[96] Michael Mates. "Report: Technology and Terrorism."

[97] Nicholas D. Kristof. "Terrorists in Cyberspace." ***New York Times,*** December 20, 2005, p. A31. Nadya Labi. "Jihad 2.0." ***Atlantic Monthly.*** (July/August 2006), pp. 102–108.

[98] Quoted in Robert Lemos. "Safety: Assessing the Infrastructure Risk." CNET News. Posted on August 26, 2002. Available online. URL: http://news.com.com/Safety+Assessing+the+infrastructure+risk/2009-1001_3-954780.html. Accessed July 15, 2006.

[99] Pierre-Arnaud Chouvy. "Narco-Terrorism in Afghanistan." ***Terrorism Monitor*** 2, no. 6 (2004). Available online. URL: http://www.jamestown.org/terrorism/news/article.php?articleid=23648. Accessed December 19, 2006.

[100] Testimony by Drug Enforcement Agency Administrator Karen P. Tandy before the U.S. House of Representatives Committee on International Relations, February 12, 2004. Transcript available online. URL: http://www.usdoj.gov/dea/pubs/cngrtest/ct021204.htm. Accessed December 19, 2006.

[101] Jeff Elliott. "The Sonoma County Connection." ***Albion Monitor.*** Posted on April 15, 1996. Available online. URL: www.albionmonitor.com/freemensr.html. Accessed April 22, 2006.

[102] Mark Pitcavage. "Every Man a King: The Rise and Fall of the Montana Freeman." ***ADL Militia Watchdog.*** (1996). Available online. URL: www.militia-watchdog.org/freemen.asp. Accessed January 12, 2006.

[103] Council of Europe. "European Convention on the Suppression of Terrorism." Strasbourg, January 27, 1977. Available online. URL: http://conventions.coe.int/Treaty/EN/Treaties/Html/090.htm. Accessed December 12, 2005.

[104] Central Intelligence Agency. "Terrorism FAQs." The War on Terrorism, November 15, 2005. Available online. URL: www.cia.gov/terrorism/faqs.html.

[105] Madrid European Council. Annex 3: Terrorism. "La Gomera Declaration." Presidency Conclusions, December 15–16, 1995. Available online. URL: http://europarl.eu.int/summits/mad2_en.htm#annex.3. Accessed December 12, 2005.

[106] European Union. "Council Framework Decision of 13 June 2002 on Combating Terrorism." November 15, 2005. Available online. URL: europa.eu.int/eur-lex/pri/en/oj/dat/2002/l_164/l_16420020622en00030007.pdf. Accessed December 12, 2005.

[107] NATO Press Release, September 12, 2001. Available online. URL: http://www.nato.int/docu/pr/2001/p01-124e.htm. Accessed December 31, 2005.

[108] UN General Assembly, 108th plenary meeting, Resolution A/RED/40/61, December 9, 1985. Available online. URL: www.un.org/documents/ga/res/40/a4r061.htm. Accessed December 12, 2005.

[109] ***Washington Post,*** July 29, 2006, p. A20.

[110] Jeremy Greenstock, report to the 4,453rd meeting of the UN Security Council, January 18, 2002 S/PV.4453. Available online. URL: http://www.un.org/terrorism/a57273.htm. Accessed July 15, 2006.

Introduction

111 Kofi Annan. speech to International Summit on Democracy, Terrorism, and Security. Madrid, Spain. October 3, 2005. Available online. URL: www.un.org/News/Press/docs/2005/sgsm9757.doc.htm.

112 "UN Seeks Definition of Terrorism." BBC News, July 26, 2005.

113 FEMA, "Mitigation Planning Resources." April 14, 2006. Available online. URL: http://www.fema.gov/plan/mitplanning/planning_resources.shtm.

114 National Commission on Terrorist Attacks upon the United States. ***The 9/11 Commission Report: Final Report of the National Commission on Terrorist Attacks upon the United States.*** Authorized edition. New York: W. W. Norton, 2004, p. 321.

115 ***The 9/11 Commission Report,*** pp. 314–15.

116 Ya'acov Lapidot. "Civil Defense in Israel during the Persian Gulf War: One Year Later." ***Doctors for Disaster Preparedness*** [n.d.]. Available online. URL: http://www.oism.org/ddp/lapidot.htm. Last Accessed July 28, 2006. Israel Home Front Command. "Questions and Answers Concerning Events in the Northern Sector." 2006. Available online. URL: http://www1.idf.il/oref/site/EN/oref.asp?pi=20131&doc_id=33993. Last Accessed July 28, 2006. "Israel in the Middle: How Should Israelis React to an Air Raid Siren?" About.com. Available online. URL: http://Judaism.about.com/library/1_security/iraq/bl_alarm.htm. Accessed July 28, 2006.

117 ***The 9/11 Commission Report,*** p. 77.

118 Thomas B. Hunter. "Wrath of God: The Israeli Response to the 1972 Munich Olympic Massacre." ***Journal of Counterterrorism and Security International*** 7, no. 4 Summer 2001. Available online. URL: http://www.specialoperations/com/Counterterrorism/operation_wrath_of_god.html. Accessed January 16, 2006.

119 For background on the development of the court see the UN Web page (www.un.org/law/icc) and the Court's own Web site (www.icc-cpi.int).

120 John R. Bolton. "The United States and the International Criminal Court." Remarks delivered November 14, 2002. Available online. URL: www.state.gov/t/us/rm/15158.htm. Accessed January 16, 2006.

2

Focus on the United States

The United States is an open, democratic political system with the rights of its residents outlined in the Constitution. These include the right to free speech, freedom of assembly, and freedom of religion. The people have a right to express their own views, to discuss them with friends, and to take their complaints to the government. Citizens can vote government officials into—or out of—office and can ask their representatives to promote or discourage particular laws. Problems can arise, however, when individuals wish to express themselves or make their opinions known by breaking laws and endangering other people. Despite these broad opportunities to express their opinions, some people still are not satisfied and may decide to take the law into their own hands. Yet even then, the Constitution guarantees criminals—and those suspected of crimes—certain rights. These include protection from unreasonable searches (the Fourth Amendment), protection from detention without formal charges (Fifth Amendment), the right to a speedy, public trial where defendants can face their accusers (Sixth Amendment), the right to a jury trial (Seventh Amendment), and protection from cruel and unusual punishment (Eighth Amendment).

Under extraordinary circumstance, such as war and other threats to national security, citizens and the government may call for curbs on these rights. They may suggest that it is necessary to curb the rights of individuals in order to protect the broader community. Terrorism raises many difficult questions about how to balance individual rights against national security. As the number of terrorist attacks within and against the United States increase, the number of complicating factors increases. The stakes also become higher as the number of potential casualties increase. Should rules be bent if they could stop an attack that would kill thousands? How can you serve warrants against people who refuse to acknowledge the authority of the U.S. legal system or who are not even on U.S. soil? How can you uncover conspiracies without invading privacy? How can you have a fair trial when evidence was obtained through clandestine measures or when potential witnesses are fugitives protected by other countries? The federal government still is looking for procedures that will protect Americans while not violating the principles on which the country was founded. It has proved to be an exceedingly difficult dilemma to resolve.

Prior to the World Trade Center bombing in 1993, the United States largely had been insulated from foreign terrorist groups. Most of the groups that challenged U.S. sovereignty in the second half of the 20th century were based within the United States and were run largely by U.S. citizens. Like terrorists in other countries, these groups tried to keep the casualty rate low and the publicity high. They were more interested in making their point than staging a massacre. This dramatically changed when Timothy McVeigh bombed a federal office building in Oklahoma City in April 1995, killing 168 people.

DOMESTIC TERRORISM

The language and terminology used to describe domestic unrest in the United States can be confusing. Prior to the Oklahoma City attack many incidents were interpreted as isolated examples of hate crimes. According to the FBI:

> *A hate crime, also known as a bias crime, is a criminal offense committed against a person, property, or society that is motivated, in whole or in part, by the offender's bias against a race, religion, disability, sexual orientation, or ethnicity/national origin.*[1]

The Ku Klux Klan (KKK) and the Aryan Nations are traditional examples of hate-crime groups. However, some analysts are wondering whether hate crimes are that different from terrorism. What originally appeared to be isolated, usually racially motivated attacks have been linked to larger, organized groups located across the country. The resurgence of religious-based terrorist groups since the 1990s has seen deliberate efforts to exterminate entire categories of people in campaigns that somewhat resemble those of hate-crime groups. Like the jihadists of al-Qaeda, White Supremacists believe their activities are sanctioned by their God, while members of the American militia movement decide to live apart from what they perceive as a corrupt secular state. Whether quoting Marx, the Bible, or the Koran, groups such as the Weathermen, the KKK, and al-Qaeda believe they follow a more enlightened doctrine. It may be prudent for analysts and law-enforcement agencies to remove the boundaries between hate crimes and terrorism in order to benefit from intelligence gathering and law-enforcement techniques developed by experts on both issues.

Mirroring the pattern seen with international terrorism, the ideology, motives, and tactics of U.S.-based terrorist groups have changed over time. In the 1960s and 1970s, left-wing, communist, or socialist groups such as the Weathermen and the Symbionese Liberation Army prevailed. There were also nationalist groups focusing on Puerto Rican independence and Native American sovereignty. The American Indian Movement (AIM) successfully occupied several symbolic facilities, including Alcatraz prison in San Francisco Bay (1969), the Bureau of Indian Affairs offices in Washington, D.C. (1972), and the Pine Ridge reservation in South Dakota (1973), to press the U.S. government to honor the commitments of previous treaties and improve living conditions on the Indian reservations. However, Washington dismissed AIM activities as intertribal conflicts rather than terrorist incidents. But because of the unique legal status of Native Americans, which are considered independent nations whose relations with the United States are regulated by treaties, AIM had potential for being an "international" group seeking changes in U.S. government policy. They could have been an attractive venue for terrorist groups wanting to infiltrate the United States. The harshness of the U.S. crackdown on AIM activities—such as dispatching 300 FBI agents overnight to investigate the deaths of two FBI agents on a reservation in 1975—suggests that Washington was significantly worried about the group's potential.[2]

In the 1990s, right-wing antigovernment groups became the norm. The FBI believes the shift was a reaction to several changes at the federal level of government. First, the Brady Bill was passed in 1993. Named for and inspired by former White House press secretary James Brady who was severely injured during the attempted assassination of Ronald Reagan in 1981, the Brady Bill regulates the sale of firearms, adding such provisions as a five-day waiting period and background checks on potential buyers. Many Americans believed this violated their constitutional right to bear arms, and some people—including Timothy McVeigh—even believed it was the first step in a government campaign to confiscate weapons and decided to create their own private stockpiles. Second, as the United Nations became more assertive, some Americans believed Washington intended to turn over some federal authority to the United Nations.[3] Consequently, some individuals decided they would no longer observe the authority—sovereignty—of the U.S. government. The Patriot Act of 2001, discussed below, only fueled their paranoia.

National Self-Determination

Small nationalist groups have made self-rule demands against the U.S. government. The most violent movement has been for Puerto Rican independence, and Cuba is believed to have supported the movement for decades.[4] Since the United States won the island in the Spanish-American War in 1898, Puerto Rico has been a U.S. territory. Its residents are U.S. citizens and are self-governing, although ultimate control lies with the U.S. Congress; Puerto Rico has a nonvoting delegate in the U.S. House of Representatives. The political limbo has led to local frustrations punctuated by occasional violence.

At least two Puerto Rican nationalist groups have carried out anti-U.S. attacks. On November 1, 1950, Oscar Collaza (1914–94) and Griselio Torresola (1925–50) of the Puerto Rican Nationalist Party attempted to assassinate President Harry Truman as he napped at Blair House, his temporary home while the White House was under renovation. Torresola and one police officer were killed in the resulting shootout.[5] Collaza was sentenced to death, but Truman commuted the sentence to life. President Jimmy Carter pardoned and released Collaza in 1979, and he returned to Puerto Rico.

Four years after the Blair House incident, on March 1, 1954, Puerto Rican nationalists began to shoot inside the U.S. Capitol, ultimately wounding five congressmen.[6] That attack was carried out by the Armed Forces of National Liberation (Fuerzas Armadas de Liberación Nacional, FALN). The FALN also carried out a series of more than 100 bombings during the 1970s, including attacks in New York City and Chicago. The group faded as members were arrested, and it has largely been inactive since the mid-1980s.

In contrast, the Popular Puerto Rican Army, "Los Macheteros," (the Cane Cutters) remains active; most of its activities take place on the island of Puerto Rico itself, mainly against U.S. military facilities and personnel. The group robbed a Wells Fargo bank in Connecticut in 1983, reportedly taking $7 million. Eleven Macheteros were arrested and sentenced to extensive jail terms for the Wells Fargo heist, but President Bill Clinton granted them clemency in 1999 provided they would renounce violence.[7]

The nationalist movement waned while the Macheteros leaders were in prison. There were protests related to the U.S. military test site in Puerto Rico, Vieques, but independence-oriented political parties polled below 5 percent and three successive referenda (1967, 1993, 1998) rejected independence. Apathy increased and "None of the above" won the 1998 referendum out of a list of possible governance systems.

Independence suddenly became an issue again in September 2005, after FBI agents shot and killed Los Macheteros founder Filiberto Ojedo Ríos (1933–2005). Ojedo Ríos had been a fugitive since escaping from U.S. custody in 1990 in connection with the Wells Fargo robbery. Amnesty International, among other groups, called for an investigation into the circumstances of Ojedo Ríos's death.[8] Thousands of Puerto Ricans turned out for Ojedo

Ríos's funeral, and talk of independence resumed among the population. In late December 2005, President George W. Bush suggested readdressing the issue by holding another referendum on independence.[9]

A variety of nationalist-oriented groups have based their operations in the United States but have seldom directly attacked U.S. citizens or facilities. These include the Armenian Revolutionary Army, the Cambodian Freedom Fighters, the Free Vietnam Revolutionary Group, World Formosans for Independence (of Taiwan), and the Yemen Islamic Jihad. Such groups tend to attack embassies, airline offices, and other sites linked to the government they want to overthrow in their homeland. Although these groups generally did not target U.S. citizens, the Croatian Freedom Fighters hijacked a TWA airliner en route to Chicago from New York's LaGuardia airport in 1976 and bombed the base of the Statue of Liberty in 1980.[10] The group eventually surrendered, its leader was jailed, and Croatia received its independence from Yugoslavia in 1991 without the CFF's help.

Left-Wing/Counterculture Organizations

Left-wing groups embrace socialist or communist ideals to bring about economic equality through revolution. The FBI notes that members of these groups "view themselves as protectors of the American people against capitalism and imperialism."[11] While working toward the eventual revolution, many left-wing groups have engaged in criminal activities thought to damage the economy, such as robbing banks and bombing corporate headquarters. They also may try to damage the government's credibility by targeting symbols of federal authority, such as courthouses or military recruiting centers. The two best-known left-wing U.S. groups were the Weather Underground and the Symbionese Liberation Army.

Weather Underground (or the Weathermen)[12] were a U.S.-based group in the 1960s and 1970s that opposed the Vietnam War and economic privilege. Only about a dozen strong, members tended to be white, 20-something college students from middle-class families. "They came off as articulate, committed, and chic, and they called for the immediate overthrow of the government."[13] Member Bill Ayers summed up their philosophy as: "Kill all the rich people. Break up their cars and apartments. Bring the revolution home, kill your parents, that's where it's really at."[14] In an effort to destroy "American imperialism," the Weathermen bombed banks, university departments, and military facilities in New York City and Chicago. The group arranged protests outside the Democratic National Convention in 1968 and staged their own "Days of Rage" in Chicago's posh Gold Coast retail district in October 1969 but attracted crowds of only a few hundred. Three members were killed trying to build a bomb at a Greenwich Village townhouse in 1970, but the group successfully planted some two dozen bombs, including ones at the U.S. Capitol and Pentagon in 1971, after bombing the New York City police headquarters and National Guard offices in Washington, D.C., in 1970. The attacks were less glamorous than they sounded—it was the U.S. Capitol barber shop and a Pentagon bathroom. The group's downfall was an armored car robbery in Nyack, New York, on August 20, 1981. Members walked away with $1.6 million, but three people, two police officers and a security guard, were killed in the attack. Kathy Boudin (1943–) and her husband, David Gilbert (1944–), were arrested and sentenced to jail. Boudin was paroled in 2003, Gilbert remains in prison.[15]

SYMBIONESE LIBERATION ARMY

The Symbionese Liberation Army was described previously in terms of its skills in kidnapping and media manipulation. Their public relations proficiency may in part have resulted from the fact that the "Army" started as a theater group.[16] The group flickered out after six members died in a police shootout and fire at their base in Los Angeles on May 17, 1975. Others, including Patty Hearst, were arrested, tried, and jailed in 1975–76. A few survivors tried to keep the movement alive but eventually returned to normal life. The SLA made headlines again in 1999 when four fugitives were arrested on charges dating to 1975. Specifically, members had tried to place pipe bombs under two Los Angeles Police Department vehicles and killed a bank customer when robbing the Crocker National Bank outside Sacramento. One member, Kathleen Ann Soliah, had been quietly living in Minnesota [using the name Sara Jane Olson] despite outstanding warrants for possession of explosives and attempted murder. Soliah initially planned to plead innocent to the bombing charges and face a trial, but after 9/11 she feared that the public anger toward terrorism might result in the maximum prison sentence possible. Instead Soliah pleaded guilty and received two terms of 10 years to life. In 2002 Soliah and three other SLA members pleaded guilty to second degree murder, receiving sentences between six and eight years.

M-19

In the 1980s a group known variously as the "May 19 Communist Order" or the "Resistance Conspiracy" robbed a series of banks in the United States and used the money to stage at least eight bombings. On November 7, 1983, M-19 bombed the U.S. Capitol building to protest U.S. military action in Grenada and Lebanon. Since the explosion occurred at 10:58 P.M., no injuries were reported.[17] The group was a fund-raising arm—or at least a front operation—for a coalition of neo-communist groups, including the Weathermen, the

Black Liberation Army, and the Palestine Liberation Organization. The name was derived from the birth dates of Vietnam's Ho Chi Minh and Malcolm X, both born on May 19. The group never had more than about 20 members, and most had been arrested by the mid-1980s.

Single-Issue Groups

The United States has also produced several small extremist groups with very narrow agendas. According to the FBI, "extremist special interest groups seek to resolve specific issues, rather than effect widespread political change." This movement has eclipsed the right-wing terrorism of Timothy McVeigh and now is the primary domestic terrorist threat.[18] The activities of these single-issue groups tend to be symbolic and destructive, but the damage so far has been measured in terms of property loss, not human lives. However, law-enforcement officials believe that fatalities are only a matter of time. John Lewis, FBI deputy assistant director for counterterrorism, warns, "Plainly, I think we're lucky. Once you set one of these fires they can go way out of control."[19]

The largest category of such groups emerged in the 1990s around environmental causes, such as preserving forests, not wearing fur, and ending scientific testing on animals. The two best-known "eco-terrorist" groups are the Animal Liberation Front (ALF) and the Earth Liberation Front (ELF). The FBI considers ALF to be "a terrorist group whose purpose is to bring about social and political change through use of force and violence."[20] The boundaries between the two groups are fluid, as they appear to share members and to cooperate.

Between 1990 and 2005 ALF and ELF claimed responsibility for 1,200 criminal attacks causing more than $110 million in damages. Arson is their weapon of choice. ALF attacks have targeted medical testing laboratories, meat packing companies, the Big Apple Circus, and a Bureau of Land Management horse corral in Oregon, while the Earth Liberation Front set fire to the offices of an Oregon logging company, an SUV dealership in Eugene, Oregon, and a Vail, Colorado, ski resort. Damages in the Vail attack exceeded $12 million.[21]

Anti-Federalist/Right-Wing/Militia

The majority of U.S. terrorist groups in the 1980s and 1990s are labeled as "anti-federalist" or "right wing." Groups in the first category resist what they see as the federal government's intrusion into their private lives. They may object to paying taxes, disagree with gun control regulations, or object to paper money—the "paper terrorists" mentioned earlier wanted their court victories paid in gold. Right-wing groups tend to espouse racial superiority and Christianity and preach the need to reduce the influence—"purify" the country—of nonwhites and non-Christians in U.S. society. This "Christian Identity" movement preaches that white people are the true children of God and that believers should only obey the law of God, not the law of the government. They have been more violent and less secretive than the KKK. Followers embrace a variety of conspiracy theories that often speak of a Jewish plot to control the world.[22] Their philosophy was aptly summed up in one comment about the 9/11 terrorists: "We may not want them marrying our daughters . . . but anyone willing to drive a plane into a building to kill Jews is alright by me. I wish our members had half as much testicular fortitude."[23]

Small, loosely coordinated Christian Identity movements are spread across the United States. As far back as 1996, the Southern Poverty Law Center calculated 441 groups active in all 50 states. A 2004 report by the Anti-Defamation League reported groups still present in 25 states.

Many movements combine elements of both anti-federalist and right-wing ideology and take the additional step of forming paramilitary units, which are outlawed in almost every state. "The most ominous aspect of the militias," according to the FBI, "is the conviction, openly expressed by many members, that an impending armed conflict with the federal government necessitates paramilitary training and the stockpiling of weapons."[24] Owning, hoarding, and using weapons are hallmarks of the right-wing movement. "Go to virtually any good-sized gun show in the country," writes the Anti-Defamation League, and you will "find dealers selling Army manuals on improvised munitions as well as a host of manuals and publications by private publishers that form a virtual literary subgenre catering to a paranoid audience."[25] Assembling this arsenal usually violates federal firearms regulations, setting the stage for a paramilitary—U.S. government confrontation. "When Congress banned certain assault weapons," Oklahoma City bomber Timothy McVeigh told his biographers, "I snapped."[26]

One of the earliest and strongest right-wing movements was the Posse Comitatus, which denies the legitimacy of the federal government. Many members are white supremacists, but that viewpoint is not central to the Posse philosophy. Since the original group's creation in 1969, members have not recognized any authority higher than the sheriff. The Posse name is taken from the Posse Comitatus Act of 1878, the legal basis of the Wild West notion of using an ad hoc volunteer corps to enforce local laws. Its symbol is a sheriff's star with a noose in the center. The movement loathes Jews and tax collectors and has attacked federal officials, particularly Internal Revenue Service agents. Numerous autonomous Posse Comitatus "franchises" have developed across the United States, such as the Montana Freemen, the West Virginia Mountaineer Militia, the South Texas Light Infantry, and the Kentucky Militia. The groups were known for their fondness for weapons and their repeated efforts to stockpile and drill for coming battles. The Montana Militia conveniently offered a $50 "do-it-yourself apocalypse kit" that contained such essentials as a gun, ammunition, a can opener, a toothbrush, and instructions on how to build a fall-out shelter.[27] The groups thrived on conspiracy theories. For example, Donald Beauregard, leader of the Florida militia, claimed to have uncovered a secret plot by Jews and the United Nations to take over the United States. The information, he explained, had been revealed to him in a map printed on the back of a box of Trix cereal.[28]

McVeigh said that his Oklahoma City attack was inspired by two events: Ruby Ridge and the Branch Davidians. In both cases, federal officials approached private citizens about alleged weapons violations, shots were fired, and women and children died. "What the U.S. government did at Waco and Ruby Ridge was dirty," McVeigh declared. "And I gave dirty back to them at Oklahoma City."[29]

RUBY RIDGE

Ruby Ridge is in a remote area of Idaho near the Canadian border that overlooks Ruby Creek. In the 1980s Randy and Vicki Weaver built a cabin in the area and moved their family there to await what they believed to be the coming Armageddon. In the meantime, they attended local meetings of the Aryan Nations, a nationwide white supremacist movement. The couple embraced some of the teachings of the Aryan Nations but never officially joined. On August 21, 1992, when federal agents tried to make an arrest in connection with illegal firearms sales, U.S. marshals went to the Weaver home with an arrest warrant for Randy. The Weavers saw strangers on their property and grabbed their guns. In the resulting shoot-out, one federal agent was mortally wounded, as were the Weavers' 14-year-old son and Vicki herself. Vicki was shot in the head while holding her baby daughter, an image that particularly enraged the militia movement.

BRANCH DAVIDIANS

One year later the Branch Davidians complex outside Waco, Texas, went up in flames on April 19, leaving 74 members—including 21 children—dead inside. Led by David Koresh, members of the religious group had refused to comply with federal laws on weapons possession or to allow an investigation into charges of child abuse. A team from the Bureau of Alcohol, Tobacco, and Firearms (ATF) descended on the Branch Davidian compound on February 28 to serve a search warrant. The armed Davidians responded with gunfire, and the ensuing battle killed four ATF agents and five Davidians. The remaining ATF agents exited the compound and began a 51-day standoff against members of the sect. On orders from U.S. Attorney General Janet Reno, on April 19 the agents fired tear gas canisters into the compound in an effort to end the siege. In response the Davidians began to set their compound on fire, and almost none exited the buildings as the compound burned, killing everyone inside.[30] The Davidians' complaint was not necessarily related to religious freedom, but rather the right to bear arms and the right to privacy.

OKLAHOMA CITY

At 9:02 A.M. on April 19, 1995, a truck loaded with 4,800 pounds of fertilizer and racing fuel exploded in front of the Alfred P. Murrah Federal Building in Oklahoma City. The entire front of the nine-story building collapsed, killing 168 people. The truck had been parked in front of the building's day-care center, and 19 of the center's 40 children also perished—"collateral damage," according to the bomber, Timothy McVeigh, that distracted the media from his real message. McVeigh said he chose the building because it housed federal offices, including a branch of the Bureau of Alcohol, Tobacco, and Firearms, and also for its *U* shape; a bomb placed in the bend of the *U* could cause extensive damage. He was disappointed, however, that the entire building did not collapse: "Damn, I didn't knock the building down. I didn't take it down."[31]

Barely an hour after the blast, police stopped McVeigh for driving a car without a license plate. They discovered loaded guns in his vehicle and took him into custody. As investigators began to examine evidence and eyewitness accounts from the bombing, they began to realize that they already had the perpetrator in custody. McVeigh had liked guns since childhood, spoke in racist terms, and hated the government. He had served in the army during the 1991 Gulf War but flunked the psychological evaluation needed to enter the elite Green Berets. Angry, he dropped out of the army and began to associate with other right-wing, antigovernment individuals. He came to believe that the U.S. government was plotting against its own citizen and would soon confiscate his personal arsenal. The tragedies at Ruby Ridge and Waco confirmed his fears; in his mindset, BATF no longer stood for "Bureau of Alcohol, Tobacco, and Firearms," but "Burn All Toddlers First."[32]

McVeigh was tried, found guilty, and executed by lethal injection. Though he never denied involvement in the explosion, McVeigh and his defense team did insist that the attack was part of a much larger operation. His lawyer filed a last-minute motion to delay McVeigh's execution to allow more time to obtain alleged U.S. government surveillance materials about a larger conspiracy, and McVeigh's execution was postponed from May 16,

2001, to June 11, 2001.[33] In bizarre coincidences noted by, among others, Clinton administration counterterrorism chief Richard A. Clarke and never quite explained, World Trade Center bomber Ramzi Yusef apparently crossed paths with McVeigh coconspirator Terry Nichols in the Philippines, and al-Qaeda members once attended a radical Islamic conference in Oklahoma City.[34] No connection was discovered, and McVeigh declined to make any statement before he was executed.

The militia movement began to wane in the late 1990s. Increased law-enforcement activities, particularly after 9/11, also took a toll on the militia membership roster.[35] According to studies by the Southern Poverty Law Center, militiamen went "home, disillusioned and tired of waiting for the revolution that never seems to come."[36] However, some experts fear that the crackdown will only strengthen resistance among the most hard-core supremacists.[37] In 2006 the movement seemed to be reviving with an anti-Hispanic orientation as a consequence of the federal government's increased focus on immigration issues.[38]

In addition to the recognized militia and white supremacist groups, individuals have been known to embrace the right-wing ideology but to act on their own. Debate continues to swirl over whether Timothy McVeigh had more help in Oklahoma City than his one convicted coconspirator, Terry L. Nichols. But a series of bombings in the South in the mid-1980s that appeared to be the work the "Army of God" was later confirmed to be the work of a lone wolf: Eric Robert Rudolph.

OLYMPIC GAMES, 1996

On July 27, 1996, a pipe bomb exploded in Centennial Olympic Park in Atlanta, Georgia, a large outdoor area where the athletes and the public could mingle and enjoy music, entertainment, and shopping during the Olympic Games. The bomber had tipped off the police 30 minutes before the actual explosion, giving security guards enough time to locate the backpack containing the bomb and to begin to evacuate bystanders. However, the bomb went off before it was defused. Hundreds of people were injured and one woman, Alice Hawthorne, was killed by flying debris. In the ensuing panic, a Turkish cameraman suffered a fatal heart attack.

Almost two years later, the FBI connected the Olympic attack to two other bombings in Atlanta in early 1997 and one in nearby Birmingham, Alabama, in January 1998. Unlike the Olympic attack, the bomber wrote to newspapers to claim responsibility for the 1997 and 1998 attacks in the name of the "Army of God." Ultimately the FBI identified Eric Robert Rudolph (1966–) as the bomber and concluded that he was acting alone rather than as part of a larger terrorist organization. A high-school dropout who briefly tried army life, Rudolph opposed abortion and homosexuality, which he argued the U.S. government supported, and embraced the Christian Identity movement.[39] Two years after his capture in 2003 he issued a statement explaining his motives: "The plan was to force the cancellation of the Games, or at least create a state of insecurity to empty the streets around the venues and thereby eat into the vast amounts of money invested."[40] Rudolph is currently serving two life sentences at a federal prison in Colorado.

FOREIGN TERRORISM

While the homeland remained relatively safe, foreign-based terrorist organizations have attacked U.S. interests overseas on several occasions with considerable loss of American lives.

Lebanon, 1980s

Lebanon was a particularly dangerous place for U.S. representatives in the 1980s. In April 1983 Islamic militants bombed the U.S. Embassy in Beirut, killing 63 people. Six months later a suicide bomber linked to Hezbollah drove a truck loaded with explosives into the U.S. Marine barracks in Beirut, killing 242 soldiers. Hezbollah, a radical Shiite Muslim group, also kidnapped a series of U.S. citizens living and working in Lebanon in the 1980s, holding them for up to seven years while demanding that Washington cease U.S. support for Israel. Yet the U.S. government under Ronald Reagan refused to retaliate for these attacks, despite convincing evidence of Iranian and Syrian complicity. Instead, the United States simply pulled its troops out of Lebanon, which some terrorists took as a victory.[41]

World Trade Center, 1993

Ten years after the Beirut embassy bombing, a truck bomb was detonated in an underground parking garage beneath the World Trade Center in New York City. The February 26, 1993, blast did not cause the towers to collapse, as would the 2001 air strikes, but it did fill the building with smoke. Investigators later learned that the bombers had wanted to fill the truck with cyanide so that poison gas would filter through the building and cause heavy casualties, but they could not afford to purchase an adequate supply. Six people died in the 1993 attack, 1,000 were wounded, and the resulting hole was seven stories high.

Unlike 2001, the 1993 attack was not conducted by al-Qaeda. Osama bin Laden's name was never even mentioned as a possible suspect.[42] Instead, investigators discovered a small group of Arab immigrants clustered around a blind Egyptian cleric, Sheikh Omar Abdel Rahman (1938–), at a mosque in New Jersey. Police had an amazing stroke of luck when they linked a truck axle found at the scene to a vehicle rental company in New Jersey. The FBI traced the rental to Mohammed Salameh (1968–) and a search of his apartment found traces of explosives. Salameh actually went back to the Ryder truck rental facility to request a refund of his $400 security deposit. He explained that he could not return the actual truck as it had been stolen. The manager said he would have to come back later, but declined to mention that FBI agents would be waiting for him.[43] Salameh was arrested and interrogated about his coconspirators.

Ultimately five men who had fled overseas were arrested and convicted of the bombing. Salameh, Mahmud Abouhalima (1959–), Nidal Ayyad (1968–), and Abdul Yasin (1960–) were convicted in 1994. A fifth conspirator, Ramzi Yusef (1968–) fled to Pakistan, where he and his uncle, Khalid Sheikh Mohammed (1965–), began to plot to blow up U.S.-flagged planes in the Philippines, but he would be convicted in 1995 for the WTC explosion. Yusef apparently was the ringleader, although the WTC cell sought and obtained approval for its plans from Sheikh Rahman. In 1995 Rahman and nine others were convicted of conspiracy to bomb a series of New York–area landmarks, including the UN headquarters and the Lincoln Tunnel. That investigation turned up two names that would soon become more familiar to the U.S. government. First, Sheikh Rahman's group was found to have ties to the al-Kifa Center in Brooklyn, which was funded by the Afghan Services Bureau—a bin Laden enterprise. Second, Yusef's uncle, Khalid Sheikh Mohammed, had played a background role in 1993 but would become the mastermind behind the 9/11 attack and a top al-Qaeda leader until his capture in 2003.[44]

Al-Qaeda and Osama bin Laden, 2001

The 9/11 hijackings were the culmination of Osama bin Laden's three-year campaign against the United States. Born to a wealthy family in Saudi Arabia in 1957, bin Laden (1957–) founded al-Qaeda ("the Base") to establish a global Islamic state (caliphate). To this end, bin Laden declared in 1998 that it is the "duty of all Muslims to kill U.S. citizens, civilian and military, and their allies everywhere." His objections to the United States are threefold: Washington's support of Israel, the U.S. military presence in the Middle East—especially Saudi Arabia, with the holy cities of Mecca and Medina, and the non-Islamic values that he believes the United States is spreading throughout the world.

Prior to 2001 al-Qaeda had made three successful attacks against U.S. interests abroad. In August 1998, suicide truck bombs almost simultaneously attacked the U.S. embassies in Dar-es-Salaam, Tanzania, and Nairobi, Kenya. Two years later, on October 12, 2000, al-Qaeda operatives attacked the USS *Cole,* moored outside Aden, Yemen. Two suicide bombers rammed the ship with a small boat loaded with explosives. The resulting blast killed 17 sailors. Al-Qaeda's most complex and most lethal attack came in September 2001.

Al-Qaeda and bin Laden were immediately suspected of masterminding the 9/11 attacks. That morning a team of 19 hijackers boarded four commercial aircraft; two departed from Boston, one from Newark, New Jersey, and one from Washington Dulles International Airport. Once the airplanes were aloft the four teams of hijackers attacked the pilots, took control of the aircraft, and turned them into lethal weapons. Two planes flew head-on into the twin towers of the World Trade Center in New York City. Loaded with thousands of pounds of jet fuel for flights to California, the planes exploded on impact, causing the buildings to erupt in flames. Within two hours, structurally weakened by the heat of the fires, the two towers collapsed, killing more than 2,700 people. The third airplane was flown into the Pentagon, headquarters of the U.S. Department of Defense just outside of Washington D.C. The airplane hit a section of building that had just been renovated and strengthened, but while the Pentagon did not collapse, it also was engulfed in flames, killing 189. The Newark plane was the last to depart, and passengers with cell phones heard of the other three hijackings as a terrorist squad took over their plane. The passengers, realizing they were likely doomed, decided to revolt and tried to overpower the terrorists, causing the plane to crash into a field outside Shanksburg, Pennsylvania. None of the 44 passengers and crew aboard the plane survived, but they prevented this terrorist squad from reaching its target, believed to be either the White House or the U.S. Capitol.

As of late 2006, bin Laden remains a fugitive. Intelligence sources believe he hides in the mountains along the Afghanistan-Pakistan border. The U.S. government is offering a $25 million bounty to anyone who helps apprehend him.

COUNTERTERRORISM

The U.S. government has adopted a variety of policies and strategies to deal with terrorism. Many predate the 2001 attacks, but legislation and regulations greatly increased following 9/11. As mentioned earlier, the U.S. government makes a formal distinction between *antiterrorism* and *counterterrorism,* separating relief efforts (*anti-*) from prevention efforts (*counter-*). However, even the government has a tendency to lump both strategies together as *counterterrorism.*

Prepare: Antiterrorism

Beginning in late 2001 Washington created a three-pronged strategy for responding to terrorist attacks, consisting of programs for the national, state/local, and individual levels.

FEDERAL

First, the White House ordered the creation of an office to coordinate the multiple agencies related to national security. Former Pennsylvania governor Thomas Ridge was appointed as head of the Office of Homeland Security, which originally was intended to be a division within the White House. Soon, however, officials realized the size of the task needed a cabinet-level post, and the Department of Homeland Security (DHS) was born. Armed with a $40 billion annual budget, Ridge was to integrate 22 agencies into a one-stop center for national defense, including Customs, Immigration, the Secret Service, the Coast Guard, Transportation Security, National Infrastructure Protection Center, the Plum Island Animal Disease Center, and the Animal and Plant Health Inspection Service.[45] To prevent turf wars, a small group of White House officials decided which agencies would be transferred. In fact, a *Washington Post* investigation discovered, "The plan had been put together with such speed and secrecy that after its release angry officials had to explain to the White House how their agencies really worked."[46] Directors of older agencies fought to keep their divisions from being reassigned to DHS, bickering over jurisdiction, supervision, even division names.

Ridge began work on January 24, 2003, without office space, without assistants and undersecretaries, and only 10 of the 300 aide positions filled. Ridge found he "had only a few dozen staffers to oversee a department that was suddenly responsible for everything from livestock inspections to floodplain mapping to the national registry for missing pets." Days later he learned from the State of the Union address that DHS would not have responsibility for a new terrorist-tracking center as promised. Frustrated, Ridge resigned after two years. "The notion that everyone was going to join hands and sing 'Kumbaya,'" Ridge told the *Washington Post,* "I don't think anybody in our leadership expected that to happen. And it didn't."

The anthrax attacks of October 2001 revealed that the United States did not have an adequate stockpile of the antibiotic Cipro, which is the preferred treatment for anthrax exposure. As early as 2000 the government had been warned that medical supplies were poorly managed, and the Strategic National Stockpile and the National Disaster Medical System were transferred to DHS despite objections from the Department of Health and Human Services. The deficiencies have not been solved, as demonstrated by the flu vaccine shortage of 2004–05 and the subsequent outbreak overseas of vaccine-resistant avian influenza ("bird flu") in 2005–06.[47]

STATE AND LOCAL

The Federal Emergency Management Agency (FEMA) was to be the focus of relief efforts, but instead it came to symbolize the problems of overbureaucratization. FEMA works to improve the U.S. ability to recover from a catastrophe, whether a terrorist attack or a natural disaster. As an independent agency, FEMA has worked with state and local first responders to train and prepare for natural emergencies such as floods and earthquakes. It provided billions of dollars to state programs to improve local readiness. However, the agency was folded into the new Department of Homeland Security in 2003, which severely reduced its flexibility. In particular, it lost control over the state and local grants, and it floundered when the agency could not quickly find replacements for key personnel who did not transfer to DHS.

FEMA antiterrorism activities encompass four broad categories: (1) improving resources, (2) conducting risk assessments, (3) identifying ways to mitigate hazards, and (4) implementing and revising plans. Ideally, FEMA would establish communication links among local rescue agencies to quickly deploy health and safety personnel to disasters, provide food and shelter for victims, determine vulnerabilities and loopholes, and propose standards for building construction to withstand terrorist attacks or design landscaping and security barriers to reduce easy access to possible targets. However, the disastrous performance by FEMA during Hurricane Katrina and Hurricane Rita in 2005 seriously called into question the agency's ability to carry out these functions and raised questions about how much had been learned since 9/11. Congress rejected a proposal to make FEMA independent of the DHS to increase its flexibility and reduce the bureaucratic red tape that slowed its response to the 2005 hurricanes.[48]

INDIVIDUAL

The federal government and the private sector are also taking practical steps to educate the public and emergency professionals about what to do in case of a terrorist attack. The Memorial Institute for the Prevention of Terrorism (MIPT), located in Oklahoma City, sponsors research to discover equipment, training, and procedures that might assist first responders—police officers, firefighters, emergency medical technicians, and all of the others who are first on the scene in the aftermath of terrorist attack. Founded in 1999 as a nonprofit corporation in Oklahoma, MIPT works to expand and disseminate the practical knowledge Oklahoma City gained after the Murrah Federal Building bombing in 1995.[49]

"Shelter in Place" is a program advocated by the American Red Cross, the Center for Disease Control, and the Department of Homeland Security, among others. It provides basic information on how families, schools, businesses, and other places where people gather can prepare to remain in one location until government help arrives. For example, schools need to be able to provide for the basic needs of students and staff if an emergency situation, such as a sniper, a tornado, or a biological attack, arises preventing them from leaving the building. Citizens are encouraged to assemble their own survival kits, including clean water, canned food, a first aid kit, duct tape to seal windows and doors, and battery-operated radios. The Rand Corporation, a think tank, provides a pocket-sized card with basic instructions for chemical, radiological, nuclear, and biological attacks.[50] The Red Cross and National Centers for Disease Control offer similar literature.

Prevent

GLOBAL COOPERATION

Washington works with global partners to prevent terror suspects from reaching the United States. The U.S. Department of State Bureau of Diplomatic Security offers antiterrorist training programs to civilians and to foreign governments. Courses offered include proper handling of weapons of mass destruction, hostage negotiation, kidnapping intervention, border management, terrorist financing, air security administration, diplomatic/VIP protection, and crime scene investigation.[51] By raising law-enforcement capacity in friendly countries through training and providing specialized equipment, the United States seeks to extend the reach of its law-enforcement investigations and to better secure the safety of U.S. citizens and interests in foreign countries. Recent initiatives include efforts to protect VIPs in Afghanistan, reduce the instances of kidnapping in Colombia, and create a national counterterrorism task force in Indonesia. Since the programs began in 1983, the Office of Antiterrorism Assistance estimates that it has trained more than 36,000 students.

Washington is cautious about which regimes it chooses to assist. Potential customers for antiterrorist training must be in high-risk areas, be of substantial interest to the United States, have regular flights to the United States, and mutual interests. Individual participants are also thoroughly screened by U.S. investigators to eliminate any person with a questionable background.

As part of its counterterrorism efforts, the United States has provided aid to countries that are known as bases for terrorist groups. Washington has provided funds to help Lebanon to contain Hezbollah, the Palestinian

Authority to counter Hamas and Palestine Islamic Jihad, and Central Asian states to counter al-Qaeda activities along their borders.[52]

Prior to 9/11 U.S. policy on terrorism evolved in reaction to specific events, rather than as a comprehensive strategy. Since domestic groups dominated, emphasis was placed on law enforcement: Efforts were focused on punishing terrorist acts, not eliminating the causes motivating terrorists. Instead of a holistic approach, terrorism was a component of regional policy: Irish terrorism was part of U.S.-British relations, for example, while the Palestinian problem was assigned to Middle East departments.[53] Emergency management was intended to be local, with the National Guard dispatched if deemed necessary. Since 1876 the U.S. military has been specifically excluded from acting as police officers on U.S. soil unless ordered by the president. If the military was to have a role, it would be to support disaster recovery efforts following a terrorist attack, not to prevent or intercept an attack.[54]

Six events in particular made Washington turn serious attention to the problem of potential terrorist attacks on U.S. soil: the Munich Olympics of 1972, the 1993 World Trade Center bombing, the Tokyo subway and Oklahoma City attacks of 1995, the 1996 Atlanta Olympics bombing, and the terrorist attacks of September 11, 2001. From the 1970s to September 10, 2001, the U.S. approach to terrorism was based on criminal law, law enforcement, and international cooperation. After 9/11 Washington adopted a unilateral military strategy, launching a "War on Terrorism."

1970s–1980s

First, after Munich, the U.S. government implemented a "lead-agency" strategy. This meant formally assigning the FBI to deal with domestic terrorism and the State Department to focus on attacks on Americans abroad. Little consideration was given to foreign attacks inside the United States. However, responsibility for specific actions under these broad divisions was less clear-cut and encouraged interdepartmental rivalries. According to David Long, former deputy director of the State Department Counterterrorism Office, U.S. counterterrorism plans were ill defined and overlapping: "In addition to diplomacy and law enforcement, they include military operations, intelligence operations, security, and public affairs."[55]

Second, the government worked to codify intelligence-gathering procedures. "Intelligence" comes generally from four sources: photo reconnaissance (spy satellites), telecommunication interception (wire-tapping), human agents (spies, informers, double-agents), and foreign intelligence agencies, such as Great Britain's MI-5 and MI-6.[56] The 1978 "Foreign Intelligence Surveillance Act" (FISA) established parameters for collecting telecommunications information, including when a court order is—or is not—required to establish a wiretap against a U.S. citizen suspected of involvement in foreign terrorist operations. Special Foreign Intelligence Surveillance Courts were created so that the attorney general of the United States could receive permission for surveillance without having to present potentially classified evidence in a public court. Persons found to be conducting unauthorized surveillance related to terrorism faced fines of $10,000 and/or five years in jail. The law was part of a series of measures designed to protect Americans from groundless, personally motivated surveillance that the Federal Bureau of Investigation was accused of engaging in during the 1960s and 1970s. In another effort to stress the rule of law, in December 1981 President Ronald Reagan signed Executive Order 12333 banning political assassination, after reports indicated that the CIA had tried to assassinate Cuban leader Fidel Castro.[57]

Third, since 1979 the State Department has identified countries that sponsor terrorism. The governments of these countries may directly provide funds or weapons to a terrorist group or allow them to operate within their borders with impunity. As of April 2006, six countries have been classified as state sponsors of terrorism: Cuba, Iran, Libya, North Korea, Sudan, and Syria.[58] The list is dynamic and may change from year to year. Iraq, for example, has been added and removed several times, and Libya was removed two weeks after the 2006 list was published. States on this list face bans on arms sales and economic assistance, while private firms and international organizations are advised to avoid financial transactions involving these states.

Fourth, the United States enacted laws that made it easier to prosecute crimes targeting Americans in U.S. courts, even if the crime took place outside U.S. territory. The laws are effective only if the United States can gain physical custody of a suspect, however, and often countries refuse to hand over a suspect if they disagree with U.S. laws (for example, if the suspect would face the death penalty) or fear reprisals from a third country (perhaps where the suspect lived) more than from the United States. The changes came as a result of the 1985 hijacking of the Italian cruise ship *Achille Lauro.* Palestinian terrorists killed Leon Klinghoffer, an elderly wheelchair-bound U.S. citizen aboard the ship but were eventually persuaded to surrender the ship in Egypt. However, neither Egypt nor Italy would deliver the suspects to U.S. authorities.

Finally, the government and airlines began to adopt policies in reaction to the wave of terrorist hijackings that began in the late 1960s and early 1970s. By 1973 the Federal Aviation Administration required passenger and baggage screening, and later sky marshals were put aboard planes. After the

Lockerbie crash of 1988, baggage could not be carried aboard a plane unless the owner was also aboard because Libyan terrorists had planted their bomb in unaccompanied baggage. However, there have always been more flights than sky marshals and few airlines and airports willing to bear the full price of screening equipment and staff.

1990s

The World Trade Center bombing in 1993 and the Oklahoma City bombing in 1995 propelled the White House and Congress to cooperate on a new package of terrorism legislation. Unlike the World Trade Center attackers, McVeigh was a home-grown terrorist who sympathized with the right-wing militia movement. Two months before his attack, on February 10, 1995, new terrorism laws were introduced in both houses of Congress. In the immediate aftermath of the Oklahoma City attack, congressional leaders promised to pass the legislation in six weeks. It actually took 12 months to hammer out a deal, but on April 24, 1996, President Bill Clinton signed the Antiterrorism and Effective Death Penalty Act into law.[59] The $1 billion package was primarily aimed at domestic terrorists and emphasized increasing law-enforcement funding, imposing stricter penalties, and streamlining death-row appeals. It also made it harder for members of known international terrorist groups to enter the United States or request political asylum.

The act also created a formal mechanism to sanction foreign terrorist groups. Under the new law, the State Department, at the president's direction, can formally identify insurgency movements as "Foreign Terrorist Organizations" (FTOs) if they threaten U.S. citizens or the country's national security. Once that terminology is applied, a series of sanctions comes into force against the group and its members. Sanctions include restrictions on visa applications by members and freezing group assets held in U.S. banks.[60] Furthermore, aiding any organization designated as an FTO is a criminal offense.

No sooner had this legislation been enacted than a new wave of terrorist attacks rocked the United States in summer 1996. First the radical group Hezbollah detonated a truck bomb outside Khobar Towers, a complex housing U.S. Air Force personnel in Saudi Arabia, on June 25, killing 19 U.S. soldiers and one Saudi. On July 17, TWA flight 800 exploded over Long Island as it departed for Paris, killing 230 passengers and crew. Though later determined to have been caused by a mechanical failure, the tragedy was initially blamed on terrorists. Ten days later, a pipe bomb exploded at the 1996 Olympics in Atlanta, Georgia, causing two deaths. The White House used this opening to introduce a revised Federal Aviation Administration Reauthorization Act that beefed up airport screening, passenger profiling, and baggage handling security.[61] The package, priced at $1 billion on top of the

$1 billion allocated in April, also took steps to improve security at U.S. facilities, such as embassies, weapons laboratories, and military bases.[62]

Osama bin Laden and al-Qaeda were largely unknown to U.S. intelligence in 1993, but bin Laden's name began to turn up as a donor to organizations linked to the World Trade Center bombers. White House security staff asked the CIA to begin to track bin Laden closely and, as they came to realize his influence, they even considered a covert action to take bin Laden into custody.[63] While that action was dismissed as too risky, attacks on U.S. interests increased, including the August 7, 1998, truck bombs that destroyed the U.S. embassies in Tanzania and Kenya. U.S. president Bill Clinton ordered surgical strikes against al-Qaeda targets in retaliation for the embassy bombings, which had caused the death of 301 people and injured more than 5,000. The strikes included dual raids on August 20, 1998, against an al-Qaeda training camp in Afghanistan and against a laboratory in Sudan, erroneously thought to be producing chemical weapons.[64] Bin Laden escaped unharmed.

The increased government attention to terrorism in general—and al-Qaeda in particular—paid off when plans were discovered to stage several attacks on New Year's Eve 1999. As intelligence sources reported increased activity by suspected terrorists, the White House put together a Millennium Alert strategy. FBI agents were deployed to investigate any potential leads and suspects. The State Department issued a travel alert to all Americans overseas in December and January.[65] More important, federal agents also put state and local officials on alert as well. Everyone from rookie cops to border guards to the director of the FBI was watching for terrorists.

On December 14, 1999, a customs officer in Washington state thought a passenger on a ferry from British Columbia was acting oddly. The passenger seemed nervous and avoided eye contact. When customs officer Diana Dean called him over for further questioning, the man ran away. After the suspect, Ahmed Ressam, was captured, officers searched his car—and found 100 pounds of bomb-making equipment. Ressam, a 32-year old Algerian living in Canada, had planned to bomb Los Angeles International Airport on New Year's Eve and had been trained by al-Qaeda. As the FBI traced Ressam's steps, they discovered an al-Qaeda cell in Montreal. Meanwhile, the CIA uncovered additional al-Qaeda operations to bomb a hotel in Amman, Jordan, as well as Christian shrines in the Middle East, and a navy ship, the USS *The Sullivans.*[66] In July 2005 Ressam was convicted and sentenced to 22 years in prison. The judge, John C. Coughenour, emphasized to the media that Ressam was convicted in a civilian court; justice had been served without the secret military tribunals established in 2001 and discussed below.[67]

According to White House counterterrorism chief Richard Clarke, "Clinton left office with bin Laden alive, but having authorized accounts to eliminate him and to step up attacks on al-Qaeda . . . many people, including the incoming Bush administration leadership, thought that he and his administration were overly obsessed with al-Qaeda. After all, al-Qaeda had killed only a few Americans."[68] Clarke, who remained in his post as the new Bush administration began, immediately requested an opportunity to brief the principal figures in the new administration about al-Qaeda, but the Bush White House had other priorities. Clarke requested the meeting in January 2001. It took place September 4, 2001.

2001–2006

Following 9/11, the White House launched a massive military campaign to hunt down bin Laden and to eliminate "those who hate democracy." Clearly preferring a military approach to diplomacy or economic sanctions, President George W. Bush presented the campaign as a "War on Terror." The war opened with new laws in the United States and the October 2001 invasion of Afghanistan. In his January 2002 State of the Union address, Bush defined an "Axis of Evil" consisting of Iraq, Iran, and North Korea, warning, "Some governments will be timid in the face of terror. And make no mistake about it: If they do not act, America will."[69]

The Axis of Evil speech was widely criticized, even by U.S. allies. Bush was accused of acting before creating a fully thought-out strategy, criticized for expanding the War on Terror to include Iraq without a concrete link between Baghdad and bin Laden, and denounced for acting unilaterally. European Union international relations chief Chris Patten called the speech "absolutist and simplistic" and called upon Europe to intervene before the White House went into "unilateralist overdrive."[70] The Bush administration would not tolerate any criticisms of its actions nor did it have patience to make its case before the international community. Instead, President Bush simply declared: "You are either with us or against us."[71]

Within days of the 9/11 attacks, Congress and the White House began work on a new legal framework for gathering intelligence to identify and prosecute suspected terrorists. Under the new system, terrorist-related investigations would now be modeled on military law, as well as including indefinite detention and the refusal to share incriminating information on a suspect that might compromise national security. The legal framework is examined in the Prosecute section below, but first we need to look at new efforts to identify terrorists, collect the evidence needed to prosecute them, and bring them into U.S. custody.

PATRIOT Act

The new investigative provisions are codified in the PATRIOT Act, which was enacted by the U.S. Congress in response to 9/11. Formally, the law is titled the "Uniting and Strengthening America by *P*roviding *A*ppropriate *T*ools *R*equired to *I*ntercept and *O*bstruct *T*errorism Act of 2001." Signed into law by President Bush on October 26, 2001, the act consists of amendments to a number of existing laws, legislation proposed prior to September 11, 2001, and a series of new laws. The package was widely criticized for being hastily pushed through Congress, violating the privacy rights of citizens, and denying suspects the right to due process and legal representation.

The PATRIOT Act provides yet another government definition of terrorism by creating a new law-enforcement category, "domestic terrorism." According to the text, the term *domestic terrorism* means activities that:

> *(A) involve acts dangerous to human life that are a violation of the criminal laws of the United States or of any State;*
>
> *(B) appear to be intended—*
>
> *(i) to intimidate or coerce a civilian population;*
>
> *(ii) to influence the policy of a government by intimidation or coercion; or*
>
> *(iii) to affect the conduct of a government by mass destruction, assassination, or kidnapping; and*
>
> *(C) occur primarily within the territorial jurisdiction of the United States.*[72]

After defining domestic terrorism, the PATRIOT Act then applies all existing U.S. laws aimed at foreign terrorist activities to actions on U.S. soil. These provisions include mechanisms to investigate suspicious financial transactions, to conduct physical searches, and to monitor communications. It also criminalizes money laundering related to terrorist activities.[73] Under an expanded definition, any person who "lends support" to a terrorist organization is now subject to the same laws as terrorist operatives.

The PATRIOT Act flew through Congress with unprecedented speed. The Bush administration presented it to Congress within a week of the September 11, 2001, attacks and President Bush signed the legislation into law on October 26, 2001. The administration actually wanted an even faster turnaround: Attorney General John Ashcroft had requested that Congress pass the bill in three days—essentially without study, debate, or revision.[74] The lightning pace made many congressmen balk. "Why is it necessary to rush this through?" asked Congressman Robert Barr (R-Ga.). "Does it have anything to do with the fact that the department has sought many of these authorities on numerous other occasions, has been unsuccessful in obtaining them, and now seeks to take advantage of what is obviously an emergency situation to obtain authorities that it has been unable to obtain previously?"[75] The media also criticized the haste, with the *New York Times* calling the legislation "Ashcroft's carelessly written anti-terrorism package"[76] and the *Washington Post* complaining, "Ashcroft continues implicitly to flog Congress for engaging in the balancing act that should have been his responsibility but that he skipped past."[77] The only senator to vote against the bill, Russell Feingold (D-Wis.), told the press that other legislators held deep reservations about the law but felt pressured into complying. He also noted that the name "PATRIOT Act" was a deliberate choice to press for passage; no government leader wanted to seem "unpatriotic."[78]

Controversy erupted particularly over Section 215 of the PATRIOT Act, which allows the U.S. government to investigate business, school, telephone, library, employment, medical, and Internet records without probable cause and without notifying the suspect before the search. While previously courts could authorize wiretapping of one particular telephone, the new law allows surveillance of all modes of communication (including cellular phones and e-mail) connected to a particular individual. Before the PATRIOT Act, investigators had to obtain a warrant by applying to the Foreign Intelligence Surveillance Court, a seven-member secret court established under the 1978 Foreign Intelligence Surveillance Act, and state that the information is needed in connection with a terrorism investigation. But under the PATRIOT Act, the Department of Justice and FBI could issue their own requests, known as National Security Letters, without court review. Furthermore, at the discretion of the FBI director, some subjects of these "sneak-and-peek" investigations may never be informed that a search has taken place. Individuals or companies receiving such a request were barred from telling anyone that they had received the letter. In 2005 the FBI issued 19,000 National Security Letters requesting 47,000 pieces of information.[79]

The loudest critics of this provision have been librarians. The American Library Association (ALA) has taken active measures to criticize the PATRIOT Act, educate patrons about the law, and develop guidelines for responding to government requests. The ALA issued a formal resolution stating, "The American Library Association (ALA) opposes any use of governmental power to suppress the free and open exchange of knowledge and information or to intimidate individuals exercising free inquiry. . . . ALA considers that sections of the USA PATRIOT ACT are a present danger to the constitutional rights and privacy rights of library users."[80] In February 2004, the ALA, the PEN writers group, and the American Booksellers Association launched a petition drive to collect 1 million signatures to press Congress to amend this provision of the PATRIOT Act.[81] They collected more than 200,000 signatures in the first year.

In December 2005 the *New York Times* revealed that President Bush had allowed the National Security Agency (NSA) to eavesdrop on communications within the United States. Not only had domestic wiretapping been moved from the purview of the FBI, but also the White House had exempted the NSA from obtaining warrants prior to the eavesdropping, even from the special Foreign Intelligence Surveillance Court. Critics labeled the process unconstitutional, as it violated the constitutional right to privacy by allowing unlawful searches.[82] When asked to explain to Americans why the policy did not violate their privacy, Bush dodged the issue, saying, "If somebody from al-Qaeda is calling you, we'd like to know why."[83] After Congress launched hearings on the NSA domestic eavesdropping issue, the White House argued that its actions were justified because the country was in a state of war. In January 2007 Executive officials eventually agreed to submit requests for warrants to monitor U.S. citizens, but only to the secret FISA court.[84]

Under the original terms of the PATRIOT Act, 16 key provisions were set to expire on December 31, 2005. The Bush administration sought to continue these provisions indefinitely, but Congress initially only agreed to a one-month extension. A four-year reauthorization was approved in March 2006; it refined—but did not eliminate—the Section 215 provisions. Now individuals served with National Security Letters can petition a court to allow them to reveal that they had received such a request. It also clarified that only libraries that are Internet service providers—rather than just access points—are subject to the requests for information.[85]

Prosecute

Once suspected terrorists are identified, the United States has several methods it can use to punish them or their sponsors. The fastest, and often most satisfying to U.S. voters, is military action, such as destroying terrorist camps or foreign military bases. State sponsors of terrorism, as discussed earlier, face a variety of economic sanctions; they can also face U.S. military action if they are harboring suspected terrorists. Individuals taken into custody through capture, arrest, or extradition face interrogation and prosecution before U.S. civilian courts, military tribunals, or both.

MILITARY MEASURES

In the 1980s and 1990s the United States on occasion took military action to punish terrorists, to mixed success. Retaliation can unleash a chain reaction of strike and counterstrike, as Washington faced with Libya in the 1980s. On April 2, 1986, the Anti-American Arab Liberation Front, Red Army Faction, and Holger Meins Commandos bombed a discotheque in West Berlin popular with U.S. servicemen. Two U.S. soldiers were killed and more than 60 injured. When intelligence data indicated that Libya had sponsored the attack, the White House decided to react. On April 15, 1986, President Ronald Reagan dispatched more than 100 aircraft to bomb military facilities in Libya. The U.S. air raid killed 60 people, including Libyan leader Muammar Qaddafi's daughter. Enraged, Qaddafi paid the Japanese Red Army to carry out a series of small-scale attacks against U.S. facilities in Indonesia, Rome, and Madrid; one member was even discovered with plans to bomb a USO club in New York City. Ultimately Qaddafi dispatched a team to bomb Pan Am flight 103 in December 1988; the explosion killed 259 people aboard the plane and another 11 on the ground when it crashed outside Lockerbie, Scotland, making it the bloodiest terrorist attack on U.S. interests prior to 9/11.

International sanctions neutralized Qaddafi in the 1990s, but Washington found terrorist threats from other sources. In June 1993 U.S. president Bill Clinton ordered a bombing raid on Iraqi intelligence headquarters in Baghdad after the government of Kuwait discovered a plot to assassinate former president George H. W. Bush during a planned visit to Kuwait City. The plot was foiled when the truck carrying the bomb was in a traffic accident en route to the attack.[86] The Clinton White House also launched several surgical strikes against al-Qaeda targets in retaliation for the bombings of the U.S. embassies in Kenya and Tanzania. The strikes included dual raids on August 20, 1998, against an al-Qaeda training camp in Afghanistan and a laboratory in Sudan, erroneously thought to be producing chemical weapons.[87] Clinton considered air strikes after al-Qaeda attacked the USS *Cole* on October 12, 2000, but with a presidential election barely two weeks away, decided to concentrate his efforts on the Middle East peace process.[88]

President Bush responded to the 9/11 attacks with two military operations. First, backed by a broad international coalition of countries providing troops, the U.S.-led Operation Enduring Freedom began by invading Afghanistan in October 2001. The mission was, first, to hunt down Osama bin Laden and, second, to remove the hard-line Islamist Taliban regime that had provided a haven for bin Laden. By March 2002 the Taliban was out of power, but as of late 2006 bin Laden is still at large. The international community oversaw the election of a new Afghan president and parliament under free-and-fair circumstances, but the Taliban have switched to insurgent tactics and are working to destabilize the regime.

After the Taliban had been removed, the White House turned its attention to Iraq and its president, Saddam Hussein. As with bin Laden, the war rhetoric was highly personalized, focusing more on Hussein than Iraq. Bush's argument was that Hussein was developing weapons of mass destruction and sponsoring terrorism, a potentially lethal combination. Despite repeated UN inspections that found no weapons of mass destruction, Bush pushed ahead with plans to remove Hussein. With considerable international protest—and no UN Security Council authorization—Operation Iraqi Freedom began in March 2003. Great Britain provided troops, but other U.S. allies either abstained from participation or sent only token forces. Hussein fled and was arrested in December 2003. An Iraqi court sentenced him to death in November 2006, and he was executed on December 30, 2006. As with Afghanistan, a new government has been selected; yet insurgent movements continue to destabilize the country.

RULE-OF-LAW APPROACH

The U.S. legal framework for prosecuting suspected terrorists has already been outlined. These judicial efforts have been aided by the remarkable ability of U.S. agencies to reconstruct crime scenes. Whether rebuilding Pan Am Flight 103 in a hangar in New York or tracing vehicle parts to bombers in Oklahoma City and the first World Trade Center attack, the problem is often less identifying the suspects than subsequently locating them. Prior to the 9/11 attacks, the United States had limited success in prosecuting perpetrators of terrorist attacks against U.S. citizens. Difficulties arise in identifying the actors, finding an appropriate venue, and bringing the suspects before that venue. Chance encounters led to the arrest of Timothy McVeigh. Mohammed Salameh as good as turned himself in when he requested a refund of his security deposit for the rented truck that housed his bomb, but other suspects in the 1993 World Trade Center attack fled abroad. Ramzi Yusef was not apprehended for another two years.

Scenarios to snatch wanted terrorists abroad and bring them to justice in the United States may sound forceful and appealing, but the operations are difficult and risky. For example, Mir Amal Kansi, who murdered three people at a traffic light outside CIA headquarters in January 1993, fled to Pakistan and eventually assumed he had been forgotten. However, CIA agents had carefully tracked him over the years and successfully snatched him from a hotel room in Pakistan and spirited him back to the United States in 1997. Many Pakistanis objected to Kansi's removal without a trial in Pakistan, and the "Amal Secret Committee" killed four Americans working in Pakistan following Kansi's trial.[89] A similar plan to snatch bin Laden in 1996 failed.[90]

Foreign countries may refuse to participate in investigations or to extradite suspects to the United States. Saudi Arabia, for example, did not want to cooperate with an FBI investigation of the Khobar Towers attack because it would have meant admitting security lapses and given more fuel to groups already critical of Saudi-U.S. ties. Consequently Saudi Arabia conducted its own investigation and refused to give the FBI access to evidence or suspects.[91] Even supposedly allied countries may refuse to prosecute or turn over suspected hijackers to the United States if the domestic cost would be too high. Italy opted to place priority on its ties with Egypt and to prosecute the Palestinians suspected of murdering an American citizen when they hijacked the *Achille Lauro* cruise ship in 1985 rather than handing them over to Washington. One of the Palestinians was never actually in Italian custody—he was convicted in absentia—and the other three escaped "while on leave from Italian prison."[92]

American refusal to accede to a variety of international legal conventions, such as the International Court of Justice and International Criminal Court, has undercut Washington's ability to seek cooperation with other countries. Similarly, countries that oppose the death penalty may refuse to remand criminals who would face such a sentence in a U.S. court. The hijackers responsible for capturing TWA Flight 847 in 1985 were not arrested as part of the deal to release the terrorists. But one of the hijackers, Mohammed Ali Hamadi, was arrested when he entered West Germany in 1987. Wary of the U.S. death penalty, Bonn decided to try him in German courts for the murder of navy diver Robert Stethem and sentenced him to life. Even when Hamadi was paroled in December 2005, Germany released him to Lebanon rather than the United States, much to Washington's anger.[93]

Finally, it is difficult to punish terrorists even if they are in U.S. custody. Zacarias Moussaoui confessed to being in on the plot of the 9/11 suicide bombers, so the issue of revealing possibly classified evidence was not a major concern. Instead, prosecutors focused on securing the death penalty for him. Yet Moussaoui turned out to be an unstable individual, who even volunteered to testify for the prosecution, and the trial gave him an audience for his regular outbursts and bizarre behavior At the death-penalty phase of his trial his own lawyers were reduced to depicting Moussaoui as "an arrogant, hate-filled wannabe terrorist who lied in court about his involvement."[94] Moussaoui apparently wanted to be executed to help him complete his path to martyrdom, and a death sentence would have risked creating a martyr. In May 2006 the jury sentenced him to life in prison without the possibility of parole. Rather than dying for his cause, Moussaoui instead will likely become a footnote to history as he joins other has-been terrorists, such as Ramzi Yusef and Eric Rudolph, in the U.S. supermax federal prison in Colorado.

WAR ON TERROR

When President Bush announced a "War on terror," the United States switched its approach to prosecuting terrorists from one based on law enforcement to a military operation. Since al-Qaeda was based in Afghanistan, whose Taliban regime had no diplomatic relations with the United States, U.S. forces had to go get them. As mentioned above, the main components of this strategy were the invasion of Afghanistan in October 2001 and the invasion of Iraq in March 2003. The problem, however, was what to do with the suspects once they had been captured. They could be tried in civilian court, like the men behind the 1993 World Trade Center attack or the Millennium plotters, Timothy McVeigh, or Eric Rudolph. Alternatively, they could be tried by a military commission observing the Uniform Code of Military Justice. Instead, the Bush administration opted to create a third venue, the secret military tribunal, which has more flexible rules than either of the two existing systems. This solution provoked widespread international and domestic protests that captured enemy combatants were not being treated fairly or even humanely. Critics have accused the Bush administration of failing to provide due process to suspects and condoning torture of prisoners.

Treatment of Enemy Combatants

Arrests or captures made in the course of war are governed by international and military law. The basic guiding document is known as the Geneva Convention. Last revised in 1949 following World War II, the international treaty establishes minimum standards for the treatment of prisoners of war. Two portions of the convention are relevant for this discussion: Articles Three and Four.[95]

Referring to domestic conflicts, such as the U.S. Civil War, Article Three specifies how enemy combatants—whether wounded, surrendered, or captured—are to be treated. Such persons "shall in all circumstances be treated humanely, without any adverse distinction founded on race, color, religion or faith, sex, birth or wealth, or any other similar criteria." Four types of activities are strictly prohibited:

> *(a) Violence to life and person, in particular murder of all kinds, mutilation, cruel treatment and torture;*
>
> *(b) Taking of hostages;*

(c) Outrages upon personal dignity, in particular, humiliating and degrading treatment;

(d) The passing of sentences and the carrying out of executions without previous judgment pronounced by a regularly constituted court affording all the judicial guarantees which are recognized as indispensable by civilized peoples.

Article Four clarifies further who is considered a "prisoner of war" under the Convention.

A. Prisoners of war, in the sense of the present Convention, are persons belonging to one of the following categories, who have fallen into the power of the enemy:

1. Members of the armed forces of a Party to the conflict as well as members of militias or volunteer corps forming part of such armed forces.

2. Members of other militias and members of other volunteer corps, including those of organized resistance movements, belonging to a Party to the conflict and operating in or outside their own territory, even if this territory is occupied, provided that such militias or volunteer corps, including such organized resistance movements, fulfil the following conditions:

(a) That of being commanded by a person responsible for his subordinates;

(b) That of having a fixed distinctive sign recognizable at a distance;

(c) That of carrying arms openly;

(d) That of conducting their operations in accordance with the laws and customs of war.

3. Members of regular armed forces who profess allegiance to a government or an authority not recognized by the Detaining Power.

4. Persons who accompany the armed forces without actually being members thereof, such as civilian members of military aircraft crews, war correspondents, supply contractors, members of labour units or of services responsible for the welfare of the armed forces, provided that they have received authorization from the armed forces which they accompany, who shall provide them for that purpose with an identity card similar to the annexed model.

5. Members of crews, including masters, pilots and apprentices, of the merchant marine and the crews of civil aircraft of the Parties to the conflict, who do not benefit by more favourable treatment under any other provisions of international law.

6. Inhabitants of a non-occupied territory, who on the approach of the enemy spontaneously take up arms to resist the invading forces, without having had time to form themselves into regular armed units, provided they carry arms openly and respect the laws and customs of war.

The problem with the War on Terror, however, is that the enemy does not neatly fall into any of the above categories. Al-Qaeda was located in Afghanistan but was not linked officially to the Afghan government, and its fighters certainly did not wear uniforms or have insignia. They did target civilians, which violates the provision to "respect the laws and customs of war." Consequently, the White House declared that captured terror suspects were not subject to the Geneva requirements.

Terror suspects captured in Afghanistan were classified as enemy combatants, not prisoners of war, and were transported to Guantánamo Bay, a U.S. naval facility in Cuba. At any time since January 2002, there have been about 700 detainees at Guantánamo. Washington valued the safety provided by an island, as escape would be nearly impossible. Technically, the United States merely leases the land from Cuba—Guantánamo therefore is not U.S. soil. Washington argued that if the detainees are not being held on U.S. territory, they could not appeal their detention in the U.S. court system, (but in 2004 the U.S. Supreme Court ruled that detainees could appeal in civilian courts.)

Secret Military Tribunals and Rendition

After 9/11 President Bush authorized the creation of secret military tribunals to try suspected terrorists. Compared to civilian courts, the tribunals require lower standards of evidence, and the "beyond a reasonable doubt" provision does not apply. "Advocates say it might be the only way a suspect can be held to account for a plot with alleged al-Qaeda ties," writes the *Wall Street Journal*, "because a civilian trial might entitle the defendant to subpoena al-Qaeda leaders the U.S. holds abroad—exposing intelligence sources and methods."[96] However, holding suspects in military custody opens the door to charges of torture and confessions obtained under duress. The proceedings not only would be closed to the public, but the defendant might not be allowed to attend portions that related to classified evidence.

Open-Ended Detention of Suspects

However, few detainees were ever brought before the secret tribunals. Detainees began to arrive at Guantánamo in January 2002. In August 2004 the Pentagon created "Combatant Status Review Tribunals" that were to screen the detainees and determine which cases would be heard by the secret tribunals. Nearly two years later, only 14 of the nearly 500 suspects then held in Guantánamo had been designated for trial, and no trials had been decided.[97]

The detainees in Guantánamo were essentially left in limbo. Without formal charges or access to U.S. courts, they could not petition for their release. Had they been classified as prisoners of war, the U.S. government would have to release them at the conclusion of hostilities, but the War on Terror has no clear ending. Washington further argues that many detainees are too dangerous to be released and repatriated.[98] Critics argue that this practice violates the constitutional right to a speedy trial and prohibition of cruel punishment.

Jose Padilla

The case of Jose Padilla illustrates the issues involved. A U.S. citizen, Padilla (1970–   ) was arrested in May 2002 but was held in a military prison for more than three years before being indicted—formally charged with a crime—in November 2005 on completely different grounds. A former gang member in Chicago, Padilla converted to Islam while in prison; reports sometimes refer to his Muslim name, Abdullah al-Muhajir. He later traveled throughout the Middle East and Asia, including Pakistan, where al-Qaeda members taught him bomb-making techniques. The FBI arrested Padilla when he landed at Chicago's O'Hare airport, and he was accused of planning to make a "dirty" (radiation) bomb. Oddly, U.S. investigators did not opt to put Padilla under surveillance, a usual practice to discover coconspirators, and admitted that he had not actually acquired bomb materials nor chosen a target.[99]

After spending one month in the Metropolitan Corrections Center in Manhattan, Padilla was transferred to the Charleston Naval Weapons Station in South Carolina. President Bush, in a personal order, designated Padilla as an "enemy combatant," a legal classification not normally applied to a U.S. citizen.[100] This status change shifted Padilla's case from the civilian court system to the military justice system. The jurisdiction change also changed the rules of the game: Evidence can be presented in a military court without revealing its source in order to protect spies and informants, and there is no limit to how long a suspect can be held without being formally charged. In a

Catch-22 introduced by the PATRIOT Act, Padilla could not actually read the evidence against him because the government argued it would reveal classified national security information.

This left Padilla in judicial limbo—he could not petition for his release because he could not defend himself against evidence he could not see. He also was denied direct access to an attorney. So began three years of legal wrangling over the principle of habeas corpus—that a suspect cannot be detained without charges. In December 2004, the U.S. Court of Appeals for the Second Circuit ruled that Padilla was to be released from military custody if charges were not filed within 30 days; further charges could then be pursued in the civilian court system. The White House appealed this ruling to the U.S. Supreme Court, and Padilla was ordered to remain in military custody in the interim. In September 2005, the U.S. Court of Appeals for the Fourth Circuit[101] ruled that Padilla actually could be held indefinitely in a military prison; Padilla's lawyers appealed to the U.S. Supreme Court.

Civil charges were finally brought against Padilla in November 2005 for recruiting and fund-raising for al-Qaeda in Chechnya, Bosnia, Somalia, and Kosovo. Handed down by a federal grand jury in Miami, the indictment never mentioned the alleged dirty bomb plot or plans for any activities on U.S. soil.[102] The timing of the indictment raised eyebrows. The indictment came days before the White House was to respond to Padilla's Supreme Court appeal. In addition, the White House said that with the civilian indictment in place, there was no need for a military trial and that Padilla could drop his Supreme Court appeal. The administration even asked the Fourth Circuit Court to overturn its September 2005 ruling that the administration could hold Padilla as an enemy combatant and authorize his transfer to Miami. A panel of judges from the Fourth Circuit Court not only turned down the requests, but it also accused the White House of "attempting to avoid consideration of our decision by the Supreme Court" and accused the Bush administration of undermining public confidence in the War on Terror.[103]

Experts who followed the Padilla case thought there was another reason the dirty bomb charges were dropped. According to the *New York Times*, the source of the dirty bomb story was two al-Qaeda members in U.S. custody: Khalid Sheikh Mohammed[104] and Abu Zubaydah. A CIA investigation revealed that the two had been tortured at a secret CIA prison. Had they testified, Padilla's lawyers could have objected that the information had been obtained under duress—and simultaneously confirmed rumors about torture in secret U.S. prisons. Had the two men not testified, there likely would not be enough evidence to convict Padilla in a civilian court, where the standards of evidence are higher.[105]

Padilla's attorneys refused to withdraw their Supreme Court appeal, as the government had not lifted the "enemy combatant" label and could therefore still send him back to military prison. On January 4, 2006, the Supreme Court authorized Padilla's transfer to Miami but did not rule on his appeal at that time.

Meanwhile, another case about the right of the United States to hold enemy combatants had already made it to the Supreme Court. In June 2004 the Supreme Court had declared that Mohammed Ali Hamadi had been improperly held in a military prison indefinitely and that he should be able to consult an attorney while held in Afghanistan.[106] Hamadi was also a U.S. citizen and had also been declared an enemy combatant, but he had been arrested in Afghanistan and held dual citizenship with Saudi Arabia. He was transferred from Afghanistan into Saudi custody, flew to Saudi Arabia, and was released. The Hamadi case seemed to be a precedent that would favor Padilla's arguments in favor of his release.

On April 4, 2006, the Supreme Court declined to hear Padilla's appeal, but he had already been released from military into civilian custody. By not hearing the case, the justices effectively upheld the 4th Circuit Court ruling that the president could designate a citizen as an enemy combatant and hold him indefinitely. In a separate decision, on July 5, 2006, a U.S. district court ruled that Padilla could finally see the evidence against him in order to prepare for trial, scheduled for 2007.[107]

International Condemnation

In mid-2006 U.S. policy regarding detainees and the Guantánamo facility came under fire at home and abroad. Reports by visitors and released detainees describe numerous forms of prisoner mistreatment, including beatings, humiliation, sleep deprivation, cultural insults, and force-feeding.[108] Prisoners still at Guantánamo have reacted to their circumstances by attacking guards, staging hunger strikes, and in June 2006 three inmates committed suicide. While human rights monitors called the suicides "acts of despair," Guantánamo's commanding officer, Admiral Harry Harris, branded the incidents "an act of asymmetric warfare waged against us."[109]

Criticism also mounted over the policy of rendition. Extradition is a formal practice whereby a suspect wanted in the United States who was caught, for example, in Spain would face a hearing in the Spanish judicial system to determine whether or not to send the suspect to the United States. Rendition, however, bypasses the local court system and immediately puts the suspect in U.S. custody. This is the principle behind the "snatch and grab" arrests of Ramzi Yusef and CIA shooter Mir Amal Kansi. The White House is accused of using rendition to facilitate the torture of suspected terrorists. Specifically, the United States flies suspects to countries that practice torture, where they stand accused of crimes. Critics accuse the United States of encouraging states known to interrogate suspects using torture to concoct charges in order to justify rendition. A suspect unwilling to speak to U.S. investigators is thus sent to Egypt, Syria, Morocco, or another country where local law enforcement may literally beat the information out of them.

International complaints about rendition have increased as countries realize that the United States may have used their airspace in a rendition operation or kidnapped suspects on their territory. In 2005 Canada, Germany, Italy, and Sweden opened their own investigations into the rendition and torture allegations.[110] The European Parliament opened its own investigation in spring 2006, and discovered that the "CIA carried out as many as 1,000 secret flights throughout Europe since the 9/11 attacks."[111] The Council of Europe opened its own investigation as well.

In early 2006 the UN Commission on Human Rights issued a report that called upon Washington to shut down the Guantánamo camp immediately and either to bring to trial or simply to release the approximately 500 individuals still held there. The report specifically condemned the practice of rendition and called the indefinite detentions a form of torture.[112] The UN Committee against Torture subsequently issued its own report that said many components of the War on Terror violate the 1994 UN Convention against Torture, to which the United States is a signatory.

In June 2006 the Supreme Court struck down the White House policy of using secret military tribunals to decide the fate of the detainees. The Court ruled that terrorism suspects are indeed protected under Article 3 of the Geneva Convention, as if they were regular prisoners of war. The justices ordered the White House either to use conventional instruments of military justice (courts martial) or, if civilian courts are unsuitable, to ask Congress for permission to pursue other options. The Supreme Court decision directly rejected the White House argument that the president should be allowed to conduct a war as he sees fit, and it opens the door to challenges to other components of the War on Terror, such as the PATRIOT Act and surveillance measures.[113]

Within a week of the Supreme Court decision, the Pentagon announced that it would abide by the Geneva Conventions where the Guantánamo detainees are concerned. Congress also opened hearings to explore new rules for the detainees, and administration officials indicated that, rather than a new system, it would prefer Congress simply to ratify the tribunal system with few changes.[114]

However, Congressional approval would not necessarily change practice. When challenged, the Bush White House has used a technique known as a "signing statement." Specifically, the president may sign a law or a treaty but may issue a separate document declaring that, as commander-in-chief, he will ignore the restrictions when it is vital to national security. Such statements were issued after President Bush signed the 2005 Detainee Treatment Act, prohibiting the torture of detainees.[115] A similar signing statement accompanied the reauthorization of the PATRIOT Act in March 2006.[116]

CONCLUSION

During the past three decades, the United States has increasingly had to face the problem of terrorism. From home-grown terrorists with nationalist or communist goals in the 1960s and 1970s, American terrorist movements took a sharp turn against the federal government in the 1980s, culminating in Timothy McVeigh's 1995 attack on the Murrah Federal Building in Oklahoma City. At the same time, U.S. citizens increasingly became vulnerable to terrorist attacks when they were abroad. U.S. embassies, military bases, and aircraft were targeted by bombers, while individual citizens were kidnapped in the Middle East and Latin America. Then in 1993 foreign terrorists made their first major strike on U.S. soil—the World Trade Center. Eight years later, terrorists affiliated with the same group, al-Qaeda, returned to New York and reduced the trade center to dust.

As the nature of the attacks changed, so did the U.S. response. The federal government created a framework to identify, prosecute, and punish terrorists under the rule of law. Whatever the motivations of the perpetrators, terrorists were treated as criminals. Strict adherence to the law was praised by U.S. allies, facilitating international cooperation.

After 9/11, however, the United States switched tactics. The White House decision to consider terrorism an act of war rather than a crime alienated many U.S. allies, who agreed to participate in the War on Terror reluctantly, if at all. International and domestic criticism of the conduct of the War on Terror culminated in summer 2006 with both the United Nations and the U.S. Supreme Court ruling that two key components of the War on Terror—indefinite detentions and domestic surveillance—violated U.S. law, international law, and human rights. Critics and even the U.S. Supreme Court argue that the Bush White House has overstepped its bounds and is ignoring the principle of checks and balances and rule of law. How the U.S. government chooses to address these criticisms and remedy the perceived procedural and legal violations will likely determine whether the next phase in the War on Terror will be conducted by an international alliance or by the United States alone.

[1] Federal Bureau of Investigation. "Crime in the United States 2004: Hate Crime." Available online. URL: http://www.fbi.gov/ucr/cius_04/offenses_reported/hate_crime/index.html. Accessed July 18, 2006.

[2] Angie Cannon. "Healing Old Wounds." *U.S. News and World Report,* December 22, 2003, pp. 34–39.

[3] Federal Bureau of Investigation. *Terrorism in the United States: 1999.* Washington, D.C.: FBI, 2000, p. 18.

[4] This is one reason Cuba remains classified as a state sponsor of terrorism. See Diego A. Abich. "The Americas: Puerto Rico's Struggle with Cuban-Sponsored Terrorism," *Wall Street Journal,* May 9, 1986.

[5] Stephen Hunter and J. S. Bainbridge. *American Gunfight: The Plot to Kill Harry Truman—and the Shoot-out that Stopped It.* New York: Simon and Schuster, 2005.

[6] Manuel Roig-Franzia. "A Terrorist in the House." *Washington Post Magazine,* February 22, 2004, p. W12.

[7] Charles Babington. "Puerto Rican Nationalists Freed from Prison." *Washington Post,* September 11, 1999, p. A2.

[8] "USA: Amnesty International calls for independent inquiry into shooting of Filiberto Ojedo Ríos." Amnesty International Press Release, September 27, 2005.

[9] Abby Goodnough. "A Moribund Independence Stirs Anew." *New York Times,* November 6, 2005, p. A25. See also "Bush Administration Proposes Vote by Puerto Ricans on Status." *New York Times,* December 23, 2005, p. A23.

[10] Other groups claimed credit for the attack, but authorities believed the Croatian claim, as the group had simultaneously bombed homes of Yugoslav diplomats in Washington, D.C. See "Croatians Are Suspected in Blast at Statue of Liberty." *New York Times,* June 6, 1980, p. B3.

[11] Federal Bureau of Investigation. "Terrorism in the United States: 1996," p. 17.

[12] The group's name came from the Bob Dylan song "Subterranean Homesick Blues," specifically the line: "you don't need a weatherman to know which way the wind blows."

[13] Ty Bur. "'Underground' a History Lesson on How Idealism Can Breed Terror," *Boston Globe,* August 22, 2003, p. C5.

[14] Quoted in Dinitia Smith. "In a Memoir of Sorts, a War Protestor Talks of Life with the Weathermen." The article appeared, ironically, in the *New York Times* on September 11, 2001, p. E1, under the header "No Regrets for Love of Explosives."

[15] Mark Honigsbaum. "The Americans Who Declared War on Their Country." *The Observer,* September 21, 2003; John Patterson. "All the Rage." *The Guardian,* July 4, 2003.

[16] William Booth. "Four SLA Members Plead Guilty in Slaying." *Washington Post,* November 8, 2002.

[17] U.S. Senate: Historical Minute Essays. "November 7, 1983, Bomb Explodes in Capitol." Available online. URL: www.senate.gov/artandhistory/history/minute/bomb_explodes_in_capitol.htm. Accessed November 22, 2006.

[18] Valerie Richardson. "FBI Targets Domestic Terrorists." *Insight.* (April 22, 2002), pp. 30–33.

[19] "FBI, ATF Address Domestic Terrorism." CNN.com (May 19, 2005).

[20] Testimony of James F. Jarboe, domestic terrorism section chief, Counterterrorism Division, FBI, before the House Resources Committee, Subcommittee on Forests and Forest Health. Posted on February 12, 2002. Available online. URL: http://www.fbi.gov/congress/congress02/jarboe021202.htm. Accessed July 19, 2006.

[21] Federal Bureau of Investigation, *Terrorism in the United States: 1999.* Washington, D.C.: FBI, 2000.

[22] Bruce Hoffman. *Inside Terrorism.* New York: Columbia University Press, 1998, pp. 110–111. Also see Anti-Defamation League, *Extremism in America,* a regularly updated report available at www.adl.org.

[23] Quoted in Anti-Defamation League. *Extremism in America,* Introduction.

[24] Federal Bureau of Investigation. "Terrorism in the United States: 1996." Washington, D.C.: FBI, 1997, p. 17.

[25] Anti-Defamation League. "Beyond Anthrax: Extremism and the Bioterrorism Threat." New York: Anti-Defamation League, 2001, p. 2. Available online. URL: http:// www.adl.org/learn/Anthrax/beyond_anthrax.pdf. Accessed November 15, 2005.

[26] "McVeigh Remorseless About Bombing." *AP,* March 29, 2001.

[27] Hoffman, *Inside Terrorism,* p. 117.

[28] Quoted in Judy L. Thomas. "Movement's Leadership left in Disarray." *Kansas City Star.* Posted on April 20, 2005. Available online. URL: http:// http://www.religionnewsblog.com/10650/movements-leadership-left-in-disarray. Accessed December 19, 2006.

[29] Ibid.

[30] While many died from the fire, autopsies found single gunshots to the heads of several corpses. See Sue Anne Pressley, "Waco Siege Ends in Dozens of Deaths as Cult Site Burns after FBI Assault." *Washington Post,* April 20, 1993, p. A1. Sue Anne Pressley and Mary Jordan. "Cultists May Have Been Forced to Stay; Agent: Bullet Hole Found in Burned Body." *Washington Post,* April 21, 1993, p. A1.

[31] Quoted in "McVeigh Remorseless about Bombing." Associated Press, March 29, 2001.

[32] Evan Thomas. "The Plot." *Newsweek,* May 8, 1995, pp. 29–34.

[33] Lois Romano. "McVeigh Asks for Delay of Execution." *Washington Post,* June 1, 2001, p. A1.

[34] Richard A. Clarke. *Against All Enemies: Inside America's War on Terror* New York: Free Press, 2004.

[35] Lois Romano. "Since Oklahoma City, Extremist Groups Wane but Remain Threats." *Seattle Times.* Posted on April 20, 2005. Available online. URL: http://www.rickross.com/reference/hate_groups/hategroups394.html. Accessed December 19, 2006.

[36] Southern Poverty Law Center. "The Rise and Decline of the 'Patriots.'" *Intelligence Report,* Summer 2001. Available online. URL: http://www.splcenter.org/intel/intelreport/article.jsp?aid=195. Accessed December 19, 2006.

[37] Brad Knickerbocker. "New Tactics Rein in Radicals." *Christian Science Monitor,* March 30, 1998, p. 1.

[38] "White Supremacists Ratchet Up Anti-Hispanic Action as U.S. Immigration Debate Rages." Anti-Defamation League Press Release, May 24, 2006.

[39] "Backgrounder: Eric Robert Rudolph." Anti-Defamation League, June 5, 2003.

[40] Quoted in Wikipedia entry for "Centennial Olympic Park Bombing." Available online. URL: http://en.wikipedia.org/wiki/Centennial_Olympic_Park_bombing. Accessed November 17, 2005.

[41] Richard A. Clarke. *Against All Enemies: Inside America's War on Terror.* New York: Free Press, 2004, pp. 40–41.

[42] Clarke. *Against All Enemies,* p. 79.

[43] Carl Weiser. "Rubble Yielded Key Clue." *USA Today,* March 5, 1993, p. A3.

[44] National Commission on Terrorist Attacks Upon the United States. *The 9/11 Commission Report: Final Report of the National Commission on Terrorist Attacks Upon the United States,* authorized ed. New York: W. W. Norton, 2004, pp. 145–150.

[45] "History: Who Became Part of the Department?" Department of Homeland Security Web site. Available online. URL: http://www.dhs.gov/xabout/history/editorial_0133.shtm. Accessed December 19, 2006.

[46] Susan B. Glasser and Michael Grunwald. "Department's Mission Was Undermined from Start." *Washington Post,* December 22, 2005, p. A1.

[47] Testimony of Cynthia A. Bascetta, associate director of veterans' affairs and military health care issues, health, education, and human services division, to House Subcommittee on National Security, Veterans Affairs, and International Relations, March 8, 2000.

[48] Spencer S. Hsu. "Can Congress Rescue FEMA?" *Washington Post,* June 26, 2006, p. A19.

[49] See www.mipt.org for more information on the institute.

[50] The card can be downloaded online. URL: www.rand.org/publications/MR/MR1731.

[51] For a list of courses see the Office of Anti-Terrorism Assistance Web site at www.diplomaticsecurity.org.

[52] Kenneth Katzman. "Terrorism: Near Eastern Groups and State Sponsors, 2002." In *CRS Reports for Congress* Washington, D.C.: Congressional Research Service, 2002, pp. 41–42. Available online. URL: http://www.fas.org/irp/crs/RL31119.pdf. Accessed December 19, 2006.

[53] David E. Long. "Coming to Grips with Terrorism after 11 September." *Brown Journal of World Affairs* 8, no. 2 (2002), p. 238.

[54] Jeffrey D. Brake. "Terrorism and the Military's Role in Domestic Crisis Management: Background and Issues for Congress." In *CRS Report for Congress.* Washington, D.C.: Congressional Research Service, 2001.

[55] Long. "Coming to Grips with Terrorism after 11 September," p. 40.

[56] This section is based on Philip B. Heymann. *Terrorism and America: A Commonsense Strategy for a Democratic Society.* Cambridge, Mass.: MIT Press, 1998), especially chapter 2.

[57] Elizabeth B. Bazan. "Assassination Ban and E.O. 12333: A Brief Summary." *CRS Report for Congress* No. RS21037, January 4, 2002.

[58] U.S. Department of State, Country Reports on Terrorism, April 28, 2006. Available online. URL: http://www.state.gov/s/ct/rls/crt/2005/64337.htm. Accessed July 16, 2006.

[59] John F. Harris. "Clinton Signs 'Mighty Blow' against Terrorism." *Washington Post,* April 25, 1996, p. A4; Allison Mitchell. "Clinton Signs Measure on Terrorism and Death Penalty Appeals." *New York Times,* April 25, 1996, p. A18.

[60] Mark P. Sullivan. "Latin America: Terrorism Issues." In *CRS Report for Congress.* Washington, D.C.: Congressional Research Service, 2005. Available online. URL: http://www.fas.org/sgp/crs/terror/RS21049.pdf. Accessed December 19, 2006.

[61] Todd S. Purdum. "Clinton Signs a Wide-Ranging Measure on Airport Security." *New York Times,* October 10, 1996, p. B13.

[62] Todd S. Purdum. "Clinton Suggests an Array of Steps to Foil Terrorism." *New York Times,* September 10, 1996, p. A1.

[63] Clarke. *Against All Enemies,* chapter 6.

[64] Tim Weiner and Steven Lee Myers. "Flaws in U.S. Account Raise Questions on Strike in Sudan." *New York Times,* August 29, 1998, p. A1.

[65] Vernon Loeb and Steven Pearlstein. "U.S. Puts Borders on High Alert." *Washington Post,* December 19, 1999, p. A1.

[66] Clarke. *Against All Enemies,* pp. 111–114.

[67] "22 Years for Millennium Bomb Plot." *CBS News,* July 27, 2005. Available online. URL: http://www.cbsnews.com/stories/2005/07/27/national/main712240.shtml. Accessed December 19, 2006.

[68] Clarke. *Against All Enemies,* p. 225.

[69] Peter Ford. "'Evil Axis' and Others Talk Back; State of Union Raises Hackles Worldwide, Even among Allies." *Christian Science Monitor,* January 31, 2002, p. 1.

[70] Jonathan Freedland. "Patten Lays into Bush's America." *Guardian.* Posted on February 9, 2002. Available online. URL: http://www.guardian.co.uk/bush/story/0,7369,647554,00.html. Accessed December 19, 2006.

[71] Michael J. Jordan. "'With or against Us War Irks Many UN Nations." *Christian Science Monitor,* November 14, 2001, p. 7.

[72] Section 802, H.R. 3162. "Uniting and Strengthening America by Providing Appropriate Tools Required to Intercept and Obstruct Terrorism Act of 2001." Available online. URL: http://thomas.loc.gov/cgi-bin/query/z?c107:H.R.3162.ENR:. Accessed December 19, 2006.

[73] Charles Doyle. "The USA Patriot Act: A Sketch." *CRS Report for Congress,* Washington, D.C., Congressional Research Service, 2002.

[74] John Lancaster. "Hill Puts Brakes on Expanding Police Powers." *Washington Post,* September 30, 2001, p. A6.

[75] John Lancaster and Walter Pincus. "Proposed Anti-Terrorism Laws Draw Tough Questions." *Washington Post,* September 25, 2001, p. A5.

[76] "Toward a Balanced Terrorism Bill." *New York Times,* October 4, 2001, p. A26.

[77] "An Improving Anti-Terror Bill." *Washington Post,* October 3, 2001, p. A30.

[78] Robert E. Pierre. "Wisconsin Senator Emerges as a Maverick." *Washington Post,* October 27, 2001, p. A8.

[79] John Soloman and Barton Gellman. "Frequent Errors in FBI's Secret Records Requests." *Washington Post,* March 9, 2007, p. A1.

[80] American Library Association. "Resolution on the USA Patriot Act and Related Measures That Infringe on the Rights of Library Users." 2003. Text available online. URL: http://www.ala.org/ala/oif/statementspols/ifresolutions/usapatriotactresolution.pdf.

[81] David Mehegan. "Reading over Your Shoulder: The Push Is on to Shelve Part of the Patriot Act." *Boston Globe,* March 9, 2004, p. E5.

[82] James Risen and Eric Lichtblau. "Bush Lets U.S. Spy on Callers without Courts." *New York Times,* December 16, 2005, p. A1. The reporters revealed that they had delayed publication of this information for one year at the request of the White House.

[83] "Bush Defends NSA Spying Program." Cable News Network. Posted on January 1, 2006. Available online. URL: http://www.cnn.com/2006/POLITICS/01/01/nsa.spying/.com. Accessed January 8, 2006.

[84] Dan Eggen. "Court Will Oversee Wiretap Program." *Washington Post,* January 18, 2007, p. A1.

[85] Peter Grief. "How the Patriot Act Came in from the Cold." *Christian Science Monitor,* March 3, 2006, p. 1.

[86] Clarke. *Against All Enemies,* pp. 78–84.

[87] Tim Weiner and Steven Lee Myers. "Flaws in U.S. Account Raise Questions on Strike in Sudan." *New York Times,* August 29, 1998, p. A1.

[88] Clarke. *Against All Enemies,* pp. 222–224.

[89] John F. Burns. "Spiriting Off of Fugitive by U.S. Irks Pakistanis." *New York Times,* June 23, 1997, p. A9; "In Wake of Karachi Killings, Americans Keep Low Profile." *New York Times,* November 14, 1997, p. A3.

[90] Clarke, *Against All Enemies,* pp. 148–150.

[91] Clarke, *Against All Enemies,* pp. 114–120.

[92] Heymann, *Terrorism and America,* p. 33.

[93] Richard Bernstein. "Germany Frees '85 Hijacker Who Killed American Sailor." *New York Times,* December 21, 2005, p. A14.

[94] Jerry Markon and Timothy Dwyer. "In Closing, Moussaoui Trial Rests on His Lies." *Washington Post,* March 30, 2006, p. A5.

[95] The full text of the Geneva Convention is available from the United Nations Office of the High Commissioner for Refugees. Available online. URL: www.unhchr.ch/html/menu3/b/91.htm.

[96] Jess Bravin. "Court on Trial." *Wall Street Journal,* March 29, 2006, p. A1.

[97] Charles Lane. "High Court Rejects Detainee Tribunals." *Washington Post,* June 30, 2006, p. A1.

[98] Michael C. Dorf. "What Is an 'Unlawful Combatant.' and Why It Matters: The Status of Detained al-Qaeda and Taliban Fighters." FindLaw.com. Posted on January 23, 2002. Available online. URL: http://writ.news.findlaw.com/dorf/20020123.html. Accessed December 19, 2006.

[99] James Risen and Philip Shenon. "U.S. Says It Halted Qaeda Plot to Use Radioactive Bomb." *New York Times,* June 11, 2002, p. A1.

[100] The document was an order from Bush to Secretary of Defense Donald Rumsfeld, signed June 9, 2002. Available online. URL: http://www.sourcewatch.org/index.php?title=GW_Bush%27s_Padilla_Designation. Accessed July 16, 2006.

[101] The case was moved from the 2nd Circuit to the 4th as a result of à June 2004 U.S. Supreme Court ruling that determined the case had been filed in the wrong jurisdiction; the 2nd Circuit was for New York, but the 4th is for South Carolina, where Padilla was then being held.

[102] David Stout. "U.S. Indicts Padilla After 3 Years in Pentagon Custody." *New York Times,* November 22, 2005, p. A1.

[103] Quoted in Warren Richey. "Terror Case Challenges White House Strategy." *Christian Science Monitor,* December 23, 2005, p. 2.

[104] Khalid Sheikh Mohammed is usually described as the "mastermind" of the 9/11 attacks. His nephew, Ramzi Yusef, remains in a U.S. prison as the ringleader of the 1993 World Trade Center bombing.

[105] Douglas Jehl and Eric Lichtblau. "Shift on Suspect Is Linked to Role of Qaeda Figures." *New York Times,* November 24, 2005, p. A1.

[106] Dan Eggen. "Padilla Is Indicted on Terrorism Charge." *Washington Post,* November 23, 2005, p. A1.

[107] "Judge Allows Padilla to See Secrets." *Washington Post,* July 14, 2006, p. A12.

[108] "Doctors Demand End to Guantánamo Force-Feeding." *Guardian.* Posted on March 10, 2006. Available online. URL: http://www.guardiaiin.co.uk/print/0,,329431566-111575,00.html. Accessed August 1, 2006.

[109] "Guantánamo Suicides 'Acts of War.'" BBC News. Posted on June 11, 2006. Available online. URL: http://newsvote.bbc.co.uk/mpapps/pagetools/print/news.bbc.co.uk/2/hi/Americas/5068606.stm. Accessed July 24, 2006.

[110] Daniel Byman. "Reject the Abuses, Retain the Tactic." *Washington Post,* April 17, 2005, p. B1.

[111] Howard LaFranchi. "Why the CIA's Secret Flights Irk Europeans." *Christian Science Monitor,* April 28, 2006, p. 1.

[112] "Annan: Shut Guantánamo Prison Camp." CNN.com. Posted on February 16, 2006. Available online. URL: http://www.cnn.com/2006/US/02/17/un.guantánamo/index.html?eref=sitesearch. Accessed December 19, 2006.

[113] Charles Lane. "High Court Rejects Detainee Tribunals." *Washington Post,* June 30, 2006, p. A1.

[114] Jonathan Weisman and Michael Abramowitz. "White House Shifts Tack on Tribunals." *Washington Post,* July 20, 2006, p. A3.

[115] Charlie Savage. "Monitors of Torture Treaty Rebuke US." *Boston Globe,* May 20, 2006, p. A1.

[116] Charlie Savage. "Bush Shuns Patriot Act." *Boston Globe,* March 24, 2006, p. A1.

3

Global Perspectives

INTRODUCTION

Terrorism is based often on historical grievances. The individuals and groups pursuing terrorist campaigns may seek to redress some historical wrongdoing or to implement laws and social codes with ancient roots that they believe are somehow superior to modern society.

Historical Grievances

National self-determination already has been cited as the motivating factor for many terrorist movements. Groups such as the Basque ETA (Euskadi Ta Askatasuna) movement in Spain and the Palestine Liberation Organization (PLO) believe that state boundaries were improperly drawn at some point in time; they want to redraw international boundaries so that they have their own country and are no longer subject to the rules of societies that, they feel, do not represent them. In the case of Palestine, national leaders believe that Israel was formed on land that was rightfully and historically Palestinian but that this was taken away when the state of Israel was formed in 1948. More moderate leaders, such as Yasser Arafat and the PLO, have sought ways to coexist with Israel, while more radical groups, such as Hamas and Hezbollah, seek the complete destruction of the Israeli state.

The Basque case provides examples of three aspects of dealing with history. First, the Basque terrorists sought to resolve a mistake of history, namely their inclusion in the Spanish state. Second, it shows that a group with a violent past may distract authorities from new threats. Finally, it also demonstrates the problem of how to come to terms with a terrorist past after a settlement has been reached. The Basques are an ethnic group of about 3 million people living in northern Spain and southwestern France, with the largest concentration on the Spanish side.[1] The Basque nationalist movement emerged as a reaction to the authoritarian rule of General Francisco Franco, who forced Basques to assimilate into the dominant Castilian culture and adopt its language. Basque nationalists formed the Basque Fatherland and Freedom group (ETA) in 1959 and seek the creation of a self-governed Basque homeland. After Franco's death in 1975 Spain adopted a constitutional monarchy, and the Basque region was granted a significant degree of autonomy, but it still did not satisfy nationalist leaders who wanted complete independence. ETA terrorist incidents continued through the 1990s and primarily consisted of bombings and murders of prominent public figures. The group declared a cease-fire in 1998 but ended the declaration after 14 months when the government showed no interest in negotiating.

A New Type of Terrorism

Then on March 11, 2004, bombs exploded aboard four commuter trains in Madrid, Spain, killing 191 and injuring 1,500. When news of the attack broke, the public and government's first response was to blame ETA.[2] But as the investigation unfolded, attention soon turned to al-Qaeda and the possibility that the attack was related to Spain's participation in the Iraq War. Police had been so focused on their familiar enemy, ETA, that they were not vigilant against Islamic terrorism. "We didn't see the immense face of Islamist terrorism at the time," said a Spanish counterterrorism expert.[3] Leaders of ETA, however, were concerned about the public backlash inside Spain and already had realized that, since 9/11, the international community had grown even more opposed to terrorism as means to political ends. The United States designated ETA as a foreign terrorist organization, severely cutting into its funding.[4]

Sobered by the reaction to the Madrid bombings, the ETA announced a partial cease-fire on June 19, 2005, and a permanent cease-fire on March 22, 2006. (ETA claimed responsibility for a December 30, 2006, bombing at Madrid's main airport that killed two people but nevertheless released a statement saying, "ETA affirms that the permanent cease-fire started on March 24, 2006, still stands."[5] The apparent contradiciton may indicate a rift inside ETA.) Now the question became amnesty: in return for laying down their weapons, should former ETA members be forgiven for their crimes? Will jailed ETA members be released? How can ETA's 800 victims be appropriately honored? What about human rights violations committed by Spanish security forces during ETA interrogations?

Truth Commissions

One option would be to institute a truth commission to allow the public to close a violent chapter in national history and to look ahead. Popular since the 1970s, truth commissions are panels established by governments to investigate past abuses by both insurgent and government forces. They do not prosecute past crimes but allow the opportunity for victims to tell their story and for the perpetrators to confess their actions and provide details, such as the fate of citizens who "disappeared" during a conflict.[6] Truth commissions have been established for Peru, East Timor, Yugoslavia, and Burundi, for example. The best-known truth commission was the postapartheid commission in South Africa.

Past Actions Constrain Today's Options

History can also constrain how a government responds to terrorism. Countries that fought wars to achieve their independence from colonial rulers, such as Algeria or India, may find it difficult to condemn self-determination movements that erupt within their borders or elsewhere in the world. One reason the United Nations has such difficulty formulating a policy on terrorism is Resolution 1514, passed in 1960, which legitimizes actions to achieve national self-determination. One man's terrorist is another man's freedom fighter.

Countries with an embarrassing history of militarism, intrusive police, and severe limits on civil rights may hesitate to formulate and implement laws that protect society but infringe upon individual freedoms. As will be discussed further below, Germany and Japan are two often-cited cases of the past influencing the present response to terrorism. Not only do memories of the Nazi state and imperial Japan make leaders hesitant to enact stricter rules, their post–World War II constitutions formally limit the types of responses available. With an aversion to military force—and, in Japan's case, no significant military at all—these countries have approached terrorism as a legal problem, best left to law enforcement, with perhaps some economic incentives thrown in.[7]

Finally, countries with a long history as targets of terrorism naturally have the most developed strategies and legal frameworks for identifying, prosecuting, and punishing suspected terrorists. They also probably have extensive practical experience with antiterrorism efforts, including public awareness and emergency response procedures. Such experiences help in regional cooperation efforts, which increasingly substitute for the lack of international laws and agencies to combat terrorism.

This chapter examines terrorism in five countries. Great Britain has developed numerous strategies and laws to deal with Irish terrorism, but London was caught off guard by home-grown Islamic terrorists that struck in 2005. Both Germany and Japan faced left-wing groups in the 1970s and found that the laws developed to eliminate those groups were not appropriate when religious-based terrorism emerged in the 1990s and early 2000s. Peru and Colombia chose different approaches to dealing with communist insurgencies in the 1980s and 1990, with Peru resorting to one-man rule while Colombia allowed the United States to dictate its antiterrorist policy.

GREAT BRITAIN/UNITED KINGDOM

Since the Easter Rebellion of 1916, Great Britain has had problems with Irish nationalism, and the greatest terrorist threat to the country in the last half of the 20th century came from the Irish Republican Army and its splinter groups. Then in July 2005 London was rocked by one of the bloodiest terrorist attacks in recent history, but the enemy in this case was Islamic fundamentalism, not Irish nationalism.

Domestic Terrorist Groups

IRISH REPUBLICAN ARMY

The conflict over Northern Ireland began before World War I, but participants believed the long-standing conflict might be resolved as part of Britain's drive to divest itself of its overseas colonies. In 1920 the British government granted home rule to the majority of Ireland. However, the northern city of Belfast had become the largest city on the Irish island and was strongly tied to the British economy. Business leaders in Northern Ireland did not want to sever their ties to the British crown and became politically active to prevent this occurrence. Eventually Ireland was partitioned, with six northern counties remaining part of Great Britain and the other 26 becoming an independent Irish state with a sovereign government based in Dublin.

Despite the leadership's decision to remain under London's control, Northern Ireland had a sizable population that wanted to be governed from Dublin. The Unionist (pro-London) leaders stacked the political system to weaken the Nationalist (pro-Dublin) sympathizers and correspondingly worked to marginalize them economically as well. Ultimately the Unionists pushed too hard, and a portion of the Nationalists took up arms, forming the Irish Republican Army.

Starting in the late 1960s, the IRA conducted a series of bombings against British targets such as the prime minister, Harrods department store, the royal family, and banks and other financial institutions. Rather than perpetrating any massacres, however, the IRA obtained its strength from its constancy and unpredictability. A body count of some 3,500 dead built up, but very slowly and incrementally, rather than in massive attacks on the scale of Oklahoma City or 9/11. London responded by stripping Northern Ireland of its legislature and instituting direct rule in 1972. The consequent permanent sense of insecurity and unease affected society and industry, draining the economy.

The Northern Ireland conflict is described frequently—and inaccurately—as a religious war. While it is easy and statistically correct to label the Unionists as Protestants and the Nationalists as Catholic, those categories distract from the real issue. The dispute is not over which religion to observe but rather about which political system will govern two distinct sets of people.

The conflict waxed and waned as different British governments came and went. Cease-fires were negotiated and broken. By the early 1990s IRA leaders became increasingly weary of the ongoing conflict and began to turn their focus toward a political settlement, and by 1994 they had agreed in principle to cease military activity. A major breakthrough came in 1998 when London agreed in the Good Friday Accord to restore the Northern Ireland assembly and home rule and released IRA members then in prison. By 2005, Gerry Adams, head of the IRA's political branch, Sinn Féin, called upon remaining IRA militants to demobilize. "In the past I have defended the right of the IRA to engage in armed struggle. I did so because there was no alternative for those who would not bend the knee, or turn a blind eye to oppression, or for those who wanted a national republic. Now there is an alternative."[8]

Foreign Groups Targeting London

While al-Qaeda has not made any direct attacks inside Great Britain, it appears to be training and advising a home-grown terrorist movement populated by young, disaffected British Muslims with ties to southern Asia, particularly Pakistan. According to this theory, London's generous asylum laws, relaxed political climate, and multiethnic environment made it a popular destination for Muslims who were exiled from other countries in the 1990s. There are some 1.6 million Muslims in Great Britain, and half of that number are younger than 25; 1 million Muslims live in London—one-eighth of its population—giving the capital its nickname "Londonistan."[9] According to the *Washington Post,* many of these Muslim youth, especially children of immigrants, "have risen so far, so fast in the dizzying culture of the West that they have become enraged, disoriented, and vulnerable to manipulation. Their spiritual leader is [Osama bin Laden] a Saudi billionaire's son who grew up with big ideas and too much money."[10] While British officials knew of restive segments of this population, they did not realize how organized they were becoming.

On July 7, 2005, three near-simultaneous explosions ripped through London's Underground system, turning the morning commute into a nightmare. Barely one hour later, a fourth bomb exploded on the top level of a London double-decker bus.[11] All four bombers died along with 52 transit riders.

The four men behind the July 7/7 bombings in London had been born in England, and their high-school friends regarded them as remarkably assimilated.[12] However, they had become drawn to the fundamentalist Islam practiced in Central and South Asia. Mohammad Sidique Khan (age 30), Hasib Hussein (18), and Shehzad Tanweer (22) were children of Pakistani immigrants and had recently visited Pakistan where they attended radical Islamic schools. They returned with a deeper focus on religion and began to withdraw from secular activities before they traveled from the town of Leeds to London.[13] The fourth bomber, Jermaine Lindsay (19) was a Jamaican who had converted to Islam. Al-Qaeda claimed responsibility for the bombings. Near the first anniversary of the attacks an Arab-language television network released a videotape of Tanweer threatening, "What you have witnessed now is only the beginning of a string of attacks that will continue and become stronger until you pull your forces out of Afghanistan and Iraq and until you stop your financial and military support to America and Israel."[14]

Exactly two weeks later bombs were discovered at four London transit locations: three Underground stations and one bus. However, these attacks were different. They occurred midday, rather than during rush hour, meaning fewer potential casualties, and there were no real explosions. The four would-be bombers tried to detonate items in backpacks, but none succeeded. There were thus no casualties. The incident turned out to be a copycat attack. One suspect told investigators that "We didn't want to kill, just sow terror."[15] The four suspects denied any connections with al-Qaeda or the 7/7 bombs, and no ties were discovered by the authorities.

Antiterrorism Efforts

Living with the perpetual threat of terrorism led the British government to create a flexible system to detect and respond to suspicious persons or objects. The program's main characteristics were decentralization and public awareness. Unusually, both programs were made possible by the cooperation of the IRA. Several IRA bombings ir the early 1970s killed civilians—rather than soldiers, police, or politicians—and generated quite negative publicity.

Consequently, the IRA developed a warning system, where a member would telephone the police to warn that an attack was imminent. The tipster used special code words agreed upon in advance with the police, to demonstrate that it was not a crank call, and the tipster would call early enough to allow the police to evacuate the area around a bomb. The police fanned out to warn the public through a combination of technologies, from shrill whistles to dedicated pagers.

The British system makes local police chiefs (constables) the first line of defense in a terrorist situation. The theory is to have contingency plans in place so that if an attack is suspected or actually called in, local law enforcement can immediately get to work, rather than having to wait for orders from London.[16] According to an FBI report, "For every incident, the police control and coordinate the response, from initially ensuring public safety through the final stages of investigation."[17] Drills are practiced three times a year and there was even a drill for a mock subway attack in 2003.[18]

The British public receives constant messages reminding them to be vigilant to the possibility of an attack. Both the London Underground system and the major airports have numerous signs and constant announcements to be on the lookout for unguarded packages, luggage, or suspicious objects. Citizens take this duty seriously; the *Washington Post* related an incident that took place in London on July 21, 2005, shortly after that day's failed bomb attacks:

> *On one double-decker bus route in south London, the driver was forced to stop suddenly when passengers reported an unattended gray duffel bag on the floor. When no one claimed the bag immediately, the bus emptied in a panic—until a middle-aged man stepped forward and sheepishly admitted that the bag was his.*
>
> *As the riders filed slowly back onto the bus, one woman let loose with frustration. She walked up to the forgetful passenger and screamed obscenitics in his face.*
>
> *"You should be skinned alive!" she shouted. "How could you do that to people? You should be arrested!"*
>
> *Nobody intervened.*[19]

The government also encourages businesses to prepare their own contingency plans to protect their employees in case of an attack. London has even produced guidebooks for businesses, including *Bombs: Protecting People and*

Property (1994) and *Maximising Business Resilience to Terrorist Bombings* (1996).[20] Both books resulted from the same incident. When the IRA tipped off police about a bomb in Bishopsgate, London, on April 24, 1993, the 60 employees of the nearby Hong Kong and Shanghai Bank followed their company's emergency plan and took cover in their building's basement. Although dozens of pedestrians were wounded by flying glass, none of the bank employees suffered injuries. The government held up the Bishopsgate contingency plan as a model for other companies.[21]

Legal Framework

Before the 7/7 terrorist attacks in London, the British government had not given much thought to domestic terrorism by non-Irish groups. From a legal standpoint, writes Terrence Taylor of the London-based International Institute for Strategic Studies: "Terrorism was defined as either Irish or international terrorism. The law allowed for no other domestic terrorism."[22]

Terrorism was treated as an occasional law-enforcement issue governed by the 1920 Emergency Powers Act, which allowed for temporary measures to restore and maintain public order but not to restrict individual rights permanently. When the Irish Republican Army became more active and more violent in the early 1970s, new laws were added to supplement the Emergency Powers Act. Specifically, the 1974 Prevention of Terrorism Act banned the Irish Republican Army and made it illegal to be a member of the group or to facilitate its activities in any way, such as fund-raising. It also allowed the government to deport IRA members or supporters and to ban their entry into Great Britain.[23]

While the IRA remained the only group to carry out attacks within Great Britain, by the 1990s British tourists, diplomats, and businesspeople had been victims of other groups abroad. Therefore a new law was enacted, the Terrorism Act of 2000, to broaden the legal framework to include groups other than the IRA. A second law was added in late 2001, the Anti-Terrorism, Crime, and Security Act, to enhance surveillance and intelligence-gathering authority.

Great Britain prides itself on taking cautious, measured approaches to terrorist cases, preferring to build a solid case to heighten the prospects of criminal convictions rather than to rush to action. Indeed, the "rush to action" following the 7/7 bombing proved disastrous. British authorities began to establish a descriptive profile for a suspected terrorist based on the background and characteristics of the four suicide bombers. When a man apparently fitting the profile left an apartment complex in London that happened to be under surveillance, he was followed. Rumors grew that he was wearing oddly heavy clothing for the summer and that he had jumped a turnstile at a subway station. Police closed in, threw Jean-Charles de Menezes to the floor of a subway car, and shot him eight times in the head—police protocol had said this was the safest way to subdue a person who might be wearing a bomb. Menezes turned out to be an unarmed electrician from Brazil. The rush to create antiterrorist tactics produced poorly conceived strategies and near hysteria among the public and left one innocent man dead.[24]

A new set of counterterror legislation was introduced following the 7/7 attacks. The government asked for the right to hold suspects for 90 days without charges, but the final law cut that down to 28 days. Another initiative that made it a crime to "glorify" terrorism was prompted by reports of people celebrating the 9/11 hijackers as "the Magnificent 19." Critics complained that the government bent over backward *not* to make the new policies appear to be aimed at Muslims, in particular pointing to a "law against incitement to religious hatred," designed to prevent Muslim-bashing.[25]

Counterterrorism Strategies

Great Britain uses extensive intelligence-gathering capabilities to prevent terrorist attacks in combination with specialized military units for rescue attempts.

Structurally, terrorism is the responsibility of the Home Office, which has an Organized and International Crime Directorate that supervises a separate Terrorism Protection Unit. Intelligence is collected by the Security Service (MI-5, for internal security), Secret Intelligence Service (MI-6, external security), and Government Communications Headquarters (GCHQ, similar to the U.S. National Security Agency). The Joint Terrorism Analysis Center (JTAC) serves as a clearinghouse for all relevant intelligence.[26] Working together, in March 2004 police, intelligence, and the Special Air Service (SAS) disrupted a plot to bomb parts of London. Like the 7/7 bombers, eight of these men were ethnic Pakistanis—the ninth was Algerian—who had grown up in London; all were between 18 and 25 years old.[27] Prior to 7/7 most intelligence efforts focused on overseas threats, but emphasis since has shifted to terror groups based in Great Britain, a reorientation that led to the discovery of a major hijacking plot in August 2006.

Britain's SAS, which was established in 1941 as an elite division of its army, is a highly trained reconnaissance unit intended to discover and disarm potential attacks before they happen. It is thus proactive, not reactive. Like most special operations squads, the SAS maintains a high level of secrecy and generates a certain level of glamour that makes it popular for recruits and movie producers. Their 1980 assault on the Iranian Embassy in London is still considered a stunning success; not only were 22 of 24 hostages rescued within moments, but the entire assault also was broadcast on live television. The Iranian Embassy operation, according to Terrence Taylor, "added greatly to the United Kingdom's terrorism deterrence by creating a myth, understandably not confirmed by the government, that it was British policy in such cases to kill all but one of the hostage takers, leaving that one alive for debriefing to provide information that would help improve further counterterrorism procedures."[28]

SAS units long have been posted in Northern Ireland to counteract attacks by the Irish Republican Army, especially in bomb disposal activities. Before the Good Friday Agreement, primary control in Northern Ireland fell to the Royal Ulster Constabulary (RUC), which was the provincial police force from 1922 until 2001. As often happens in divided societies, the RUC was a controversial group, seen as a vital source of protection by the pro-London faction and as oppressors by the pro-Dublin faction.

With little success through violence, the IRA began to work toward a permanent truce with Great Britain. On July 28, 2005, three weeks after Islamic terrorists detonated bombs in London, the Irish Republican Army declared the Irish conflict over.[29] In a first step, the IRA agreed to disarm. Once that process was completed, in September 2005,[30] the two sides began to clean up remnants of the past. First, families want to know the fate of nine individuals who simply vanished during The Troubles.[31] Second, and the more heated debate, London wants to bring to justice a group of IRA fugitives through an amnesty program that would hand down convictions but not require jail time. As Prime Minister Tony Blair explained, "Under the Good Friday Agreement in 1998, people who were convicted and in prison for terrorist offenses pre-1998 got released. How can you possibly say they [the fugitives] should be put in prison if the people already convicted have been let out?"[32] Ultimately the deal fell through; not only did relatives of victims object to the amnesty, but IRA representatives realized it would also apply tc police and military who had committed human rights violations in Northern Ireland.[33]

LEFT-WING TERRORISM IN GERMANY AND JAPAN

In the 1960s and 1970s Western Europe and Japan began to pull out of the economic slump caused by World War II. But the new economic wealth was not spread evenly. The people who worked the hardest, the factory workers producing the new consumer goods, did not enjoy the fruits of their labor as much as the factory managers and owners did. A backlash against this uneven development began, often within the younger generation. West European and Japanese 20-somethings had not experienced World War II, and in Germany, Italy, and Japan many youths felt a sense of shame that their parents had cooperated with the Nazis, the Fascists, or the Japanese empire. Communist ideology was attractive doubly to these youths: It preached economic equality and was the polar opposite of the defeated World War II regimes.[34] This intellectual tendency combined with the global anticapitalist anti–Vietnam War sentiment of the late 1960s, and new left-wing groups began to emerge in the early 1970s.

Left-wing terrorists such as the Baader-Meinhof group focus on economic issues and seek to equalize the distribution of wealth. They oppose capitalism as an economic system that disproportionately rewards business owners, while workers or farmers see little benefit from their labors. Most left-wing terrorists draw upon the principles of Marxism and class struggle, taking either Vladimir Lenin's Russian version (workers lead the revolution) or Mao Zedong's Chinese version (peasants lead the revolution), depending on local circumstances.

The most visible left-wing terrorist organizations were the Japanese Red Army, the Red Army Faction (RAF or, more commonly, Baader-Meinhof Gang) in West Germany, and the Red Brigades (Italy). These groups advocated Marxist class struggle and sought to remove their respective countries from Western, "capitalist-dominated" organizations such as NATO and the European Economic Community, the forerunner of the European Union. They targeted the local business community and government leaders with business ties. They also were small—usually fewer than 50 active members—and often had high-ranking women among their leadership. Members tended to be in their 20s.

Germany

DOMESTIC TERRORIST GROUPS

Red Army Faction

West Germany's home-grown left-wing terrorists date to 1968, when Andreas Baader (1943–77), a small-time thief, and Gudrun Ensslin (1940–77), a brilliant college student and minister's daughter, set fire to two department stores in Frankfurt as part of a misguided protest of the Vietnam War. They were arrested and convicted of arson but two years later broke out of jail with the help of Ulrike Meinhof (1934–76), a well-known journalist. The group fled to Lebanon, where they trained with the Popular Front for the Liberation of Palestine and, upon their return to Germany, founded the Baader-Meinhof Gang. (While Meinhof was more famous, Ensslin actually outranked her within the group.) They sought to expose the "Fascist" underpinning of the West German state and robbed banks to fund their activities.

Baader-Meinhof found a small following among German youth, drawn more to the glamour of rebellion than the Marxist theory it offered. According to Ben Lewis, director of the documentary, "Baader-Meinhof: In Love with Terror," the RAF offered a glamorous antidote to German guilt over the Nazi past:

> *A lot of school children thought they were cool. They wore leather jackets and were full of sexy girls and were run by a sexy guy. This was the German answer to the Rolling Stones. Typically, Germans couldn't come up with the Rolling Stones because they have to be very serious about things; so they came up with a terrorist group rather than a rock group.*[35]

Baader-Meinhof members conducted a series of bombings and political killings, including a stream of attacks in May 1972 on a U.S. military barracks in Frankfurt, the U.S. embassy in Bonn,[36] and the West German embassy in Stockholm. Baader, Meinhof, Ensslin, and a fourth member, Jan-Carl Raspe (1944–77), were arrested, convicted of murder and terrorism in 1975, and sentenced to life in prison; Meinhof, however, committed suicide during her trial. Other group members hijacked an Air France airplane in 1976 and diverted it to Entebbe, Uganda, asking the German government to swap the 80 hostages for Baader, Ensslin, and Raspe. When Bonn refused, the jailed leaders lost hope and committed suicide.

Their followers renamed the movement Red Army Faction and continued to attack prominent German business leaders sporadically until 1991. The collapse of the Soviet Union and German unification in 1990 marked the end of the Red Army Faction, as communism had lost its international appeal. In 1998 the RAF issued a press release announcing that it was disbanding.[37]

FOREIGN GROUPS: HAMBURG CELL

While there do not appear to be non-German terrorist groups that target Germans, al-Qaeda members prepared for the 9/11 attacks from an apartment in the city of Hamburg. At least three of the 19-man 9/11 squad had lived in Hamburg, and investigators believe that at least four senior al-Qaeda members were also in the city. The group had not raised any suspicions, however, and local investigators did not know of their link to the city prior to a tip received on September 12, 2001. The city was a good base because the cell members could easily blend in. Hamburg is a multiethnic port city with some 130,000 Muslims: 8 percent of the city is Muslim, compared to a national average of 4 percent.[38] The city also has a history with extreme political groups, including anarchists and anticapitalists.[39] Finally, Hamburg Technical University has a very large foreign student population, and the al-Qaeda members seemed to be just more university students.[40]

ANTITERRORISM EFFORTS

Unlike Great Britain, Germany has been fortunate not to face widespread terrorist attacks that would require extensive contingency planning and disaster-preparedness drills. Red Army Faction attacks tended to be small in scale and were easily handled by conventional police procedures. Germans were alarmed when two unexploded bombs were discovered in luggage aboard trains on July 31, 2006, but the subsequent investigation suggests that the incidents were the work of two disgruntled Lebanese immigrants and not part of an international conspiracy.[41] The only two attacks by external groups were those at the 1972 Olympic Games in Munich and Libya's April 5, 1986, bombing of the La Belle disco in Berlin. Investigators in the La Belle incident were stymied until East and West Germany were unified in 1990. Key evidence on the bombers was discovered in the files of the Stasi—East Germany's secret police. That evidence led to the arrest of five suspects in 1996; their trial began in 1997, but a verdict did not come until November 2001.

For the Munich Olympics, wishful thinking and concern for Germany's public image took precedence over disaster preparedness. The last time Germany had hosted the Olympic games was in Berlin in 1932, and those games went down in history as a massive propaganda event for the Nazi regime of Adolf Hitler, so the 1972 organizers had made a deliberate decision to keep security to a minimum in what planners called the "Carefree Games." Barely $2 million was spent on security.[42] Rather than a menacing black-shirted security corps, Olympic officials had inconspicuous, unarmed "Olys" who responded to a group of several hundred Maoist demonstrators by handing out candy.[43]

On September 5, 1972, at about 4:00 A.M., Palestinian terrorists from Black September, a group tied to the Palestine Liberation Organization (PLO), scaled a fence outside the Olympic Village, entered the athletes' dormitory, and seized 11 members of the Israeli Olympic team. The terrorists wanted to trade the hostages for 234 Palestinians held in Israel, as well as two leaders of the German Red Army Faction, Andreas Baader and Ulrike Meinhof. Two athletes were killed in the initial assault, and the captors declared they would execute one of the other nine every hour until their demands were met.

The Munich hostage crisis played out live on international television. Negotiations continued throughout the day, as German officials stalled for time and the terrorists extended their deadline. Israeli Prime Minister Golda Meir flatly refused to negotiate with terrorists, much less release the prisoners as demanded. The German government, desperate to avoid having more Jews executed on German soil, offered the terrorists an unlimited amount of money to release the hostages, but to no avail. Efforts to sneak in police disguised as athletes were thwarted when the terrorists saw the assault unfold on televisions inside the dormitory and heard the crowd gathered outside shouting directions to the police squad. By 5:00 P.M. the terrorists demanded an airplane to take them to Egypt. Again the negotiators stalled, while they hastily assembled a poorly equipped assault team at a nearby airbase. The nine surviving athletes and the eight terrorists then boarded two helicopters at 10:10 P.M. for a brief flight to the airbase.

When the helicopters landed, the terrorists realized they had flown into a trap, and bullets flew for more than two hours. Four hostages died when their helicopter caught fire, the other five were executed by their captors. One German policeman also was fatally shot. Five of the terrorists were killed, and the other three were captured.[44] Two months later, on October 29, hijackers from the Popular Front for the Liberation of Palestine (another PLO subsidiary) commandeered a Lufthansa jet, demanding the release of the three jailed Black September members. Germany immediately complied, conveniently avoiding the spectacle of a trial. To this day, many observers believe the Lufthansa hijacking was staged by the West German government to avoid having to conduct a very difficult criminal investigation.[45]

Ironically, the largest and best prepared group at the Olympics was not the security detail, but the media. Around 4,000 print and radio journalists plus another 2,000 television reporters were on site, waiting for news to report home. The first communications satellite had been launched only four years earlier, and live international broadcasts were still a novelty that news crews used to great effect.[46] Broadcast live around the globe, the image of a masked Black September gunman prowling the dormitory balcony proved indelible. It remains one of the 10 most frequently viewed television news clips.[47]

Within two weeks of the murders, Bonn established Grenzschutzgruppe 9 (GSG-9), an elite special forces unit modeled on Britain's SAS. In 1977 GSG-9 successfully stormed a Lufthansa flight hijacked by the Red Army Faction and flown to Mogadishu, Somalia. While the plane was parked at the airport, GSG-9 operatives scaled the aircraft, blasted the door open, and rescued the 91 passengers and crew.

LEGAL FRAMEWORK

Germany's current legal system is also a reaction to its Nazi past. Compared with other European countries, German prosecutors must present a much higher standard of evidence, and German police and intelligence units must operate more transparently, making it difficult to conduct sensitive investigations. Family members of victims are allowed to assist in prosecution efforts, including questioning witnesses in court.[48] Due to the presumption of innocence, it can even be difficult to detain suspects to assure that they actually will appear for trial. Suspected al-Qaeda financier Mounir al-Mottasadeq, discussed below, not only was free during his trial, but he did not even have a police escort during his daily walks to the courthouse.[49]

Reacting to the central police force created by the Nazis, the architects of postwar Germany opted for extreme decentralization. Intelligence and police functions are completely separate. Instead of one police force, there are 16 separate ones, one for each state (laander). Consequently there was a mixture of turf wars and buck-passing—either every law-enforcement agency wanted in on the action or they all wanted to avoid the problem and pass it to someone else. Although there are current efforts to create centralized agencies for terrorist prevention and investigation, state leaders have resisted, not wanting to lose their current autonomy. While Great Britain gives local police great leeway to initiate investigations, in Germany the federal attorney general must grant permission before the Federal Crime Office can launch an inquiry. However, often the only way to gain sufficient evidence to convince the prosecutor is through an investigation—an almost impossible situation.[50]

When faced with a violent left-wing insurgency in the 1970s, West Germany promulgated the "Baader-Meinhof Laws," to facilitate prosecution of members of the Baader-Meinhof Gang. The laws allowed for trials in absentia, restricted access by "sympathetic" lawyers, and allowed civil servants to be screened for radical activities. A new centralized police structure emerged, and surveillance of civilians suspected of domestic terrorism was expanded to include investigations of such seemingly mundane items as utility bills.[51] The government also began to conduct broad, dragnet searches for individuals who matched profiles created to describe the "typical" left-wing terrorist.[52]

However, those laws were drafted specifically for fighting Baader-Meinhof; prior to 9/11 Germany had no laws banning foreign terrorist organizations from working in Germany. In fact, many German postwar laws made it an attractive location for militant Islamic groups. First, Germany had extremely liberal immigration and asylum laws. A person could claim to be a university student for years on end, without paying tuition or even attending classes.[53] Second, after the Nazi policy of targeting and exterminating Jews,

Germany adopted a liberal, hands-off policy regarding religious organizations and their activities. Third, Germany had become a popular destination for Muslims, particularly for Muslims driven out of France. By the end of the 1990s Germany was home to 3 million Muslims.

On December 8, 2001, Germany introduced a new law making it illegal for residents and citizens to join or otherwise help foreign terrorist organizations. It also gave the government the power to ban religious groups that they believe promote terrorism. Three groups were immediately outlawed: Kalifatstaat (Caliph State), al-Aksa, and Hizb-ut-Tahrir. A second set of legislation, known as the "Second Counterterrorism Packet," was implemented on January 2, 2002, and made it easier for German officials to monitor the activities, communications, and financial transactions of suspects, provided nearly $2 billion in additional funding, and improved coordination among law-enforcement agencies and security organs. Previously, intelligence gathering was extremely restricted and generally could not be shared among the leading agencies: the Federal Intelligence Service, the Federal Bureau for the Protection of the Constitution, and the Military Counterintelligence Service.[54] The Second Counterterrorism Packet also implemented advanced technology to monitor immigration flows better. Passports, residency permits, and other identification papers were now to include biometric information such as fingerprints and DNA for the holders, and the documents themselves would use holograms and other printing techniques to reduce counterfeiting.[55] To identify potential suspects, Berlin turned to a technique developed for the Red Army Faction: computer profiling. In the first two months after the 9/11 attack, a computer profiling system identified 10,000 "suspicious students" in Hamburg who warranted additional investigation.[56]

COUNTERTERRORISM STRATEGIES

Given Germany's violent history of militarism, Nazi storm troopers (Waffen SS), and secret police (Gestapo), post–World War II leaders have opposed war and promoted pacifism. While German armies bulldozed through Europe during World War I and World War II, the contemporary German state long avoided dispatching troops outside Europe. Consequently Germany's primary approach toward countering terrorism is based on diplomacy, not military action.

Germany was quick to back Washington during the initial stages of the War on Terror and agreed to contribute 3,900 troops to the war in Afghanistan. However, according to Cornell University's Peter J. Katzenstein, "After the defeat of the Taliban government in Afghanistan, Germany saw September 11 as a 'crime' for which military instruments were largely unsuitable."[57] Berlin did not agree with the need for regime change in Baghdad and refused to back the Bush administration on the war in Iraq, a decision, according to then U.S. Secretary of Defense Donald Rumsfeld, that had "the effect of poisoning the relationship" between Germany and the United States.[58]

The rift over Iraq severely damaged German efforts to prosecute Mounir al-Motassadeq, an Algerian national living in Hamburg, because the United States refused to provide key evidence to German investigators. Motassadeq was accused of being the "financial officer" for the 9/11 terrorists and was charged with being a member of a terrorist organization and with more than 3,000 counts of accessory to murder. Motassadeq was convicted in 2003, but that conviction was overturned in April 2004 due to a lack of convincing evidence. Washington had provided evidence to German intelligence, but it was conditioned on an agreement to keep it secret and not present it in court.[59]

Japan

When Japan ended a long period of isolationism in the 1880s, the government sought to prevent incursions by Western powers by strengthening the military. At the same time it launched a massive industrialization campaign. Leaders also emphasized nationalism, including loyalty to the emperor, and sought to control public thought through censorship, the Shinto religion, and rigorous, standardized education. A "special higher police" force was created to monitor antigovernment activities and to enforce a series of laws that limited the right of association. In 1925 a "Peace Preservation Law" was introduced to ban groups formally that seemed to oppose the government.

At the same time, the military grew increasingly strong during these years, and by the 1930s it completely controlled the government. When Japan surrendered at the end of World War II, the Allied powers drafted a new constitution to prevent a replay of Japan's recent history. The emperor was no longer considered to be a god, rights to privacy and individual liberty were introduced, the powers of the police were curtailed severely, the secret police were abolished, and Tokyo was stripped of an army. These reforms created a pacifist Japanese state but also severely handicapped the Japanese government when it was challenged by a home-grown terrorist movement in the 1970s.

DOMESTIC TERRORIST GROUPS

Japanese Red Army (JRA)

By far the bloodiest of the 1970s left-wing groups was the Japanese Red Army. With no more than three dozen members, the JRA was notorious for its airplane hijackings. It maintained ties with the Popular Front for the Liberation of Palestine and worked with the PFLP to bomb Tel Aviv's Lod Airport in 1972, causing more than a dozen fatalities. Libya hired the group to bomb several locations in New York City in 1988.[60] It was also one of the rare international terrorist groups led by a woman, Fusako Shigenobu (1945–). Founded in 1970–71, the JRA sought to overthrow Japan's constitutional monarchy and launch a global communist revolution. Experts believe its membership never exceeded 40 people. Once Tokyo successfully expelled the JRA from Japan, it largely ignored the movement's violent campaign abroad; it was now somebody else's problem.[61]

In 1973 the JRA stormed the Japanese embassy in Kuwait, taking 16 staff members hostage. The next year they took hostages at the French embassy in The Hague, Netherlands, and the American embassy in Kuala Lumpur, Malaysia. (Starting in 1986 the JRA often used the name Anti-Imperialist International Brigade.) In 1988 a JRA operative was arrested and accused of planning to bomb sites in New York City, possibly at the request of Libyan leader Muammar Qaddafi.[62] Shigenobu long based her operations in Lebanon, but the country expelled the remaining JRA members in March 2000.[63] Following her arrest in November 2000 in Osaka, Shigenobu announced that the group would cease operations.

Aum Shinrikyo

As the JRA reduced its activities, a new domestic terror group emerged in Japan: Aum Shinrikyo. This cult drew upon Buddhism, Hinduism, and Taoism to prepare its members to survive the forthcoming apocalypse.[64] Led by Shoko Asahara (born Chizuo Matsumoto in 1955), the group attracted an extremely well-educated membership and demanded absolute loyalty. Members were expected to surrender all of their money and possessions upon joining and lived in austere conditions at the cult's compound on Mount Fuji.

Asahara expected members to prove their loyalty through acts of violence and suffering. Members would starve themselves, abstain from sex, or immerse themselves in icy or boiling water. Members who began to doubt the movement were often murdered, as were family members who tried to bring their relatives home and back to normal life.

Experts attribute the group's attraction to the social dislocation in Japan following World War II. The U.S. decision to declare that the emperor was an ordinary man, not a god, undermined the traditional belief system in Japan, and some citizens were disturbed by the growing materialism brought by the country's economic expansion. Many Japanese turned to nontraditional movements to give their lives a focus.[65] Aum had 10,000 members scattered in 36 branches across Japan, and by 1994 the group had branches in Asia, Europe, the United States, and Russia.

Aum Shinrikyo is best known for spreading poisonous sarin gas inside the Tokyo subway system on March 20, 1995, an assault that killed 12 and injured more than 5,000 passengers and workers. Aum has already been mentioned in the discussion regarding weapons of mass destruction, cyberterrorism, and the high educational levels of its members. It is also significant because the group's success stemmed from Aum leaders' ability to exploit the loopholes in the Japanese legal system: the 1951 Religious Corporation law decreed that registered religious organizations were tax-exempt and that the government was not allowed to intrude on their activities. As in Germany, by making religious groups exempt from surveillance, they became attractive covers for unscrupulous leaders. While Aum expanded beyond Japan's borders, there have not been instances of foreign terrorist groups operating inside Japan. Instead, Japanese citizens are targeted when overseas.

FOREIGN GROUPS TARGETING TOKYO

Japan's extensive economic holdings abroad could make it an attractive target, particularly for leftist groups. According to one study, "As businesspeople, tourists, scholars, and the like, private Japanese citizens live all over the world without any Japanese military or security presence; they are easy, visible targets."[66] In November 1986 the New People's Army of the Philippines captured the head of a Japanese trading firm's Manila office, reportedly with the help of the JRA. Similarly, the Peruvian terrorists that seized the Japanese ambassador's residence claimed that Japanese businesses were exploiting Peruvian workers.[67]

ANTITERRORISM EFFORTS

Back home, Japan's antiterrorism program focuses on crisis management. However, no one had anticipated a chemical weapons attack like that staged by Aum in 1995. Caught off guard, two hours passed before authorities in Tokyo recognized what was making people sick. Furthermore, communications coordination was insufficient; the Tokyo Metropolitan Fire Department received calls about problems in 15 different subway stations, however, more than an hour passed before anyone realized that these events were connected and dispatched emergency teams to the area. Compounding the problem, nearly *all* of the city's rescue teams scrambled to the first reported incident; as other calls came in, there were no crews on standby.[68]

The Tokyo subway incident raised public concerns that the Japanese government was not able to respond properly to disasters. The sarin attack came only two months after a huge earthquake hit Kobe, killing more than 6,000 people, and people criticized the government's response to both incidents. As later reports made clear, a primary problem during the response to the sarin attack had been uncertainty over what measures the government was allowed to take under the constitution.[69] Consequently a new government position, deputy chief cabinet secretary for crisis management, was created, and a new emergency secretariat was formed to coordinate efforts of other agencies. A police Special Assault Team was also created but can only be used under very narrowly defined conditions. The reorganization included a reconceptualization of terrorism: "Terrorism [is] a subset of consequence management for all natural and manmade disaster. The government views the threat of terrorism through a broader lens and no longer focuses solely on left-wing activities and hostage taking in its response plans."[70]

LEGAL FRAMEWORK

Article Nine of the Japanese Constitution of 1947 renounces the country's right of war. Specifically, Japan "forever renounces the threat or use of force as a means of settling international disputes" and "land, sea, and air forces . . . will never be maintained." Japan has no military, aside from the small Self-Defense Forces. The National Police Agency has minimal intelligence-gathering capabilities. Given these small institutions, Tokyo has very limited options for countering terrorist groups.

In the 1970s Tokyo's guiding principle was to protect the lives of hostages seized by terrorists. When the JRA bombed Shell Oil storage tanks in Singapore in 1973, members asked the Japanese government to dispatch a plane to take them to safety in South Yemen. Tokyo complied. When the JRA hijacked a Japanese Airlines flight in September 1977, they requested—and received—a $6 million ransom from Tokyo. Soon, however, the government realized this policy would backfire. Rather than protecting the lives of Japanese citizens, the prospect of a huge ransom payment actually made them more attractive targets for terrorists.

In September 1978, leaders of the Group of Seven industrialized countries (G7) addressed the issue of hijacking at their annual summit. They agreed to cooperate on international terrorism, including a unified approach toward ransom demands. Specifically, governments would no longer negotiate with terrorists. However, the law applies only to governments; private companies and families can still pay ransoms for employees or family members. Mexican terrorists, for example, received a $2 million ransom when they kidnapped the head of the Japanese Sanyo electronics company's Mexican office.[71]

The 9/11 attacks in the United States prompted the Japanese government to take action to increase its terrorist awareness far more than did the Aum Shinrikyo attack. Following the Aum attack, the Liberal Democratic Party, the majority in parliament in 1995, tried to increase police powers and introduced a wiretapping provision but faced stiff resistance. Ultimately a bill passed, the "Law to Control Organizations That Engage in Acts of Indiscriminate Mass Murder," but its focus was so narrow as only to be applicable really to Aum Shinrikyo.[72] In fact, investigations can begin only *after* the group has committed "indiscriminate mass murder"; no advance surveillance is allowed, which makes it very difficult to detect and thwart an attack.

The 9/11 attacks, on the other hand, triggered a significant change in Japanese military strategy. Tokyo had been condemned for not participating in the 1990–91 Gulf War, and Prime Minister Junichiro Koizumi was not going to allow a repeat with the War on Terror. He introduced a seven-point plan into parliament that, after much debate, allowed three Japanese Aegis cruisers to offer logistical support to U.S. forces in Afghanistan and to establish a refugee camp and hospital in Pakistan. Three Japanese destroyers and other small ships accompanied U.S. forces to the Middle East in late September 2001, where they would carry out support operations, such as refueling.[73] Tokyo also agreed to provide humanitarian relief and to share intelligence with the United States and coalition countries.[74] On December 11, 2001, the Japanese parliament passed a new "Law to Support Counter-Terrorism," but experts dismissed it as an incremental change in existing policy. According to David Leheny, the law "is not real counterterrorism legislation, but rather an initiative to help U.S. action in this specific instance."[75]

COUNTERTERRORISM STRATEGIES

Japan's primary counterterrorism strategy is international cooperation. Since 1960 its security largely has been guaranteed by a treaty with the United States. Because its own intelligence gathering and analysis efforts are weak, it maintains close ties with countries that can share information, particularly the United States. Since 1995 the government has worked to upgrade the country's intelligence capabilities, primarily through better technology, and to improve knowledge about chemical and biological weapons. New management bodies have been created under the police, such as an Office for Counterterrorism and Office for Suspicious Groups, and a Public Security Investigation Agency under the Ministry of Justice. Yet coordination remains weak due to constitutional limits and public opinion concerns about creating national police structures. The Self-Defense Forces readily acknowledge that their best source of information is "newspaper clippings."[76]

However, since the Aum incident in 1995 there has been no domestic terrorist incident to test the new provisions. The one major terrorist attack against Japan actually occurred in Lima, Peru, where indigenous terrorists invaded the residence of the Japanese ambassador, initially taking more than 700 hostages. The Japanese prime minister dispatched his foreign minister, Yukihiko Ikeda, to Lima to persuade the Peruvian president to concede to demands in order to save lives.[77]

PERU

Beginning in 1982 Peru experienced a bloody campaign by two distinct communist insurgencies that for nearly 15 years often fought each other as well as the government. Both sought to impose communist regimes and remove foreign influence, but their tactics differed. Together the rebellions and counterinsurgencies they triggered caused more than 60,000 deaths and $25 billion in damages.[78]

Domestic Terrorist Groups

The older group is commonly known as Shining Path (Sendero Luminoso, SL); it was established in the 1960s by Abimael Guzmán (1934–), a university professor who recruited students to his cause. After years of spouting Maoist propaganda, in 1980 SL turned to a bloody campaign of bombing, assassination, and kidnapping, killing some 30,000 Peruvians to force the revolution. The peasantry eventually grew tired of SL's stranglehold and formed their own paramilitary group to defend themselves. Following Guzmán's arrest in 1992 the group significantly dwindled in numbers and influence, but his conviction was overturned in 2003 because it was handed down by a military court and technically Guzmán is a civilian.[79] In October 2006 a civilian court sentenced Guzmán to life in prison.

The second left-wing group is the Túpac Amaru Revolutionary Movement (MRTA), which is named for a famous Inca leader. Founded in 1983, Túpac Amaru seeks to establish a Marxist-Leninist regime in Peru and to eliminate U.S. and Japanese economic influence in the country. It had much better relations with the peasantry than did SL. Fourteen members of Túpac Amaru seized the residence of the Japanese ambassador during a party in December 1996. Most of the 700 party guests taken hostage were soon released, but MRTA members kept 72 VIP guests in custody until 140 police officers stormed the compound in April 1997.[80] The group had demanded the release of jailed comrades and changes to the government's economic policies. All 14 terrorists died in the raid, including leader Nestor Cerpa (1953–97), which generally marked the end of the movement. Later reports that many of the terrorists had been executed while trying to surrender tainted President Alberto Fujimori.[81] The incident contributed to Fujimiro's decision to resign and flee the country in late 2000.

Foreign Groups Targeting Lima

Peru faces outside terrorism threats from two sources, one indirect and one direct. In recent years the U.S. State Department has been concerned with potential terrorist activity in the "Triborder Area" of South America. This zone is where the borders of Argentina, Paraguay, and Brazil meet, and the region has a growing Muslim population. Terror experts believe Hamas and Hezbollah are interested in the area as a source of both funding and potential recruitment. The region is an area known for drug and arms smuggling, and the State Department believes that Middle Eastern terrorist groups may launder money and acquire weapons in this area.[82] Such activities could potentially spill over to Peru or draw support from SL. A more direct threat comes from the Revolutionary Armed Forces of Colombia (FARC), whose members apparently use remote Peruvian territory for downtime and for arms purchases.[83]

Antiterrorism Efforts

When SL and Túpac Amaru began their insurgencies in the 1980s, the Peruvian government was structurally unprepared to fight an insurgency movement. The country had been run as a military dictatorship from 1968 to 1980, and even after the restoration of democracy in 1980 the public remained wary of the military due its history of violence against the peasantry. Furthermore, the national government had very little infrastructure or effective control outside of the capital city, Lima.[84] There was not even a national police force until 1988. SL leader Guzmán successfully exploited Lima's lack of control in the countryside and gradually took over entire peasant towns. However, he preferred violence over persuasion, a strategy that eventually led the peasants to form their own defensive regiments, the *rondas,* to drive the SL out. In time, the Peruvian military regained the confidence of the peasantry and provided weapons and training to the rondas.

Legal Framework

On April 5, 1992, President Fujimori moved to seize power from other branches of government so that he could implement the laws he believed necessary to eradicate the insurgencies. Known as the "Autocoup," Fujimori suspended the constitution, dissolved parliament, and shut down the judicial system. Article 2 of Decree Law 25475, which created a new framework for combating terrorism, defines terrorism as:

> *[an act that] provokes, creates, or maintains a state of anxiety, alarm, or fear in the population or in a sector thereof, performs acts against life, the body, health, personal liberty and security, or against property, against*

the security of public buildings, roads, or means of communication or of transport of any type, energy or explosive materials or artifacts, or any other means capable of causing damage or grave disturbance of the public peace, or affect the international relations or the security of society and the State.[85]

Other components of the decree set a minimum prison sentence for terrorism at 20 years for collaborators, 30 years for active terrorists, and life for terrorist leaders (Article 4), allowed the police to hold suspects without warrants and without outside contact for up to 15 days (Article 12), and specified that trials would be heard by judges alone in closed courtrooms and could not last longer than 15 days (Article 13). To prevent potential retaliation, judges were allowed to remain anonymous—they would not affix their name to any document and could disguise their identity by wearing hoods and using voice-altering equipment (Article 15).

The Repentant Terrorist Law (Decree law 25499, issued in May 1992) allowed convicted terrorists to reduce their sentences possibly if they could provide "useful, truthful, and detailed information" about other terrorist activities.

In 2000 the Inter-American Commission on Human Rights, part of the Organization of American States, struck down significant parts of Decree Law 25475. Judges said that the definition of terrorism was too vague and the sentencing guideline too extreme.[86] They deemed that the law compromised basic human rights, including the freedom of expression and freedom of assembly, and violated due process, including the right to know the charges against a suspect and the right to legal representation.

The commission's ruling on Article 12 was particularly crucial because the 15-day period gave police the opportunity to torture suspects before they had lawyers or even had been charged with a specific crime. Paragraph 95 of the report confirms these fears:

The Commission considers that the authority given the Police by Decree Law No. 25,475, to hold a detainee incommunicado for up to 15 days, creates conditions that lend themselves to violations of physical integrity. The Commission has received numerous complaints consistently alleging acts of torture committed during this phase. Concretely, the complaints indicate that torture is used to obtain the signing of "confessions" that have later become the main evidentiary basis of the conviction. Such acts constitute violations of Article 5 of the American Convention, which sets forth the right of all persons not to be subjected to torture or to cruel,

> *inhuman, or degrading treatment, and of all detainees to be treated with respect for the inherent dignity of the human person.*

The commission also condemned the process of secret military tribunals, citing numerous procedural flaws. The commission's ruling quoted a UN Rapporteur's description of these trials:

> *The main characteristic of the proceedings before "faceless" courts, both civilian and military, is secrecy. Judges and prosecutors are identified by codes. When handling treason cases, Supreme Court judges also identify themselves by secret codes. The judges are at all times invisible to the defendants and their counsel, and trial proceedings are conducted in private. Hearings take place in specially equipped courtrooms inside high-security prisons or, in treason cases, at military bases. The courtrooms are small, with a single door and a large one-way mirror along one wall. In an adjoining room on the other side of the mirror, the judges, prosecutor and court secretaries have their seats. They communicate with the accused persons and their counsel through voice-distorting microphones. Since the sound system does not always function properly, it is sometimes impossible for the defendant or his or her counsel to understand what is being said, which has in many cases seriously obstructed the proceedings or affected the defense.*[87]

Despite its legal flaws, Fujimori's framework considerably reduced the terrorist threat in the country. Peruvian forces captured SL leader Guzmán on September 12, 1992. As Guzmán preferred to lead without deputies, there was no one to replace him, and the leaderless group soon collapsed. Guzmán appeared before one of the secret military tribunals and was sentenced to life. The success against the terrorists came at great human cost, however. Subsequent investigations revealed that the police and military used forced enlistment, arbitrary arrest, rape, torture, and kidnapping to extract confessions and the security services operated a death squad that carried out summary executions.[88]

The terrorism laws were amended in 2000 to address the commission's concerns, but few of the violations would be punished. In 1995 Fujimori amnestied military and police personnel and civilians who committed human-rights abuses in the course of terrorism investigations. The amnesty prevented further investigation into allegations of torture. The tribunal system was declared unconstitutional in 2000 and some 2,000 cases were annulled—including Guzmán's—and transferred to civilian jurisdictions. Guzmán's civilian trial was scheduled to begin in 2004 but has been plagued with resignations of the judges and courtroom protests.

Counterterrorism Strategies

Initially Peruvian president Fernando Belaúnde (1980–85) chose simply to ignore SL. Although the group burst onto the scene with an assault on Chuschi on May 17, 1980, one day before the first democratic elections in more than a decade, he did not order the armed forces to attack SL until December 1982—some 32 months later.

While Belaúnde dithered, Peruvian peasants took matters into their own hands, forming *rondas campesinas,* a civil-defense force with a long tradition in Peru. Gradually the military began to work with the *rondas* and eventually trained and supplied the *rondas* with weapons. Belaúnde's solution was to designate portions of the country as "emergency zones" in which the military could impose martial rule if needed to restore the peace. The number of zones expanded as terrorist attacks increased; at one point nearly 60 percent of the population lived in territories designated as emergency zones. Fujimori reduced the number of zones but did not eliminate them completely. The bulk of the human-rights violations mentioned above are believed to have taken place in the emergency zones.[89]

As discussed above, Fujimori's decrees gave the police, specifically the National Counterterrorism Directorate (DINCOTE), primary authority to investigate suspected terrorists, using evidence collected by the National Intelligence Service (SIN). With the two terrorist groups quickly subdued, Fujimori dissolved DINCOTE in late 1992 and ordered the National Intelligence Service to concentrate on his political opponents. As reports about the abuses of the SIN began to emerge in late 2000, Fujimori dissolved the organization and announced his own resignation.[90] His successor recreated a police counterterror unit known as DIRCOTE.

While Fujimori's crackdown eliminated most of the SL and Túpac Amaru, his decision to abolish the counterterror police units allowed the groups to hibernate. A small contingent of SL fighters remains active in Huallaga Valley, a major cocaine-producing region. Some experts suggest that SL may be able to draw a new cadre of members from younger Peruvians who are dissatisfied with President Alejandro Toledo's policies and who do not remember the terror of the 1980s.[91] "The drug trade," according to the U.S. Department of State, "provides SL a greater source of funding to conduct operations, improve relations with local communities in remote areas, and gain recruits."[92] In March 2002 a car bomb exploded outside the U.S. embassy in Lima, killing 10 people, three days before U.S. president George W. Bush was scheduled to visit. Lima blamed SL for the attack. The group also began to ambush and kill police officers in the area in late 2005. The government in Lima has responded with several initiatives, including increased funding for the security service. Now the military and national police work jointly as needed for both terrorism and narcotics-related incidents. Finally, the president has authorized the military to impose a form of martial law for no longer than 60 days in areas of the country where public order is threatened by SL activities.

MRTA was largely destroyed following the Japanese hostage incident. Perhaps the most famous remaining member of Túpac Amaru is Lori Berenson (1969–). A U.S. citizen, Berenson dropped out of the Massachusetts Institute of Technology and moved to El Salvador and then Peru in the early 1990s, where she became acquainted with MRTA members. She was arrested following a raid on a MRTA safe house on November 30, 1995, and sentenced to life in prison by a military tribunal. When military tribunals were declared unconstitutional, Berenson was retried in a civilian court in 2001 and sentenced to 20 years in jail in Peru.

In June 2001 the Peruvian government launched a Truth and Reconciliation Commission. Consisting of 11 prominent citizens, the commission spent 23 months holding public hearings in which victims of terrorism could describe the events they had witnessed.[93]

COLOMBIA

Colombia has at least four separate terrorist problems. First, two left-wing insurgencies have disturbed public order since the 1960s. Second, a right-wing paramilitary group, separate from the government, emerged to fight the left-wing insurgents. Third, all three insurgent groups have been lured into the cocaine trade by the huge amounts of money available in that industry. Finally, the country faces outside pressure, if not outright interference, primarily from the United States, which wants the government to crack down on the cocaine industry and ties assistance programs to antinarcotics efforts. The terrorist and narcotics networks have become intertwined, as the drug cartels seek protection from the insurgencies and the insurgencies seek funding from the cartels.

Domestic Terrorist Groups

For several decades two rival left-wing groups have carried out a bloody civil war in Colombia. With more than 12,000 soldiers, the Revolutionary Armed Forces of Colombia (FARC) is the leading Latin American guerrilla group. Founded in 1964 to be the military branch of the Colombian Communist Party, FARC has now diversified into bombing, kidnapping, and drug running. Although FARC has strayed from its Marxist roots, it continues to receive aid from Cuba. It also easily moves in and out of neighboring Venezuela and considers the Venezuelan government to be an ally.

The National Liberation Army (ELN) is the smaller of Colombia's two left-wing insurgent movements. Fabio Vásquez Castaqo, after training in Cuba, founded ELN in 1964. The movement seeks to end Colombia's uneven distribution of wealth with a blend of Castro-style guerrilla combat and liberation theology. Both groups frequently kidnap foreign nationals and raise most of their funds through ransom demands, local "tax" levies, and the drug trade. In 2000 FARC held a five-year-old U.S. citizen captive for six months until the police staged a rescue operation. The ongoing battle between the FARC and ELN is increasingly evolving from disputes about ideology to competition for the illegal drug industry.[94]

While FARC and ELN see themselves as rival representatives for the peasants, a right-wing militia sprouted among the targets of left-wing terrorism. The United Self-Defense Forces of Colombia (AUC) was formed in April 1997 to coordinate the activities and demobilization of nationalist paramilitary forces in Colombia. AUC forces are made up of groups frequently targeted by Marxist guerrillas: economic leaders, narcotics traffickers, and rural communities. The group claims to earn 70 percent of its income from cocaine.

Foreign Groups Targeting Bogotá

As previously mentioned, in recent years the U.S. State Department has been concerned with potential terrorist activity in the Triborder Area of South America. Such activities potentially could spill over to Colombia or could draw support from indigenous terrorist groups. Venezuelan president Hugo Chávez, a leader of the democratic socialist movement in Latin America, is known to sympathize with both ELN and FARC and could provide potentially destabilizing support to the rebels.

Antiterrorism Efforts

The Colombian government does very little in the way of antiterrorist activities. Because the country's insurgent groups prefer kidnappings and assassinations to bombings, there are seldom major crime scenes to analyze or extensive victims to treat. At one point Bogotá moved to make paying ransom illegal, but rather than stopping kidnappings it merely stopped citizens from reporting the disappearance of their relatives or coworkers.

Legal Framework

According to James Zackrison of Oxford University, "Colombian society does not recognize or admit that terrorism exists." Without acknowledging the problem, the government cannot outlaw terrorism. The closest legislation is Article 187 of the Criminal Code, which addresses terrorist-type activities as violations of public security. This blindness is part of a larger preference to avoid security and defense issues. Colombia does not even have a national security policy, so the police, armed forces, and intelligence agencies have no clearly defined purpose and therefore cannot formulate a strategy to protect the country.[95] Like the Peruvian peasants, Colombians created the ad hoc United Self-Defense Forces of Colombia to fill this need.

With no clear law on terrorism in Colombia, the main laws that cause anxiety for drug dealers and terrorists alike are extradition laws with the United States. In 1987, the Medellín drug cartel created the "Extraditables," a terrorist branch that launched a bombing campaign to pressure the government not to send suspects to the United States. That same year Colombia's Supreme Court overturned the U.S.–Colombian Extradition Treaty, paving the way for several top criminal figures to surrender if they could be assured of prosecution and punishment in Colombia. The new 1991 Colombian constitution explicitly banned the extradition of Colombian citizens. Pablo Escobar (1949–93), the infamous leader of the Medellín drug cartel, agreed to surrender to Colombian authorities only after the extradition ban in 1991 so that he could serve any sentence in Colombia, where his money and contacts allowed him to build his own maximum-luxury prison. He spent the next two years in a lush prison he built himself but escaped during a transfer on July 22, 1992. He died in a shoot-out with government forces on December 2, 1993.

Colombia's passivity toward its security allows outside forces, primarily the United States, to both define the problem and to prescribe how to eradicate it. Washington views Colombia through its broader security vocabulary. During the cold war, when the United States opposed communism, Colombia's problem was left-wing insurgents. In the 1990s when Washington was concerned about drug abuse, Colombia was the focus of antinarcotics programs. After 9/11 the United States framed all of its security problems in terms of terrorism, and Colombia's problem was redefined as narco-terrorism.[96]

In June 2000 the United States launched "Plan Colombia," a major policy package to eradicate cocaine production in Colombia. However, the program has had mixed results. The massive aerial spraying of coca fields has ruined many coca crops; it also ruined many legitimate crops growing nearby and sickened people living in the vicinity.[97] Plan Colombia also changed the institutional focus of counternarcotics efforts. While previously U.S. funding had favored the national police, now it dramatically shifted to the military. The 2000–01 package offered $416.9 million to the Colombian army, compared to $115.6 million to the national police. Unfortunately the Colombian army had a long history of human-rights abuses, and the U.S. aid package was conditioned on certifying that the military units receiving counternarcotics funding were not tainted by human-rights violations.

After the Plan Colombia package was unveiled, President Andres Pastrana began to extradite drug trafficking suspects to the United States at a rapid pace. While only 22 extraditions from Colombia to the United States took place from 1997 to 2000, Pastrana sent 26 in 2001. His successor, Alvaro Uribe, continued the trend, sending more than 200 in the first two years of his administration. Both presidents saw extradition as a way to pressure the drug dealers and insurgents into disarmament, and it seemed to work. AUC agreed to enter negotiations in 2002 after two of its top commanders were arrested and sent to the United States.[98]

Counterterrorism Strategies

Bogotá has not addressed terrorism consistently or as a specific phenomenon. "The society is so acculturated to violence," writes Zackrison, "that everyone talks about specific acts of terrorism but few treat the issue as a whole."[99] The government may make statements and try to take actions, but it has repeatedly caved in to pressure from the insurgents and from the drug dealers, and criminals assume they can bend laws as they see fit. Therefore efforts to negotiate cease-fires have been fitful.

To encourage negotiations, in November 1998 government representatives withdrew from designated portions of southeastern Colombia to create demilitarized zones (*zona de despeja*) where peace talks could be held. Instead FARC has been accused of using these neutral areas to grow coca and to hold training exercises led by the Irish Republican Army.[100] The FARC talks began in January 1999, but President Andres Pastrana canceled them in September 2000, accusing FARC of harboring a hijacker who had landed in the demilitarized zone. Talks resumed in February 2001, and that October FARC and the government signed a deal indicating their commitment to negotiate a cease-fire. However, talks were canceled on February 20, 2002, when FARC hijacked an airplane and kidnapped a member of the Colombian senate.

Alvaro Uribe was elected president in 2002 with pledges to end the rebel insurgencies. Part of his determination is personal: His father was killed in an attempted FARC kidnapping in 1983, and insurgents have attempted to assassinate him at least 15 times.[101] His plan included doubling the size of the military and creating a citizen intelligence corps, but because of Bogotá's small budget, he must rely on Washington to fund the project.

AUN began negotiations with Uribe in July 2004 and in October offered to disarm 3,000 of their fighters. Again, the sticking point is extradition—tapes from the negotiations were leaked to the press that "showed paramilitary leaders in a state of near panic over the possibility of being extradited to the United States on drug charges."[102]

Aware of this perpetual problem, Uribe introduced the Justice and Peace Law, an amnesty program that encourages insurgents to lay down arms, confess their terrorist activities, and surrender any financial assets gained through terrorism. By early 2006 an estimated 24,000 insurgents had accepted amnesty, leaving only 4,000 in the field.[103] While that offer would keep them out of Colombian jails—and earn them job-training programs—the United States has insisted that it will not drop drug charges against amnestied individuals.[104] The amnesty encourages ELN to consider negotiations.

In June 2006 FARC offered to begin talks with Uribe, provided the president backed off on his anti-insurgent programs. Leaders even offered to release some 60 hostages, some of whom are believed to have been held for at least four years, in exchange for 500 jailed comrades.[105] Uribe refused.

CONCLUSION

Prior to 9/11, books about terrorism predicted that insurgents would stage increasingly deadly attacks and likely would turn to weapons of mass destruction. So far, that ominous prediction has not come to pass. While 21st-century terrorists apparently want to maximize the body count, there are much simpler ways to do it than to build or steal a nuclear weapon. The 9/11 attackers demonstrated that 19 men armed with box-cutter knives could kill more than 3,000 people efficiently.

Throughout history, terrorism has operated in cycles. After decades of focusing on nationalism and self-determination movements, 21st-century terrorists seem to have returned to religious motivations. Defending against attacks from this "modern" terrorist presents several specific challenges.

First, religious motivations tend to raise the death toll. The terrorist feels less restraint on his (her) actions because he fervently believes that he is carrying out the will of his god. Furthermore, instead of seeking limited, symbolic activities—hijacking airplanes but not executing passengers, for example—the terrorist now desires to eliminate an entire group of people.

Second, the 21st-century terrorist is becoming increasingly isolated. The Internet has revolutionized the structure of terrorist organizations. Instead of large, centralized bureaucracies, small cells and individuals can communicate and form bonds of allegiance electronically. Al-Qaeda, in fact, has become "the first guerrilla movement in history to migrate from physical space to cyberspace."[106]

But physical isolation is not the pressing threat, it appears to be social isolation. More and more terrorists are striking out at their own governments, angry young men such as Timothy McVeigh, Eric Rudolph, Mohammad Sidique Khan, Hasib Hussein, and Shehzad Tanweer who feel they have been rejected by the societies in which they live. Disaffected individuals seek a better life through messianic cults, such as Aum Shrinikyo, religions that promise martyrdom for suicide terrorists, or they simply may have given up, as have the Tamil Tigers and the Chechen Black Widows.

Third, terrorism can only be defeated by observing the rule of law. Increasingly groups from Northern Ireland or Spain or Peru are realizing that violent approaches are less effective in realizing their goals than working through political channels. But more important, the governments seeking to prosecute terrorists must themselves observe the rule of law. They must find ways to help societies heal wounds of the past that were committed by insurgents but also by the governments themselves. Political leaders need to find ways to achieve public safety without sacrificing individual liberty. Endless detentions, torture, and pervasive surveillance perpetuate the cycle of grievances.

---

[1] For an overview, see Gorka Espiau Idoiaga. "The Basque Conflict: New Ideas and Prospects for Peace." U.S. Institute of Peace Special Report no. 161, April 2006.

[2] Tom Regan. "Was It ETA or Al Qaeda?" *Christian Science Monitor.* Posted on March 12, 2004. Available online. URL: www.csmonitor.com/2004/0312/dailyUpdate.html. Accessed January 15, 2006.

[3] Lisa Abend. "Spaniards United in Loss but Divided on Lessons." *Christian Science Monitor,* March 11, 2005, p. 7.

[4] Keith B. Richburg. "Long Basque Rebellion Losing Strength; International Effort Squeezes Underground Separatist Group." *Washington Post,* December 11, 2003, p. A1.

[5] Elaine Sciolino. "Separatists Admit to Madrid Airport Attack but Stand by Cease-Fire," *New York Times,* January 10, 2007, p. A8.

[6] See Eric Brahm. "Truth Commissions," www.beyondintractability.org/essay/truth_commissions. Accessed August 13, 2006. Brahm's work draws on Priscilla Haymer, *Unspeakable Truths* (New York: Routledge, 2001).

[7] Peter J. Katzenstein. "Same War, Different Views: Germany, Japan, and the War on Terrorism." *Current History* 57, no. 4 (Fall 2003), pp. 731–760.

[8] Text of Gerry Adams speech of April 6, 2005, BBC News. Available online. URL: http://news.bbc.co.uk/2/low/uk_news/northern_ireland/4417575.stm. Accessed April 11, 2006.

[9] Stephen Ulph. "Londonistan." *Terrorism Monitor.* Posted on February 26, 2004. Available online. URL: http://www.jamestown.org/terrorism/news/article.php?issue_id=2914. Accessed December 20, 2006.

[10] David Ignatius. "Revolt of Privilege, Muslim Style." *Washington Post,* July 27, 2005, p. A21.

[11] House of Commons, Intelligence and Security Committee. "Report into the London Terrorist Attacks on 7 July 2005." May 2006, p. 11. Available online. URL: http://www.official-documents.gov.uk/document/cm67/6785/6785.asp. Accessed December 20, 2006.

[12] Tom Hundley. "Attacks Spur Identity Crisis for Britain." *Chicago Tribune,* December 16, 2005, p. 6.

[13] Charles M. Sennott and Kevin Cul. "Video Shows Bomb Suspects' Final Steps." *Boston Globe,* July 17, 2005, p. A1.

[14] Kevin Sullivan. "Video Broadcast Warns Britons of More Attacks." *Washington Post,* July 7, 2006, p. A10.

[15] Charles M. Sennott. "Suspect Said to Tell of London Attack Role." *Boston Globe,* July 31, 2005, p. A1.

[16] Terrence Taylor. "United Kingdom." In *Combating Terrorism: Strategies of Ten Countries,* edited by Yonah Alexander. Ann Arbor: University of Michigan Press, 2002, pp. 187–223.

[17] Timothy Hillier. "Bomb Attacks in City Centers." *FBI Law Enforcement Bulletin,* September 1, 1994, pp. 13–17.

[18] Lars Langenau. "How London Prepared for Terror." *Der Spiegel* Online. Posted on July 7, 2005. Available online. URL: http://www.Spiegel.de/international/0,1518,364214,00.html. Accessed January 16, 2006.

[19] Craig Whitlock and Tamara Jones. "Not Much Damage but Plenty of Uncertainty and Fear." *Washington Post,* July 22, 2005, p. A17.

[20] Home Office. "Business As Usual: Maximising Business Resilience to Terrorist Bombings." London: Home Office Communication Directorate, 1999. Available online. URL: http://www.bedfordshire.police.uk/CrimeInfo/CounterTerrorism/documents/Business%20As%20Usual.pdf. Accessed December 20, 2006.

[21] William Miller. "Bomb in London Wounds More Than 30." *Boston Globe,* April 25, 1993, p. 4.

[22] Terrence Taylor. "United Kingdom." In *Combating Terrorism: Strategies of Ten Countries,* edited by Yonah Alexander. Ann Arbor: University of Michigan Press, 2002, p. 188.

[23] British Government. "Prevention of Terrorism Temporary Provisions Act 1974." Available online. URL: http://cain.ulst.ac.uk/hmso/pta1974.htm. Accessed December 20, 2006.

[24] Elaine Sciolino. "Regrets, but No Apology, in London Shooting." *New York Times,* July 25, 2005, p. A12.

[25] Christopher Caldwell. "After Londonistan." *New York Times Magazine,* June 25, 2006, p. 46; Kevin Sullivan. "Terrorism Bill Passes House of Commons." *Washington Post,* February 16, 2006, p. A14.

[26] House of Commons, Intelligence and Security Committee. "Report into the London Terrorist Attacks on 7 July 2005," May 2006.

[27] Elaine Sciolino and Don Van Natta, Jr. "2004 British Raid Sounded Alert on Pakistani Militants." *New York Times,* July 14, 2005, p. A12.

[28] Taylor. "United Kingdom." p. 192.

[29] Kevin Cullen. "IRA Announces End of Violent Campaign." *Boston Globe,* July 29, 2005, p. A1.

[30] "IRA 'Has Destroyed All Its Arms." BBC News. Posted on September 26, 2005. Available online. URL: http://news.bbc.co.uk/go/pr/fr/-/1/hi/northern_Ireland/4283444.stm. Accessed August 13, 2006.

[31] "IRA Urged to Locate Bodies." BBC News. Posted on August 28, 2003. Available online. URL: http://news.bbc.co.uk/go/pr/fr/-/1/hi/northern_Ireland/3189437.stm. Accessed August 13, 2006. "IRA 'Sorry' for Disappeared." BBC News. Posted on October 24, 2003. Available online. URL: http://news.bbc.co.uk/go/pr/fr/-/1/hi/northern_Ireland/3210967.stm. Accessed August 13, 2006. "New Efforts to Find Bodies of IRA 'Disappeared." Agence France-Presse. Posted on August 4, 2006. Available online. URL: http://www.chanelnewsasia.com/stories/afp_world/print/223005/1/.html. Accessed August 13, 2006.

[32] "Blair Defends 'On-the-Runs' Plan." BBC News. Posted on November 7, 2005. Available online. URL: http://newsvote.bbc.co.uk/mpapps/pagetools/print/news.bbc.co.uk/2/hi/uk_news/northern_Ireland/4414724.stm. Accessed August 13, 2006.

[33] "Sinn Féin Rejects On-the-Run Bill." BBC News, December 20, 2005.

[34] This is the argument made by Jillian Becker in *Hitler's Children: The Story of the Baader-Meinhof Terrorist Gang.* London: Michael Joseph, 1977.

[35] Interview with Ben Lewis, BBC Four. Available online. URL: http://www.bbc.co.uk/bbcfour/documentaries/features/baader-meinhof.shtml. Also see personal recollections at www.baader-meinhof.com.

[36] From 1945 to 1990 Germany was divided into two states: West Germany (with its capital in Bonn) and East Germany (with its capital in Berlin). Following German unification in October 1990, Berlin became the sole capital city.

[37] Denise Noe. "Baader-Meinhof Gang." Court TV Crime Library. Available online. URL: http://www.crimelibrary.com/terrorists_spies/terrorists/meinhof/1.htm. Accessed January 9, 2006.

[38] "Al-Qaeda in Germany." *NewsHour with Jim Lehrer,* PBS October 25, 2002, transcript available at www.pbs.org/newshours/bb/terrorism/july-dec02/germanycell_10-25.html. Accessed July 16, 2006; Peter Finn. "Suspects Used German Rental as Headquarters." *Washington Post,* September 15, 2001, p. A15.

[39] Arie Farnam. "Germany's Counterterror Push." *Christian Science Monitor,* November 7, 2001, p. 6.

[40] John Tagliabue. "Retracing a Trail to Sept. 11 Plot." *New York Times,* November 18, 2001, p. A1.

[41] Mark Landler, "In Reversal, Germany Will Join Lebanon Force," *New York Times,* September 21, 2006, A19.

[42] Alexander Wolff. "Munich 1972: When the Terror Began." *Time.* Posted on August 25, 2002. Online edition. URL: http://www.time.com/time/europe/magazine/printout/0,13155,901020902-340700,00.html. Accessed November 15, 2005.

[43] Alexander Wolff. "Munich 1972: When the Terror Began." *Time,* August 25, 2002.

[44] "Munich Massacre Remembered." CBS News, September 5, 2002. Available online. URL: http://www.cbsnews.com/stories/2002/09/05/world/main520865.shtml. Accessed November 15, 2005.

[45] This theory is also discussed in the 1999 documentary. "One Day in September," documentary directed by Kevin McDonald, released by Sony Pictures.

[46] Hoffman, *Inside Terrorism,* p. 137.

[47] According to Britain's ITN archive. "Most Like to Watch Moonwalk." *The Australian,* September 4, 2003, p. 7.

[48] Craig Whitlock. "9/11 Cases Proving Difficult in Germany." *Washington Post,* December 13, 2004, p. A1.

[49] Ibid.

[50] Ian Johnson. "In Hamburg Terror Probe, Grim Lessons." *Wall Street Journal,* November 14, 2001, p. A17.

[51] Curtis Wilkie. "Terrorism; Freedom, too, Was Maimed by the Baader-Meinhof Gang." *Boston Globe,* September 22, 1981, p. A1.

[52] Francis T. Miko and Christian Froehlich. "Germany's Role in Fighting Terrorism: Implications for U.S. Policy." Congressional Research Service Report RL-32710, December 27, 2004.

[53] "Al-Qaeda in Germany." *NewsHour with Jim Lehrer,* PBS October 25, 2002, transcript available at www.pbs.org/newshours/bb/terrorism/july-dec02/germanycell_10-25.html. Accessed July 16, 2006.

[54] Francis T. Miko and Christian Froehlich. "Germany's Role in Fighting Terrorism: Implications for U.S. Policy." Congressional Research Service Report RL-32710, December 27, 2004.

[55] German Embassy. "Counter-Terrorism Laws Take Effect." Fact Sheet at www.germany.info.relaunch/politics/new/pol_anti-terror.html. Accessed January 15, 2006.

[56] Arie Farnam. "Germany's Counterterror Push." *Christian Science Monitor,* November 7, 2001, p. 6; Ian Johnson. "Germany Set to Use 'Profiling' to Nab Terrorists." *Wall Street Journal,* September 19, 2001, p. A12.

[57] Katzenstein. "Same War, Different Views."

[58] Charles M. Sennott. "Washington Seethes as Schroeder Tries to Make Amends." *Boston Globe,* September 24, 2002, p. A1.

[59] Craig Whitlock. "9/11 Cases Proving Difficult in Germany." *Washington Post,* December 13, 2004, p. A1; John Crewdson. "Only 9/11 Conviction Tossed Out in Germany." *Chicago Tribune,* March 5, 2004, p. 1.

[60] John Walcott. "Evidence Suggests Japanese Terrorist Was to Plant Bombs in New York City." *Wall Street Journal,* May 2, 1988, p. 1.

[61] Katzenstein. "Same War, Different Views."

[62] John Walcott. "Evidence Suggests Japanese Terrorist Was to Plant Bombs in New York City." *Wall Street Journal,* May 2, 1988, p. 1.

[63] John F. Burns. "Japanese Terrorist Case Inspires Accusations against Lebanon." *New York Times,* March 23, 2000, p. A9.

[64] This section is based on David Van Biema. "Prophet of Poison." *Time,* April 3, 1995, pp. 27–33.

[65] T. R. Reid. "New Cults Flourish in a Changed Japan." *Washington Post,* March 27, 1995, p. A1.

[66] Isao Itabashi and Masamichi Ogawara, with David Leheny. "Japan." In *Combating Terrorism: Strategies of Ten Countries,* edited by Yonah Alexander. Ann Arbor: University of Michigan Press, 2002, p. 351.

[67] Isao Itabashi and Masamichi Ogawara, with David Leheny. "Japan." In *Combating Terrorism: Strategies of Ten Countries,* edited by Yonah Alexander. Ann Arbor: University of Michigan Press, 2002, p. 351.

[68] Robyn Pangi. "Consequence Management in the 1995 Sarin Attacks on the Japanese Subway System." BCSIA Discussion Paper 2002-4, ESDP Discussion Paper ESDP-2002-01, John F. Kennedy School of Government, Harvard University, February 2002.

[69] David Leheny. "Tokyo Confronts Terror." *Policy Review,* December 2001/January 2002, pp. 37–47.

[70] Pangi. "Consequence Management in the 1995 Sarin Attacks on the Japanese Subway System." p. 18.

[71] Jathon Sapsford. "Tokyo Gets a Rude Awakening in Peru." *Wall Street Journal,* December 20, 1996, p. A13.

[72] Isao Itabashi and Masamichi Ogawara, with David Leheny. "Japan." In *Combatting Terrorism: Strategies of Ten Countries,* edited by Yonah Alexander. Ann Arbor: University of Michigan Press, 2002, pp. 337–373.

[73] "Japan Decides to Continue to Dispatch MSDF Vessels to the Indian Ocean in Order to Support International Efforts to Fight Against Terrorism." Ministry of Foreign Affairs of Japan press release, October 27, 2005. Available online. URL: http://www.mofa.go.jp/policy/terrorism/measure0510.html. Accessed July 5, 2006.

[74] Larry Wortzel. "Joining Forces Against Terrorism: Japan's New Law Commits More than Words to U.S. Effort." Heritage Foundation background report, November 5, 2001. Available online. URL: http://www.heritage.org/Research/NationalSecurity/BG1500.cfm. Accessed July 5, 2006.

[75] Leheny. "Japan Confronts Terror."

[76] Isao Itabashi and Masamichi Ogawara, with David Leheny. "Japan." In *Combatting Terrorism: Strategies of Ten Countries,* edited by Yonah Alexander. Ann Arbor: University of Michigan Press, 2002, p. 357.

[77] Nicholas D. Kristof. "Tokyo Takes Usual Path: Conciliation and Caution." *New York Times,* December 20, 1996, p. A14.

[78] Peter Eisner. "60,000 May Have Died in Peru Violence." *Washington Post,* June 21, 2003, p. A12.

[79] Scott Wilson. "Peruvian Guerrillas Fight New Battle in Court." *Washington Post,* March 23, 2003, p. A16.

[80] Gabriel Escobar and Molly Moore. "Peru's Hostage Gamble: The Drama and Danger." *Washington Post,* April 27, 1997, p. A1.

[81] The government refused to return the rebels' bodies to their families or to conduct autopsies. Calvin Sims. "Peru Hears Report Some Rebels Were Slain Trying to Surrender." *New York Times,* April 25, 1997, p. A1.

[82] U.S. Department of State. *Country Reports on Terrorism, 2005,* p. 157.

[83] U.S. Department of State. *Country Reports on Terrorism, 2005,* p. 169.

[84] Alberto Bolivar. "Peru." In *Combating Terrorism: Strategies of Ten Countries,* edited by Yonah Alexander. Ann Arbor: University of Michigan Press, 2002, p. 84–115.

[85] For an excellent outline of the Peruvian antiterrorism laws, see Ralph Ruebner et al. "The War on Terrorism: Peru's Past and Present: A Legal Analysis." mimeo. John Marshall School of Law, Chicago, August 2004. Available online. URL: http://www.jmls.edu/facultypubs/ruebner/perureport.pdf. Accessed December 20, 2006.

[86] Inter-American Commission on Human Rights, Organization of American States, chapter 2. "Administration of Justice and Rule of Law." Available online. URL: http://www.cidh.org/countryrep/Peru2000en/chapter2a.htm. Accessed December 20, 2006.

[87] IACHR at paragraph 106, citing United Nations, Commission on Human Rights, Report of the Special Rapporteur on the independence of judges and lawyers, Mr. Param Cumaraswamy, Mission to Peru, Doc. E/CN.4/1998/39/Add.1 (1998), paragraph 73.

[88] U.S. Department of Justice, Immigration and Naturalization Service. "Peru: Human Rights and Political Developments through December 1994." Profile Series, June 1995.

[89] U.S. Department of Justice, Immigration and Naturalization Service. "Peru: Human Rights and Political Developments through December 1994." Profile Series, June 1995.

[90] Anthony Faiola. "Army Played 'A Key Role' in Departure of Fujimori." *Washington Post,* September 18, 2000, p. A1; Alberto Bolivar. "The Return of Shining Path." Foreign Policy Research Institute e-Note April 5, 2002. Available online. URL: http://www.fpri.org/enotes/latin.20020405.bolivar.returnofshiningpath.html. Accessed July 16, 2006.

[91] Juan Forero. "Shining Path Rebels are Spreading Terror again in Peru," *New York Times,* July 23, 2003, p. A4.

[92] U.S. Department of State. *Country Reports on Terrorism, 2005,* p. 168.

[93] Lucien Chauvin. "Peru Goes Public on 20 Years of Guerrilla and Army Violence." *Washington Post,* May 30, 2002, p. A21.

[94] U.S. Department of State. "Latin America Overview." *Patterns of Global Terrorism, 2001* Washington, D.C.: GPO, 2002. Available online. URL: www.state.gov/ct/rls/pgtrpt/2001/html/10246.htm. Accessed October 3, 2005.

[95] James Zackrison. "Colombia." In *Combating Terrorism: Strategies of Ten Countries,* edited by Yonah Alexander. Ann Arbor: University of Michigan Press, 2002, pp. 116–159.

[96] James Zackrison. "Colombia," p. 133; Arlene B. Tucker. "Colombia and the United States: From Counternarcotics to Counterterrorism." *Current History,* February 2003, p. 77–85.

[97] Tucker. "Colombia and the United States."

[98] Juan Forero. "Surge in Extradition of Colombia Drug Suspects to U.S." *New York Times,* December 6, 2004, p. A3.

[99] Zackrison. "Colombia." p. 128.

[100] Tucker. "Colombia and the United States."

[101] Kirk Semple. "Undaunted, Colombia's Uribe Presses Security Plan." *Christian Science Monitor,* August 9, 2002, p. 7.

[102] Juan Forero. "Rightist Militias in Colombia Offer to Disarm 3,000 of Their Fighters." *New York Times,* October 9, 2004, p. A5.

[103] International Crisis Group. "Colombia: Towards Peace and Justice?" ICG Latin America Report No. 16, March 14, 2006.

[104] "FARC Wants Colombia Peace Talks." BBC News, Posted on June 24, 2006. Available online. URL: http://newsvote.bbc.co.uk/mpappa/pagetools/print/news.bbc.co.uk/2/hi/Americas/5112418.stm. Accessed August 12, 2006.

[105] "FARC Wants Colombia Peace Talks." BBC News, June 24, 2006.

[106] Steve Coll and Susan B. Glasser. "Terrorists Turn to the Web as Base of Operations." *Washington Post,* August 7, 2005, p. A1.

PART II

Primary Sources

4

United States Documents

The primary sources reproduced in this chapter are divided into three sections: background information on types of terrorism, statements related to domestic terrorist groups and incidents, and official U.S. government counterterrorism legislation and policy. The first section is arranged thematically, while the other sections are given in chronological order. Documents that have been excerpted are identified as such; all others are reproduced in full.

FORMS OF TERRORISM

Graham Allison testifies before Congress on the issue of weapons of mass destruction (August 1995)

Arms control expert Graham Allison describes the danger of terrorists acquiring nuclear weapons and criticizes the U.S. government for ignoring this threat. Drawing on a Harvard study, Allison provides many detailed examples of poorly guarded Russian nuclear facilities and argues that terrorists could easily steal any of these weapons.

Testimony by Graham Allison, . . . to the Senate Committee on Foreign Relations, Subcommittee on European Affairs, August 23, 1995 (excerpts)

Let me then summarize the major findings of our Harvard study [Avoiding Nuclear Anarchy: Containing the Threat of Loose Nuclear Weapons and Fissile Material] in seven brief propositions. These propositions are, in the main, quite consistent with those that you have heard from the first two experts.

Proposition one. Loose Nukes the loss, theft, or sale of weapons-usable nuclear materials or nuclear weapons themselves is not a hypothetical threat. It is today a brute fact hard to ignore. In the past 4 years since the disappearance of the Soviet Union, the number of reported, suspected, and documented cases of diversion of weapons-usable nuclear material has been increasing steadily at a sharp pace.

Instance: Murmansk. One night in November 1993, a Russian naval officer entered a shipyard near Murmansk, located a building used for naval reactor fuel storage, removed fuel containing about 10 pounds of weapons-usable, highly-enriched uranium smaller than this can of Coca-Cola, put the fuel in a bag and walked out of the shipyard the same way he came.

The officer had been briefed beforehand by his brother, a civilian employee of the shipyard. He was aware that the flimsy security protecting the substantial inventory of highly-enriched uranium fuel for naval nuclear reactors was easily penetrated. He penetrated it successfully, put the material in his garage and was searching for a buyer when Russian police caught him.

Second instance: Plutonium seized in Munich in August, 1994. Almost a pound of weapons-usable plutonium seized by German police at the Munich Airport. The plutonium had been carried in a suitcase on a flight from Moscow to Munich. Two passengers on the flight were arrested along with a third man in Munich who was the intended buver. [. . .]

If these examples leave any lingering doubt about this threat, consider the largest and most dramatic case in which the American Government purchased and removed about 1,000 pounds of highly-enriched uranium from Kazakhstan just last year, material sufficient to allow a terrorist or rogue state to build a serious arsenal of 20 nuclear weapons.

In this case, when the Kazakh Government discovered the material that had been left at a former submarine fuel facility, it contacted the U.S. Government. The U.S. Government purchased this thousand pounds of highly-enriched uranium, took it, and brought it to Oak Ridge, Tennessee, paying for it an amount that has been reported to be about $20 million. $20 million paid; 20 weapons equivalents received; 20 potential terrorist weapons now safely protected at Oak Ridge. This threat is not hypothetical.

Proposition two. If a rogue actor, a state like Iran or Iraq or Libya or Cuba, or a terrorist group like Hamas [. . .], or a drug cartel, obtained as little as 30 pounds of highly-enriched uranium, or less than half that weight in plutonium, they could produce a nuclear device in a matter of a month or two with design information that is publicly available, equipment that is readily available in the commercial market, and modest levels of technical competence found in graduates of any respectable engineering program. How much is 30 pounds of highly-enriched uranium or half that of plutonium? Tom Cochran's Coke can here could be filled with just such material.

I carry this briefcase with me everywhere, as you know from having seen me in other settings. In this briefcase, I carried today in addition to the pile of papers, first one softball. It is an American softball. If this softball were highly-enriched uranium, it would weigh 30 pounds. It fits in my briefcase quite well. Actually, I could carry several softballs of highly-enriched uranium in my case.

If we were talking about plutonium, enough plutonium to make a bomb, a second item in this same briefcase is more than enough. This is an American baseball. Several of them can fit alongside the softball very well. So the amounts of weapons-usable material [. . .] are very small. Once this amount of material is in-hand, the rest of the problem is relatively easy.

As Johnny Foster, the former Director of Livermore Lab, wrote in the Encyclopedia Americana more than 20 years ago: "If the essential nuclear materials like these are in-hand, it is possible to make an atomic bomb using the information that is available in the open literature."

Proposition three. If the terrorists who attacked the 110-story World Trade Center in 1993 or, more recently last April, the Federal Office Building in Oklahoma City, killing 162 men, women, and children, had used the same minivan they drove, but filled it not with the explosives they used, but rather with a weapon that started with this softball, what would have been the consequences?

They could have created an explosion of 10,000 to 20,000 tons of TNT which would demolish an area of about 3 square miles.

[. . .]

For those who live in New York, it is worth considering what would have happened if the terrorist van at the World Trade Center had carried just the softball or the baseball rather than the explosives that it carried. As chart three illustrates, lower Manhattan basically disappears, including the financial district up to Gramercy Park.

[. . .]

Proposition four. As the most open society in the world, the U.S. is also most vulnerable to nuclear terrorist attack. My personal bet is that we will not be the most likely first target. As I try to explain to my Russian friends, the threat of loose nukes is greater to them than it is to us, since Russia is an attractive first target.

I believe the Middle East offers the second most attractive target. But the United States is indeed the most open and therefore most vulnerable set of targets. If a rogue state or terrorist group acquired this softball of HEU, could they transport it to the U.S.? As one of my colleagues at Harvard likes to say, if they have any doubt, they could always wrap it in a bail of marijuana, since they know that can be delivered to any of our major cities.

How many uninspected packages arrive in the U.S. every day? The answer is literally millions. The irony will be if the first one of these softballs comes in a Federal Express package.

Proposition five. [. . . It] is hard for us to appreciate the depth oı what is happening in Russia today. We are witnessing a historically unique and unprecedented event, whose consequences we still can't seem to take seriously.

Russia is *a state in revolution:* a genuine sinew-shaking transformation in its economy, its government, its society, every aspect of life. This revolution is shredding the fabric of a command and control society, in a state that houses a superpower nuclear arsenal and a superpower nuclear enterprise.

This ongoing Russian revolution is driven by the deepest and most powerful forces, none more important than individuals demand for freedom. As we watch the Russian reformers attempt to deconstruct what was actually a prison in which they lived for 70 years and create a society in which they can live free from the fear that was the backbone of Soviet society, we have to applaud.

But the same forces that are tearing down the old prison state are also liberating the individuals and systems charged with controlling more than 30,000 nuclear weapons that are still left there; more than 1,000 tons of highly-enriched uranium that remain in scores of locations; more than 100 tons of plutonium still there in place.

[. . .] While I am optimistic about Russia, and hopeful about the current economic and political reforms, I ncte that in every other area of life, significant quantities of every other item of value have been "liberated," as people there often say. Individual entrepreneurs, new businessman, and criminals have seized assets for themselves and exported them for money.

Consider precious metals and ask how Estonia can be the second largest exporter of precious metals in the world when it produces no precious metals? Consider diamonds and ask how many show up in the gray market. Take gold. Take any other item of value. To date, we have no evidence that a nuclear weapon's equivalent of highly-enriched uranium or indeed a bomb itself has been successfully exported. But this is something for which I give thanks. We are living on borrowed time.

Proposition six. How big is this problem? My colleagues on this panel have already noted the more than 100 sites across Russia at which nuclear weapons can be found. [. . .] There are an additional hundred sites at which there are significant quantities, that is numbers of bombs' worth, of highly-enriched uranium or plutonium. [. . .]

These locations include weapons storage depots. They include deployed weapons. They include research laboratories. They include abandoned research facilities. There are many, many different sites. [. . .] First one has to mine the uranium. Then you have to refine it. Then you assemble weapons. You then have stockpiles, deployment, and maintenance. As one dismantles weapons, one dismantles components. Then highly-enriched uranium and plutonium must be safely stored.

If one takes as a defining example the case that we know best, namely Project Sapphire, which removed more than 1,000 pounds of highly-enriched uranium from Kazakhstan, what was the story? This facility had been producing highly-enriched uranium for naval fuel in the late 1970s and early 1980s. Production ceased in the mid-80s when facilities elsewhere in Russia were producing sufficient amounts of submarine fuel to meet the Soviet navy's needs. The Soviet Union disappeared in the end of 1991. A thousand pounds of highly-enriched uranium remained in place at this facility in what became a newly-independent country. The Russian Government took no action to recover this material. Indeed, the best evidence suggests that the Russian Government was not aware that this material had been left there.

As the Kazakh national security adviser explained to us at this meeting that Senator Nunn and I were just attending in California, he and President Nazarbayev had no idea that this material was there. The new facility director discovered the material, and said, aha, here we have a thousand pounds of highly-enriched uranium.

As Secretary Christopher has testified publicly, the Iranian Government was in Kazakhstan actively pursuing this material. Fortunately, because of good relations between the Kazakh Government and the U.S. Government and effectiveness on both sides, this material is in Tennessee today rather than in Tehran.

This outcome is the result of hard work and very good fortune. It is not an isolated case. I believe that we will discover over time a number of additional facilities at which there are weapons equivalents of materials still left at sites that we and the Russian Government have still not identified.

In fact, in this Project Sapphire case, when the highly enriched uranium arrived at Oak Ridge, we found that we had 4 percent more material than we had purchased. I think this answers the earlier question about the reliability of current accounting procedures.

My seventh and final proposition. Is there anything we can do to prevent this? Or is this just inevitable?

In the light of our stakes, is the current program of action, level of effort, urgency of effort, timetable, and commitment of funds consistent with American vital national security interests? I think the answer is certainly no.

Our Report has a final chapter that states an agenda for action in a much more substantial effort that would be undertaken by a government that really believed this was the number one threat to American security today. But I understand that this is not the subject for today's hearings. I look forward to the subsequent hearings you and Senator Nunn are planning where that will be the focus of debate.

Source: John F. Kennedy School of Government, Harvard University. Available online. URL: http://www.fas.org/spp/starwars/congress/1995_h/allison1.htm.

Statement to Congress by Jessica Eve Stern on weapons proliferation (October 1997)

Appearing before Congress two years after Professor Allison, Stern warns that the threat of terrorists acquiring weapons of mass destruction remains and that the U.S. public has become aware of this danger. This nightmare scenario was dramatized in the 1997 movie The Peacemaker, *with Nicole Kidman playing a character based on Dr. Stern.*

Statement of Jessica Eve Stern, former National Security Council staff director, Russian, Ukrainian, and Eurasian Affairs
House of Representatives, Committee on National Security, Military Research and Development Subcommittee
Washington, D.C., Wednesday, October 1, 1997

I have three points today. First, constraints are eroding against terrorism involving nuclear, chemical, and biological weapons. Second, we are not doing enough about the threat. Third, Americans are increasingly afraid of nuclear terrorism. According to a recent poll, some 76 percent of those polled said that they were afraid of nuclear terrorism.

It is worth considering our particular vulnerabilities right now. First of all, our population is highly concentrated, making us quite vulnerable to nuclear, chemical, and biological agents. Second is the approach of the millennium and the possibility that heretofore peace-loving millenarian groups might become violent. The millenarian idea is that the present age is corrupt and there will be a cleansing apocalypse, and then the lucky few will survive that apocalypse.

Terrorists who believe in this millenarian idea might be attracted to these kind of weapons. For example, the fifth plague, murrain, was actually anthrax, so there is a kind of mystical aura to, in my view, chemical and biological weapons.

There are three constraints that I believe are eroding. The first is loose nukes, and I know that you, Congressman [Curt] Weldon, know more than almost anyone about this issue, but I will just very briefly point out that there are vulnerable sites in Russia.

Of particular concern is a site in Kazakhstan, Aktau, and also a couple sites in Georgia. As a friend of mine described what he saw when he got to Russia, he saw a nuclear site that was guarded by Aunt Masha with a cucumber.

The second constraint that is eroding is a proliferation of know-how. As you know, weapons scientists who were formerly treated as the elite are now poverty stricken. But I would like to alert you to another area where know-how is proliferating, and that is in books and on the Internet.

There are many, many books that provide instructions about how to use weapons of mass destruction. When I was a graduate student, I learned about some of these books, and I called one of the publishers, and I did a little experiment. I said, I understand you have books that tell you how to poison people, and I would like to poison someone. I wrote down very carefully what the operator said. She asked me a few questions, and then she basically just wanted to know my credit card number.

. . . . .

The third constraint that is eroding is that a new breed of terrorist seems to be emerging. We know that terrorists have always been capable of significantly more lethal acts than they have actually carried out. That is because many terrorists up until now have had very clear political constraints. They have had real constituencies.

For example, I grew up in Boston. The IRA was out there on the Boston Common fundraising. I think the IRA [Irish Republican Army] is going to be much less successful if they decide to use bubonic plague as a mass destruction weapon. But there are new terrorists with apocalyptic ideas, religious and right wing extremists. They don't have clear constituencies. For some of them their main constituent is God, and usually the ones who have direct phone lines with God, the God that they talk to is a very violent one, unfortunately.

I had the opportunity to interview William Pierce, who wrote *The Turner Diaries,* the book that inspired the Oklahoma bombing. I would like to tell you one of the things he said to me. I am quoting. "This society is in the process of self-destruction. Society will descend into chaos or civil war, and speeding up that process is in the interest of the country."

Clearly someone who believes that chaos is beneficial will not face the kind of political and moral constraints that some terrorists have faced in the past.

I have also been spending quite a bit of time lately searching the web, and some of the things you find on the web are quite horrifying. One of the most prolific writers in the ultra right wing, Louie Beam, is exhorting extremists to form "leaderless cells" precisely to avoid government detection.

It is a new doctrine. He calls it a doctrine of leaderless resistance. He encourages followers to form cells numbering between 1 and 12 men to circumvent the FBI's intelligence gathering capabilities.

The bottom line is that we need to do much more than we are doing.

The Nunn-Lugar-Domenici acts have made very significant strides in combating this threat, but I think the funding level is not appropriate to the level of the threat.

In my statement for the record, I spell out some concrete proposals, and I would actually propose that you sponsor legislation, and I would be thrilled and honored to work with you and your staff, to work out more ideas. I will just give you a couple of examples.

One is to create a nuclear emergency fund. [Russian] General [Alexander] Lebed, as you pointed out, we do not know whether he was telling the truth, but one interesting thing he said is that he would like an international commission to come in and help locate those allegedly missing suitcase bombs. I think it is imperative when a person like General Lebed makes a statement like that that we follow up immediately. We should be in there. He wants help, let's give him help.

Similarly, during Project Sapphire, when the Government of Kazakhstan asked the United States Government for assistance in securing vulnerable materials, we were delayed by difficulties with funding. So this nuclear emergency fund could be used to carry out operations of this kind, that are clear emergencies and essential to all Americans' security.

Source: U.S. House of Representatives. Available online. URL: http://commdocs.house.gov/committees/security/has274010.000/has274010_0f.htm.

"Effective Multilateralism: The U.S. Strategy for Dealing with Global Nuclear Proliferation" by Andrew K. Semmel (November 2005)

The danger of individuals, terrorist groups, or rogue countries acquiring nuclear weapons persists, but Assistant Secretary Semmel outlines U.S. government efforts to prevent such proliferation.

Effective Multilateralism: The U.S. Strategy for Dealing with Global Nuclear Proliferation (excerpts)
Andrew K. Semmel, deputy assistant secretary for nuclear nonproliferation
Address to the National Strategy Forum
Chicago, Illinois, November 14, 2005

[. . .]

The Bush Administration has constructed a comprehensive strategy against proliferation that was outlined in the December 2002 National Strategy to Combat Weapons of Mass Destruction. The three pillars of that strategy are: proliferation prevention; counterproliferation; and consequence management. To prevent proliferation, the Administration has launched dramatically expanded efforts to prevent rogue states and terrorists from acquiring WMD, their related materials, and delivery systems. Counterproliferation recognizes that prevention does not always succeed and that we must have the capabilities to deter, detect, defend against, and defeat WMD and those who would use them for malevolent purposes. Consequence management aims to reduce the consequences or tragic effects of a WMD attack at home or abroad.

A central element of all three pillars of the Administration's strategy against proliferation is a commitment to "effective multilateralism," to confronting the real problems that we face with realism and determination in league with our international partners. [. . .]

Effective multilateralism has meant strengthening existing tools and developing new ones. Before turning to some specific Administration proposals for strengthening nuclear nonproliferation, let me outline for you some of those tools.

One essential tool is the Treaty on the Nonproliferation of Nuclear Weapons or NPT. The NPT, the cornerstone of the nuclear nonproliferation regime, has created an international norm against nuclear proliferation and established the legal basis for actions against those that violate this norm. I would argue that the NPT and the associated system of International Atomic Energy Agency (IAEA) safeguards involving international inspections and verification procedures designed to protect against the diversion of nuclear material from peaceful to non-peaceful weapons programs have had more success than setbacks in 35 years of attempting to prevent the proliferation of nuclear weapons. . . .

Another tool includes multilateral export control regimes: principally the forty-five member Nuclear Suppliers Group and the Zangger Committee. To make a nuclear weapon, a country must possess separated plutonium or high enriched uranium. These export control regimes seek to establish guidelines to prevent a country from acquiring the technology needed to obtain either of these. [. . .] They also establish a set of common export standards to which all nuclear supplier countries agree to abide.

However, continued proliferation by rogue states and networks has made clear that strong supplier commitments and solid national control lists do not automatically translate into prevention of illicit exports associated with WMD. We require multilateral action to enforce those standards. The disruption of the A.Q. Khan supply network and the subsequent decision by Libya to abandon its WMD and longer-range missile programs, would not have been possible without effective multilateral action, based on strong intelligence, close cooperation, and active interdiction. Central to those successes was the Proliferation Security Initiative, or PSI, which had been proposed by President Bush only a few months before. . . .

Another tool in our nonproliferation arsenal includes programs to secure and eliminate nuclear weapon-related facilities and materials and to redirect scientists and scientific communities involved in these projects into civilian sectors. The United States has been engaged in such programs since the launch of the Cooperative Threat Reduction program by Senator Lugar—my former boss in the U.S. Senate—and Senator Nunn in December 1991, just after the collapse of the Soviet Union, and has worked cooperatively with the Russian Federation and other former Soviet states since that time on nuclear as well as chemical and biological threats.

Strengthening Nuclear Nonproliferation

[. . .]

We have seen progress on many of these fronts. In June of this year, the IAEA Board of Governors agreed to establish the new Committee on Safeguards and Verification to examine measures to strengthen the Agency's ability to ensure that nations comply with their international obligations. The Committee met for the first time last week. Likewise, we have seen an increase in the number of NPT parties with Additional Protocols. So far 104 NPT parties have signed Additional Protocols, and seventy of these are in force. [. . .]

In April 2004, the UN Security Council adopted UN Security Council Resolution 1540, establishing for the first time binding, i.e., mandatory, obligations on all UN member states to criminalize WMD proliferation, enforce effective export controls, and secure nuclear materials. Resolution 1540, if implemented as intended, will be an extraordinarily effective tool against the spread of nuclear and other dangerous materials to dangerous groups. It seeks to meet proliferators' lethal flexibility with the firm resolve of states to cut off the path to proliferation. UNSCR 1540 places a premium on establishment of legal and regulatory measures at the national level. It seeks to build capacity from the bottom up rather than attempting to impose it from above. We strongly support these efforts and have signaled our willingness to provide assistance to other governments to implement these obligations.

International engagement on cooperative threat reduction activities has greatly increased since the inauguration of the Global Partnership Against the Threat of Weapons and Materials of Mass Destruction by the G-8 in 2002. The United States provides about $1 billion annually for these programs for Russia and the FSU (Former Soviet Union) alone, and looks to our G-8 partners to fulfill their commitment to match that level. Russia and the FSU continue to be critical areas of focus, but we are addressing nuclear proliferation threats worldwide through assistance to other countries to strengthen their export and border control efforts to prevent illicit trafficking.

In July of this year, President Bush and Indian Prime Minister Singh announced a joint U.S.-India partnership that has the potential to yield important benefits for the United States, India, and the international community. Under this partnership, India has committed to a series of actions including implementing strong and effective export control legislation, adhering to the NSG Guidelines on exports, separating its civil and military facilities and placing all its civilian facilities and activities under IAEA safeguards, signing and adhering to an Additional Protocol, and maintaining its nuclear testing moratorium. In return, the United States will pursue the necessary changes to U.S. national laws and international regimes to allow full civil nuclear cooperation with India.

In a March statement on the NPT, the President stressed, "NPT Parties must take strong action to confront the threat of noncompliance with the NPT in order to preserve and strengthen the Treaty's nonproliferation undertakings. We cannot allow rogue states that violate their commitments and defy the international community to undermine the NPT's fundamental role in strengthening international security." We have faced Libyan, North Korean and Iranian noncompliance with their nonproliferation obligations and addressed each with a targeted strategy. Libya had a secret nuclear weapons program, but it made the strategic decision to renounce and transparently dismantle that program and return to full compliance with its NPT nonproliferation obligations. We expect North Korea to implement fully and promptly the commitment it made in the last round of the Six Party Talks to abandon its nuclear weapons and all nuclear programs, and we expect it to do so in a complete, verifiable and irreversible manner. Iran's clandestine nuclear program has stretched over two decades. As a result of Iran's pattern of deception and denial, lack of full cooperation with the IAEA, and pursuit of nuclear fuel cycle capabilities in defiance of the international community, the IAEA Board of Governors found Iran in formal noncompliance with its safeguards obligations on September 24, a decision which triggers a report to the UNSC. We continue to urge Iran to make the strategic decision to abandon its nuclear weapons pursuits. One lesson comes across clearly from all these cases: the NPT has established an invaluable norm against nuclear proliferation, but the NPT's ability to stem nuclear proliferation is only as strong as its parties' willingness to comply with their obligations and the resolve of compliant parties to hold others to those obligations. . . .

Nuclear Material Security

[. . .] The United States is aggressively committed to improving the physical protection of nuclear weapons and materials though a number of nonproliferation assistance programs. Through a variety of State, Energy, and Defense Department programs, the U.S. is working with states around the globe to better secure and prevent the illicit trafficking of nuclear materials. We believe that the best odds for prohibiting the spread of nuclear materials to dangerous states or terrorists lay with strong and effective prevention at their source.

The Department of Energy launched the Global Threat Reduction Initiative or GTRI in 2004. The GTRI has given new emphasis to programs to secure HEU fresh and spent fuel for research reactors and to convert those reactors to LEU fuel, as well as programs to secure radiological sources that could used for "dirty bombs." Along with IAEA programs and other international initiatives to secure radioactive sources, a strong foundation to address nuclear terrorism is being built.

President Bush and Russian President Putin took a major step in this effort at their February meeting in Bratislava. We achieved substantial gains in agreements with the Russian Federation for security upgrades of nuclear facilities and for transportation of nuclear warheads slated for disposal. We are also working closely at many facilities to replace high-enriched uranium, which can be used in a nuclear explosive device, with low enriched uranium, which cannot. These efforts will ensure that large quantities of materials will be removed as a potential terrorist target. Anytime or anywhere HEU fuel is made secure or repatriated back to Russia or the U.S., anytime a nuclear reactor anywhere that uses weapons-sensitive HEU is converted to LEU, or anytime another nuclear facility is placed under reliable physical protection, the world is made a safer place.

Multilaterally, the United States is deeply committed to strengthening international frameworks and regimes. The United States is the leading supporter of the IAEA's Nuclear Security Plan, donating over twenty five million dollars to it since September 11th, 2001. The Plan provides assistance to states in the physical protection of their civil nuclear materials and facilities, prevention of illicit trafficking, and security of radioactive materials.

In July, a diplomatic conference of over eighty-five States Parties to the 1979 Convention on the Physical Protection of Nuclear Material (CPPNM) adopted a crucial Amendment that significantly strengthens that Convention to address illicit trafficking in nuclear and non-nuclear radiological material and the potential for malevolent use. The Amendment is intended to accomplish three purposes:

- to achieve and maintain worldwide effective physical protection of nuclear material and nuclear facilities used for peaceful purposes;
- to prevent and combat offenses relating to such material and facilities worldwide; and
- to facilitate co-operation among States Parties to those ends.

In sum, it provides a treaty-based anchor for an international regime for the physical protection worldwide of nuclear material and facilities used for peaceful purposes.

Conclusion

In conclusion, the United States is working daily, effectively, and multilaterally to prevent proliferation, to counter proliferation, and to prepare for possible consequence management. I have presented today an amalgam of program and initiatives designed to make the world safe from the scourge of weapons of mass destruction. More than any other country, the United States has taken the leading role in fashioning a set of tools to prevent, protect, deter, interdict and prohibit the spread of WMD, their associated materials and technology from acquisition and use by terrorists and those who support them. We have witnessed some truly impressive successes in our efforts, but much more needs to be done. Success can be fleeting as new challenges or threats arise. We must be as agile and aggressive in preventing and countering proliferation as those who seek these deadly capabilities.

Success requires active collaboration with others, vigilance, and commitment. It is what we are calling "effective multilateralism." The task is simply too big, too important and too complex for any one nation, for any one tool, for any one international organization or voluntary arrangement to tackle alone. The United States will continue to do its part to develop and improve solutions that work.

Source: U.S. Department of State. Available online. URL: http://www.state.gov/t/np/rls/rm/56942.htm.

"Narco-Terror: The International Connection between Drugs and Terror" by Asa Hutchinson (April 2002)

Narco-terrorism is a mixture of the illegal drug trade and terrorism. Terrorists may use money from the illegal drug market to fund their activities or to threaten to kill government officials who want to shut down their operation. Hutchinson outlines the issue country by country.

Narco-Terror: The International Connection between Drugs and Terror Speech by Asa Hutchinson, director, Drug Enforcement Administration, Washington, D.C., April 2, 2002

[. . .]

THE FACTS ON DRUGS AND TERRORISM

Afghanistan. [. . .] Afghanistan, as you know, is a major source of heroin in the world, producing in the year 2000 some 70 percent of the world's supply of opium, which is converted to heroin.

The Taliban, the ruling authority at the time, benefited from that drug trade by taxing and, in some instances, being involved in the drug trafficking. Taxation was institutionalized to the extent that they actually issued tax receipts when they collected the revenue from the heroin traffickers. [. . .]

Taken a step further, the DEA has also received multi-source information that Osama bin Laden himself has been involved in the financing and facilitation of heroin-trafficking activities. That is history now with the operation that has been taking place by our military in Afghanistan.

Now we can look to the future in Afghanistan. We're pleased that the interim president, Chairman [Hamid] Karzai, has banned poppy cultivation and drug production; but the United Nations, despite this ban that is currently in place, estimates that the area that is currently under cultivation could potentially produce up to 2,700 metric tons of opium in Afghanistan this coming year.

[. . .]

Colombia. In Colombia, we deal with three groups designated as terrorist organizations by the State Department: the revolutionary group called the FARC (Revolutionary Armed Forces of Colombia); the ELN (National Liberation Army); and a paramilitary group, the AUC (United Self-Defenses of Colombia). At least two of those, without any doubt, are heavily engaged in drug trafficking, receiving enormous funds from drug trafficking: the AUC and the FARC.

In the case of the FARC, the State Department has called them the most dangerous international terrorist group based in the Western Hemisphere. Two weeks ago, the Department of Justice indicted three members of the 16th Front of the FARC, including their commander, Tomas Molina, on charges of conspiracy to transport cocaine and distribute it in the United States. It was the first time that members of a known terrorist organization have been indicted on drug trafficking charges.

The 16th Front operates out of a remote village in Eastern Colombia where they operate an air strip, where they engage in their trafficking activities, where they control all the operations in that particular arena. The cocaine that is transported by the 16th Front out of that area is paid for with currency, with weapons, and with equipment; and, of course, you know the activities that that terrorist organization has been engaged in, in which they would use that currency, the weapons, and the equipment.

But the 16th Front is not the only front of the FARC that is engaged in drug trafficking activity. Ninety percent of the cocaine Americans consume comes from Colombia; the FARC controls the primary coca cultivation and processing regions in that country, and they have controlled it for the past two decades.

The State Department estimates that the FARC receives $300 million a year from drug sales to finance its terrorist activities.

In March of this year, under the direction of President Pastrana, the Colombian Army and the Colombian National Police reclaimed the demilitarized zone from the FARC, based upon intelligence the DEA was able to provide. The police went in, and in the demilitarized zone that was supposed to be a peaceful haven, they found two major cocaine laboratories. The police seized five tons of processed cocaine from that particular site, so you can imagine the enormity of this processing site. They destroyed the labs as well as a 200-foot communications tower that the FARC operated to use in their communications efforts.

Prior to the seizure, we knew the FARC was engaged in trafficking activities, but this is the first time we have had solid evidence that the FARC is involved in the cocaine trade from start to finish, from cultivation to processing and distribution.

[. . .]

Peru. In Peru, you have the Shining Path. There's evidence that they were responsible for the car bombing that occurred just two weeks ago that killed nine people prior to President Bush's visit to Peru. They have historically also benefited from the taxation of coca cultivation in the region of Peru that they control.

So, yes, the facts demonstrate that drugs are a funding source for terrorism and violence against government. But it's not just the facts that are involved here; it's also the lives that are impacted to such an extraordinary extent.

Mexico. When I went to Mexico City in February, I had a meeting with the Attorney General, Macedo de la Concha, and in that meeting, I shook hands with the prosecutors that were on the back row as I was leaving. One of the prosecutors, Mario Roldan Quirino, was handling a case that we were involved in that was a multi-ton seizure of cocaine off of a fishing vessel. I shook hands with that prosecutor. Within one hour after I left Mexico City, Mario Roldon was shot 28 times outside of Mexico City and assassinated.

The Toll on Law Enforcement. In the first few months of 2002, 13 law enforcement officers have been murdered in Mexico. You say, "this may not be terrorism." When you're going after government officials, judicial officials, to impact the stability of a government, in my judgment, it is terrorism.

Last week, I visited the Colombian National Police—not just their police building, but also their hospital. In that hospital, I visited with five officers who were wounded in an attack by the FARC while they were doing coca eradication and providing protection for that operation. [. . .]

America's National Interest. What is the national interest when it happens in faraway countries? It should be elementary: Drug production in Mexico, in Colombia, in Thailand, and in Afghanistan produces the supply of drugs that devastates our families and our communities.

The same illegal drug production funds that attack civilized society also destabilize democracies across the globe. Illegal drug production undermines America's culture; it funds terror; and it erodes democracy. And they all represent a clear and present danger to our national security.

A COMPREHENSIVE STRATEGY

What is our strategy to address this international difficulty?

Keeping Our Focus. First of all, from the DEA's perspective, we intend to keep our focus. Since September 11, DEA's mission has not changed. Our focus is still the enforcement of our anti-narcotics laws domestically, but also to support the enforcement of the international laws against international drug trafficking.

So we intend to keep our focus; to engage in this effort; to be focused on our counter-narcotics mission knowing the contribution that that, in and of itself, makes to our effort against terrorism.

Adding Value to Intelligence Collection. The second thing that the DEA intends to do is to add value to our intelligence collection. Since September 11, our sources have been worked not just to identify narcotics trafficking, but also to learn information on terrorist activity. [. . .]

Another illustration of this added value in our intelligence collection is Operation Mountain Express, which is an investigation that we conducted in order to reduce the amount of pseudoephedrine coming into the United States that goes to produce methamphetamine, particularly in the superlabs in California.

The latest source of the pseudoephedrine is Canada, where pseudoephedrine is not regulated. It comes across the border from Canada into Chicago and Detroit, and is transported by semi-trailer trucks in multi-ton quantities into California.

Our investigation led to the arrest of over 100 defendants. Almost all of the defendants were of Mid-Eastern origin. And because they many times have connections with countries that export terrorism, we furthered the investigation, our intelligence gathering activities, and were able to establish linkages to terrorist groups as well as funding of certain organizations that support terrorism.

[. . .]

Accepting International Responsibility. The third part of our strategy is to accept our increased responsibilities internationally. The DEA has offices in 56 countries. We develop intelligence. We train and we build effective law enforcement in other countries, and this has given us successes in recent weeks. [. . .]

KEYS TO FUTURE SUCCESS

I also want to look at the keys to future success. We have to capitalize on this unique opportunity in history in which the international community is looking to the United States for consistent, dynamic, and timely leadership in going after the international criminal organizations that traffic in drugs and support terrorism.

Enhancing DEA's International Presence. To carry out that strategy, we have sent to the Hill, and OMB has approved, an Afghan initiative that includes enhancing our DEA presence in Afghanistan, opening an office there in Pakistan and Uzbekistan, in that region of the world, but developing that with a world-wide heroin strategy, looking at Southeast Asia and Mexico and Colombia, the four regions of the world that produce heroin.

It's like a commodity such as corn: If we reduce the supply in Afghanistan, that helps us on the streets of the United States. We have that strategy on the Hill waiting for the reprogramming approval.

Enhancing Intelligence Sharing. Second, it is important that we continue to enhance our intelligence sharing, and I want to compliment the great study by the Heritage Foundation, Defending the American Homeland, and the work that was done there putting out ideas on intelligence fusion centers that will bring people together in our community as well as internationally to share greater intelligence more effectively.

Focusing American Support. Third, to have success in the future in Colombia, we must recognize that there is no distinction between the terrorists who kidnap presidential candidates and the traffickers who operate the cocaine labs and protect the coca fields. U.S. support should be limited in scope and restricted to avoid support for units that violate human rights.

But our logistical support for the Colombian government should not be restricted to the extent that we become ineffective in our primary mission of reducing illegal drug production and our secondary goal of strengthening the institutions of democracy in Colombia.

Under the current law, as you know, we have restrictions on our support in the counter-narcotics arena, but what if intelligence indicates that the FARC is going to set up a roadblock? Can we provide that intelligence to our counterparts in Colombia? Is it a counter-narcotics mission? Is it a counter-kidnapping mission? Is it a counter-terrorism mission? When they have a multifaceted problem facing them, then certainly our support should be in a broader context. [. . .]

Source: U.S. Department of Justice, Drug Enforcement Agency. Available online. URL: http://www.usdoj.gov/dea/speeches/s040202p.html.

Statement by Richard Boucher on the issue of international terrorism: American hostages (February 2002)

Meeting the ransom demands of kidnappers may save hostage lives, but it may also encourage further kidnappings. Indeed, in Colombia hostage-taking is a major industry. The U.S. government, however, maintains a strict policy of not negotiating with hostage-takers and encourages the private sector to follow the same policy.

International Terrorism: American Hostages
Statement by Richard Boucher, U.S. Department of State spokesman
Washington, D.C., February 20, 2002

U.S. Government Policy

The U.S. Government will make no concessions to individuals or groups holding official or private U.S. citizens hostage. The United States will use every appropriate resource to gain the safe return of American citizens who are held hostage. At the same time, it is U.S. Government policy to deny hostage takers the benefits of ransom, prisoner releases, policy changes, or other acts of concession.

Basic Premises

It is internationally accepted that governments are responsible for the safety and welfare of persons within the borders of their nations. Aware of both the hostage threat and public security shortcomings in many parts of the world, the United States has developed enhanced physical and personal security programs for U.S. personnel and established cooperative arrangements with the U.S. private sector. It has also established bilateral assistance programs and close intelligence and law enforcement relationships with many nations to prevent hostage-taking incidents or resolve them in a manner that will deny the perpetrators benefits from their actions. The United States also seeks effective judicial prosecution and punishment for hostage takers victimizing the U.S. Government or its citizens and will use all legal methods to these ends, including extradition. U.S. policy and goals are clear, and the U.S. Government actively pursues them alone and in cooperation with other governments.

U.S. Government Responsibilities When Private U.S. Citizens Are Taken Hostage

Based upon past experience, the U.S. Government concluded that making concessions that benefit hostage takers in exchange for the release of hostages increased the danger that others will be taken hostage. U.S. Government policy is, therefore, to deny hostage takers the benefits of ransom, prisoner releases, policy changes, or other acts of concession.

At the same time, the U.S. Government will make every effort, including contact with representatives of the captors, to obtain the release of hostages without making concessions to the hostage takers.

Consequently, the United States strongly urges American companies and private citizens not to accede to hostage-taker demands. It believes that good security practices, relatively modest security expenditures, and continual close cooperation with embassy and local authorities can lower the risk to Americans living in high-threat environments.

The U.S. Government is concerned for the welfare of its citizens but cannot support requests that host governments violate their own laws or abdicate their normal enforcement responsibilities.

If the employing organization or company works closely with local authorities and follows U.S. policy, U.S. Foreign Service posts can be involved actively in efforts to bring the incident to a safe conclusion. This includes providing reasonable administrative services and, if desired by local authorities and the American entity, full participation in strategy sessions. Requests for U.S. Government technical assistance or expertise will be considered on a case-by-case basis. The full extent of U.S. Government participation must await an analysis of each specific set of circumstances.

The host government and the U.S. private organizations or citizen must understand that if they wish to follow a hostage resolution path different from that of U.S. Government policy, they do so without U.S. Government approval. In the event a hostage-taking incident is resolved through concessions, U.S. policy remains steadfastly to pursue investigation leading to the apprehension and prosecution of hostage takers who victimize U.S. citizens. [. . .]

Source: U.S. Department of State Press Briefing. Available online. URL: http://www.state.gov/r/pa/prs/ps/2002/8190.htm.

DOMESTIC TERRORIST GROUPS AND INCIDENTS

Criminal Complaint against Timothy McVeigh, Oklahoma City (April 1995)

At 9:02 A.M. on April 19, 1995, a truck loaded with 4,800 pounds of fertilizer and racing fuel exploded in front of the Alfred P. Murrah Federal Building in Oklahoma City. The entire front of the nine-story building collapsed, killing 168 people. Barely an hour after the blast, police stopped Timothy McVeigh for driving a car without a license plate. Investigators later realized he was their primary suspect in the bombing. The first document below outlines the U.S. government's case against McVeigh. The second document outlines McVeigh's argument that other forces were responsible for the explosion and that his trial should be delayed while additional information was requested regarding alleged U.S. government surveillance materials.

Affidavit in Support of the Criminal Complaint against Timothy McVeigh

United States District Court

WESTERN DISTRICT OF OKLAHOMA

UNITED STATES OF AMERICA

V.

TIMOTHY JAMES McVEIGH CRIMINAL COMPLAINT

CASE NUMBER: M-95-98-H

I, HENRY C. GIBBONS, being duly sworn, do hereby state that I am an agent with the Federal Bureau of Investigation, having been so employed for 26 years and as such am vested with the authority to investigate violations of federal laws, including Title 18, United States Code, Section 844 (f).

Further, the Affiant states as follows:

1. The following information has been received by the Federal Bureau of Investigation over the period from April 19 through April 21, 1995;

2. On April 19, 1995, a massive explosion detonated outside the Alfred P. Murrah building in Oklahoma City, Oklahoma, at approximately 9:00 a.m.

3. Investigation by Federal agents at the scene of the explosion have determined that the explosive was contained in a 1993 Ford owned by Ryder Rental company. [. . .]

4. The rental agent at Elliot's Body Shop in Junction City, Kansas, was interviewed by the FBI on April 19, 1995. The individual who signed the rental agreement provided the following information:
a. The person who signed the rental agreement identified himself as BOB KLING, SSN: 962-42-9694, South Dakota's driver's license number YF942A6, and provided a home address of 428 Malt Drive, Redfield, South Dakota. The person listed the destination as 428 Maple Drive, Omaha, Nebraska.
b. Subsequent investigation conducted by the FBI determine all this information to be bogus.

5. On April 20, 1995, the rental agent was recontacted and assisted in the creation of composite drawings. The rental agent has told the FBI that the composite drawings are fair and accurate depictions of the individuals who rented the truck.

6. On April 20, 1995, the FBI interviewed three witnesses who were near the scene of the explosion at Alfred P. Murrah Federal Building prior to the determination of the explosives. The three witnesses were shown a copy of the composite drawing of Unsub #1 and identified him as closely resembling a person the witnesses had seen in front of the Alfred P. Murrah Building where the explosion occurred on April 19, 1995. The witnesses advised the FBI that they observed a person identified as Unsub #1 at approximately 8:40 a.m. on April 19, 1995, when they entered the building. They again observed Unsub #1 at approximately 8:55 a.m., still in front of the 5th Road entrance of the building when they departed just minutes before the explosion.

7. The Alfred P. Murrah building is used by various agencies of the United States, including Agriculture Department of the Army, the Defense Department, Federal Highway Administration, General Accounting Office, General Services Administration, Social Security Administration, Labor Department, Marine Corps, Small Business Administration, Transportation

Department, United States Secret Service, Bureau of Alcohol, Tobacco and Firearms, and Veteran's Administration.

8. The composite drawings were shown to employees at various motels and commercial establishments in the Junction City, Kansas, vicinity. Employees of the Dreamland Motel in Junction City, Kansas, advised FBI agents that an individual resembling Unsub #1 depicted in the composite drawings had been a guest at the Motel from April 14 through April 18, 1995. This individual had registered at the Motel under the name of Tim McVeigh, listed his automobile as bearing an Oklahoma license plate with an illegible plate number, and provided a Michigan address, on North Van Dyke Road in Decker, Michigan. The individual was seen driving a car described as a Mercury from the 1970's.

9. A check of Michigan Department of Motor Vehicle records shows a license in the name of Timothy J. McVeigh , date of birth April 23, 1968, with an address of 3616 North Nan Dyke Road, Decker, Michigan. This Michigan license was renewed by McVeigh on April 8, 1995. McVeigh had a prior license issued in the state of Kansas on March 21, 1990, and surrendered to Michigan in November 1993, with the following address: P.O. Box 2153, Fort Riley, Kansas.

10. Further investigation shows that the property at 3616 North Van Dyke Road, Decker, Michigan, is associated with James Douglas Nichols and his brother Terry Lynn Nichols. The property is a working farm. Terry Nichols formerly resided in Marion, Kansas, which is approximately one hour from Junction City.

11. A relative of James Nichols reports to the FBI that Tim McVeigh is a friend and associate of James Nichols, who has worked and resided at the farm on North Van Dyke Road in Decker, Michigan. This relative further reports that she had heard that James Nichols had been involved in constructing bombs in approximately November 1994, and that he possessed large quantities of fuel oil and fertilizer.

12. On April 21, 1995, a former co-worker of Tim McVeigh's reported to the FBI that he had seen the composite drawing of Unsub #1 on the television and recognized the drawing to be a former co-worker, Tim McVeigh. He further advised that McVeigh was known to hold extreme rightwing views, was a military veteran, and was particularly agitated about the conduct of the federal government in Waco, Texas, in 1993. In fact, the co-worker further reports that McVeigh had been so agitated about the deaths of the Branch Davidians in Waco, Texas, on April 19,

1993, that he personally visited the site. After visiting the site, McVeigh expressed extreme anger at the federal government and advised that the Government should never had done what it did. He further advised that the last known address he had for McVeigh is 1711 Stockton Hill Road, #206, Kingman, Arizona.

13. On April 21, 1994 [sic], investigators learned that a Timothy McVeigh was arrested at 10:30 a.m. on April 19, 1995, in Perry, Oklahoma, for not having a license tag and for possession of a weapon approximately 1-1/2 hours after the detonation of the explosive device at the Alfred P. Murrah Federal Building in Oklahoma City, Oklahoma. Perry, Oklahoma, is approximately a 1- 1/2 hour drive from Oklahoma City, Oklahoma. McVeigh, who has been held in custody since his arrest on April 19, 1995, listed his home address as 3616 North Van Dyke Road, Decker, Michigan. He listed James Nichols of Decker, Michigan, as a reference. McVeigh was stopped driving a yellow 1977 Mercury Marquis.

14. The detonation of the explosive in front of the Alfred P. Murrah Federal Building constitutes a violation of 18 U.S.C. Section 844(f), which makes it a crime to maliciously damage or destroy by means of an explosive any building or real property, in whole or in part owned, possessed or used by the United States, or any department or agency thereof.

Source: Court TV Crime Library. Available online. URL: http://www.courttv.com/archive/casefiles/oklahoma/documents/complaint1.html.

Petition for Writ of Mandamus of Petitioner-Defendant, Timothy James McVeigh and Brief in Support (March 25, 1997) (excerpted)

IN THE UNITED STATES COURT OF APPEALS FOR THE TENTH CIRCUIT

TIMOTHY JAMES McVEIGH,

Petitioner-Defendant,

v.

HONORABLE RICHARD P. MATSCH,

Respondent.

Case No. 96 (Case No. 96-CR-68-M below)

[. . .]

OVERVIEW

The McVeigh defense, based upon the material provided to it, suggests the following hypothesis: A foreign power, probably Iraq, but not excluding the possibility of another foreign state, planned a terrorist attack(s) in the United States and that one of those targets was the Alfred P. Murrah Building in Oklahoma City. The Murrah Building was chosen either because of lack of security (i.e. it was a "soft target"), or because of available resources such as Iraqi POW's who had been admitted into the United States were located in Oklahoma City, or possibly because the location of the building was important to American neo-Nazis such as those individuals who supported Richard Snell who was executed in Arkansas on April 19, 1995.

The plan was arranged for a Middle Eastern bombing engineer to engineer the bomb in such a way that it could be carefully transported and successfully detonated. There is no reported incident of neo-Nazis or extreme right-wing militants in this country exploding any bomb of any significant size let alone one to bring down a nine (9) story federal building and kill 168 persons. In fact, not even members of the left-wing militant groups such as the Weatherman were ever able to accomplish anything of this magnitude.

This terrorist attack was "contracted out" to persons whose organization and ideology was friendly to policies of the foreign power and included dislike and hatred of the United States government itself, and possibly included was a desire for revenge against the United States, with possible anti-black and anti-semitic overtones. Because Iraq had tried a similar approach in 1990, but had been thwarted by Syrian intelligence information given to the United States, this time the information was passed through an Iraqi intelligence base in the Philippines.

Operating out of the Philippines as a base, the state-sponspored [sic] terrorists, with the Murrah Building already chosen as the target, enlisted the support and assistance of members of the Radical American Right. The defense believes the evidence suggests that American neo-Nazis were chosen to carry out the bombing of the Murrah Building because of a shared ideological bent of hatred against the American government. It is possible that those who carried out the bombing were unaware of the true sponsor.

The evidence collected by the defense suggests that the desired ideology was found by the state-sponsored terrorists in Elohim City,

Oklahoma, a small compound near Muldrow, Oklahoma, consisting of between 25 and 30 families and described as a terrorist organization which preaches white supremacy, polygamy and overthrow of the government. Elohim City was a haven for former members of The Covenant, The Sword and the Arm of the Lord ("CSA"), another extremist organization that had been raided by the federal government on April 19, 1995, exactly ten years to the day prior to the Oklahoma City bombing. One member of CSA turned on the organization and testified in court at the trial of Richard Snell and others who were charged in Arkansas with sedition in that they conspired to destroy the Alfred P. Murrah Building in Oklahoma City with a rocket launcher in the early 1980's. Snell was convicted on unrelated capital charges and sentenced to death in Arkansas. He was executed the day of the Oklahoma City bombing—April 19, 1995—and is buried at Elohim City. It is from this group of people that the defense believes that the evidence suggests foreign, state-sponsored terrorists groomed the most radical persons associated with Elohim City and extracted monumental revenge against the federal government by destroying the Murrah Building on the day of Richard Snell's execution and the anniversary date of the federal raid.

But the defense hypothesis also entails evidence, very strong evidence, that the federal government, through the Bureau of Alcohol, Tobacco & Firearms, had an informant in Elohim City, an informant who warned federal law enforcement prior to April 19, 1995, that former residents, including the former chief of security, of Elohim City were planning to "target for destruction" federal buildings in Oklahoma, including the Alfred P. Murrah Building. The defense believes this scenario is true, that is is [sic] eerily similar to the World Trade Center bombing where the FBI had an informant infiltrate the terrorist group but failed to stop that criminal act, and that, absent judicial intervention, information concerning these matters in the possession of the federal government will be forever buried.

The defense for Mr. McVeigh is not engaged in a fishing expedition. As the information set forth in this Petition demonstrates, the McVeigh defense, using resources provided to it by the district court, has conducted a wide-ranging and increasingly narrow focused investigation. But without subpoena power, without the right to take depositions, and without access to national intelligence information, the McVeigh defense can go no further.

Source: Federation of American Scientists, Intelligence Resource Program, Intelligence Threat Assessments. Available online. URL: http://www.fas.org/irp/threat/mcveigh/part02.htm.

Confession by Eric Robert Rudolph (for attacks in 1996 and 1997)

Eric Robert Rudolph, suspected of bombing the 1996 Atlantic Olympic Games and a series of abortion clinics and gay bars in Atlanta and Birmingham, was apprehended in 2003. Two years later Rudolph agreed to plead guilty to the charges against him in return for not seeking the death penalty. He issued a written confession that outlined the reasoning behind his violent attacks.

Text of Eric Rudolph's Confession (excerpts)

After much thought and consideration, I entered into an agreement with the government. After potentially facing 4 trials in 4 separate jurisdictions on circumstantial evidence that would likely lead to a conviction in at least one of these jurisdictions, I have deprived the government of its goal of sentencing me to death.

The fact that I have entered an agreement with the government is purely a tactical choice on my part and in no way legitimates [sic] the moral authority of the government to judge this matter.

Abortion is murder. And when the regime in Washington legalized, sanctioned and legitimized this practice, they forfeited their legitimacy and moral authority to govern. At various times in history men and women of good conscience have had to decide when the lawfully constituted authorities have overstepped their moral bounds and forfeited their right to rule. This took place in July of 1776 when our Forefathers decided that the British Crown had violated the essential rights of Englishmen, and therefore lost its authority to govern. And, in January of 1973 the government in Washington decided to descend into barbarism by sanctioning the ancient practice of infanticide by that act consigned 50 million unborn children to their graves. There is no more legitimate reason to my knowledge, for renouncing allegiance to and if necessary using force to drag this monstrosity of a government down to the dust where it belongs.

I am not an anarchist. I have nothing against government or law enforcement in general. It is solely for the reason that this govt [sic] has legalized the murder of children that I have no allegiance to nor do I recognize the legitimacy of this particular government in Washington.

Along with abortion, another assault upon the integrity of American society is the concerted effort to legitimize the practice of homosexuality. Homosexuality is an aberrant sexual behavior, and as such I have complete sympathy and understanding for those who are suffering from this condition. Practiced by consenting adults within the confines of their own private lives, homosexuality is not a threat to society. Those consenting adults practicing this behavior in privacy should not be hassled by a society which respects the sanctity of private sexual life. But when the attempt is made to drag this practice out of the closet and into the public square in an "in your face" attempt to force society to accept and recognize this behavior as being just as legitimate and normal as the natural man/woman relationship, every effort should be made, including force if necessary, to halt this effort.

For many years I thought long and hard on these issues and then in 1996 I decided to act. In the summer of 1996, the world converged upon Atlanta for the Olympic Games. Under the protection and auspices of the regime in Washington millions of people came out celebrate the ideals of global socialism. Multinational corporations spent billions of dollars, and Washington organized an army of security to protect these best of all games. Even though the conception and purpose of the so-called Olympic movement is to promote the values of global socialism, as perfectly expressed in the song "Imagine" by John Lennon, which was the theme of the 1996 games—even though the purpose of the Olympics is to promote these despicable ideals, the purpose of the attack on July 27th was to confound, anger and embarrass the Washington government in the eyes of the word for its abominable sanctioning of abortion on demand.

The plan was to force the cancellation of the Games, or at least create a state of insecurity to empty the streets around the venues and thereby eat into the vast amounts of money invested. The plan was conceived in haste and carried out with limited resources, planning and preparation—it was a monster that kept getting out of control the more I got into it. Because I could not acquire the necessary high explosives, I had to dismiss the unrealistic notion of knocking down the power grid surrounding Atlanta and consequently pulling the plug on the Olympics for their duration.

The plan that I finally settled upon was to use five low-tech timed explosives to be placed one at a time on successive days throughout the Olympic schedule, each preceded by a forty to fifty minute warning given to 911. The location and the time of detonation was to be given, and the intent was to thereby clear each of the areas, leaving only uniformed arms-carrying government personnel exposed to potential injury.

The attacks were to have commenced with the start of the Olympics, but due to a lack of planning this was postponed a week. I had sincerely hoped to achieve these objections without harming innocent civilians. However, I knew that the weapons used (highly uncontrollable timed explosives) and the choice of tactics (placing them in areas frequented by large numbers of civilians) could potentially lead to a disaster wherein many civilians could be killed or wounded. There is no excuse for this, and I accept full responsibility for the consequences of using this dangerous tactic.

The first and largest device was placed in Centennial Park. There was a 55 [minute] delay on the device. After placing the device it took approximately 10 minutes to walk to the telephone booth where a call was placed immediately. The 911 operator answered the call, and after acknowledging that she could understand my voice (I was using a little plastic contraption to disguise my voice), I proceeded to deliver my message and much to my chagrin the operator terminated the call.

I had to assume that the call had been traced and that in less than a few minutes a responder would be headed to that particular booth. So I walked approximately one block and frantically sought out a booth to make another call. I was not paying attention to the time as the minutes ticked off. Thinking perhaps the operator was put off by the sound of my distorted voice coming through the plastic device, I ditched the contraption and sought out a booth by the Days Inn where I then tried to deliver a clear message while holding my nose. The crowd was pushing in and after the first couple of sentences, I was eyeballed closely by at least two individuals. This caused me to leave off the last sentence which indicated the exact location of the device. The result of all this was to produce a disaster—a disaster of my making and for which I do apologize to the victims and their families.

This second call that was made is the only one that has been made public. Unfortunately, Washington's government has not released all of the recordings of the 911 calls made within the hours before the blast. If they had, the public would discover that a call was made from the immediate area approximately 40 to 45 minutes before the blast. The call began with the words, "Do you understand me?" After an acknowledgement by the operator the message began: "We defy your . . ." and at this point the call was terminated.

After the blast and the consequent chaos, I decided to discontinue the operation. I hurried back to the vacant lot I had used as a staging area which was east of Atlanta on I-20. Off to the right side of the interstate is what appeared to be a huge vacant lot with woods and bulldozing excavations, perhaps the place where a mall would be erected. Amid the piles of illegal garbage dumpings, I primed and detonated the other four devices and left Atlanta with much remorse.

After the disaster at Centennial Park, I resolved to improve my devices and focus the blasts upon a very narrow target. Toward this end I acquired a quantity of high explosives (dynamite). I shaped the charges in order to minimize the potential range of their destruction. However, I was still using clock timers which put the detonation outside of my control, thus leaving room for the same kind of disaster that occurred at the Park. Fortunately this did not happen and my intended targets were the only ones placed in jeopardy from that point on.

Two attacks were carried out in the winter of 1997. The first in January was an abortion mill (Northside Family Planning). The second was a homosexual establishment (The Otherside Lounge). The abortion mill was closed that day but occasionally there was staff on hand to clean their blood-stained equipment, and these minions and the facility itself were the targets of the first device. The second device placed at the scene was designed to target agents of the Washington government.

The next attack in February was at The Otherside Lounge. Like the assault at the abortion mill, two devices used. The first device was designed not necessarily to target the patrons of this homosexual bar, but rather to set the stage for the next device, which was again targeted at Washington's agents. The attack itself was meant to send a powerful message in protest of Washington's continued tolerance and support for the homosexual political agenda.

Despite the inherent dangers involved in timed devices, all of these devices used in both of these assaults functioned within the parameters of the plan, and I make no apologies.

After laying low for a year, I succeeded in making operations a command-detonated focused device that would greatly reduce the risk for harming innocent civilians when carrying out these operations. Over a million human beings had died in the past year, and as the anniversary of Roe v. Wade approached, the idea was to send yet another message to the killers and who protected them.

Birmingham and that particular abortion mill were chosen purely for tactical reasons. The city was a sufficient distance away from any location I was known to have frequented. Three abortion mills were looked at in Birmingham, none of which I truly liked for a target. New Woman All Women was tactically the least objectionable. [. . .]

Washington was lucky that day in Birmingham, they had a witness who happened into a fortuitous position, and my truck was identified. I knew something was amiss based upon the early reports coming out of Birmingham so I prepared to make a move as I debated within myself whether or not to run or fight them in court. I chose the woods.

The next year was a starving time. Hunted and haggard, I struggled to survive. But I am a quick study, and so I learned to adapt to my situation. [. . .]

The next three years were spent living a fairly comfortable routine, which involved mostly hunting and camp life. After so many years ducking and hiding and eating crappy foods you tend to let your guard down, and this is what led to my capture in Murphy in 2003. It has been a long journey up to this pint, but I still have a ways to go.

When I was in the woods I used a small dugout underneath a rock to avoid helicopters and their heat sensitive equipment. One cold day in December of 1998 I huddled underneath the rock for half an hour as the chopper slowly hovered overhead scanning the ridge. The whir of his blades became less audible and finally he was over the ridge, and then there was silence. I climbed out of my hide brushing off the icy dirt and remembered thinking about the words of the Psalmist who wrote about seeing his enemies in "great power, spreading his branches and roots like a large tree," but after a little while he looked and beheld his enemies were "nowhere to be found." In defiance I looked toward the ridge into which the chopper had just gone and said, "I am still here."

And now after the agreement has been signed the talking heads on the news opine that I am "finished," that I will "languish broken and unloved in the bowels of some supermax," and but I say to you people that by the grace of God I am still here—a little bloodied, but emphatically unbowed.

Source: National Public Radio, April 14, 2005. Available online. URL: http://www.npr.org/templates/story/story.php?storyId=4600480.

Press briefing on the "Report of the Accountability Review Boards on the Embassy Bombings in Nairobi and Dar es Salaam" by Admiral William J. Crowe (January 8, 1999)

On August 7, 1998, members of al-Qaeda simultaneously detonated truck bombs at the U.S. embassies in Kenya and Tanzania, killing 224 people. As with the Khobar Towers attack two years earlier, the attacks prompted congressional and Department of Defense reviews of security deficiencies at U.S. facilities abroad. The Accountability Review Boards on the Embassy Bombings did not single out individuals for blame but, rather, uncovered a legacy of U.S. administrations failing to maintain adequate security at their diplomatic facilities abroad. The report and related questions reveal the contradiction between maintaining open access to the public and security.

Press briefing on the Report of the Accountability Review Boards on the Embassy Bombings in Nairobi and Dar es Salaam
Admiral William J. Crowe, chairman
Washington, D.C., January 8, 1999

[. . .] The [Accountability Review] boards did not find reasonable cause to believe that any employee of the United States Government or member of the uniform services breached his or her duty in connection with the August 7 bombings. However, we found that security affairs in today's complex bureaucracy are widely dispersed. Consequently, it is difficult to pinpoint responsibility.

Nevertheless, we believe that there was a collective failure by several Administrations and Congresses over the past decade to reduce the vulnerability of US diplomatic missions adequately.

In this regard, the boards were most disturbed by two inter-connected issues: First, the inadequacy of resources to provide protective measures against terrorist attacks; and second, the relative low priority accorded security concerns throughout the US Government by the Congress, the Department, other agencies in general, and on the part of many employees—both in Washington and in the field.

Saving lives and adequately addressing our security vulnerabilities on a sustained basis must, in our judgment, be a given higher priority by all those involved if we are to prevent such tragedies in the future. Let me stress a clause in the last sentence: "by all those involved." We discovered that many people want to continue to do their work as always, but consider it the job of someone else to make them safe. In today's world, I'm afraid it's not that simple. Security—to use a Navy expression—is an "all-hands" proposition. All employees serving overseas must adapt their lifestyles to make their workplace and their residences more safe.

The security systems and procedures of both posts at the time of the bombings were in general accord with current Department policy. Alarmingly, those procedures and systems followed by the embassies under the Department's direction did not speak to large vehicular bombs with any specificity or trans-national terrorism, nor the dire consequences that would result from them. This gap existed throughout the system.

Both embassies were located immediately adjacent or close to public streets and were especially vulnerable to large vehicular bombs. The boards found that too many of our overseas missions are similarly situated. Unless these vulnerabilities are addressed on a sustained and realistic basis, the lives and safety of US Government employees and the public in many of our facilities abroad will continue to be at risk from further terrorist bombings.

The boards further found that intelligence provided no immediate tactical warning of the August 7 attacks. We understand the difficulty—in fact, more than we did when we started—of monitoring terrorist networks, and concluded that the current role or state or play in the intelligence community and intelligence expertise offers us no assurance that we will have tactical warning and that our missions which are vulnerable will have such warning.

In any case, there are instances, of course, that we have tactical warning, but they are more the exception than the rule. We must consider that a bonus rather than a normal event. We found, however, that both policy and intelligence officials have relied in the past on warning intelligence to measure threats; whereas experience has shown, that trans-national terrorists often strike without warning at vulnerable targets in areas where expectations of terrorist acts against the United States are relatively low.

In our investigations of the bombings, the boards were struck by how similar the lessons were to those drawn by the Inman Commission over 14 years ago. What is most troubling is the failure of the US Government to take the necessary step to prevent such tragedies through an unwillingness to give sustained priority and funding to security improvements. We viewed as our primary and overriding responsibility the submission of recommendations that will save lives of personnel serving at US missions abroad in the future.

We are advancing, in this report, a number of proposals that deal with a handling of terrorist threats and attacks; the review and revision of standards, including a review of the Inman Report; also, a review of procedures to improve security readiness and crisis management; the size and composition of our missions; and the need to have adequate and sustained funding for safe buildings and security programs in the future.

Some of these recommendations are, of necessity, classified. We recognize that the Department of State and other US Government agencies are already making adjustments. In fact, we have cooperated with that by, as our investigation proceeded, occasionally telling various concerned departments of some of the things that we were encountering and some of the measures that we might suggest. They are in essence taking measures now to enhance the protection of our personnel in facilities abroad. It is clear, however, that still much more needs to be done.

While many of the recommendations in our report identify problems which we found in various areas of security, none of this should obscure the outstanding and often heroic efforts made by the diplomatic and Marine security guard personnel in the field in the wake of the horrific terrorist attacks. They often save lives and acted in the highest traditions of government service. It was a very moving experience to encounter this.

In closing, I would like to express both a warning and a plea. The boards concluded early in their deliberations that the appearance of large bomb attacks and the emergence of sophisticated and global terrorist networks aimed at US interests abroad have dramatically and irrevocably changed the threat environment. Old assumptions are no longer valid.

Today, US Government employees from many departments and agencies overseas work and live in harm's way just as military people do.

We must acknowledge this fact of life and bend every effort to continually remind Congress and our citizenry of this reality. In turn, I would vigorously argue that the nation must make greater exertions to provide for their safety. Service abroad can never be made completely safe; we fully understand that. But we can reduce some of the risks to the survival and security of our men and women who conduct the nation's business far from home. This will require a much greater effort in terms of national commitment, resources and procedures than in the past.

In fact, it involves a sea-change in the way we do our business. We have a choice, of course: we can continue as we have been, we can continue to see our embassies blown away, our people killed and our nation's foreign reputation eroded. I would hope we would not take that choice.

Source: Federation of American Scientists, Intelligence Resource Program, Intelligence Threat Assessments. Available online. URL: http://www.fas.org/irp/threat/arb/990108_emb_rpt.html.

9/11: Testimony of Richard Clarke to 9/11 Commission (March 24, 2004)

The National Commission on Terrorist Attacks Upon the United States was an independent, bipartisan commission created by congressional legislation and the signature of President George W. Bush in late 2002. Using hearings, testimony, interviews, and documentary evidence, the commission was tasked with preparing a full and complete account of the circumstances surrounding the September 11, 2001, terrorist attacks, including preparedness for and the immediate response to the attacks. The commission was also mandated to provide recommendations designed to guard against future attacks. Below are three excerpts from the testimony by White House Counter-Terrorism Chief Richard Clarke. The commission's final report was issued in 2004 both as a bound volume, The 9/11 Commission Report, *and as a PDF file available at http://www.9-11 commission.gov/report/index.htm.*

TESTIMONY OF RICHARD A. CLARKE BEFORE THE NATIONAL COMMISSION ON TERRORIST ATTACKS UPON THE UNITED STATES (March 24, 2004)

I am appreciative of the opportunity the Commission is offering for me to provide my observations about what went wrong in the struggle against al Qaeda, both before and after 9-11. I want the families of the victims to know that we tried to stop those attacks, that some people tried very hard. I want them to know why we failed and what I think we need to do to insure that nothing like that ever happens again.

I have testified for twenty hours before the House-Senate Joint Inquiry committee and before this Commission in closed hearings. Therefore, I will limit my prepared testimony to a chronological review of key facts and then provide some conclusions and summary observations, which may form the basis for further questions. My observations and answers to any questions are limited by my memory, because I do not have access to government files or classified information for purposes of preparing for this hearing.

I was assigned to the National Security Council staff in 1992 and had terrorism as part of my portfolio until late 2001. Terrorism became the predominant part of my duties during the mid-1990s and I was appointed National Coordinator for Counter-terrorism in 1998.

1. *Terrorism without US Retaliation in the 1980s:* In the 1980s, Hizballah killed 278 United States Marines in Lebanon and twice destroyed the US embassy. They kidnapped and killed other Americans, including the CIA Station chief. There was no direct US military retaliation. In 1989, 259 people were killed on Pan Am 103. There was no direct US military retaliation. The George H.W. Bush administration did not have a formal counter-terrorism policy articulated in an NSC Presidential decision document.

2. *Terrorism Early in the Clinton Administration:* Within the first few weeks of the Clinton administration, there was terrorism in the US: the attack on the CIA gatehouse and the attack on the World Trade Center. CIA and FBI concluded at the time that there was no organization behind those attacks. Similarly, they did not report at the time that al Qaeda was involved in the planned attack on Americans in Yemen in 1992 or the Somali attacks on US and other peacekeepers in 1993. Indeed, CIA and FBI did not report the existence of an organization named al Qaeda until the mid-1990s, seven years after it was apparently created. Nonetheless, the 1993 attacks and then the terrorism in the Tokyo subway and the Oklahoma City bombing caused the Clinton Administration to increase its focus on terrorism and to expand funding for counter-terrorism programs.

As a result of intelligence and law enforcement operations, most of those involved in the World Trade Center attack of 1993, the planned attacks on the UN and New York tunnels, the CIA gatehouse shootings, the Oklahoma City bombing, and the attempted assassination of former President Bush were successfully apprehended.

The Clinton Administration responded to Iraqi terrorism against the US in 1993 with a military retaliation and against Iranian terrorism against the US in 1996 at Khobar Towers with a covert action. Both US responses were accompanied by warning that further anti-US terrorism would result in greater retaliation. Neither Iraq nor Iran engaged in anti-US terrorism subsequently. (Iraqis did, of course, later engage in anti-US terrorism in 2003–4.)

3. *Identifying the al Qaeda Threat:* The White House urged CIA in 1994 to place greater focus on what the Agency called "the terrorist financier, Usama bin Ladin." After the creation of a "virtual station" to examine bin Ladin, CIA identified a multi-national network of cells and of affiliated terrorist organizations. That network was attempting to wage "jihad" in Bosnia and planned to have a significant role in a new Bosnian government. US and Allied actions halted the war in Bosnia and caused most of the al Qaeda related jihadists to leave. The White House asked CIA and DOD to develop plans for operating against al Qaeda in Sudan, the country of its headquarters. Neither department was able successfully to develop a plan to do so. Immediately following Usama bin Ladin's move to Afghanistan, the White House requested that plans be developed to operate against al Qaeda there. CIA developed ties to a group which reported on al Qaeda activity, but which was unable to mount successful operations against al Qaeda in Afghanistan. CIA opposed using its own personnel to do so.

4. *Sudan:* While bin Ladin was in Sudan, he was hosted by its leader, Hasan Turabi. Under Turabi, Sudan had become a safe haven for many terrorist groups, but bin Ladin had special status. He funded many development programs such as roads and dined often with Turabi and his family. Turabi and bin Ladin were ideological brethren. Following the assassination attempt on Egyptian President Mubarek, the US and Egypt successfully proposed UN sanctions on Sudan because of its support of terrorism. Because of the growing economic damage to Sudan due to its support of terrorism, bin Ladin offered to move to Afghanistan. Sudan at no time detained him, nor was there ever a credible offer by Sudan to arrest and render him. This is in contrast to Sudan's arrest of the terrorist known as Carlos the Jackal, who the Sudanese then handed over in chains to French authorities.

5. *1998 Turning Point:* In 1996, CIA had been directed to develop its capability to operate against al Qaeda in Afghanistan and elsewhere. CIA operations identified and disrupted al Qaeda cells in several countries. In 1997, a federal grand jury began reviewing evidence against al Qaeda and in 1998

indicted Usama bin Ladin. Several terrorists, including bin Ladin, issued a fatwa against the United States.

In August, al Qaeda attacked two US embassies in East Africa. Following the attacks, the United States responded militarily with cruise missile attacks on al Qaeda facilities. President Clinton was widely criticized for doing so. A US Marine deployment, combined with CIA activity, disrupted a third attack planned in Tirana, Albania.

President Clinton requested the Chairman of the Joint Chiefs to develop follow-on military strike plans, including the use of US Special Forces. The Chairman recommended against using US forces on the ground in Afghanistan, but placed submarines with cruise missiles off shore awaiting timely intelligence of the location of Usama bin Ladin.

The President also requested CIA to develop follow-on covert action plans. He authorized lethal activity in a series of directives which progressively expanded the authority of CIA to act against al Qaeda in Afghanistan.

Diplomatic activity also increased, including UN sanctions against the Taliban regime in Afghanistan and pressure on Pakistan to cooperate further in attempts to end the Taliban support for al Qaeda.

6. *National Coordinator:* In 1998, I was appointed by the President to a newly created position of National Coordinator for Security, Infrastructure Protection and Counter-terrorism. Although the Coordinator was appointed to the Cabinet level NSC Principals Committee, the position was limited at the request of the departments and agencies. The Coordinator had no budget, only a dozen staff, and no ability to direct actions by the departments or agencies. The President authorized ten security and counter-terrorism programs and assigned leadership on each program (e.g. Transportation Security) to an agency lead.

7. *1999:* The Clinton Administration continued to pursue intelligence, including covert action, military, law enforcement, and diplomatic activity to disrupt al Qaeda.

CIA was unable to develop timely intelligence to support the planned follow-on military strikes. On three occasions, CIA reported it knew where Usama bin Ladin was, but all three times the Director of Central Intelligence recommended against military action because of the poor quality of the intelligence. Eventually, the US submarines on station for the military operation returned to normal duties. CIA's assets in Afghanistan were unable to utilize the lethal covert action authorities and CIA recommended against placing its own personnel in Afghanistan to carry out the operations. Captures of al Qaeda personnel outside of Afghanistan continued.

In December 1999, intelligence and law enforcement information indicated that al Qaeda was planning attacks against the US. The President ordered the Principals Committee to meet regularly to prevent the attacks. That Cabinet level committee met throughout December 1999, to review intelligence and develop counter-measures. The planned al Qaeda attacks were averted.

Despite our inability to locate Usama bin Ladin in one place long enough to launch an attack, I urged that we engage in a bombing campaign of al Qaeda facilities in Afghanistan. That option was deferred by the Principals Committee.

8. *Terrorists in the US:* FBI had the responsibility for finding al Qaeda related activities or terrorists in the US. In the 1996–1999 timeframe, they regularly responded to me and to the National Security Advisor that there were no known al Qaeda operatives or activities in the US. On my trips to FBI field offices, I found that al Qaeda was not a priority (except in the New York office). Following the Millennium Alert, FBI Executive Assistant Director Dale Watson attempted to have the field offices act more aggressively to find al Qaeda related activities. The Bureau was, however, less than proactive in identifying al Qaeda related fund raising, recruitment, or other activities in the United States. Several programs to increase our ability to respond to terrorism in the US were initiated both in the FBI and in other departments, including programs to train and equip first responders.

9. *2000:* The President, displeased with the inability of CIA to eliminate the al Qaeda leadership, asked for additional options. The NSC staff proposed that the Predator, unmanned aerial vehicle, be used to find the leadership. CIA objected. The National Security Advisor, however, eventually obtained Agency agreement to fly the Predator on a "proof of concept" mission without any link to military or CIA forces standing by. CIA wanted to experiment with the concept before developing a command and control system that incorporated Predator information with attack capabilities. The flights ended when the high winds of winter precluded the operation of the aircraft. The experiment had proved successful in locating the al Qaeda leadership.

In October 2000, the USS Cole was attacked in Yemen. Following the attack, the Principals considered military retaliation. CIA and FBI were, however, unwilling to state that those who had conducted the attack were al Qaeda or related to the facilities and personnel in Afghanistan. The Principals directed that the Politico-Military Plan against al Qaeda be updated with additional options. Among those options were aiding Afghan factions to fight the Taliban and al Qaeda and creating an armed version of the Predator unmanned aircraft to use against the al Qaeda leadership. Military strike options, including cruise missiles, bombing, and use of US Special Forces were also included.

As the Clinton Administration came to an end, three attacks on the US had been definitively tied to al Qaeda, (the World Trade Center 1993, the Embassies in 1998 and the Cole in 2000), in which a total of 35 Americans had been killed over eight years.

To counter al Qaeda's growing threat, a global effort had been initiated involving intelligence activities, covert action, diplomacy, law enforcement, financial action, and military capability. Nonetheless, the organization continued to enjoy a safe haven in Afghanistan.

10. *2001:* On January 24, 2001, I requested in writing an urgent meeting of the NSC Principals committee to address the al Qaeda threat. That meeting took place on September 4, 2001. It was preceded by a number of Deputies Committee meetings, beginning in April. Those meetings considered proposals to step up activity against al Qaeda, including military assistance to anti-Taliban Afghan factions.

In June and July, intelligence indicated an increased likelihood of a major al Qaeda attack against US targets, probably in Saudi Arabia or Israel. In response, the interagency Counter-terrorism Security Group agreed upon a series of steps including a series of warning notices that an attack could take place in the US. Notices were sent to federal agencies (Immigration, Customs, Coast Guard, FAA, FBI, DOD, and State), state and local police, airlines, and airports.

In retrospect, we know that there was information available to some in the FBI and CIA that al Qaeda operatives had entered the United States. That information was not shared with the senior FBI counter-terrorism official (Dale Watson) or with me, despite the heightened state of concern in the Counter-terrorism Security Group.

Observations and Conclusions

Although there were people in the FBI, CIA, Defense Department, State Department, and White House who worked very hard to destroy al Qaeda before it did catastrophic damage to the US, there were many others who found the prospect of significant al Qaeda attacks remote. In both CIA and the military there was reluctance at senior career levels to fully utilize all of the capabilities available. There was risk aversion. FBI was, throughout much of this period, organized, staffed, and equipped in such a way that it was ineffective in dealing with the domestic terrorist threat from al Qaeda.

At the senior policy levels in the Clinton Administration, there was an acute understanding of the terrorist threat, particularly al Qaeda. That understanding resulted in a vigorous program to counter al Qaeda including lethal covert action, but it did not include a willingness to resume bombing of Afghanistan. Events in the Balkans, Iraq, the Peace Process, and domestic politics occurring at the same time as the anti-terrorism effort played a role.

The Bush Administration saw terrorism policy as important but not urgent, prior to 9-11. The difficulty in obtaining the first Cabinet level (Principals) policy meeting on terrorism and the limited Principals' involvement sent unfortunate signals to the bureaucracy about the Administration's attitude toward the al Qaeda threat.

The US response to al Qaeda following 9-11 has been partially effective. Unfortunately, the US did not act sufficiently quickly to insert US forces to capture or kill the al Qaeda leadership in Afghanistan. Nor did we employ sufficient US and Allied forces to stabilize that country. In the ensuing 30 months, al Qaeda has morphed into a decentralized network, with its national and regional affiliates operating effectively and independently. There have been more major al Qaeda related attacks globally in the 30 months since 9-11 than there were in the 30 months preceding it. Hostility toward the US in the Islamic world has increased since 9-11, largely as a result of the invasion and occupation of Iraq. Thus, new terrorist cells are likely being created, unknown to US intelligence.

To address the continuing threat from radical Islamic terrorism, the US and its allies must become increasingly focused and effective in countering the ideology that motivates that terrorism.

Source: GlobalSecurity.org. Available online. URL: http://www.globalsecurity.org/security/library/congress/9-11_commission/040324-clarke.pdf.

COUNTER-TERRORISM LEGISLATION AND POLICY

Fact Sheet: Foreign Terrorist Organizations (FTOs) U.S. Department of State Office of Counterterrorism Washington, D.C., October 11, 2005

The 1996 Effective Death Penalty and Anti-Terrorism Act instructs the State Department to identify formally insurgency movements as "Foreign Terrorist Organizations" (FTOs) if they threaten U.S. citizens or the country's national security. Once that terminology is applied, a series of sanctions comes into force against the group and its members, including restrictions on visa applications by members and freezing group assets held in U.S. banks. Aiding any organization designated as an FTO is a criminal offense. The list is updated annually.

Foreign Terrorist Organizations (FTOs) are foreign organizations that are designated by the secretary of state in accordance with section 219 of the

Immigration and Nationality Act (INA), as amended. FTO designations play a critical role in our fight against terrorism and are an effective means of curtailing support for terrorist activities and pressuring groups to get out of the terrorism business.

Identification

The Office of the Coordinator for Counterterrorism in the State Department (S/CT) continually monitors the activities of terrorist groups active around the world to identify potential targets for designation. When reviewing potential targets, S/CT looks not only at the actual terrorist attacks that a group has carried out, but also at whether the group has engaged in planning and preparations for possible future acts of terrorism or retains the capability and intent to carry out such acts.

Designation

Once a target is identified, S/CT prepares a detailed "administrative record," which is a compilation of information, typically including both classified and open sources information, demonstrating that the statutory criteria for designation have been satisfied. If the secretary of state, in consultation with the attorney general and the secretary of the treasury, decides to make the designation, Congress is notified of the secretary's intent to designate the organization and given seven days to review the designation, as the INA requires. Upon the expiration of the seven-day waiting period and in the absence of congressional action to block the designation, notice of the designation is published in the Federal Register, at which point the designation takes effect. By law an organization designated as an FTO may seek judicial review of the designation in the United States Court of Appeals for the District of Columbia Circuit not later than 30 days after the designation is published in the Federal Register.

Until recently the INA provided that FTOs must be redesignated every two years or the designation would lapse. Under the Intelligence Reform and Terrorism Prevention Act of 2004 (IRTPA), however, the redesignation requirement was replaced by certain review and revocation procedures. IRTPA provides that an FTO may file a petition for revocation two years after its designation date (or in the case of redesignated FTOs, its most recent redesignation date) or 2 years after the determination date on its most recent petition for revocation. In order to provide a basis for revocation, the petitioning FTO must provide evidence that the circumstances forming the basis for the designation are sufficiently different as to warrant revocation. If no such review has been conducted during a five-year period with respect to a designation, then the secretary of state is required to review the designation to determine whether revocation would be appropriate. In addition, the secretary of state may at any time revoke a designation upon a finding that the circumstances forming the basis for the designation have changed in such a manner as to warrant revocation, or that the national security of the United States warrants a revocation. The same procedural requirements apply to revocations made by the secretary of state as apply to designations. A designation may be revoked by an act of congress, or set aside by a court order.

Legal Criteria for Designation under Section 219 of the INA as amended

It must be a foreign organization.

The organization must engage in terrorist activity, as defined in section 212 (a)(3)(B) of the INA (8 U.S.C. § 1182(a)(3)(B)), or terrorism, as defined in section 140(d)(2) of the Foreign Relations Authorization Act, Fiscal Years 1988 and 1989 (22 U.S.C. § 2656f(d)(2)), or retain the capability and intent to engage in terrorist activity or terrorism.

The organization's terrorist activity or terrorism must threaten the security of U.S. nationals or the national security (national defense, foreign relations, or the economic interests) of the United States.

Legal Ramifications of Designation

It is unlawful for a person in the United States or subject to the jurisdiction of the United States to knowingly provide "material support or resources" to a designated FTO. (The term "material support or resources" is defined in 18 U.S.C. § 2339A(b)(1) as "any property, tangible or intangible, or service, including currency or monetary instruments or financial securities, financial services, lodging, training, expert advice or assistance, safehouses, false documentation or identification, communications equipment, facilities, weapons, lethal substances, explosives, personnel (1 or more individuals who may be or include oneself), and transportation, except medicine or religious materials." 18 U.S.C. § 2339A(b)(2) provides that for these purposes "the term 'training' means instruction or teaching designed to impart a specific skill, as opposed to general knowledge." 18 U.S.C. § 2339A(b)(3) further provides that for these purposes the term 'expert advice or assistance' means advice or assistance derived from scientific, technical or other specialized knowledge."

Representatives and members of a designated FTO, if they are aliens, are inadmissible to and, in certain circumstances, removable from the United States (see 8 U.S.C. §§ 1182 (a)(3)(B)(i)(IV)-(V), 1227 (a)(1)(A)).

Any U.S. financial institution that becomes aware that it has possession of or control over funds in which a designated FTO or its agent has an interest must retain possession of or control over the funds and report the funds to the Office of Foreign Assets Control of the U.S. Department of the Treasury. [. . .]

Source: U.S. Department of State, Office of Counterterrorism. Available online. URL: http://www.state.gov/s/ct/rls/fs/37191.htm.

Presidential Declaration of National Emergency by Reason of Terrorist Attacks (September 14, 2001)

A declaration of national emergency allows the president to assume extra powers to deal with a crisis. However, any actions must still comply with the Constitution.

Proclamation 7463 of September 14, 2001
Declaration of National Emergency by Reason of Certain Terrorist Attacks
By the President of the United States of America

A Proclamation

A national emergency exists by reason of the terrorist attacks at the World Trade Center, New York, New York, and the Pentagon, and the continuing and immediate threat of further attacks on the United States.

NOW, THEREFORE, I, GEORGE W. BUSH, President of the United States of America, by virtue of the authority vested in me as President by the Constitution and the laws of the United States, I hereby declare that the national emergency has existed since September 11, 2001, and, pursuant to the National Emergencies Act (50 U.S.C. 1601 et seq.), I intend to utilize the following statutes: sections 123, 123a, 527, 2201(c), 12006, and 12302 of title 10, United States Code, and sections 331, 359, and 367 of title 14, United States Code.

This proclamation immediately shall be published in the Federal Register or disseminated through the Emergency Federal Register, and transmitted to the Congress.

This proclamation is not intended to create any right or benefit, substantive or procedural, enforceable at law by a party against the United States, its agencies, its officers, or any person.

IN WITNESS WHEREOF, I have hereunto set my hand this fourteenth day of September, in the year of our Lord two thousand one, and of the Independence of the United States of America the two hundred and twenty-sixth.

[signed:] George W. Bush

Source: Federal Register: September 18, 2001 (Volume 66, Number 181)
Presidential Documents , Page 48199. Available online. URL: http://www.fas.org/irp/news/2001/09/fr091801.html.

Presidential Military Order on Detention, Treatment, and Trial of Certain Non-Citizens in the War Against Terrorism (November 13, 2001)

The White House argued that irregular forces such as al-Qaeda insurgents are not subject to Geneva Convention restrictions on prisoners of war. The following presidential order was issued to provide a legal basis for detaining al-Qaeda insurgents in Afghanistan and transferring them to the U.S. Naval Base at Guantánamo Bay, Cuba, and trying them under military jurisdiction.

By the authority vested in me as President and as Commander in Chief of the Armed Forces of the United States by the Constitution and the laws of the United States of America, including the Authorization for Use of Military Force Joint Resolution (Public Law 107-40, 115 Stat. 224) and sections 821 and 836 of title 10, United States Code, it is hereby ordered as follows:

Section 1. Findings.

(a) International terrorists, including members of al Qaeda, have carried out attacks on United States diplomatic and military personnel and facilities abroad and on citizens and property within the United States on a scale that has created a state of armed conflict that requires the use of the United States Armed Forces.

(b) In light of grave acts of terrorism and threats of terrorism, including the terrorist attacks on September 11, 2001, on the headquarters of the United States Department of Defense in the national capital region, on the World Trade Center in New York, and on civilian aircraft such as in Pennsylvania, I proclaimed a national emergency on September 14, 2001 (Proc. 7463, Declaration of National Emergency by Reason of Certain Terrorist Attacks).

(c) Individuals acting alone and in concert involved in international terrorism possess both the capability and the intention to undertake further terrorist attacks against the United States that, if not detected and prevented, will cause mass deaths, mass injuries, and massive destruction of property, and may place at risk the continuity of the operations of the United States Government.

(d) The ability of the United States to protect the United States and its citizens, and to help its allies and other cooperating nations protect their nations and their citizens, from such further terrorist attacks depends in significant part upon using the United States Armed Forces to identify terrorists and those who support them, to disrupt their activities, and to eliminate their ability to conduct or support such attacks.

(e) To protect the United States and its citizens, and for the effective conduct of military operations and prevention of terrorist attacks, it is necessary for individuals subject to this order pursuant to section 2 hereof to be detained, and, when tried, to be tried for violations of the laws of war and other applicable laws by military tribunals.

(f) Given the danger to the safety of the United States and the nature of international terrorism, and to the extent provided by and under this order, I find consistent with section 836 of title 10, United States Code, that it is not practicable to apply in military commissions under this order the principles of law and the rules of evidence generally recognized in the trial of criminal cases in the United States district courts.

(g) Having fully considered the magnitude of the potential deaths, injuries, and property destruction that would result from potential acts of terrorism against the United States, and the probability that such acts will occur, I have determined that an extraordinary emergency exists for national defense purposes, that this emergency constitutes an urgent and compelling government interest, and that issuance of this order is necessary to meet the emergency.

Sec. 2. Definition and Policy.

(a) The term "individual subject to this order" shall mean any individual who is not a United States citizen with respect to whom I determine from time to time in writing that:

(1) there is reason to believe that such individual, at the relevant times,
(i) is or was a member of the organization known as al Qaeda; (ii) has engaged in, aided or abetted, or conspired to commit,
acts of international terrorism, or acts in preparation therefor,
that have caused, threaten to cause, or have as their aim to
cause, injury to or adverse effects on the United States, its

citizens, national security, foreign policy, or economy; or
(iii) has knowingly harbored one or more individuals described in subparagraphs (i) or (ii) of subsection 2(a)(1) of this order;
and
(2) it is in the interest of the United States that such individual be subject to this order.

(b) It is the policy of the United States that the Secretary of Defense shall take all necessary measures to ensure that any individual subject to this order is detained in accordance with section 3, and, if the individual is to be tried, that such individual is tried only in accordance with section 4.

(c) It is further the policy of the United States that any individual subject to this order who is not already under the control of the Secretary of Defense but who is under the control of any other officer or agent of the United States or any State shall, upon delivery of a copy of such written determination to such officer or agent, forthwith be placed under the control of the Secretary of Defense.

Sec. 3. Detention Authority of the Secretary of Defense.

Any individual subject to this order shall be—

(a) detained at an appropriate location designated by the Secretary of Defense outside or within the United States;

(b) treated humanely, without any adverse distinction based on race, color, religion, gender, birth, wealth, or any similar criteria;

(c) afforded adequate food, drinking water, shelter, clothing, and medical treatment;

(d) allowed the free exercise of religion consistent with the requirements of such detention; and

(e) detained in accordance with such other conditions as the Secretary of Defense may prescribe.

Sec. 4. Authority of the Secretary of Defense Regarding Trials of Individuals Subject to this Order.

(a) Any individual subject to this order shall, when tried, be tried by military commission for any and all offenses triable by military commission that such individual is alleged to have committed, and may be punished in accordance with the penalties provided under applicable law, including life imprisonment or death.

(b) As a military function and in light of the findings in section 1, including subsection (f) thereof, the Secretary of Defense shall issue such orders and regulations, including orders for the appointment of one or more military commissions, as may be necessary to carry out subsection (a) of this section.

(c) Orders and regulations issued under subsection (b) of this section shall include, but not be limited to, rules for the conduct of the proceedings of military commissions, including pretrial, trial, and post-trial procedures, modes of proof, issuance of process, and qualifications of attorneys. [. . .]

GEORGE W. BUSH
THE WHITE HOUSE,
November 13, 2001.

Source: White House Press Release, November 13, 2001. Available online. URL: http://www.whitehouse.gov/news/release/2001/11/20011113-27.html.

Bush Addresses Joint Session of Congress and the American People (September 20, 2001)

President George W. Bush's first major public statement following the 9/11 attacks was this speech addressed to Congress and the American people. Bush uses the speech to praise the solidarity exhibited by U.S. citizens in the days following the attacks. He also recognizes the losses of citizens of other countries and notes expressions of sympathy from abroad. Bush explicitly blames Osama bin Laden for the 9/11 attacks and announces the appointment of a homeland security coordinator, Tom Ridge, who later became the first secretary of the new Department for Homeland Security.

Address to a Joint Session of Congress and the American People
United States Capitol
Washington, D.C.
September 20, 2001

[. . .] Tonight we are a country awakened to danger and called to defend freedom. Our grief has turned to anger, and anger to resolution. Whether we bring our enemies to justice, or bring justice to our enemies, justice will be done. (Applause.)

I thank the Congress for its leadership at such an important time. All of America was touched on the evening of the tragedy to see Republicans and

Democrats joined together on the steps of this Capitol, singing "God Bless America." And you did more than sing; you acted, by delivering $40 billion to rebuild our communities and meet the needs of our military. [. . .]

And on behalf of the American people, I thank the world for its outpouring of support. America will never forget the sounds of our National Anthem playing at Buckingham Palace, on the streets of Paris, and at Berlin's Brandenburg Gate. [. . .]

On September the 11th, enemies of freedom committed an act of war against our country. Americans have known wars—but for the past 136 years, they have been wars on foreign soil, except for one Sunday in 1941. Americans have known the casualties of war—but not at the center of a great city on a peaceful morning. Americans have known surprise attacks—but never before on thousands of civilians. All of this was brought upon us in a single day—and night fell on a different world, a world where freedom itself is under attack.

Americans have many questions tonight. Americans are asking: Who attacked our country? The evidence we have gathered all points to a collection of loosely affiliated terrorist organizations known as al Qaeda. They are the same murderers indicted for bombing American embassies in Tanzania and Kenya, and responsible for bombing the USS Cole.

Al Qaeda is to terror what the mafia is to crime. But its goal is not making money; its goal is remaking the world—and imposing its radical beliefs on people everywhere.

The terrorists practice a fringe form of Islamic extremism that has been rejected by Muslim scholars and the vast majority of Muslim clerics—a fringe movement that perverts the peaceful teachings of Islam. The terrorists' directive commands them to kill Christians and Jews, to kill all Americans, and make no distinction among military and civilians, including women and children.

This group and its leader—a person named Osama bin Laden—are linked to many other organizations in different countries, including the Egyptian Islamic Jihad and the Islamic Movement of Uzbekistan. There are thousands of these terrorists in more than 60 countries. They are recruited from their own nations and neighborhoods and brought to camps in places like Afghanistan, where they are trained in the tactics of terror. They are sent back to their homes or sent to hide in countries around the world to plot evil and destruction.

The leadership of al Qaeda has great influence in Afghanistan and supports the Taliban regime in controlling most of that country. In Afghanistan, we see al Qaeda's vision for the world. [. . .]

The United States respects the people of Afghanistan—after all, we are currently its largest source of humanitarian aid—but we condemn the Taliban regime. (Applause.) It is not only repressing its own people, it is threatening people everywhere by sponsoring and sheltering and supplying terrorists. By aiding and abetting murder, the Taliban regime is committing murder.

And tonight, the United States of America makes the following demands on the Taliban: Deliver to United States authorities all the leaders of al Qaeda who hide in your land. (Applause.) Release all foreign nationals, including American citizens, you have unjustly imprisoned. Protect foreign journalists, diplomats and aid workers in your country. Close immediately and permanently every terrorist training camp in Afghanistan, and hand over every terrorist, and every person in their support structure, to appropriate authorities. (Applause.) Give the United States full access to terrorist training camps, so we can make sure they are no longer operating.

These demands are not open to negotiation or discussion. (Applause.) The Taliban must act, and act immediately. They will hand over the terrorists, or they will share in their fate. [. . .]

Our war on terror begins with al Qaeda, but it does not end there. It will not end until every terrorist group of global reach has been found, stopped and defeated. (Applause.)

Americans are asking, why do they hate us? They hate what we see right here in this chamber—a democratically elected government. Their leaders are self-appointed. They hate our freedoms—our freedom of religion, our freedom of speech, our freedom to vote and assemble and disagree with each other.

They want to overthrow existing governments in many Muslim countries, such as Egypt, Saudi Arabia, and Jordan. They want to drive Israel out of the Middle East. They want to drive Christians and Jews out of vast regions of Asia and Africa.

These terrorists kill not merely to end lives, but to disrupt and end a way of life. With every atrocity, they hope that America grows fearful, retreating from the world and forsaking our friends. They stand against us, because we stand in their way. [. . .]

Americans are asking: How will we fight and win this war? We will direct every resource at our command—every means of diplomacy, every tool of intelligence, every instrument of law enforcement, every financial influence, and every necessary weapon of war—to the disruption and to the defeat of the global terror network.

This war will not be like the war against Iraq a decade ago, with a decisive liberation of territory and a swift conclusion. It will not look like the air war above Kosovo two years ago, where no ground troops were used and not a single American was lost in combat.

Our response involves far more than instant retaliation and isolated strikes. Americans should not expect one battle, but a lengthy campaign, unlike any other we have ever seen. It may include dramatic strikes, visible on TV, and covert operations, secret even in success. We will starve terrorists of funding, turn them one against another, drive them from place to place, until there is no refuge or no rest. And we will pursue nations that provide aid or safe haven to terrorism. Every nation, in every region, now has a decision to make. Either you are with us, or you are with the terrorists. (Applause.) From this day forward, any nation that continues to harbor or support terrorism will be regarded by the United States as a hostile regime.

Our nation has been put on notice: We are not immune from attack. We will take defensive measures against terrorism to protect Americans. Today, dozens of federal departments and agencies, as well as state and local governments, have responsibilities affecting homeland security. These efforts must be coordinated at the highest level. So tonight I announce the creation of a Cabinet-level position reporting directly to me—the Office of Homeland Security.

And tonight I also announce a distinguished American to lead this effort, to strengthen American security: a military veteran, an effective governor, a true patriot, a trusted friend—Pennsylvania's Tom Ridge. (Applause.) He will lead, oversee and coordinate a comprehensive national strategy to safeguard our country against terrorism, and respond to any attacks that may come.

These measures are essential. But the only way to defeat terrorism as a threat to our way of life is to stop it, eliminate it, and destroy it where it grows. (Applause.) [. . .]

This is not, however, just America's fight. And what is at stake is not just America's freedom. This is the world's fight. This is civilization's fight. This is the fight of all who believe in progress and pluralism, tolerance and freedom.

We ask every nation to join us. We will ask, and we will need, the help of police forces, intelligence services, and banking systems around the world. The United States is grateful that many nations and many international organizations have already responded—with sympathy and with support. Nations from Latin America, to Asia, to Africa, to Europe, to the Islamic world. Perhaps the NATO Charter reflects best the attitude of the world: An attack on one is an attack on all.

The civilized world is rallying to America's side. They understand that if this terror goes unpunished, their own cities, their own citizens may be next. Terror, unanswered, can not only bring down buildings, it can threaten the stability of legitimate governments. And you know what—we're not going to allow it. (Applause.)

Americans are asking: What is expected of us? I ask you to live your lives, and hug your children. I know many citizens have fears tonight, and I ask you to be calm and resolute, even in the face of a continuing threat.

I ask you to uphold the values of America, and remember why so many have come here. We are in a fight for our principles, and our first responsibility is to live by them. No one should be singled out for unfair treatment or unkind words because of their ethnic background or religious faith. (Applause.) [. . .]

I ask your continued participation and confidence in the American economy. Terrorists attacked a symbol of American prosperity. They did not touch its source. America is successful because of the hard work, and creativity, and enterprise of our people. These were the true strengths of our economy before September 11th, and they are our strengths today. (Applause.) [. . .]

Tonight, we face new and sudden national challenges. We will come together to improve air safety, to dramatically expand the number of air marshals on domestic flights, and take new measures to prevent hijacking. We will come together to promote stability and keep our airlines flying, with direct assistance during this emergency. (Applause.)

We will come together to give law enforcement the additional tools it needs to track down terror here at home. (Applause.) We will come together to strengthen our intelligence capabilities to know the plans of terrorists before they act, and find them before they strike. (Applause.)

We will come together to take active steps that strengthen America's economy, and put our people back to work. [. . .]

After all that has just passed—all the lives taken, and all the possibilities and hopes that died with them—it is natural to wonder if America's future is one of fear. Some speak of an age of terror. I know there are struggles ahead, and dangers to face. But this country will define our times, not be defined by them. As long as the United States of America is determined and strong, this will not be an age of terror; this will be an age of liberty, here and across the world. (Applause.) [. . .]

Fellow citizens, we'll meet violence with patient justice—assured of the rightness of our cause, and confident of the victories to come. In all that lies before us, may God grant us wisdom, and may He watch over the United States of America.

Thank you. (Applause.)

Source: White House Press Office. Available online. URL: http://www.whitehouse.gov/news/releases/2001/09/20010920-8.html.

Fact Sheet: Executive Order to Curtail Financial Support of Terrorism (September 24, 2001)

Two weeks after 9/11, President George W. Bush issued an executive order expanding the mechanisms to deprive terrorists of funding.

"We will starve terrorists of funding, turn them against each other, rout them out of their safe hiding places, and bring them to justice."

President George W. Bush, September 24, 2001

The President has directed the first strike on the global terror network today by issuing an Executive Order to starve terrorists of their support funds. The Order expands the Treasury Department's power to target the support structure of terrorist organizations, freeze the U.S. assets and block the U.S. transactions of terrorists and those that support them, and increases our ability to block U.S. assets of, and deny access to U.S. markets to, foreign banks who refuse to cooperate with U.S. authorities to identify and freeze terrorist assets abroad.

Disrupting the Financial Infrastructure of Terrorism

- Targets all individuals and institutions linked to global terrorism.
- Allows the Treasury Department to freeze U.S. assets and block U.S. transactions of any person or institution associated with terrorists or terrorist organizations.
- Names specific individuals and organizations whose assets and transactions are to be blocked.
- Identifies charitable organizations that secretly funnel money to al-Qaeda.
- Provides donors information about charitable groups who fund terrorist organizations.
- States the President's intent to punish those financial institutions at home and abroad that continue to provide resources and/or services to terrorist organizations.

Authorities Broadened

The new Executive order broadens existing authority in three principal ways:

- It expands the coverage of existing Executive orders from terrorism in the Middle East to global terrorism;
- The Order expands the class of targeted groups to include all those who are "associated with" designated terrorist groups; and
- Establishes our ability to block the U.S. assets of, and deny access to U.S. markets to, those foreign banks that refuse to freeze terrorist assets.

Blocking Terrorist Assets

- The Order prohibits U.S. transactions with those terrorist organizations, leaders, and corporate and charitable fronts listed in the Annex.
- Eleven terrorist organizations are listed in the Order, including organizations that make up the al-Qaeda network.
- A dozen terrorist leaders are listed, including Osama bin Ladin and his chief lieutenants, three charitable organizations, and one corporate front organization are identified as well.
- The Order authorizes the Secretary of State and the Secretary of the Treasury to make additional terrorist designations in the coming weeks and months.

Other Actions in War on Terrorist Financing

This Executive Order is part of a broader strategy that we have developed for suppressing terrorist financing:

- A Foreign Terrorist Asset Tracking Center (FTAT) is up and running. The FTAT is a multi-agency task force that will identify the network of terrorist funding and freeze assets before new acts of terrorism take place.
- The President, the Secretary of the Treasury, the Secretary of State and others are working with our allies around the world to tackle the financial underpinnings of terrorism. We are working through the G-8 and the United Nations. Already, several of our allies, including Switzerland and Britain, have frozen accounts of suspected terrorists.

Source: White House Press Office. Available online. URL: http:/www.whitehouse.gov/news/releases/2001/09/print/20010924-2.html.

State of the Union Address (January 29, 2002)

President George W. Bush used his 2002 State of the Union Address to request increased funding for homeland security programs. He also detailed the U.S. defeat of the Taliban forces (al-Qaeda sponsors) in Afghanistan. Most important, in this speech Bush first invoked the concept of an "axis of evil," consisting of Iran, North Korea, and Iraq as sponsors of terrorism.

The President's State of the Union Address
The United States Capitol
Washington, D.C.
January 29, 2002

THE PRESIDENT: Thank you very much. Mr. Speaker, Vice President Cheney, members of Congress, distinguished guests, fellow citizens: As we gather tonight, our nation is at war, our economy is in recession, and the civilized world faces unprecedented dangers. Yet the state of our Union has never been stronger. (Applause.) [. . .]

Our cause is just, and it continues. Our discoveries in Afghanistan confirmed our worst fears, and showed us the true scope of the task ahead. We have seen the depth of our enemies' hatred in videos, where they laugh about the loss of innocent life. And the depth of their hatred is equaled by the madness of the destruction they design. We have found diagrams of American nuclear power plants and public water facilities, detailed instructions for making chemical weapons, surveillance maps of American cities, and thorough descriptions of landmarks in America and throughout the world.

What we have found in Afghanistan confirms that, far from ending there, our war against terror is only beginning. Most of the 19 men who hijacked planes on September the 11th were trained in Afghanistan's camps, and so were tens of thousands of others. Thousands of dangerous killers, schooled in the methods of murder, often supported by outlaw regimes, are now spread throughout the world like ticking time bombs, set to go off without warning.

Thanks to the work of our law enforcement officials and coalition partners, hundreds of terrorists have been arrested. Yet, tens of thousands of trained terrorists are still at large. These enemies view the entire world as a battlefield, and we must pursue them wherever they are. (Applause.) So long as training camps operate, so long as nations harbor terrorists, freedom is at risk. And America and our allies must not, and will not, allow it. (Applause.)

Our nation will continue to be steadfast and patient and persistent in the pursuit of two great objectives. First, we will shut down terrorist camps, disrupt terrorist plans, and bring terrorists to justice. And, second, we must prevent the terrorists and regimes who seek chemical, biological or nuclear weapons from threatening the United States and the world. (Applause.)

Our military has put the terror training camps of Afghanistan out of business, yet camps still exist in at least a dozen countries. A terrorist underworld—including groups like Hamas, Hezbollah, Islamic Jihad, Jaish-i-Mohammed—operates in remote jungles and deserts, and hides in the centers of large cities. [. . .]

My hope is that all nations will heed our call, and eliminate the terrorist parasites who threaten their countries and our own. Many nations are acting forcefully. Pakistan is now cracking down on terror, and I admire the strong leadership of President Musharraf. (Applause.)

But some governments will be timid in the face of terror. And make no mistake about it: If they do not act, America will. (Applause.)

Our second goal is to prevent regimes that sponsor terror from threatening America or our friends and allies with weapons of mass destruction. Some of these regimes have been pretty quiet since September the 11th. But we know their true nature. North Korea is a regime arming with missiles and weapons of mass destruction, while starving its citizens.

Iran aggressively pursues these weapons and exports terror, while an unelected few repress the Iranian people's hope for freedom.

Iraq continues to flaunt its hostility toward America and to support terror. The Iraqi regime has plotted to develop anthrax, and nerve gas, and nuclear weapons for over a decade. This is a regime that has already used poison gas to murder thousands of its own citizens—leaving the bodies of mothers huddled over their dead children. This is a regime that agreed to international inspections—then kicked out the inspectors. This is a regime that has something to hide from the civilized world.

States like these, and their terrorist allies, constitute an axis of evil, arming to threaten the peace of the world. By seeking weapons of mass destruction, these regimes pose a grave and growing danger. They could provide these arms to terrorists, giving them the means to match their hatred. They could attack our allies or attempt to blackmail the United States. In any of these cases, the price of indifference would be catastrophic.

We will work closely with our coalition to deny terrorists and their state sponsors the materials, technology, and expertise to make and deliver weapons of mass destruction. We will develop and deploy effective missile defenses to protect America and our allies from sudden attack. (Applause.)

And all nations should know: America will do what is necessary to ensure our nation's security.

We'll be deliberate, yet time is not on our side. I will not wait on events, while dangers gather. I will not stand by, as peril draws closer and closer. The United States of America will not permit the world's most dangerous regimes to threaten us with the world's most destructive weapons. (Applause.)

Our war on terror is well begun, but it is only begun. This campaign may not be finished on our watch—yet it must be and it will be waged on our watch. [. . .]

Our first priority must always be the security of our nation, and that will be reflected in the budget I send to Congress. My budget supports three great goals for America: We will win this war; we'll protect our homeland; and we will revive our economy. [. . .]

My budget nearly doubles funding for a sustained strategy of homeland security, focused on four key areas: bioterrorism, emergency response, airport and border security, and improved intelligence. We will develop vaccines to fight anthrax and other deadly diseases. We'll increase funding to help states and communities train and equip our heroic police and firefighters. (Applause.) We will improve intelligence collection and sharing, expand patrols at our borders, strengthen the security of air travel, and use technology to track the arrivals and departures of visitors to the United States. (Applause.)

Homeland security will make America not only stronger, but, in many ways, better. Knowledge gained from bioterrorism research will improve public health. Stronger police and fire departments will mean safer neighborhoods. Stricter border enforcement will help combat illegal drugs. (Applause.) And as government works to better secure our homeland, America will continue to depend on the eyes and ears of alert citizens. [. . .]

Once we have funded our national security and our homeland security, the final great priority of my budget is economic security for the American people. (Applause.) To achieve these great national objectives—to win the war, protect the homeland, and revitalize our economy—our budget will run a deficit that will be small and short-term, so long as Congress restrains spending and acts in a fiscally responsible manner. (Applause.) We have clear priorities and we must act at home with the same purpose and resolve we have shown overseas: We'll prevail in the war, and we will defeat this recession. (Applause.) . . .

The last time I spoke here, I expressed the hope that life would return to normal. In some ways, it has. In others, it never will. Those of us who have lived through these challenging times have been changed by them. We've come to know truths that we will never question: evil is real, and it must be opposed. (Applause.) Beyond all differences of race or creed, we are one country, mourning together and facing danger together. Deep in the American character, there is honor, and it is stronger than cynicism. And many have discovered again that even in tragedy—especially in tragedy—God is near. (Applause.)

In a single instant, we realized that this will be a decisive decade in the history of liberty, that we've been called to a unique role in human events. Rarely has the world faced a choice more clear or consequential.

Our enemies send other people's children on missions of suicide and murder. They embrace tyranny and death as a cause and a creed. We stand for a different choice, made long ago, on the day of our founding. We affirm it again today. We choose freedom and the dignity of every life. (Applause.)

Steadfast in our purpose, we now press on. We have known freedom's price. We have shown freedom's power. And in this great conflict, my fellow Americans, we will see freedom's victory.

Thank you all. May God bless. (Applause.)

Source: White House Press Office. Available online. URL: http://www.whitehouse.gov/news/releases/2002/01/print/20020129-11.html.

George W. Bush Classifies Jose Padilla as Enemy Combatant (June 9, 2002)

In this letter to Defense Secretary Donald Rumsfeld, President George W. Bush classifies Jose Padilla as an enemy combatant. A suspected al-Qaeda sympathizer, Padilla had been exempt from the military tribunal investigation system because he was a U.S. citizen.

TO THE SECRETARY OF DEFENSE:

Based on the information available to me from all sources,

REDACTED

In accordance with the Constitution and consistent with the laws of the United States, including the Authorization for Use of Military Force Joint Resolution (Public Law 107-40);

I, GEORGE W. BUSH, as President of the United States and Commander in Chief of the U.S. armed forces, hereby DETERMINE for the United States of America that:

(1) Jose Padilla, who is under the control of the Department of Justice and who is a U.S. citizen, is, and at the time he entered the United States in May 2002 was, an enemy combatant;

(2) Mr. Padilla is closely associated with al Qaeda, an international terrorist organization with which the United States is at war;

(3) Mr. Padilla engaged in conduct that constituted hostile and war-like acts, including conduct in preparation for acts of international terrorism that had the aim to cause injury to or adverse effects on the United States;

(4) Mr. Padilla possesses intelligence, including intelligence about personnel and activities of al Qaeda, that, if communicated to the U.S., would aid U.S. efforts to prevent attacks by al Qaeda on the United States or its armed forces, other governmental personnel, or citizens;

(5) Mr. Padilla represents a continuing, present and grave danger to the national security of the United States, and detention of Mr. Padilla is necessary to prevent him from aiding al Qaeda in its efforts to attack the United States or its armed forces, other governmental personnel, or citizens;

(6) it is in the interest of the United States that the Secretary of Defense detain Mr. Padilla as an enemy combatant; and

(7) it is, REDACTED consistent with U.S. law and the laws of war for the Secretary of Defense to detain Mr. Padilla as an enemy combatant.

Accordingly, you are directed to receive Mr. Padilla from the Department of Justice and to detain him as an enemy combatant.

DATE: [June 9, 2002]
George W. Bush
[Signature]

Source: White House Office-controlled Document. Available online. URL: http://www.sourcewatch.org/index.php?title=GW_Bush%27s_Padi!!a_Designation.

5

International Documents

The primary sources reproduced in this chapter are divided into three sections: international treaties, regional agreements, and documents related to specific countries or groups. The first section is arranged thematically, while the other sections are in chronological order. Documents that have been excerpted are identified as such; all others are reproduced in full.

INTERNATIONAL CONVENTIONS AND TREATIES RELATING TO TERRORISM

Convention on Offences and Certain Other Acts Committed On Board Aircraft (1963) (excerpts)

This first international terrorism agreement, known as the Tokyo Convention, focuses on in-flight safety only. It authorizes the aircraft commander (pilot) to impose reasonable measures, including restraint, on any person he or she has reason to believe has committed or is about to commit such an act, when necessary to protect the safety of the aircraft. Once the disrupted flight lands, the convention requires contracting states to take custody of offenders and to return control of the aircraft to the lawful commander.

CHAPTER I
SCOPE OF THE CONVENTION

Article 1

1. This Convention shall apply in respect of:

offences against penal law;

a. acts which, whether or not they are offences, may or do jeopardize the safety of the aircraft or of persons or property therein or which jeopardize good order and discipline on board.

2. Except as provided in Chapter III, this Convention shall apply in respect of offences committed or acts done by a person on board any aircraft registered in a Contracting State, while that aircraft is in flight or on the surface of the high seas or of any other area outside the territory of any State.

3. For the purposes of this Convention, an aircraft is considered to be in flight from the moment when power is applied for the purpose of take-off until the moment when the landing run ends.

4. This Convention shall not apply to aircraft used in military, customs or police services.

Article 2

Without prejudice to the provisions of Article 4 and except when the safety of the aircraft or of persons or property on board so requires, no provision of this Convention shall be interpreted as authorizing or requiring any action in respect of offences against penal laws of a political nature or those based on racial or religious discrimination.

CHAPTER III

POWERS OF THE AIRCRAFT COMMANDER

Article 5

1. The provisions of this Chapter shall not apply to offences and acts committed or about to be committed by a person on board an aircraft in flight in the airspace of the State of registration or over the high seas or any other area outside the territory of any State unless the last point of take-off or the next point of intended landing is situated in a State other than that of registration, or the aircraft subsequently flies in the airspace of a State other than that of registration with such person still on board.

2. Notwithstanding the provisions of Article 1, paragraph 3, an aircraft shall for the purposes of this Chapter, be considered to be in flight at any time from the moment when all its external doors are closed following embarkation until the moment when any such door is opened for disembarkation. In the case of a forced landing, the provisions of this Chapter shall continue to apply with respect to offences and acts committed on board until competent authorities of a State take over the responsibility for the aircraft and for the persons and property on board.

Article 6

1. The aircraft commander may, when he has reasonable grounds to believe that a person has committed, or is about to commit, on board the aircraft, an offence or act contemplated in Article 1, paragraph 1, impose upon such person reasonable measures including restraint which are necessary:

- to protect the safety of the aircraft, or of persons or property therein; or
- to maintain good order and discipline on board; or
- to enable him to deliver such person to competent authorities or to disembark him in accordance with the provisions of this Chapter.

2. The aircraft commander may require or authorize the assistance of other crew members and may request or authorize, but not require, the assistance of passengers to restrain any person whom he is entitled to restrain. Any crew member or passenger may also take reasonable preventive measures without such authorization when he has reasonable grounds to believe that such action is immediately necessary to protect the safety of the aircraft, or of persons or property therein.

Article 8

1. The aircraft commander may, in so far as it is necessary for the purpose of subparagraph (a) or (b) or paragraph 1 of Article 6, disembark in the territory of any State in which the aircraft lands any person who he has reasonable grounds to believe has committed, or is about to commit, on board the aircraft an act contemplated in Article 1, paragraph 1(b).

2. The aircraft commander shall report to the authorities of the State in which he disembarks any person pursuant to this Article, the fact of, and the reasons for, such disembarkation.

Article 9

1. The aircraft commander may deliver to the competent authorities of any Contracting State in the territory of which the aircraft lands any person who he has reasonable grounds to believe has committed on board the aircraft an act which, in his opinion, is a serious offence according to the penal law of the State of registration of the aircraft.

2. The aircraft commander shall as soon as practicable and if possible before landing in the territory of a Contracting State with a person on board whom

the aircraft commander intends to deliver in accordance with the preceding paragraph, notify the authorities of such State of his intention to deliver such person and the reasons therefor.

3. The aircraft commander shall furnish the authorities to whom any suspected offender is delivered in accordance with the provisions of this Article with evidence and information which, under the law of the State of registration of the aircraft, are lawfully in his possession.

Article 10

For actions taken in accordance with this Convention, neither the aircraft commander, any other member of the crew, any passenger, the owner or operator of the aircraft, nor the person on whose behalf the flight was performed shall be held responsible in any proceeding on account of the treatment undergone by the person against whom the actions were taken.

Source: United Nations Office on Drugs and Crime. Available online. URL: http://www.unodc.org/unodc/terrorism_convention_aircraft.html. Accessed on April 2, 2007.

Convention for the Suppression of Unlawful Acts Against the Safety of Civil Aviation (1971) (excerpts)

Known as the "Montreal Convention," this act focuses on specific types of aviation sabotage, such as bombings aboard an aircraft already in flight. Specifically, it becomes unlawful for any person to perform an act of violence intentionally against a person on board an aircraft in flight, if that act is likely to endanger the safety of that aircraft; to place an explosive device on an aircraft; and to attempt such acts or be an accomplice of a person who performs or attempts to perform such acts. As with other Conventions, this agreement requires cooperation in extradition and prosecution.

The States Parties to the Convention

[. . .]

Have agreed as follows:

Article 1

1. Any person commits an offence if he unlawfully and intentionally:

- performs an act of violence against a person on board an aircraft in flight if that act is likely to endanger the safety of that aircraft; or

- destroys an aircraft in service or causes damage to such an aircraft which renders it incapable of flight or which is likely to endanger its safety in flight; or
- places or causes to be placed on an aircraft in service, by any means whatsoever, a device or substance which is likely to destroy that aircraft, or to cause damage to it which renders it incapable of flight, or to cause damage to it which is likely to endanger its safety in flight; or
- destroys or damages air navigation facilities or interferes with their operation, if any such act is likely to endanger the safety of aircraft in flight; or
- communicates information which he knows to be false, thereby endangering the safety of an aircraft in flight.

2. Any person also commits an offence if he:

- attempts to commit any of the offences mentioned in paragraph 1 of this Article; or
- is an accomplice of a person who commits or attempts to commit any such offence.

Article 2

For the purposes of this Convention:

- an aircraft is considered to be in flight at any time from the moment when all its external doors are closed following embarkation until the moment when any such door is opened for disembarkation; in the case of a forced landing, the flight shall be deemed to continue until the competent authorities take over the responsibility for the aircraft and for persons and property on board;
- an aircraft is considered to be in service from the beginning of the preflight preparation of the aircraft by ground personnel or by the crew for a specific flight until twenty-four hours after any landing; the period of service shall, in any event, extend for the entire period during which the aircraft is in flight as defined in paragraph (a) of this Article.

Article 3

Each Contracting State undertakes to make the offences mentioned in Article 1 punishable by severe penalties.

Source: United Nations Office on Drugs and Crime. Available online. URL: http://www.unodc.org/unodc/terrorism_convention_civil_aviation.html.

International Convention Against the Taking of Hostages (1979) (excerpt)

The Hostages Convention makes it illegal to seize or detain an individual in order to compel a third party, such as a state or international intergovernmental organization, to take a particular action to secure the release of the hostage. Article 3 does not prohibit states from paying ransoms. In 1978 members of the Group of Seven industrialized countries had mutually agreed to not pay ransoms.

ARTICLE 1

1. Any person who seizes or detains and threatens to kill, to injure or to continue to detain another person (hereinafter referred to as the "hostage") in order to compel a third party, namely, a State, an international intergovernmental organization, a natural or juridical person, or a group of persons, to do or abstain from doing any act as an explicit or implicit condition for the release of the hostage commits the offence of taking of hostages ("hostage-taking") within the meaning of this Convention.

2. Any person who:

- attempts to commit an act of hostage-taking, or
- participates as an accomplice of anyone who commits or attempts to commit an act of hostage-taking likewise commits an offence for the purposes of this Convention.

ARTICLE 4

States Parties shall co-operate in the prevention of the offences set forth in article 1, particularly by:

- taking all practicable measures to prevent preparations in their respective territories for the commission of those offences within or outside their territories, including measures to prohibit in their territories illegal activities of persons, groups and organizations that encourage, instigate, organize or engage in the perpetration of acts of taking of hostages;
- exchanging information and co-ordinating the taking of administrative and other measures as appropriate to prevent the commission of those offences.

Source: United Nations Office on Drugs and Crime. Available online. URL: http://www.unodc.org/unodc/terrorism_convention_hostages.html. Accessed on April 2, 2007.

Convention on the Physical Protection of Nuclear Material (1980) (excerpt)

Commonly known as the Nuclear Materials Convention, this agreement criminalizes the unlawful possession, use, transfer, etc., of nuclear material, the theft of nuclear material, and threats to use nuclear material to cause death or serious injury to any person or substantial property damage. The convention is binding upon states, thereby undercutting its usefulness for prosecuting individuals or non-state terrorist groups that acquire nuclear materials.

ARTICLE 1

For the purposes of this Convention:

- "nuclear material" means plutonium except that with isotopic concentration exceeding 80% in plutonium-238; uranium-233; uranium enriched in the isotopes 235 or 233; uranium containing the mixture of isotopes as occurring in nature other than in the form of ore or ore-residue; any material containing one or more of the foregoing;

- "uranium enriched in the isotope 235 or 233" means uranium containing the isotopes 235 or 233 or both in an amount such that the abundance ratio of the sum of these isotopes to the isotope 238 is greater than the ratio of the isotope 235 to the isotope 238 occurring in nature;

- "international nuclear transport" means the carriage of a consignment of nuclear material by any means of transportation intended to go beyond the territory of the State where the shipment originates beginning with the departure from a facility of the shipper in that State and ending with the arrival at a facility of the receiver within the State of ultimate destination.

ARTICLE 2

1. This Convention shall apply to nuclear material used for peaceful purposes while in international nuclear transport.

2. With the exception of articles 3 and 4 and paragraph 3 of article 5, this Convention shall also apply to nuclear material used for peaceful purposes while in domestic use, storage and transport.

3. Apart from the commitments expressly undertaken by States Parties in the articles covered by paragraph 2 with respect to nuclear material used for peaceful purposes while in domestic use, storage and transport, nothing in this Convention shall be interpreted as affecting the sovereign rights of a State regarding the domestic use, storage and transport of such nuclear material.

ARTICLE 3

Each State Party shall take appropriate steps within the framework of its national law and consistent with international law to ensure as far as practicable that, during international nuclear transport, nuclear material within its territory, or on board a ship or aircraft under its jurisdiction insofar as such ship or aircraft is engaged in the transport to or from that State, is protected at the levels described in Annex 1.

Source: United Nations Office on Drugs and Crime. Available online. URL: http://www.unodc.org/unodc/terrorism_convention_nuclear_material.html. Accessed on April 2, 2007.

Convention on the Marking of Plastic Explosives for the Purpose of Detection (1991) (excerpts)

Pan Am Flight 103 was destroyed in 1988 by a bomb using a plastic explosive that was not detectable using conventional X-ray scans. Therefore, this treaty has two purposes: It requires chemical marking to facilitate detection of plastic explosives and also requires parties to ensure effective control over any "unmarked" plastic explosive. It details a variety of detection agents in an accompanying Technical Annex to the treaty.

Article 1

For the purposes of this Convention:

1. "Explosives" mean explosive products, commonly known as "plastic explosives", including explosives in flexible or elastic sheet form, as described in the Technical Annex to this Convention.

2. "Detection agent" means a substance as described in the Technical Annex to this Convention which is introduced into an explosive to render it detectable.

3. "Marking" means introducing into an explosive a detection agent in accordance with the Technical Annex to this Convention.

4. "Manufacture" means any process, including reprocessing, that produces explosives.

5. "Duly authorized military devices" include, but are not restricted to, shells, bombs, projectiles, mines, missiles, rockets, shaped charges, grenades and perforators manufactured exclusively for military or police purposes according to the laws and regulations of the State Party concerned.

6. "Producer State" means any State in whose territory explosives are manufactured.

Article 2

Each State Party shall take the necessary and effective measures to prohibit and prevent the manufacture in its territory of unmarked explosives.

Article 3

1. Each State Party shall take the necessary and effective measures to prohibit and prevent the movement into or out of its territory of unmarked explosives.

2. The preceding paragraph shall not apply in respect of movements for purposes not inconsistent with the objectives of this Convention, by authorities of a State Party performing military or police functions, of unmarked explosives under the control of that State Party in accordance with paragraph 1 of Article IV. . . .

Source: United Nations Office on Drugs and Crime. Available online. URL: http://www.unodc.org/unodc/terrorism_convention_plastic_explosives.html. Accessed on April 2, 2007.

International Convention for the Suppression of Terrorist Bombing (1998) (excerpt)

The UN General Assembly formulated this convention as a response to the increasing occurrence of terrorist attacks by means of explosives or other lethal devices and the lack of multilateral legal provisions to address adequately such attacks. The Convention seeks to enhance international cooperation between states in devising and adopting effective and practical measures for the prevention of such acts of terrorism and for the prosecution and punishment of their perpetrators. Specifically, it focuses on actions intentionally using explosives and other lethal devices in, into, or against various public places with intent to kill, cause serious bodily injury, or cause extensive destruction.

Article 1

For the purposes of this Convention

1. "State or government facility" includes any permanent or temporary facility or conveyance that is used or occupied by representatives of a State, members of Government, the legislature or the judiciary or by officials or employees of a

State or any other public authority or entity or by employees or officials of an intergovernmental organization in connection with their official duties.

2. "Infrastructure facility" means any publicly or privately owned facility providing or distributing services for the benefit of the public, such as water, sewage, energy, fuel or communications.

3. "Explosive or other lethal device" means:

- An explosive or incendiary weapon or device that is designed, or has the capability, to cause death, serious bodily injury or substantial material damage; or
- A weapon or device that is designed, or has the capability, to cause death, serious bodily injury or substantial material damage through the release, dissemination or impact of toxic chemicals, biological agents or toxins or similar substances or radiation or radioactive material.

4. "Military forces of a State" means the armed forces of a State which are organized, trained and equipped under its internal law for the primary purpose of national defence or security and persons acting in support of those armed forces who are under their formal command, control and responsibility.

5. "Place of public use" means those parts of any building, land, street, waterway or other location that are accessible or open to members of the public, whether continuously, periodically or occasionally, and encompasses any commercial, business, cultural, historical, educational, religious, governmental, entertainment, recreational or similar place that is so accessible or open to the public.

6. "Public transportation system" means all facilities, conveyances and instrumentalities, whether publicly or privately owned, that are used in or for publicly available services for the transportation of persons or cargo.

Article 2

1. Any person commits an offence within the meaning of this Convention if that person unlawfully and intentionally delivers, places, discharges or detonates an explosive or other lethal device in, into or against a place of public use, a State or government facility, a public transportation system or an infrastructure facility:

- With the intent to cause death or serious bodily injury; or
- With the intent to cause extensive destruction of such a place, facility or system, where such destruction results in or is likely to result in major economic loss.

2. Any person also commits an offence if that person attempts to commit an offence as set forth in paragraph 1 of the present article.

3. Any person also commits an offence if that person:

- Participates as an accomplice in an offence as set forth in paragraph 1 or 2 of the present article; or
- Organizes or directs others to commit an offence as set forth in paragraph 1 or 2 of the present article; or
- In any other way contributes to the commission of one or more offences as set forth in paragraph 1 or 2 of the present article by a group of persons acting with a common purpose; such contribution shall be intentional and either be made with the aim of furthering the general criminal activity or purpose of the group or be made in the knowledge of the intention of the group to commit the offence or offences concerned.

Source: United Nations Office on Drugs and Crime. Available online. URL: http://www.unodc.org/unodc/terrorism_convention_terrorist_bombing.html. Accessed on April 2, 2007.

International Convention for the Suppression of the Financing of Terrorism (1999) (excerpt)

This convention requires governments to eliminate activities that finance terrorists, such as groups claiming to have charitable, social, or cultural goals or that also engage in such illicit activities as drug trafficking or gun running. The agreement calls on states to prosecute individuals or organizations who finance or assist terrorism and allows for the identification, freezing, and seizure of funds allocated for terrorist activities. Most important, it eliminates many arguments for refusing to cooperate, such as the invocation of bank secrecy.

Article 1

For the purposes of this Convention:

1. "Funds" means assets of every kind, whether tangible or intangible, movable or immovable, however acquired, and legal documents or instruments in any form, including electronic or digital, evidencing title to, or interest in, such assets, including, but not limited to, bank credits, travellers cheques, bank cheques, money orders, shares, securities, bonds, drafts and letters of credit.

2. "State or government facility" means any permanent or temporary facility or conveyance that is used or occupied by representatives of a State,

members of Government, the legislature or the judiciary or by officials or employees of a State or any other public authority or entity or by employees or officials of an intergovernmental organization in connection with their official duties.

3. "Proceeds" means any funds derived from or obtained, directly or indirectly, through the commission of an offence set forth in article 2.

Article 2

1. Any person commits an offence within the meaning of this Convention if that person by any means, directly or indirectly, unlawfully and wilfully, provides or collects funds with the intention that they should be used or in the knowledge that they are to be used, in full or in part, in order to carry out:

(a) An act which constitutes an offence within the scope of and as defined in one of the treaties listed in the annex; or

(b) Any other act intended to cause death or serious bodily injury to a civilian, or to any other person not taking an active part in the hostilities in a situation of armed conflict, when the purpose of such act, by its nature or context, is to intimidate a population, or to compel a Government or an international organization to do or to abstain from doing any act.

3. For an act to constitute an offence set forth in paragraph 1, it shall not be necessary that the funds were actually used to carry out an offence referred to in paragraph 1, subparagraph (a) or (b).

4. Any person also commits an offence if that person attempts to commit an offence as set forth in paragraph 1 of this article.

5. Any person also commits an offence if that person:

(a) Participates as an accomplice in an offence as set forth in paragraph 1 or 4 of this article;

(b) Organizes or directs others to commit an offence as set forth in paragraph 1 or 4 of this article;

(c) Contributes to the commission of one or more offences as set forth in paragraph 1 or 4 of this article by a group of persons acting with a common purpose.

Source: United Nations Office on Drugs and Crime. Available online. URL: http://www.unodc.org/unodc/resolution_2000-02-25_1.html. Accessed on April 2, 2007.

International Convention for the Suppression of Acts of Nuclear Terrorism, April 13, 2005 (excerpt)

This 13th international convention was adopted by the UN General Assembly on April 13, 2005. This convention focuses on the potential problem of nonstate actors (individuals or groups) acquiring nuclear weapons and calls upon members to enact legislation to prevent and prosecute persons attempting to do so.

Article 1

For the purposes of this Convention:

1. "Radioactive material" means nuclear material and other radioactive substances which contain nuclides which undergo spontaneous disintegration (a process accompanied by emission of one or more types of ionizing radiation, such as alpha-, beta-, neutron particles and gamma rays) and which may, owing to their radiological or fissile properties, cause death, serious bodily injury or substantial damage to property or to the environment.

2. "Nuclear material" means plutonium, except that with isotopic concentration exceeding 80 per cent in plutonium-238; uranium-233; uranium enriched in the isotopes 235 or 233; uranium containing the mixture of isotopes as occurring in nature other than in the form of ore or ore residue; or any material containing one or more of the foregoing; Whereby "uranium enriched in the isotope 235 or 233" means uranium containing the isotope 235 or 233 or both in an amount such that the abundance ratio of the sum of these isotopes to the isotope 238 is greater than the ratio of the isotope 235 to the isotope 238 occurring in nature.

3. "Nuclear facility" means:

(a) Any nuclear reactor, including reactors installed on vessels, vehicles, aircraft or space objects for use as an energy source in order to propel such vessels, vehicles, aircraft or space objects or for any other purpose;

(b) Any plant or conveyance being used for the production, storage, processing or transport of radioactive material.

4. "Device" means:

(a) Any nuclear explosive device; or

(b) Any radioactive material dispersal or radiation-emitting device which may, owing to its radiological properties, cause death, serious bodily injury or substantial damage to property or the environment.

5. "State or government facility" includes any permanent or temporary facility or conveyance that is used or occupied by representatives of a State, members of Government, the legislature or the judiciary or by officials or employees of a State or any other public authority or entity or by employees or officials of an intergovernmental organization in connection with their official duties.

6. "Military forces of a State" means the armed forces of a State which are organized, trained and equipped under its internal law for the primary purpose of national defence or security and persons acting in support of those armed forces who are under their formal command, control and responsibility.

Article 2

1. Any person commits an offence within the meaning of this Convention if that person unlawfully and intentionally:

(a) Possesses radioactive material or makes or possesses a device:

(i) With the intent to cause death or serious bodily injury; or

(ii) With the intent to cause substantial damage to property or the environment;

(b) Uses in any way radioactive material or a device, or uses or damages a nuclear facility in a manner which releases or risks the release of radioactive material:

(i) With the intent to cause death or serious bodily injury; or

(ii) With the intent to cause substantial damage to property or the environment; or

(iii) With the intent to compel a natural or legal person, an international organization or a State to do or refrain from doing an act.

2. Any person also commits an offence if that person:

(a) Threatens, under circumstances which indicate the credibility of the threat, to commit an offence as set forth in subparagraph 1

(b) of the present article; or

(b) Demands unlawfully and intentionally radioactive material, a device or a nuclear facility by threat, under circumstances which indicate the credibility of the threat, or by use of force.

3. Any person also commits an offence if that person attempts to commit an offence as set forth in paragraph 1 of the present article.

4. Any person also commits an offence if that person:

(a) Participates as an accomplice in an offence as set forth in paragraph 1, 2 or 3 of the present article; or

(b) Organizes or directs others to commit an offence as set forth in paragraph 1, 2 or 3 of the present article; or

(c) In any other way contributes to the commission of one or more offences as set forth in paragraph 1, 2 or 3 of the present article by a group of persons acting with a common purpose; such contribution shall be intentional and either be made with the aim of furthering the general criminal activity or purpose of the group or be made in the knowledge of the intention of the group to commit the offence or offences concerned.

Article 3

This Convention shall not apply where the offence is committed within a single State, the alleged offender and the victims are nationals of that State, the alleged offender is found in the territory of that State and no other State has a basis under article 9, paragraph 1 or paragraph 2, to exercise jurisdiction, except that the provisions of articles 7, 12, 14, 15, 16 and 17 shall, as appropriate, apply in those cases.

Source: United Nations Treaty Collection, Conventions on Terrorism. Available online. URL: http://untreaty.un.org/English/Terrorism.asp.

REGIONAL CONVENTIONS AND TREATIES RELATING TO TERRORISM

Council of Europe

European Convention on the Suppression of Terrorism (January 27, 1977) (excerpt)

Signed in Strasbourg on January 27, 1977, this landmark convention took the novel approach of considering terrorism as a phenomenon distinct from activities such as bombing or hijacking, but it specifically says (Article 1) terrorist actions should not be regarded as politically motivated attacks.

The member States of the Council of Europe, signatory hereto,

Considering that the aim of the Council of Europe is to achieve a greater unity between its members;

Aware of the growing concern caused by the increase in acts of terrorism;

Wishing to take effective measures to ensure that the perpetrators of such acts do not escape prosecution and punishment;

Convinced that extradition is a particularly effective measure for achieving this result,

Have agreed as follows:

Article 1

For the purposes of extradition between Contracting States, none of the following offences shall be regarded as a political offence or as an offence connected with a political offence or as an offence inspired by political motives:

a. an offence within the scope of the Convention for the Suppression of Unlawful Seizure of Aircraft, signed at The Hague on 16 December 1970;

b. an offence within the scope of the Convention for the Suppression of Unlawful Acts against the Safety of Civil Aviation, signed at Montreal on 23 September 1971;

c. a serious offence involving an attack against the life, physical integrity or liberty of internationally protected persons, including diplomatic agents;

d. an offence involving kidnapping, the taking of a hostage or serious unlawful detention;

e. an offence involving the use of a bomb, grenade, rocket, automatic firearm or letter or parcel bomb if this use endangers persons;

f. an attempt to commit any of the foregoing offences or participation as an accomplice of a person who commits or attempts to commit such an offence.

Article 2

a. For the purpose of extradition between Contracting States, a Contracting State may decide not to regard as a political offence or as an offence connected with a political offence or as an offence inspired by political motives a serious offence involving an act of violence, other than one covered by Article 1, against the life, physical integrity or liberty of a person.

b. The same shall apply to a serious offence involving an act against property, other than one covered by Article 1, if the act created a collective danger for persons.

c. The same shall apply to an attempt to commit any of the foregoing offences or participation as an accomplice of a person who commits or attempts to commit such an offence.

Article 3

The provisions of all extradition treaties and arrangements applicable between Contracting States, including the European Convention on Extradition, are modified as between Contracting States to the extent that they are incompatible with this Convention.

Article 4

For the purpose of this Convention and to the extent that any offence mentioned in Article 1 or 2 is not listed as an extraditable offence in any extradition convention or treaty existing between Contracting States, it shall be deemed to be included as such therein.

Article 5

Nothing in this Convention shall be interpreted as imposing an obligation to extradite if the requested State has substantial grounds for believing that the request for extradition for an offence mentioned in Article 1 or 2 has been made for the purpose of prosecuting or punishing a person on account of his race, religion, nationality or political opinion, or that that person's position may be prejudiced for any of these reasons.

Source: Council of Europe. Available online. URL: http://conventions.coe.int/Treaty/en/Treaties/Html/090.htm. Accessed on April 2, 2007.

Declaration on Terrorism by Committee of Ministers (November 1978)

One year after the Council of Europe's 1977 convention on terrorism, the organization moved to emphasize greater cooperation in pursuit of terrorist groups.

(Adopted by the Committee of Ministers at its 63rd Session, on 23 November 1978)

The Committee of Ministers of the Council of Europe,

1. Mindful of the recent increase in acts of terrorism in certain member states;

2. Considering that the prevention and suppression of such acts are indispensable to the maintenance of the democratic structure of member states;

3. Noting that the European Convention on the Suppression of Terrorism entered into force on 4 August 1978;

4. Considering that this convention represents an important contribution to the fight against terrorism;

5. Convinced that it is necessary further to develop and to strengthen international co-operation in this field,

I. Reaffirms the important role of the Council of Europe in the fight against terrorism as an Organisation of democratic states founded on the rule of law and committed to the protection of human rights and fundamental freedoms;

II. Emphasises the importance of the work being undertaken in the Council of Europe with a view to intensifying European co-operation in the fight against terrorism;

III. Decides that in this work priority should be given to the examination of the following questions:

a. means of rendering existing practices of international co-operation between the competent authorities simpler and more expeditious;

b. means of improving and speeding up the communication of information to any state concerned relating to the circumstances in which an act of terrorism was committeed, the measures taken against its author, the outcome of any judicial proceedings against him and the enforcement of any sentence passed;

c. problems arising where acts of terrorism have been committed within the jurisdiction of several states.

Source: The Avalon Project, Yale University. Available online. URL: http://www.yale.edu/lawweb/avalon/terrorism/t_0001.htm.

Conference of European Ministers of Justice, Resolution on Combating International Terrorism (2001)

Following the 9/11 attacks the European body called upon its members to join all existing international conventions on terrorism and the International Criminal Court. It also advocated the use of new investigative technology such as DNA.

24th Conference of European Ministers of Justice
4-5 October 2001, Moscow (Russian Federation)
Resolution No 1 on combating international terrorism

THE MINISTERS participating in the 24th Conference of European Ministers of Justice (Moscow, October 2001),

Condemning the heinous terrorist attacks in the United States of America on 11 September 2001;

Deploring the loss of life and the injuries suffered by thousands of innocent people as a result of these attacks as well as those in other regions of the world;

Expressing their deeply felt sympathy with the victims and their families;

Reaffirming their determination to combat all forms of terrorism;

Welcoming the declarations and decisions of international organisations condemning terrorism, in particular the Declaration adopted by the Committee of Ministers on 12 September 2001 and the Decision taken on 21 September 2001, and expressing their full support for the measures envisaged in this Decision;

Bearing in mind Parliamentary Assembly Recommendation 1534 (2001) on democracies facing terrorism;

Convinced of the need for a multidisciplinary approach to the problem of terrorism, involving all relevant legal aspects;

Resolved to play their part in States' efforts to reinforce the fight against terrorism and to increase the security of citizens, in a spirit of solidarity and on the basis of the common values to which the Council of Europe is firmly committed: Rule of Law, human rights and pluralist democracy;

Recognising the need to involve and motivate the public in this fight, including relevant organisational, social and educational measures;

Convinced of the urgent need for increased international co-operation,

CALL UPON member and observer States of the Council of Europe

a. to become Parties as soon as possible to the relevant international treaties relating to terrorism, in particular the International Convention for the Suppression of the Financing of Terrorism of 9 December 1999;

b. to participate actively in the elaboration of the draft United Nations comprehensive Convention on International Terrorism; and

c. to become Parties as soon as possible to the Statute of the International Criminal Court;

INVITE the Committee of Ministers urgently to adopt all normative measures considered necessary for assisting States to prevent, detect, prosecute and punish acts of terrorism, such as:

a. reviewing existing international instruments—conventions and recommendations, in particular the European Convention on the Suppression of Terrorism—and domestic law, with a view to improving and facilitating co-operation in the prosecution and punishment of acts of terrorism so that the perpetrators of such acts can speedily be brought to justice;

b. drafting model laws in this field, and codes of conduct in particular for law enforcement agencies;

c. reviewing existing or, where necessary, adopting new rules concerning:

i. the prosecution and trial of crimes of an international character, with a view to avoiding and solving conflicts of jurisdiction and, in this context, facilitating States' co-operation with international criminal courts and tribunals;

ii. the improvement and reinforcement of exchanges of information between law enforcement agencies;

iii. the improvement of the protection of witnesses and other persons participating in proceedings involving persons accused of terrorist crimes;

iv. the improvement of the protection, support and compensation of victims of terrorist acts and their families;

v. the reinforcement of the prevention and punishment of acts of terrorism committed against or by means of computer and telecommunication systems ("cyber-terrorism");

d. depriving terrorists of any financial resources which would allow them to commit acts of terrorism, including amendments to the law, in conformity with Security Council Resolution 1373 (2001);

e. reinforcing, through adequate financial appropriation, the work of Council of Europe bodies involved in the fight against money laundering, in particular the Committee evaluating States' anti-money laundering measures (PC-R-EV);

f. facilitating the identification of persons by means of appropriate identity, civil status and other documents, as well as by other means, including the possibility of using genetic prints (DNA);

g. ensuring the safety and control of dangerous or potentially dangerous substances;

DECIDE to remain in close contact on these matters, in particular in order to review the steps taken to give effect to this Resolution, at the latest on the occasion of their next Conference.

Source: The Avalon Project, Yale University. Available online. URL: http://www.yale.edu/lawweb/avalon/terrorism/t_0002.htm.

European Union

U.S.-EU Statement of Shared Objections and Close Cooperation on Counterterrorism (1998)

Following a U.S.-EU Summit meeting, leaders agreed to increase trans-Atlantic cooperation in the fight against terrorism. The framework created more concrete definitions than the UN resolutions and called for work in specific areas, such as fund-raising. However, only seven of the then-15 EU members (France, Germany, Italy, Portugal, Greece, Spain, and the United Kingdom) had specific laws against terrorism. The other eight countries treated terrorist activities as ordinary criminal crimes.

Released following the U.S.-EU Summit, Birmingham, United Kingdom, May 18, 1998

1. The United States, the European Union and its member states are strategic allies in the global fight against terrorism—a grave threat to democracy, and to economic and social development. They oppose terrorism in all its forms, whatever the motivation of its perpetrators, oppose concessions to terrorists, and agree on the need to resist extortion threats. They condemn absolutely not only those who plan or commit terrorist acts, but also any who support, finance or harbor terrorists. They recognize that terrorism operates on a transnational scale, and cannot effectively be dealt with solely by isolated action using each individual state's own resources. They work together to promote greater international cooperation and coordinated effort to combat terrorism by all legal means and in all relevant bilateral and multilateral fora—from the Transatlantic Dialogue to the United Nations.

The International Legal Framework

2. Extradition and mutual legal assistance arrangements are in operation or will be developed between the United States and EU partners. The U.S. and the EU cooperate in the United Nations framework to elaborate the necessary international legal instruments for the fight against terrorism. They work in tandem to promote universal adherence to the eleven international counter-terrorism conventions. EU partners contributed to the rapid and successful negotiation of the most recent UN Convention (for the Suppression of Terrorist Bombings) based on a draft proposed by the U.S. Now they are cooperating to consider the terms of a draft UN Convention on the Suppression of Nuclear Terrorism.

Areas of Current U.S./EU Mutual Interest

3. (i) Terrorist Fund-raising: EU partners are pooling their knowledge and experience to work to cut off terrorists' sources of funding. They have agreed to a set of action points, and their operational agencies are working on joint initiatives against terrorist funding. The U.S. participated in an EU seminar in 1997 which shaped this work, is briefed regularly on the current developments in this key area, and will take part in a follow-up EU seminar in Vienna in October 1998.

(ii) Chemical/Biological Terrorism and other threats: During the UK Presidency, the U.S. and EU have shared their thinking and compared best practice in the areas of CB terrorism, terrorist arms trafficking and bomb scene management.

(iii) The Middle East Peace Process: The EU briefs the U.S. regularly on its current 3-year program of counter-terrorism cooperation to enhance the effectiveness of the Palestinian Authority in this key area, including an extensive program of human rights training. To strengthen EU/Palestinian links still further in the fight against terrorism, a declaration creating a joint Security Committee was agreed in April 1998. The Committee now meets regularly to discuss these security issues.

U.S./EU Consultation and Information Exchange

4. Policy cooperation is developed bilaterally and at U.S./EU level. Operational cooperation, including intelligence sharing, is handled bilaterally by national law enforcement agencies, and is given high priority. To identify and assess the scale of the terrorist threat, the U.S. and the EU members states exchange information and assessments on terrorist trends and latest developments. The regular meetings on counter-terrorism between the U.S. and the EU Troika of the Second and Third Pillars are used to exchange views on all aspects of terrorism policy, including trends in countries of particular current concern in the Middle East and elsewhere. Information is also shared on significant developments on either side of the Atlantic, e.g., the creation of Europol, which will include terrorism within its remit soon after its launch. The U.S. has updated EU partners on the impact of its decision last October to designate 30 foreign terrorist organizations.

Further Cooperation

5. While recognizing the wide range of work successfully accomplished hitherto, both sides see scope to strengthen further their close ties in the field of counter-terrorism, and are working to do so—by additional information sharing at their regular Troika meetings, enhanced bilateral intelligence

exchanges, and sustained cooperation at the United Nations and ir other fora to advance their common objectives.

Source: The Avalon Project, Yale University. Available online. URL: http://www.yale.edu/lawweb/avalon/terrorism/t_0021.htm

EU Framework Decision on Combating Terrorism, 2002

European Union member states began work to create a pan-European arrest warrant and to standardize extradition provisions. This effort sought to close the gaps caused as some EU member states recognized terrorism as a distinct offense and others considered terrorism to be a form of criminal activity. First proposed in September 2001, the agreement came into force on June 13, 2002.

(Acts adopted pursuant to Title VI of the Treaty on European Union)

COUNCIL FRAMEWORK DECISION
of 13 June 2002
on combating terrorism
(2002/475/JHA)

THE COUNCIL OF THE EUROPEAN UNION,

Having regard to the Treaty establishing the European Union, and in particular Article 29, Article 31(e) and Article 34(2)(b) thereof,

Having regard to the proposal from the Commission [(1)],

Having regard to the opinion of the European Parliament [(2)],

Whereas:

(1) The European Union is founded on the universal values of human dignity, liberty, equality and solidarity, respect for human rights and fundamental freedoms. It is based on the principle of democracy and the principle of the rule of law, principles which are common to the Member States.

(2) Terrorism constitutes one of the most serious violations of those principles. The La Gomera Declaration adopted at the informal Council meeting on 14 October 1995 affirmed that terrorism constitutes a threat to democracy, to the free exercise of human rights and to economic and social development.

[(1)] OJ C 332 E, 27.11.2001, p. 300.

[(2)] Opinion delivered on 6 February 2002 (not yet published in the Official Journal).

(3) All or some Member States are party to a number of conventions relating to terrorism. The Council of Europe Convention of 27 January 1977 on the Suppression of Terrorism does not regard terrorist offences as political offences or as offences connected with political offences or as offences inspired by political motives. The United Nations has adopted the Convention for the suppression of terrorist bombings of 15 December 1997 and the Convention for the suppression of financing terrorism of 9 December 1999. A draft global Convention against terrorism is currently being negotiated within the United Nations.

(4) At European Union level, on 3 December 1998 the Council adopted the Action Plan of the Council and the Commission on how best to implement the provisions of the Treaty of Amsterdam on an area of freedom, security and justice [(3)]. Account should also be taken of the Council Conclusions of 20 September 2001 and of the Extraordinary European Council plan of action to combat terrorism of 21 September 2001. Terrorism was referred to in the conclusions of the Tampere European Council of 15 and 16 October 1999, and of the Santa María da Feira European Council of 19 and 20 June 2000. It was also mentioned in the Commission communication to the Council and the European Parliament on the biannual update of the scoreboard to review progress on the creation of an area of 'freedom, security and justice' in the European Union (second half of 2000). Furthermore, on 5 September 2001 the European Parliament adopted a recommendation on the role of the European Union in combating terrorism. It should, moreover, be recalled that on 30 July 1996 twenty-five measures to fight against terrorism were advocated by the leading industrialised countries (G7) and Russia meeting in Paris.

(5) The European Union has adopted numerous specific measures having an impact on terrorism and organised crime, such as the Council Decision of 3 December 1998 instructing Europol to deal with crimes committed or likely to be committed in the course of terrorist activities against life, limb, personal freedom or property [(4)]; Council Joint Action 96/610/JHA of 15 October 1996 concerning the creation and maintenance of a Directory of specialised counter-terrorist competences, skills and expertise to facilitate counter-terrorism cooperation between the Member States of the European Union [(5)]; Council Joint Action 98/428/JHA of 29 June 1998 on the

(3) OJ C 19, 23.1.1999, p. 1.

(4) OJ C 26, 30.1.1999, p. 22.

(5) OJ L 273, 25.10.1996, p. 1.

creation of a European Judicial Network [6], with responsibilities in terrorist offences, in particular Article 2; Council Joint Action 98/733/JHA of 21 December 1998 on making it a criminal offence to participate in a criminal organisation in the Member States of the European Union [7]; and the Council Recommendation of 9 December 1999 on cooperation in combating the financing of terrorist groups [8].

(6) The definition of terrorist offences should be approximated in all Member States, including those offences relating to terrorist groups. Furthermore, penalties and sanctions should be provided for natural and legal persons having committed or being liable for such offences, which reflect the seriousness of such offences.

(7) Jurisdictional rules should be established to ensure that the terrorist offence may be effectively prosecuted.

(8) Victims of terrorist offences are vulnerable, and therefore specific measures are necessary with regard to them.

(9) Given that the objectives of the proposed action cannot be sufficiently achieved by the Member States unilaterally, and can therefore, because of the need for reciprocity, be better achieved at the level of the Union, the Union may adopt measures, in accordance with the principle of subsidiarity. In accordance with the principle of proportionality, this Framework Decision does not go beyond what is necessary in order to achieve those objectives.

(10) This Framework Decision respects fundamental rights as guaranteed by the European Convention for the Protection of Human Rights and Fundamental Freedoms and as they emerge from the constitutional traditions common to the Member States as principles of Community law. The Union observes the principles recognised by Article 6(2) of the Treaty on European Union and reflected in the Charter of Fundamental Rights of the European Union, notably Chapter VI thereof. Nothing in this Framework Decision may be interpreted as being intended to reduce or restrict fundamental rights or freedoms such as the right to strike, freedom of assembly, of association or of expression, including the right of everyone to form and to join

[6] OJ L 191, 7.7.1998, p. 4.

[7] OJ L 351, 29.12.1998, p. 1.

[8] OJ C 373, 23.12.1999, p. 1.

trade unions with others for the protection of his or her interests and the related right to demonstrate.

(11) Actions by armed forces during periods of armed conffict, which are governed by international humanitarian law within the meaning of these terms under that law, and, inasmuch as they are governed by other rules of international law, actions by the armed forces of a State in the exercise of their official duties are not governed by this Framework Decision,

HAS ADOPTED THIS FRAMEWORK DECISION:

Article 1

Terrorist offences and fundamental rights and principles

1. Each Member State shall take the necessary measures to ensure that the intentional acts referred to below in points (a) to (i), as defined as offences under national law, which, given their nature or context, may seriously damage a country or an international organisation where committed with the aim of:

—seriously intimidating a population, or

—unduly compelling a Government or international organisation to perform or abstain from performing any act, or

—seriously destabilising or destroying the fundamental political, constitutional, economic or social structures of a country or an international organisation,

shall be deemed to be terrorist offences:

(a) attacks upon a person's life which may cause death;

(b) attacks upon the physical integrity of a person;

(c) kidnapping or hostage taking;

(d) causing extensive destruction to a Government or public facility, a transport system, an infrastructure facility, including an information system, a fixed platform located on the continental shelf, a public place or private property likely to endanger human life or result in major economic loss;

(e) seizure of aircraft, ships or other means of public or goods transport;

(f) manufacture, possession, acquisition, transport, supply or use of weapons, explosives or of nuclear, biological or chemical weapons, as well as research into, and development of, biological and chemical weapons;

(g) release of dangerous substances, or causing fires, floods or explosions the effect of which is to endanger human life;

(h) interfering with or disrupting the supply of water, power or any other fundamental natural resource the effect of which is to endanger human life;

(i) threatening to commit any of the acts listed in (a) to (h).

2. This Framework Decision shall not have the effect of altering the obligation to respect fundamental rights and fundamental legal principles as enshrined in Article 6 of the Treaty on European Union.

Article 2
Offences relating to a terrorist group

1. For the purposes of this Framework Decision, 'terrorist group' shall mean: a structured group of more than two persons, established over a period of time and acting in concert to commit terrorist offences. 'Structured group' shall mean a group that is not randomly formed for the immediate commission of an offence and that does not need to have formally defined roles for its members, continuity of its membership or a developed structure.

2. Each Member State shall take the necessary measures to ensure that the following intentional acts are punishable:

(a) directing a terrorist group;

(b) participating in the activities of a terrorist group, including by supplying information or material resources, or by funding its activities in any way, with knowledge of the fact that such participation will contribute to the criminal activities of the terrorist group.

Article 3
Offences linked to terrorist activities

Each Member State shall take the necessary measures to ensure that terrorist-linked offences include the following acts:

(a) aggravated theft with a view to committing one of the acts listed in Article 1(1);

(b) extortion with a view to the perpetration of one of the acts listed in Article 1(1);

(c) drawing up false administrative documents with a view to committing one of the acts listed in Article 1(1)(a) to (h) and Article 2(2)(b).

Article 4
Inciting, aiding or abetting, and attempting

1. Each Member State shall take the necessary measures to ensure that inciting or aiding or abetting an offence referred to in Article 1(1), Articles 2 or 3 is made punishable.

2. Each Member State shall take the necessary measures to ensure that attempting to commit an offence referred to in Article 1(1) and Article 3, with the exception of possession as provided for in Article 1(1)(f) and the offence referred to in Article 1(1)(i), is made punishable.

Article 5
Penalties

1. Each Member State shall take the necessary measures to ensure that the offences referred to in Articles I to 4 are punishable by effective, proportionate and dissuasive criminal penalties, which may entail extradition.

2. Each Member State shall take the necessary measures to ensure that the terrorist offences referred to in Article 1(1) and offences referred to in Article 4, inasmuch as they relate to terrorist offences, are punishable by custodial sentences heavier than those imposable under national law for such offences in the absence of the special intent required pursuant to Article 1(1), save where the sentences imposable are already the maximum possible sentences under national law.

3. Each Member State shall take the necessary measures to ensure that offences listed in Article 2 are punishable by custodial sentences, with a maximum sentence of not less than fifteen years for the offence referred to in Article 2(2)(a), and for the offences listed in Article 2(2)(b) a maximum sentence of not less than eight years. In so far as the offence referred to in Article 2(2)(a) refers only to the act in Article 1(1)(i), the maximum sentence shall not be less than eight years.

Article 6
Particular circumstances

Each Member State may take the necessary measures to ensure that the penalties referred to in Article 5 may be reduced if the offender:

(a) renounces terrorist activity, and

(b) provides the administrative or judicial authorities with information which they would not otherwise have been able to obtain, helping them to:

(i) prevent or mitigate the effects of the offence;

(ii) identify or bring to justice the other offenders;

(iii) find evidence; or

(iv) prevent further offences referred to in Articles 1 to 4.

Article 7

Liability of legal persons

1. Each Member State shall take the necessary measures to ensure that legal persons can be held liable for any of the offences referred to in Articles 1 to 4 committed for their benefit by any person, acting either individually or as part of an organ of the legal person, who has a leading position within the legal person, based on one of the following:

(a) a power of representation of the legal person;

(b) an authority to take decisions on behalf of the legal person;

(c) an authority to exercise control within the legal person.

2. Apart from the cases provided for in paragraph 1, each Member State shall take the necessary measures to ensure that legal persons can be held liable where the lack of supervision or control by a person referred to in paragraph 1 has made possible the commission of any of the offences referred to in Articles 1 to 4 for the benefit of that legal person by a person under its authority.

3. Liability of legal persons under paragraphs I and 2 shall not exclude criminal proceedings against natural persons who are perpetrators, instigators or accessories in any of the offences referred to in Articles 1 to 4.

Article 8

Penalties for legal persons

Each Member State shall take the necessary measures to ensure that a legal person held liable pursuant to Article 7 is punishable by effective, proportionate and dissuasive penalties, which shall include criminal or non-criminal fines and may include other penalties, such as:

(a) exclusion from entitlement to public benefits or aid;

(b) temporary or permanent disqualification from the practice of commercial activities;

(c) placing under judicial supervision;

(d) a judicial winding-up order;

(e) temporary or permanent closure of establishments which have been used for committing the offence.

Article 9
Jurisdiction and prosecution

1. Each Member State shall take the necessary measures to establish its jurisdiction over the offences referred to in Articles 1 to 4 where:

(a) the offence is committed in whole or in part in its territory. Each Member State may extend its jurisdiction if the offence is committed in the territory of a Member State;

(b) the offence is committed on board a vessel flying its flag or an aircraft registered there;

(c) the offender is one of its nationals or residents;

(d) the offence is committed for the benefit of a legal person established in its territory;

(e) the offence is committed against the institutions or people of the Member State in question or against an institution of the European Union or a body set up in accordance with the Treaty establishing the European Community or the Treaty on European Union and based in that Member State.

2. When an offence falls within the jurisdiction of more than one Member State and when any of the States concerned can validly prosecute on the basis of the same facts, the Member States concerned shall cooperate in order to decide which of them will prosecute the offenders with the aim, if possible, of centralising proceedings in a single Member State. To this end, the Member States may have recourse to any body or mechanism established within the European Union in order to facilitate cooperation between their judicial authorities and the coordination of their action. Sequential account shall be taken of the following factors:

—the Member State shall be that in the territory of which the acts were committed,

—the Member State shall be that of which the perpetrator is a national or resident,

—the Member State shall be the Member State of origin of the victims,

—the Member State shall be that in the territory of which the perpetrator was found.

3. Each Member State shall take the necessary measures also to establish its jurisdiction over the offences referred to in Articles 1 to 4 in cases where it refuses to hand over or extradite a person suspected or convicted of such an offence to another Member State or to a third country.

4. Each Member State shall ensure that its jurisdiction covers cases in which any of the offences referred to in Articles 2 and 4 has been committed in whole or in part within its territory, wherever the terrorist group is based or pursues its criminal activities.

5. This Article shall not exclude the exercise of jurisdiction in criminal matters as laid down by a Member State in accordance with its national legislation.

Article 10

Protection of, and assistance to, victims

1. Member States shall ensure that investigations into, or prosecution of, offences covered by this Framework Decision are not dependent on a report or accusation made by a person subjected to the offence, at least if the acts were committed on the territory of the Member State.

2. In addition to the measures laid down in the Council Framework Decision 2001/220/JHA of 15 March 2001 on the standing of victims in criminal proceedings [(1)], each Member State shall, if necessary, take all measures possible to ensure appropriate assistance for victims' families.

Article 11

Implementation and reports

1. Member States shall take the necessary measures to comply with this Framework Decision by 31 December 2002.

2. By 31 December 2002, Member States shall forward to the General Secretariat of the Council and to the Commission the text of the provisions transposing into their national law the obligations imposed on them under this Framework Decision. On the basis of a report drawn up from that information and a report from the Commission, the Council shall assess,

[(1)] OJ L 82, 22.3.2001, p. 1.

by 31 December 2003, whether Member States have taken the necessary measures to comply with this Framework Decision.

3. The Commission report shall specify, in particular, transposition into the criminal law of the Member States of the obligation referred to in Article 5(2).

Article 12
Territorial application

This Framework Decision shall apply to Gibraltar.

Article 13
Entry into force

This Framework Decision shall enter into force on the day of its publication in the Official Journal.

Done at Luxembourg, 13 June 2002.

For the Council
The President
M. RAJOY BREY

Source: The Avalon Project, Yale University. Available online. URL: http://www.yale.edu/lawweb/avalon/terrorism/t_0002.htm. Accessed on April 2, 2007.

Organization of American States

Inter-American Convention Against Terrorism (2002) (excerpt)

The countries of North, Central, and South America moved to standardize their approach to fighting terrorism in 2002. This agreement invokes the existing UN agreements on terrorism but also adds new dimensions specific to Latin America, such as terrorist financing and extradition. The agreement was reached in Bridgetown, Barbados, on June 3, 2002.

Article 1
Object and purposes
The purposes of this Convention are to prevent, punish, and eliminate terrorism. To that end, the states parties agree to adopt the necessary measures and to strengthen cooperation among them, in accordance with the terms of this Convention.

Article 2

Applicable international instruments

1. For the purposes of this Convention, "offenses" means the offenses established in the [ten] international instruments listed below: [. . .]

Article 3

Domestic measures

Each state party, in accordance with the provisions of its constitution, shall endeavor to become a party to the international instruments listed in Article 2 to which it is not yet a party and to adopt the necessary measures to effectively implement such instruments, including establishing, in its domestic legislation, penalties for the offenses described therein.

Article 4

Measures to prevent, combat, and eradicate the financing of terrorism

1. Each state party, to the extent it has not already done so, shall institute a legal and regulatory regime to prevent, combat, and eradicate the financing of terrorism and for effective international cooperation with respect thereto: [. . .]

2. When implementing paragraph 1 of this article, states parties shall use as guidelines the recommendations developed by specialized international and regional entities, in particular the Financial Action Task Force and, as appropriate, the Inter-American Drug Abuse Control Commission, the Caribbean Financial Action Task Force, and the South American Financial Action Task Force.

Article 5

Seizure and confiscation of funds or other assets

1. Each state party shall, in accordance with the procedures established in its domestic law, take such measures as may be necessary to provide for the identification, freezing or seizure for the purposes of possible forfeiture, and confiscation or forfeiture, of any funds or other assets constituting the proceeds of, used to facilitate, or used or intended to finance, the commission of any of the offenses established in the international instruments listed in Article 2 of this Convention.

2. The measures referred to in paragraph 1 shall apply to offenses committed both within and outside the jurisdiction of the state party.

Article 6

Predicate offenses to money laundering

1. Each state party shall take the necessary measures to ensure that its domestic penal money laundering legislation also includes as predicate

offenses those offenses established in the international instruments listed in Article 2 of this Convention.

2. The money laundering predicate offenses referred to in paragraph 1 shall include those committed both within and outside the jurisdiction of the state party.

Article 7
Cooperation on border controls

1. The states parties, consistent with their respective domestic legal and administrative regimes, shall promote cooperation and the exchange of information in order to improve border and customs control measures to detect and prevent the international movement of terrorists and trafficking in arms or other materials intended to support terrorist activities.

2. In this context, they shall promote cooperation and the exchange of information to improve their controls on the issuance of travel and identity documents and to prevent their counterfeiting, forgery, or fraudulent use.

3. Such measures shall be carried out without prejudice to applicable international commitments in relation to the free movement of people and the facilitation of commerce.

Article 8
Cooperation among law enforcement authorities

The states parties shall work closely with one another, consistent with their respective domestic legal and administrative systems, to enhance the effectiveness of law enforcement action to combat the offenses established in the international instruments listed in Article 2. In this context, they shall establish and enhance, where necessary, channels of communication between their competent authorities in order to facilitate the secure and rapid exchange of information concerning all aspects of the offenses established in the international instruments listed in Article 2 of this Convention.

Article 9
Mutual legal assistance

The states parties shall afford one another the greatest measure of expeditious mutual legal assistance with respect to the prevention, investigation, and prosecution of the offenses established in the international instruments listed in Article 2 and proceedings related thereto, in accordance with applicable international agreements in force. In the absence of such agreements, states parties shall afford one another expeditious assistance in accordance with their domestic law.

Article 10
Transfer of persons in custody
1. A person who is being detained or is serving a sentence in the territory of one state party and whose presence in another state party is requested for purposes of identification, testimony, or otherwise providing assistance in obtaining evidence for the investigation or prosecution of offenses established in the international instruments listed in Article 2 may be transferred if the following conditions are met: [. . .]

Article 11
Inapplicability of political offense exception
For the purposes of extradition or mutual legal assistance, none of the offenses established in the international instruments listed in Article 2 shall be regarded as a political offense or an offense connected with a political offense or an offense inspired by political motives. Accordingly, a request for extradition or mutual legal assistance may not be refused on the sole ground that it concerns a political offense or an offense connected with a political offense or an offense inspired by political motives.

Source: Office of International Law, Organization of American States. Available online. URL: http://www.oas.org/juridico/english/ga02/agres_1840.htm.

DOCUMENTS RELATING TO TERRORISM IN SPECIFIC COUNTRIES

Spain

ETA Declares Ceasefire (2006)

After nearly four decades of armed struggle for Basque independence, the Basque Fatherland and Freedom group (ETA) announced a permanent ceasefire in March 2006.

Message from Euskadi Ta Askatasuna [Eta] to the Basque people.
The Basque revolutionary socialist national liberation organisation Euskadi Ta Askatasuna (Eta) wishes to make known via this declaration the following decision:

Euskadi Ta Askatasuna has decided to declare a permanent ceasefire as from 0000 (2300GMT) on 24 March 2006.

The aim of this decision is to promote a democratic process in Euskal-Herria (the Basque Country) in order that the Basque people might implement the political change they need through dialogue, negotiation and agreement.

Leaving behind the current framework of negation, partition and imposition, a democratic framework must be built for Euskal-Herria, recognising the rights as a people which are its due and guaranteeing the opportunity to develop all political options in the future.

At the end of this process, Basque citizens must have the say and the decision on their future, thus giving a democratic solution to the conflict.

Eta considers that it is for all Basque agents to develop this process and to adopt the appropriate agreements for the future of Euskal-Herria, taking into account its plurality and its totality.

The Spanish and French states must recognise the results of this democratic process, without interference or limitations of any kind. The decision we Basque citizens make on our future will have to be respected.

We call on all agents to act responsibly and to be consistent with the step taken by Eta.

It is time for agreements. We must all accept our responsibilities to build together the democratic solution which the Basque people need. It is time to take important decisions, moving from words to deeds.

Eta calls on the Spanish and French authorities to respond positively to this new situation, and not to obstruct the democratic process, leaving repression aside and showing the will to give a negotiated solution to the conflict.

Lastly, we call on Basque citizens in general and the members of the radical Basque nationalist Left in particular to get involved in this process and to fight for the rights as a people which are our due.

Eta expresses its desire and will for the process which has begun to reach its end, thereby achieving a truly democratic situation for Euskal-Herria, ending the long years of conflict and building a peace based on justice.

We reaffirm our commitment to continue taking steps in the future in accordance with this will and to keep fighting until we obtain the rights of Euskal-Herria.

Ending the conflict, here and now, is possible. This is the desire and the will of Eta.

Euskal Herria, March 2006

Euskadi Ta Askatasuna

Eta

Source: BBC news, reprinted from *Gara,* March 23, 2006. Available online. URL: http://news.bbc.co.uk/2/hi/europe/4833490.stm.

United Kingdom

IRISH CONFLICT

Anglo-Irish Agreement 1985 Between the Government of Ireland and the Government of the United Kingdom (November 15, 1985) (excerpt)

Agreement between British prime minister Margaret Thatcher and Irish prime minister Garret FitzGerald that any change in the status of Northern Ireland would come only with the consent of the people of Northern Ireland. Officially gave the Republic of Ireland a voice in the settlement of Northern Ireland and did not rule out the possibility of Irish unification.

A. STATUS OF NORTHERN IRELAND

ARTICLE 1

The two Governments

(a) affirm that any change in the status of Northern Ireland would only come about with the consent of a majority of the people of Northern Ireland; **(b)** recognise that the present wish of a majority of the people of Northern Ireland is for no change in the status of Northern Ireland;

(c) declare that, if in the future a majority of the people of Northern Ireland clearly wish for and formally consent to the establishment of a united Ireland, they will introduce and support in the respective Parliaments legislation to give effect to that wish.

B. THE INTERGOVERNMENTAL CONFERENCE

ARTICLE 2

(a) There is hereby established, within the framework of the Anglo-Irish Intergovernmental Council set up after the meeting between the two Heads of Government on 6 November 1981, an Intergovernmental Conference (hereinafter referred to as "the Conference"), concerned with Northern Ireland and with relations between the two parts of the island of Ireland, to deal, as set out in this Agreement, on a regular basis with

(i) political matters;

(ii) security and related matters;

(iii) legal matters, including the administration of justice;

(iv) the promotion of cross-border co-operation. [. . .]

ARTICLE 3
[. . .]

ARTICLE 4

(a) In relation to matters coming within its field of activity, the Conference shall be a framework within which the Irish Government and the United Kingdom Government work together

(i) for the accommodation of the rights and identities of the two traditions which exist in Northern Ireland; and

(ii) for peace, stability and prosperity throughout the island of Ireland by promoting reconciliation, respect for human rights, co-operation against terrorism and the development of economic, social and cultural co-operation.

(b) It is the declared policy of the United Kingdom Government that responsibility in respect of certain matters within the powers of the Secretary of State for Northern Ireland should be devolved within Northern Ireland on a basis which would secure widespread acceptance throughout the community. The Irish Government support that policy.

(c) Both Governments recognise that devolution can be achieved only with the co-operation of constitutional representatives within Northern Ireland of both traditions there. The Conference shall be a framework within which the Irish Government may put forward views and proposals on the modalities of bringing about devolution in Northern Ireland, in so far as they relate to the interests of the minority community.

C. POLITICAL MATTERS

ARTICLE 5

(a) The Conference shall concern itself with measures to recognise and accommodate the rights and identities of the two traditions in Northern

Ireland, to protect human rights and to prevent discrimination. Matters to be considered in this area include measures to foster the cultural heritage of both traditions, changes in electoral arrangements, the use of flags and emblems, the avoidance of economic and social discrimination and the advantages and disadvantages of a Bill of Rights in some form in Northern Ireland. [. . .]

Source: CAIN (Conflict Archive on the Internet) Web Service. Available online. URL: http://cain.ulst.ac.uk/events/aia/aiadoc.htm.

Downing Street Declaration (1993)

Statement by British prime minister John Major and Irish prime minister (or Taoiseach) Albert Reynolds on improving climate of trust and working toward peace. Ireland recognized that Northern Ireland might not want unification; Britain admitted that Northern Ireland had right to choose unification.

Wednesday 15 December 1993

1. The Taoiseach, Mr. Albert Reynolds, TD and the Prime Minister, the Rt. Hon. John Major MP, acknowledge that the most urgent and important issue facing the people of Ireland, North and South, and the British and Irish Governments together, is to remove the conflict, to overcome the legacy of history and to heal the divisions which have resulted, recognising the absence of a lasting and satisfactory settlement of relationships between the peoples of both islands has contributed to continuing tragedy and suffering. They believe that the development of an agreed framework for peace, which has been discussed between them since early last year, and which is based on a number of key principles articulated by the two Governments over the past 20 years, together with adaptation of other widely accepted principles, provides the starting point of a peace process designed to culminate in a political settlement.

2. The Taoiseach and the Prime Minister are convinced of the inestimable value to both their peoples, and particularly for the next generation, of healing divisions in Ireland and of ending a conflict which has been so manifestly to the detriment of all. Both recognise that the ending of divisions can come about only through the agreement and co-operation of the people, North and South, representing both traditions in Ireland. They therefore make a solemn commitment to promote co-operation at all levels on the basis of the fundamental principles, undertakings, obligations under international

agreements, to which they have jointly committed themselves, and the guarantees which each Government has given and now reaffirms, including Northern Ireland's statutory constitutional guarantee. It is their aim to foster agreement and reconciliation, leading to a new political framework founded on consent and encompassing arrangements within Northern Ireland, for the whole island, and between these islands.

3. They also consider that the development of Europe will, of itself, require new approaches to serve interests common to both parts of the island of Ireland, and to Ireland and the United Kingdom as partners in the European Union.

4. The Prime Minister, on behalf of the British Government, reaffirms that they will uphold the democratic wish of the greater number of the people of Northern Ireland on the issue of whether they prefer to support the Union or a sovereign united Ireland. On this basis, he reiterates, on the behalf of the British Government, that they have no selfish strategic or economic interest in Northern Ireland. Their primary interest is to see peace, stability and reconciliation established by agreement among all the people inhabit the island, and they will work together with the Irish Government to achieve such an agreement, which will embrace the totality of relationships. The role of the British Government will be to encourage, facilitate and enable the achievement of such agreement over a period through a process of dialogue and co-operation based on full respect for the rights and identities of both traditions in Ireland. [. . .] The British Government agree that it is for the people of the island of Ireland alone, by agreement between the two parts respectively, to exercise their right of self-determination on the basis of consent, freely and concurrently given, North and South, to bring about a united Ireland, if that is their wish. [. . .] The Taoiseach, on behalf of the Irish Government, considers that the lessons of Irish history, and especially of Northern Ireland, show that stability and well-being will not be found under any political system which is refused allegiance or rejected on grounds of identity by a significant minority of those governed by it. For this reason, it would be wrong to attempt to impose a united Ireland, in the absence of the freely given consent of the majority of the people of Northern Ireland. He accepts, on behalf of the Irish Government, that the democratic right of self-determination by the people of Ireland as a whole must be achieved and exercised with and subject to the agreement and consent of a majority of the people of Northern Ireland and must, consistent with justice and equity, respect the democratic dignity and the civil rights and religious liberties of both communities, [. . .]

5. The Taoiseach however recognises the genuine difficulties and barriers to building relationships of trust either within or beyond Northern Ireland, from which both traditions suffer. He will work to create a new era of trust, in which suspicion of the motives and actions of others is removed on the part of either community. He considers that the future of the island depends on the nature of the relationship between the two main traditions that inhabit it. Every effort must be made to build a new series of trust between those communities. [. . .]

6. Both Governments accept that Irish unity would be achieved only by those who favour this outcome persuading those who do not, peacefully and without coercion or violence, and that, if in the future a majority of the people of Northern Ireland are so persuaded, both Governments will support and give legislative effect to their wish. But, notwithstanding the solemn affirmation by both Governments in the Anglo-Irish Agreement that any change in the status of Northern Ireland, would only come about with a consent of the majority of the people of Northern Ireland, the Taoiseach also recognises the continuing uncertainties and misgivings which dominate so much of Northern Unionist attitudes towards the rest of Ireland. He believes that we stand at a stage of our history when the genuine feelings of all traditions in the North must be recognised and acknowledged. He appeals to both traditions at this time to grasp the opportunity for a fresh start and a new beginning, which could hold such promise for all our lives and the generations to come. He asks the people of Northern Ireland to look on the people of the Republic as friends, who share their grief and shame over all the suffering of the last quarter of a century, and who wants to develop the best possible relationship with them, a relationship in which trust and new understanding can flourish and grow. The Taoiseach also acknowledges the presence in the Constitution of the Republic of elements which are deeply resented by Northern Unionists, but which at the same time reflect hopes and ideals which lie deep in the hearts of many Irish men and women North and South. [. . .]

7. The Taoiseach recognises the need to engage in dialogue which would address the honesty and integrity the fears of all traditions. But that dialogue, both within the North and between the people and their representatives of both parts of Ireland, must be entered into with an acknowledgment that the future security and welfare of the people of the island will depend on an open, frank and balanced approach to all the problems which for too long have caused division.

8. The British and Irish Governments will seek, along with the Northern Ireland constitutional parties through a process of political dialogue, to create institutions and structures which, while respecting the diversity of the people of Ireland, would enable them to work together in all areas of common interest. This will help over a period to build the trust necessary to end past divisions, leading to an agreed and peaceful future. Such structures would, of course, include institutional recognition of the special links that exist between the peoples of Britain and Ireland as part of the totality of relationships, while taking account of newly forged links with the rest of Europe.

9. The British and Irish Governments reiterate that the achievement of peace must involve a permanent end to the use of, or support for, paramilitary violence. They confirm that, in these circumstances, democratically mandated parties which establish a commitment to exclusively peaceful methods and which have shown that they abide by the democratic process, are free to participate fully in democratic politics and to join in dialogue in due course between the Governments and the political parties on the way ahead.

10. The Irish Government would make their own arrangements within their jurisdiction to enable democratic parties to consult together and share in dialogue about the political future. The Taoiseach's intention is that these arrangements could include the establishment, in consultation with other parties, of a Forum for Peace and Reconciliation to make recommendations on ways in which agreement and trust between both traditions can be promoted and established.

Source: CAIN (Conflict Archive on the Internet) Web Service. Available online. URL: http://cain.ulst.ac.uk/events/aia/aiadoc.htm.

Belfast Accord/Good Friday Agreement (1998)

An agreement between the Republic of Ireland, the United Kingdom, and Northern Ireland political parties on the need for self-determination in Northern Ireland. The UK Northern Ireland Office issued the following executive summary of the lengthy treaty.

THE AGREEMENT

The Agreement (also known as the Good Friday Agreement or Belfast Agreement) was reached in Belfast on Friday, April 10, 1998.

It sets out a plan for devolved government in Northern Ireland on a stable and inclusive basis and provided for the creation of Human Rights and Equality commissions, the early release of terrorist prisoners, the decommissioning of paramilitary weapons and far reaching reforms of criminal justice and policing.

The **Agreement** proposed an inter-connected group of institutions from three 'strands' of relationships.

Strand One deals with relationships within Northern Ireland and created the Northern Ireland Assembly, its Executive and the consultative Civic Forum. The Assembly has **108 members (MLAs),** elected by proportional representation and Ministers to the Executive are appointed according to party strength under the d'Hondt mechanism. The last Assembly election was held in November, 2003.

Strand Two deals with relationships between Northern Ireland and the Republic of Ireland. A North-South Ministerial Conference (NSMC) brings together members of the Northern Ireland Executive and the Irish Government to oversee the work of six cross-border implementation bodies.

Strand Three deals with the East-West relationships within the British Isles. A **British-Irish Inter-Governmental Conference** was established to promote bilateral co-operation between the UK and Ireland. It replaced the Anglo-Irish Inter-Governmental Council and Conference set up by the Anglo-Irish Agreement in 1985.

A British-Irish Council was also created that incorporates members of all devolved administrations within the UK and representatives of the Isle of Man and the Channel Islands as well as the British and Irish governments.

The **Equality Commission** and the **Human Rights Commission** were created under the Agreement; there was a comprehensive review of criminal justice and policing arrangements and money was allocated to help victims of violence.

Source: United Kingdom, Northern Ireland Office. Available online. URL: http://www.nio.gov.uk/the-agreement.

IRA Statement on Disarmament (2005)

On July 28, 2005, two weeks after the London transit bombings known as 7/7, the Irish Republican Army formally announced the end of its armed campaign against the British government.

July 28, 2005 IRA Statement ending its armed campaign

"The leadership of Óglaigh na hÉireann has formally ordered an end to the armed campaign. This will take effect from 4pm this afternoon.

All IRA units have been ordered to dump arms.

All Volunteers have been instructed to assist the development of purely political and democratic programmes through exclusively peaceful means. Volunteers must not engage in any other activities whatsoever.

The IRA leadership has also authorised our representative to engage with the IICD to complete the process to verifiably put its arms beyond use in a way which will further enhance public confidence and to conclude this as quickly as possible. We have invited two independent witnesses, from the Protestant and Catholic churches, to testify to this.

The Army Council took these decisions following an unprecedented internal discussion and consultation process with IRA units and Volunteers.

We appreciate the honest and forthright way in which the consultation process was carried out and the depth and content of the submissions. We are proud of the comradely way in which this truly historic discussion was conducted.

The outcome of our consultations show very strong support among IRA Volunteers for the Sinn Féin peace strategy. There is also widespread concern about the failure of the two governments and the unionists to fully engage in the peace process. This has created real difficulties. The overwhelming majority of people in Ireland fully support this process. They and friends of Irish unity throughout the world want to see the full implementation of the Good Friday Agreement.

Notwithstanding these difficulties our decisions have been taken to advance our republican and democratic objectives, including our goal of a united Ireland. We believe there is now an alternative way to achieve this and to end British rule in our country.

It is the responsibility of all Volunteers to show leadership, determination and courage. We are very mindful of the sacrifices of our patriot dead, those who went to jail, Volunteers, their families and the wider republican base. We reiterate our view that the armed struggle was entirely legitimate.

We are conscious that many people suffered in the conflict. There is a compelling imperative on all sides to build a just and lasting peace.

The issue of the defence of nationalist and republican communities has been raised with us. There is a responsibility on society to ensure that there is no re-occurrence of the pogroms of 1969 and the early 1970s. There is also a universal responsibility to tackle sectarianism in all its forms.

The IRA is fully committed to the goals of Irish unity and independence and to building the Republic outlined in the 1916 Proclamation.

We call for maximum unity and effort by Irish republicans everywhere. We are confident that by working together Irish republicans can achieve our objectives. Every Volunteer is aware of the import of the decisions we have taken and all Óglaigh are compelled to fully comply with these orders.

There is now an unprecedented opportunity to utilise the considerable energy and goodwill which there is for the peace process. This comprehensive series of unparalleled initiatives is our contribution to this and to the continued endeavours to bring about independence and unity for the people of Ireland."

Source: Sinn Féin, "Peace Process Special." Available online. URL: http://www.sinnfeinonline.com/elections.

7/7 LONDON BOMBINGS (2005)

Prime Minister Tony Blair's Statement to Parliament on the London Bombings (11 July 2005)

With your permission, Mr Speaker, I would like to make a statement on last Thursday's terrorist attacks in London. The number of confirmed dead currently stands at 52; the number still in hospital 56, some severely injured. [. . .]

I will now try to give the House as much information as I can. Some of it is already well-known. There were four explosions. Three took place on underground trains—one between Aldgate East and Liverpool Street; one between Russell Square and Kings Cross; one in a train at Edgware Road station. All of these took place within 50 seconds of each other at 8.50 a.m.

The other explosion was on the No. 30 bus at Upper Woburn Place at 9.47 a.m.

The timing of the Tube explosions was designed to be at the peak of the rush hour and thus to cause maximum death and injury.

It seems probable that the attack was carried out by Islamist extremist terrorists, of the kind who over recent years have been responsible for so many innocent deaths in Madrid, Bali, Saudi Arabia, Russia, Kenya, Tanzania, Pakistan, Yemen, Turkey, Egypt and Morocco, of course in New York on September 11th, but in many other countries too. [. . .]

I would also like to say this about our police and intelligence services. I know of no intelligence specific enough to have allowed them to prevent last Thursday's attacks. By their very nature, people callous enough to kill completely innocent civilians in this way, are hard to stop. But our services and police do a heroic job for our country day in day out and I can say that over the past years, as this particular type of new and awful terrorist threat has grown, they have done their utmost to keep this country and its people safe. As I saw again from the meeting of COBR this morning, their determination to get those responsible is total. [. . .]

There is then the issue of further anti-terrorist legislation. During the passage of the Prevention of Terrorism Act earlier this year we pledged to introduce a further counter-terrorism Bill later in this session. That remains our intention. It will give us an opportunity, in close consultation with the police and the agencies, to see whether there are additional powers which they might need to prevent further attacks. [. . .]

Mr Speaker, the 7th of July will always be remembered as a day of terrible sadness for our country and for London. Yet it is true that just four days later, London's buses, trains and as much of its underground as is possible, are back on normal schedules; its businesses, shops and schools are open; its millions of people are coming to work with a steely determination that is genuinely remarkable.

Yesterday we celebrated the heroism of WW II including the civilian heroes of London's blitz. Today what a different city London is—a city of many cultures, faiths and races, hardly recognisable from the London of 1945. So different and yet, in the face of this attack, there is something wonderfully familiar in the confident spirit which moves through the city, enabling it to take the blow but still not flinch from re-asserting its will to triumph over adversity. Britain may be different today but the coming together is the same.

And I say to our Muslim community. People know full well that the overwhelming majority of Muslims stand four square with every other community in Britain. We were proud of your contribution to Britain before last

Thursday. We remain proud of it today. Fanaticism is not a state of religion but a state of mind. We will work with you to make the moderate and true voice of Islam heard as it should be.

Together, we will ensure that though terrorists can kill, they will never destroy the way of life we share and which we value, and which we will defend with the strength of belief and conviction so that it is to us and not to the terrorists, that victory will belong.

Source: Office of the Prime Minister, United Kingdom. Available online. URL: http://www.pm.gov.uk/output/Page7903.asp.

Germany

RED ARMY FACTION

Manifesto for Armed Action (1970)

Leaders of the Red Army Faction sent the following statement to the German magazine "883" to explain their philosophy of class struggle shortly after members helped Andreas Baader escape police custody.

Comrades of 883—there is no point in trying to explain the right way to the deceitful people. That we have done long enough. We don't have to explain the Baader-Release Action to the intellectual prattlers, the know-it-alls, but rather to the potentially revolutionary segment of the people. That means to those who can immediately grasp the deed, because they themselves are imprisoned. To those who think nothing of the prattle of the Left because it has remained without consequences or deeds. [In other words] to those who have enough! [. . .]

You have to convey the Action to those who get no compensation for the exploitation which they suffer, who get no compensation through living standards, consumption, savings agreements, personal credit, middle-class autos. To those who cannot afford all the stuff [junk], to those who don't care about it. To those who have exposed as lies all of the promises of the future by their nursery teachers and school teachers and property managers and welfare workers and foremen and craft masters and union functionaries and district mayors, and still fear only the police.

To them—and not to the petit bourgeois intellectuals—you have to say: that that's enough, that it's now beginning [breaking loose], that the release of Baader is only the beginning! That an end of police power [rule] is in sight! [. . .]

What does it mean, to carry the conflicts too far? That means to not let yourselves be slaughtered. That's why we are building up the Red Army. [. . .]

Without simultaneously building up the Red Army, every conflict, every political effort in the workplace, in Wedding and in the Markisch Quarter and in the Ploetze and in the court room degenerates into reformism, i.e., you set up only better means of discipline, better methods of intimidation, better methods of exploitation. That only breaks the people, it doesn't break what breaks the people! Without building up the Red Army, the pigs can continue, they can go on locking up, dismissing, seizing, stealing children, intimidating, shooting, ruling. To bring the conflict to a fever pitch means that they no longer can do what they want, rather they must do what we want.

You have to make it clear to them, to those who gain nothing from the exploitation of the Third World, from Persian oil, Bolivia's bananas, South Africa's gold, who have no ground to identify themselves with the exploitaters. They can understand that what is now being launched here has already been launched in Vietnam, Palestine, Guatemala, in Oakland and Watts, in Cuba and China, in Angola and New York.

They'll get that, if you explain to them that the Baader-Release Action is no isolated action, never was, but [rather] only the first of this type in the FRG. Damn it!

Don't sit around on the shabby, ransacked sofa and count your loves, like the small-time shopkeeper souls. [. . .] Get out where the homes are and the big families and the sub-proletariat and the proletarian women, [they] who are only waiting to smash the right people in the chops. They will assume the leadership. And don't let yourself be nabbed and learn from them how one keeps from being nabbed—they understand more about that than you.

Let the class struggle unfold! Let the proletariat organize! Let the armed resistance begin! Build up the Red Army!

Source: "Build Up the Red Army Manifesto," at This is Baader-Meinhof. Available online. URL: http://www.baader-meinhof.com/students/resources/communique/engbuild.html.

Statement Disbanding Red Army Faction (1998)

Nearly 10 years after the collapse of Communist East Germany, the Red Army Faction abandons its struggle against capitalism.

The Urban Guerrilla Is History (excerpt)

Almost 28 years ago, on May 14, 1970, the RAF was born from an act of liberation: Today we are ending this project. The urban guerrilla in the form of the RAF is now history.

We, that is all of us who were organized in the RAF until the end, are taking this step jointly. From now on, we, like all others from this association, are former RAF militants.

We stand by our history. The RAF was the revolutionary attempt by a minority of people to resist the tendencies in this society and contribute to the overthrow of capitalist conditions. We are proud to have been part of this attempt.

The end of this project shows that we were not able to succeed on this path. But this does not speak against the necessity and legitimacy of revolt. The RAF was our decision to stand on the side of those people struggling against domination and for liberation all across the world. For us, this was the right decision to make.

Hundreds of years in prison terms for RAF prisoners were not able to wipe us out, nor could all the attempts to eradicate the guerrilla. We wanted a confrontation with the ruling powers. We acted as subjects when we decided upon the RAF 27 years ago. We remain subjects today, as we consign ourselves to history.

The results are critical of us. But the RAF—Like all of the left until now—was nothing more than a phase of transition on the path to liberation.

After fascism and war, the RAF brought something new into the society: The moment of a break with the system and the historic flash of decisive opposition to the conditions which structurally subject and exploit people and which brought about a society in which the people are forced to fight against one another. The struggle in the social cracks, which marked our opposition, pushed a genuine social liberation forward; this break with the system, a system in which profit is the subject and people are the objects, and the desire for a life without the lies and weight of this distorted society. Fed up with stooping down, functioning, kicking, and being kicked. From rejection to attack, to liberation.

Source: "Statement of the RAF," at This is Baader-Meinhof. Available online. URL: http://www.baader-meinhof.com/students/resources/communique/engrafend.html.

"Counter-Terrorism Laws Take Effect" (2002)

Germany has been at the forefront of new counterterrorism practices in Europe, particularly in terms of introducing new identification technologies such as biometric data. The German Embassy in Washington, D.C., issued the following guide detailing the new regulations.

On January 1, a host of new laws took effect in Germany. Foremost among them is the raft of regulations known as the "Second Counter-Terrorism Packet." The first packet had amended many existing laws to meet the new threats posed by international terrorism, taking effect in December. The second packet includes numerous new security laws as well as regulations pertaining to the rights of foreigners in Germany. The new laws are intended to prevent the entry of terrorists into the Federal Republic and to enable authorities to identify extremists already residing in Germany and swiftly halt their activities. Provisions to facilitate these goals include:

- using biometric characteristics in passports and personal IDs
- making more relevant data available to security authorities
- improving identification measures in the visa-issuing process
- intensifying background checks on individuals employed in the security field
- ensuring asylum seekers and temporary residents receive IDs that cannot be counterfeited, and
- using sky marshals to prevent hijackings.

Digitized fingerprints may become part of German National ID cards

To offset the increased costs of the fight against terrorism, tax levied on general and fire insurance went up by 1% on January 1, 2002, which will generate additional revenues of roughly € 1.5 billion.

In response to a United Nations Security Council call for countries to report on existing or soon to be enacted legislation for the prevention of terrorism, Germany recently filed a paper outlining steps its has taken in this area.

For details of this report, please see Report to the Security Council Committee established pursuant to Resolution 1373 (2001) concerning Counter-Terrorism AND Annex.

Source: German Embassy, "Counter-Terrorism Laws Take Effect," Fact Sheet. Available online. URL: http://www.germany.info/relaunch/politics/new/pol_anti-terror.html.

Japan

Japan's International Counter-Terrorism Cooperation (January 2005)

After being criticized for not participating in the 1990–91 Gulf War, Japanese leaders went out of their way to join the War on Terror. In the two documents below, the Japanese Ministry of Foreign Affairs outlines the county's international counterterrorism efforts and extends the historic decision to send troops to help U.S. forces in the Indian Ocean.

I. Global Cooperation

1. UN Security Council

[. . .] Japan annually reports its implementation on counter-terrorism, including domestic measures to combat the financing of terrorism, to the UNCTC (Counter-Terrorism Committee) established by the UNSCR 1373.

2. G8

With in the framework of G8, international counter-terrorism cooperation has been developed in areas including transportation security and technical assistance to developing countries since G8 leaders issued a joint statement on September 19, 2001 and instructed relevant ministers to strengthen counter-terrorism measures. [. . .]

II. Regional Cooperation

1. ASEAN+3, ASEAN Regional Forum (ARF) and APEC

At the regional level, there has been intensive development of regional cooperation in the fight against terrorism through frameworks such as ASEAN+3, APEC and ARF, and Japan has been actively engaged in the activities in these frameworks.

With regard to ASEAN, Japan hosted the Japan-ASEAN Commemorative Summit in December 2003, and adopted the Japan-ASEAN Plan of Action, which addresses enhanced counter-terrorism measures of both parties. In November 2004, Japan and ASEAN issued "the ASEAN-Japan Joint Declaration for Cooperation in the Fight against International Terrorism," which deals with enhanced cooperation on counter-terrorism between two parties.

In APEC, leaders condemned the terrorist attacks of the September 11th attacks, and agreed to take possible measures to fight against international terrorism ("Leaders' Statement on Fighting Terrorism and Promoting Growth" in October 2002). As a specific forum dealing with counter-terrorism, the Counter-Terrorism Task Force (CTTF) has been established within APEC. In November 2004, the Santiago Declaration was adopted by the leaders at the summit in Chile, and it addresses their commitment to enhanced counter-terrorism measures including the start of issuance of machine readable travel documents originally proposed by Japan. [. . .]

2. Bali Process (Ministerial Commitment on Counter-Terrorism Issues in the Asia-Pacific Region)

In February 2004, the Bali Regional Ministerial Meeting on Counter-Terrorism was held, co-chaired by Indonesia and Australia, for the purpose of exchanging the views on counter-terrorism issues in the Southeast Asia. 25 countries in the region and EU participated, and Mr. Aisawa, Japanese Senior-Vice Minister for Foreign Affairs, participated in this meeting. Participants agreed to enhance their coordination in the legal frameworks of each country, and cooperation between law-enforcement agencies in the Asia-Pacific region.

In August 2004, the Legal Issues Working Group (LIWG) was held in Canberra, Australia, and the Law-Enforcement Working Group was held in Bali, Indonesia, as follow-up of the ministerial commitment. Japan has become the coordinator concerning ratification and implementation of international counter-terrorism Conventions and Protocols in the LIWG, and held the Seminar on the Promotion of Accession to the International Convention for the Suppression of the Financing of Terrorism in December 2004.

3. Regional Talks

In Japan, Ministry of Foreign Affairs and National Police Agency have held regional counter-terrorism dialogues every year since 1996 (except 2000). Officials from Asia, Pacific, Latin America and Middle East region have been invited. Participants discussed the issues such as the situation of Islamic extremism and CT cooperation in Southeast Asia.

III. Bilateral Cooperation

1. Bilateral Dialogues

Since Ambassador in charge of International Counter-Terrorism was appointed in March 2003, Japan has actively held bilateral and trilateral consultations on counter-terrorism as follows: [meetings with South Korea, Australia, Russia, United States and European Union]

1. 12 Conventions and Protocols on Counter-Terrorism

It is important to ratify and implement 12 international counter-terrorism conventions and protocols, which criminalize acts of terrorism, and address obligations of parties to either prosecute or extradite the terrorist to another country, in order to terminate safe-haven of terrorists. In particular, the International Convention for the Suppression of the Financing on Terrorism is significant in the sense that the convention criminalizes the acts of financial support for terrorists, and aims at regulating roots of terrorist activities.

2. Ratification and Implementation

Japan had ratified 10 of them when the UNSCR 1373 was adopted. Following UNSCR 1373, Japan ratified International Convention for the Suppression of Terrorist Bombings in November 2001, and International Convention for the Suppression of the Financing on Terrorism (TFC) in June 2002, and then completed ratification of 12 international agreements relating to terrorism. Regarding its implementation of the TFC, some laws are established, and others are amended. The Act on Punishment of Financing to Offences of Public Intimidation (Law No.67 of 2002) was introduced for the purpose of punishing patron of terrorist. Law for Customer Identification (Law No.32 of 2002) was also made so that anybody whose identity is not clear cannot use financial institution. Also the Foreign Exchange and Foreign Trade Law was amended to facilitate information exchange among relevant ministries and agencies for asset freezing.

V. Fighting the Financing of Terrorism

1. Cooperation in Fighting the Financing of Terrorism

Terminating the funding of terrorism is one of the most important measures to suppress international terrorism, since it cuts off roots of terrorist activities. Japan has ratified the International Convention for the Suppression of the Financing of Terrorism. At the same time, Japan actively joins anti-terrorist financial frameworks within the UN (CTC: Counter-Terrorism Committee), G8 (CTAG: Counter-Terrorism Action Group) and the OECD (FATF: Financial Action Task Force on Money Laundering), and contributes to international effort to eradicate terrorist finance.

2. Japan's Asset-Freezing Measures

In addition to ratifying and implementing the TFC, Japan has made full use of legal instruments to give an end to international terrorism. As of January 2005, 442 individuals / entities have been covered by the decision of UN Sanctions Committee on al-Qaeda members, and 28 individuals / entities have been targeted by the decision of UNSC CTC. In December 2004, the inclusion of additional names of "JAMA'AT AL-TAWHID WA'AL-JIHAD," which the Government of Japan submitted for the first time to the UNSC Committee Established Pursuant to Resolution 1267 concerning Al-Qaeda and the Taliban and Associated Individuals and Entities with the United Kingdom and Germany, was approved.

VI. Capacity Building Assistance on Counter-Terrorism

1. Capacity Building: Its Purpose

Some of developing countries cannot afford to arrange counter-terrorism measures in both international and domestic arena. In order to deny terrorists a safe haven anywhere in the world, Japan attaches a great importance to capacity building assistance, especially to the countries in Southeast Asia.

2. Capacity Building: Japan's Concrete Assistance

Japan has extended capacity building assistance to combat terrorism, mainly to Asian countries, in the following 9 areas: (1) immigration control, (2) aviation security, (3) port and maritime security, (4) customs cooperation, (5) export control, (6) law-enforcement cooperation, (7) anti-terrorist financing, (8) counter-CBRN terrorism, and (9) international counter-terrorism conventions and protocols. Japan accepted 235 officials in FY2001 and 264 officials in FY2002 and received approximately 306 officials in FY 2003. [. . .]

Source: The Ministry of Foreign Affairs of Japan. Available online. URL: http://www.infojapan.org/policy/terrorism/cooperation.html.

"Japan decides to continue to dispatch MSDF vessels to the Indian Ocean in order to support international efforts to fight against terrorism" (Extension of the Anti-Terrorism Special Measures Law) (October 27, 2005)

1. On October 26, Japan extended the Anti-Terrorism Special Measures Law for another year until November 2006, in order to continue to support international efforts to fight against terrorism by dispatching Mari-

time Self-Defense Force (MSDF) vessels to the Indian Ocean for refueling operations.

2. Japan enacted the Anti-Terrorism Specials Measures Law in November 2001 in order to contribute to the efforts of international society in eradicating threats of international terrorism following the September 11 attacks in the United States. The law was extended once in 2003 with its expiration date on November 1, 2005.

3. Based on the law, the MSDF vessels have supplied 410,000 kilo liters of fuels ($ about 140 million worth)(as of September 2005) to the vessels of coalition forces that are engaged in the operation to prevent and deter free movement of terrorists and their related materials (Operation Enduring Freedom-Maritime Interdiction Operation: OEF-MIO).

4. The extension of the law enables the MSDF vessels to continue the refueling activity until November 2006, and shows Japan's commitment to actively participate in the international efforts to fight against terrorism.

Source: The Ministry of Foreign Affairs of Japan. Available online. URL: http://www.mofa.go.jp/policy/terrorism/measure0510.html.

Peru

Japanese Foreign Ministry Reacts to Lima Hostage Crisis (1996)

In December 1996, members of Peru's Tupac Amaru Revolutionary Movement (MRTA) stormed a party at the Japanese ambassador's residence in Lima, taking more than 700 hostages. Japan responded in typical fashion, encouraging Lima to meet the insurgents' demands rather than resort to violence. Ultimately Peruvian forces stormed the residence in April, releasing the 72 people still held hostage at that time. The summary execution of all of the MRTA members became a scandal that contributed to the downfall of Peruvian president Alberto Fujimori.

Summary of the Press Conference by Foreign Minister Yukihiko Ikeda (on the Incident at the Official Residence of the Japanese Ambassador to the Republic of Peru)

December 18, 1996 (unofficial Translation)

1. Good evening, ladies and gentlemen. I would now like to brief you on the status of the terrorist occupation of the Japanese Ambassador's residence in

Peru. Various communications, including cables from abroad, are available. However, what we can accurately say now is that there are roughly ten terrorists holding approximately 200 hostages, according to the conversation that Prime Minister [Ryutaro] Hashimoto and President [Alberto] Fujimori had by telephone a short while ago. That is basically all we can say at the moment. However, at about 16:00 we did receive word from Japanese Embassy personnel who had been able to escape and approach the residence to see what was going on. According to their observation, all of the women and elderly involved had been released, and, at the time, no gunfire could be heard from around the residence. We also received a report that approximately 20 Peruvian Government and police vehicles, had been situated around the Ambassador's residence.

2. I would now like to explain the Foreign Ministry's immediate response to this situation. At 12:30, we established a task-force headquarters in our home offices in Tokyo, headed by the Vice-Foreign Minister Sadayuki Hayashi. This headquarters is currently the cornerstone of our information-gathering efforts. In fact, I have just come from the operations room where I consulted with task force personnel. We are determined to watch the situation very carefully, and I intend to make every effort to respond to events as they unfold.

3. In closing, I know that the information currently available is incomplete, and in some cases confusing. However, we are deeply concerned about the situation, and will continue to communicate with the Government of Peru to do our utmost to resolve the situation peacefully, making the safety of the hostages our top priority. Thank you very much.

Source: The Ministry of Foreign Affairs of Japan. Available online. URL: http://www.mofa.go.jp/region/latin/peru/incident/1218.html.

Report by Prime Minister Ryutaro Hashimoto on the Release of the Hostages Held at the Residence of the Japanese Ambassador to the Republic of Peru (1997)

April 24, 1997

I would like to report to you on the occupation of the Residence of the Japanese Ambassador to the Republic of Peru, which has been a grave cause of concern for our nation since the end of last year. At 5:23 a.m. on 23 April (Tokyo time), Special Forces of the Peruvian Army implemented a rescue operation at the Residence, which had been occupied by the MRTA. As a result, 71 hostages were freed without serious harm. All of the 24 Japanese hostages were among them.

First of all, I would like to express my deepest condolences that in the rescue of these hostages, three precious lives were sacrificed, including one hostage and two members of the military force which implemented this rescue operation. I would like to express my gratitude to President Alberto Fujimori who, with a view to safely rescuing the hostages without yielding to terrorism, prepared thoroughly and conducted this rescue operation resulting in the safe release of almost all of the hostages. I would also like to express my gratitude to the concerned countries for their cooperation during this period and for the solidarity and support of the international community for the resolution of this incident.

I spoke with President Fujimori on the phone immediately after this incident ended and I expressed my gratitude for the president's efforts, to which President Fujimori responded by asking me to convey a message to the people of Japan expressing his gratitude for the trust placed in the Government of Peru despite the fact that it had not been possible to inform the Government of Japan in advance of this operation.

Moreover, last night I dispatched Minister for Foreign Affairs Yukihiko Ikeda to Peru to express our gratitude to the Government of Peru and our condolences to the bereaved families, and to handle the various issues which will arise in the aftermath of this incident.

With regard to anti-terrorism measures, at the G-7 Summit in Lyon in June 1996, the Declaration on Terrorism was adopted. I intend for Japan to learn from this incident, and together with the international community, continue to battle terrorism in the future without ever yielding.

In closing, I would like to express my heartfelt gratitude to the members of all political parties for the warm support and cooperation which they displayed across partisan lines.

Source: Office of the Prime Minister of Japan and His Cabinet, Press Release. Available online. URL: http://www.kantei.go.jp/foreign/0430peru-3.html.

Abimael Guzman Appeal to the United Nations (1998)

Sendero Luminoso leader Guzman was captured by Peruvian forces on September 12, 1992, due in part to the new counterterrorism laws enacted when President Fujimori suspended the Constitution in April 1992. Guzman argued that his capture was illegal and took his case to the UN. His appeal describes the conditions surrounding his arrest, trial, and imprisonment.

Communication in the Matter of Guzman v. Peru, January 10, 1998 Submitted on behalf of Dr. Abimael Guzman to the United Nations Working Group On Arbitrary Detention (excerpt) Section IV: Describe the circumstances of the arrest and/or the detention and indicate precise reasons why you consider the arrest or detention to be arbitrary: . . .

(1) Pre-Trial

Dr. Guzman and others were arrested during a violent raid, without legal authorization, on the premises indicated above. Almost all the detained were physically mistreated. In the following hours, Dr. Guzman was taken to the offices of DINCOTE [National Counter-Terrorism Directorate] where he was asked to undress himself for a supposedly "routine inspection." This was improperly filmed by the agents and later shown to the press with the clear intention of humiliating Dr. Guzman.

On September 26, 1992 President Alberto Fujimori ordered Dr. Guzman and the others arrested with him to be tried under military jurisdiction on the grounds of the anti-constitutional Decree Law Nos. 25.659 and 25.708. Yet Article 282 of the Political Constitution of Peru of 1979, still in effect at that time, clearly establishes that the Military Court and the Military Code of Justice cannot be applied to a civilian except in cases of treason to the fatherland in times of foreign war, which is not the case in the situation of internal war which exists in Peru.

Mr. Fujimori also ordered that Dr. Guzman be tried in a summary military trial, according to the procedural norms of the Military Code Title II: "trial in the site of operations." This violated the following rights: the complete judicial guarantee recognized in the Political Constitution of Peru Article No. 282; the right to be tried according to the norms of due process, the right to defense and the right to be judged by the jurisdiction predetermined by law. [. . .]

When on September 24, 1992, Dr. Guzman was brought before members of the international and domestic press corps, he was dressed in striped prison clothing and confined in an iron cage in an orchestrated attempt to humiliate him. This was a deliberate attempt to rob him of his dignity before the world and to make him appear as a convict. [. . .]

(2) The Trial

Dr. Guzman's trial, which took place in the context of martial law throughout Lima, was held on the military base on San Lorenzo island. The judges (and everyone else present in the courtroom except the defendant and his attorney) were all Navy officers, and thus under President Fujimori's direct orders as commander-in-chief, rendering them not competent to conduct a fair and impartial trial of Dr. Guzman. This military tribunal was conducted in the strictest secrecy violating the guarantee of an open and public trial as set forth in Article 10 of the UDHR which provides for a fair and public hearing by an independent and impartial tribunal.

The judges and their assistants all wore black hoods. Court officials were identified not by name but by numbers only, and spoke aloud only through voice-altering electronic devices. These "faceless court" procedures violated Dr. Guzman's right to challenge the judges for bias, since it is impossible for the defense to ascertain the identities of the officials.

President Fujimori ordered that Dr. Guzman and the others also arrested on September 12, 1992, be held in total isolation, with no communication at all, even with their lawyers. The lawyers turned to the judicial authorities for help in getting access to their clients, and on September 14, the Attorney General of Peru, Dr. Blanca Nelida Dolan Maguino, told Dr. Crespo the she "could not do anything at all to help" since "the government's order was not to intervene." [. . .] Just prior to the beginning of trial Dr. Crespo ultimately was allowed fifteen minutes with his client to prepare his defense and was only allowed to communicate by telephone from across the room; this was the first and last time they were allowed to discuss the case. During the interview the universally recognized right to privacy of attorney-client communications was violated by the surveillance of police agents as well as by the setting of secret microphones to record it. [. . .]

Dr. Alfredo Crespo, Dr. Guzman's attorney was advised of the trial date with only two days prior notice. Despite repeated requests he had been denied access to the case files on numerous occasions and was finally allowed only twelve hours to review eight volumes of material and prepare his arguments. This was in violation of the requirement that defendants be afforded time for the preparation of their defense as guaranteed in the ICCPR Article 14 (3b).

Dr. Crespo faced a systematic policy of harassment, being subjected to 24-hour surveillance and also death threats. On his way to the trial, Dr. Crespo was led blindfolded across minefields by soldiers who told him, "Take care,

Doctor, walk slowly, take care with the mines." During the trial Dr. Crespo was led into the courtroom blindfolded and made to sit behind a panel of thick glass. All of this was part of a policy to severely infringe upon Dr. Crespo's ability to defend his client and was in violation of Dr. Guzman's universally protected right to present a defense.

At no time before the trial and sentencing was Dr. Guzman ever informed of the charges against him. Only after the trial was over was Dr. Crespo briefly allowed to see a copy of the indictment, to which he was instructed to respond immediately in writing if he wished to appeal Dr. Guzman's conviction. Since the indictment is still secret and the lawyer is not allowed to reveal its contents, it is not clear exactly what the charges against Dr. Guzman were, although the Peruvian press has said that there were no specific charges whatsoever. [. . .]

Under the instructions of President Fujimori, the Joint Command of the Armed Forces and the Supreme Council of Military Justice, the judge ordered that Dr. Guzman be seated during the entire trial on a chair enclosed in a specially constructed steel cage. He was interrogated exclusively about his political and ideological convictions, which demonstrated that these convictions were the sole objective of the "trial," [. . .]

On October 7th, 1992 the verdict was announced: guilty of "treason to the fatherland." This announcement was delivered to the national and international press by an "Official Communique" of the Supreme Court of Military Justice—several hours *before* the sentence was actually handed down by the Instructor Judge in the hearing scheduled for that purpose. This situation confirms yet again the lack of autonomy of the judge issuing the sentence. In fact, President Fujimori had already announced the date and nature of the verdict, as well as that the sentence would be life imprisonment, *before* the trial was even conducted. Mr. Fujimori stated that sentence would be imposed on October 7, 1992, and that the second hearing to be held on October 27, 1992, would uphold the sentence from the first case. All of this clearly indicates the totally arbitrary and illegal character of this trial, as carried out under the orders of Mr. Fujimori.

(3) Post-Trial

. . . On April 3, 1993 Dr. Guzman was transferred to a newly built prison specially designed to create a sense of total isolation and deprivation. The design of the cells, built completely underground, ensures that contact, even visual, between prisoners and the outside world (including the guards) is reduced to an absolute minimum. The cells have no ventilation and no electricity or water. Because the prison is situated near the mouth of the Rimac River it may periodically flood. In short the prison facility was designed to bring about a "certain and slow" death, as stated by Mr. Fujimori in April, 1993 in the Argentinean press and transmitted on Channel 13 on Lima television. Mr. Fujimori has described the prison where Dr. Guzman is held as a "tomb for the living." These conditions of imprisonment constitute cruel and degrading treatment [. . .]

Mail to and from prisoners is strictly controlled by the National Intelligence Service (SIN). According to the government, Dr. Guzman is not allowed to receive any type of correspondence and is not permitted nor given the necessary means to conduct correspondence. President Fujimori himself controls all forms of possible communication. There is no access to books, magazines, papers, TV or radio (Dr. Guzman was also denied his eyeglasses). According to the government, the only information accessible to these prisoners is via edited videos in a TV room. President Fujimori has openly bragged to the press of keeping Dr. Guzman on "an information diet," on which Dr. Guzman has no access no knowledge of any news (e.g., press coverage or other news sources independent of his captors), and is thus kept unaware of actual developments in Peru and the world. [. . .]

Source: Committee to Support the Revolution in Peru. Available online. URL: http://www.csrp.org/iec/agunbrief.htm.

Tupac Amaru Revolutionary Movement Statement on the Global Economy (1998)

MRTA outlined its objections to capitalism and global commerce in the following statement submitted to the UN Commission on Human Rights Sub-Commission on Prevention of Discrimination and Protection of Minorities.

THE REALIZATION OF ECONOMIC, SOCIAL AND CULTURAL RIGHTS: THE QUESTION OF TRANSNATIONAL CORPORATIONS
June 22, 1998

CODE OF CONDUCT FOR TRANSNATIONAL CORPORATIONS

. . . . .

2. A response is now needed to the challenges posed by the inexorable advance of globalization worldwide, the deregulation of the international financial system, the penetration of transnational corporations in all spheres of the world economy leading to the irrational exploitation of natural

resources, the privatization of core enterprises and extreme poverty ensuing from the implementation of the structural adjustment programmes of the International Monetary Fund (IMF) and the World Bank.

3. In the context of the new international economic order, the transnational movement, as the concrete manifestation of the blind, anarchic forces of the market economy, constitutes the greatest obstacle to the effective exercise of the inherent economic, social and cultural rights of all peoples, and to the enjoyment of their basic natural resources as provided in international instruments.

4. In the face of the law of free competition—the driving force behind globalization, which sweeps away all obstacles to the unbridled determination to colonize the world, hastens the dismantling of mechanisms and rules of conduct and obstructs the economic function of the State—societies from North to South have succumbed in a world without borders, without laws and without ethical standards. After the relentless advance of the globalization of capital, the absence is being felt now more than ever before of an international legal framework that is capable of regulating the manifold activities of transnationals and their direct investments throughout the world.

5. A number of factors make the elaboration of a code of conduct for transnational corporations a matter of urgency. First, the invisible hand of powerful monopolies and holdings, which are in constant quest of profit and which, by their nature, behave irrationally and blindly, that is, without morals and outside the jurisdiction of host countries. Their prime objective consists in generating maximum profit and gain by plundering natural resources and exploiting labour.

6. Second, the demands of poor countries for the right to just and equitable development have confirmed how impossible it is to bring such supranational activities under the control of a host country's national legislation. The host States have gradually lost their bargaining power and can no longer exercise legal jurisdiction over foreign subsidiaries operating in their territories, because their legislations often contain no reference to the term or concept of "corporate nationality," or to rules of conduct or any definition of the legal status of transnational corporations.

7. Since the domestic legislation of host countries neither specifies the legal status nor clearly defines the rights and duties of the supranational enterprises they are in effect neither national nor stateless, but operate through vertical links with their parent companies which effectively means that they

are subject to the jurisdiction of decision-making centres located in the industrialized nations.

.....

18. Meanwhile, the international community, particularly environmental organizations and indigenous peoples committed to defending the Earth, to protecting the environment and to the rational use of resources, were left confused and powerless in the face of the triumph of the neoliberal and free trade policies as absolute values of the market economy.

19. In conformity with General Assembly resolution 47/212B, of 6 May 1993, on the restructuring of the United Nations, it was decided to do away with the United Nations Centre on Transnational Corporations and to replace it simply with a Division on Transnational Corporations and Investments, which under a different name is currently part of the Geneva-based UNCTAD. Its function is now limited to gathering and publishing statistical data on the flows of direct foreign investment in the world.

20. In June 1994, the Centre on Transnational Corporations submitted its fourth and final report to the Working Group on Indigenous Populations in compliance with the Sub-Commission's resolutions 1989/35 of 1 September 1989, 1990/26 of 31 August 1990, 1991/31 of 29 August 1991 and 1992/33 of 27 August 1992. The indigenous peoples of the world, who are the first victims of the negative effects of transnational capital, lamented the lack of political will on the part of States and urged the United Nations to restore the Centre on Transnational Corporations.

21. For the above reasons, and in the light of the legitimate concerns of the nations which are gradually succumbing to the dictatorship of transnational capital, the non-governmental organizations signing this declaration called on the Sub-Commission to adopt appropriate recommendations, addressed to the United Nations bodies and to the international community, for the urgent establishment of a working group or the restoration of the Centre on Transnational Corporations, with the following responsibilities:

(a) To identify the globally negative effects of transnational corporations on the enjoyment of economic, social and cultural rights;

(b) To investigate the illegal transfer of capital from poor countries to rich countries, and fraudulent and speculative operations on the stock market;

(c) To define the ownership structure of multinational corporations and their global strategies aimed at market concentration at national, regional and international levels;

(d) To examine the legality of mergers between transnational corporations and banks to form monopolies with unlimited powers, which obstruct technology transfers;

(e) To regulate the abusive use of financial mechanisms (World Bank, IMF, UNDP and other international development aid bodies) serving the interests of parent companies and their subsidiaries;

(f) To assess the interference of transnational corporations in the political life of States, through the corruption and bribery of governments, parliamentarians and the military;

(g) To determine the responsibilities of transnational corporations with respect to environmental pollution, the destruction of nature and the laundering of drug money;

(h) To compile reliable data on direct foreign investment in developing countries and on the dispossession of resources considered to be strategic for national sovereignty, and to draft a series of recommendations which could serve as a normative basis for a future code of conduct.

Source: United Nations Economic and Social Council, Document E/CN.4/Sub.2/1998/NGO/12.

President Bush Meets with President Toledo in Peru (2002) (excerpt)

Three days before U.S. president George W. Bush was to visit Peru in March 2002, a car bomb exploded outside the U.S. Embassy in Lima, killing 10 people. The Peruvian government blamed Sendero Luminoso for the attack, and Bush arrived on schedule. At their joint press conference, President Bush and President Alejandro Toledo discuss their experiences with terrorism, particularly narco-terrorism.

Remarks by President Bush and President Toledo in Joint Press Conference
Presidential Palace
Lima, Peru
March 23, 2002

PRESIDENT BUSH: Earlier today, our two governments signed an agreement that will reintroduce the Peace Corps to Peru, after an absence of nearly 30 years. The first volunteers will arrive in August, a symbol of the stronger ties between our people and the stronger relationship between our nations.

This relationship is based on common values and common interests. Our nations understand that political and economic progress depends on security—and that security is impossible in a world with terrorists. Peruvians have been reminded again this week of the terrible human toll of terror. On behalf of the people of the United States, I express our deep sympathy for the victims of the recent bombing and our deep sympathy for their loved ones.

President Toledo and I share a common perspective on terrorism: We must stop it. Since September the 11th, Peru has taken the lead in rallying our hemisphere to take strong action against this common threat. And I want to thank the President for his leadership and his strong support.

Our nations understand that freedom is only as strong as the institutions protecting it. The United States is actively supporting the President's efforts to strengthen Peru's democratic foundations. And we will continue to support the work of Peru's Truth and Reconciliation Commission, which is helping correct the abuses of the past and set the course for a better future. . . .

Q You, sir. Given increasing evidence that the FARC [Revolutionary Armed Forces of Columbia] is now operating in Peru, will you be willing to provide President Toledo extra assistance in fighting the war against terrorism here, should he ask for it? And are you concerned that what was once a regional problem in Colombia or something restricted to Colombia is now spreading across Colombia's border and threatening its neighbors?

PRESIDENT BUSH: We discussed the neighborhood at length today. President Toledo told me that he is—now that he's done a very good job, or the country's done a good job, of making sure that relations with neighbors, north and south, are peaceful, that he is moving troops and making decisions to prevent terrorists from coming into his country from Colombia. And we will help him in this effort. That's part of the reason why I'm here—is to support our mutual desire to fight terror and to help this good democracy thrive.

PRESIDENT TOLEDO: [. . .]—I repeat, the evidence that we have indicates that there is no transfer of the FARC into Peru. However, we are adopting every measure possible. The Minister of Defense was at the border very recently. We took our bases that were along the border with Ecuador—where, after signing the peace agreement, there is no need for their presence—we removed them as a precautionary measure over to the border with Colombia.

As President Bush just indicated, this is a joint task. What happens to Colombia affects us, and vice versa. But here, too, we're partners. And I think that the issues that have to do with the Andean community are issues on which President Bush is extremely interested and I'm sure that we will be working together on these. We are going to work together on this; I'm sure of that. . . .

PRESIDENT TOLEDO: [. . .] In 1990, the number of hectares with coca cultivation was approximately 140,000 total. Today, we are down to 34,000 hectares where we have coca cultivation. Enormous progress has been made.

I know it's not enough. We have a long path ahead of us yet. And we have to do this together. I know that the drug traffickers have become more sophisticated over time—they have more high-tech capabilities. And now we, too, have to push forward in that direction.

I want to be very open, and I apologize to my friend, President Bush, now. We are not fighting against drug trafficking in order to satisfy the United States or Europe. Drug trafficking, in partnership with terrorism, is an issue of national security. It's an issue of national security. On Wednesday, they killed nine people—nine of our brothers and sisters—and there are 30 people wounded. I have publicly stated—and I want to repeat this—we are not going to let this stand.

So let me respond to you. We have met a substantial reduction. We still have 34,000 hectares to go. But we are going to do this together.

Final point. I think President Bush is extremely sincere—he's extremely sincere and honest when he recognizes that as long as there is a demand out there, there will be a supply. As long as there are consumers, there will be producers. And so, together, we need to work on reducing the number of consumers, cure them better, make them better. And we need to reduce the amount of hectares under cultivation.

Source: White House Press Office. Available online. URL: http://www.whitehouse.gov/news/releases/2002/03/20020323-13.html.

Colombia

Plan Colombia (2003)

In June 2000 the United States launched "Plan Colombia," a major policy package to eradicate cocaine production in Colombia. The program changed

the institutional focus of counternarcotics efforts. While previously U.S. funding had favored the national police, now it dramatically shifted to the military. The 2000–01 package offered $416.9 million to the Colombian army, compared with $115.6 million to the national police.

The Government of Colombia has developed a multi-year, comprehensive strategy designed to bring about lasting peace by reducing the production of illegal drugs, revitalizing the economy and strengthening government institutions. This is known as Plan Colombia.

The international press tends to refer to Plan Colombia as only a military operation, but this is inaccurate. Because Plan Colombia is a social and political strategy to bring government presence to the country's frontier territories and re-unite them with the rest of the country. In other words, it seeks to strengthen public institutions and the rule of law in an area overwhelmed by lawlessness. And at the same time, bring about economic reform and sustained growth to an ailing economy, which in 1999 had negative GDP growth of 4.3%.

Of course, Plan Colombia also seeks to fight against the drug trade, because a significant portion of the multi-billion dollar profits from drug-trafficking are funding the activities of guerrillas and paramilitaries, while thousands of innocent civilians are caught in the crossfire. A final peace agreement, probably the most important of the four main objectives of Plan Colombia, will remain illusive as long as the rebel groups maintain an unlimited source of funding from drug trafficking. So it is in Colombia's national interest to crack-down on this illegal industry.

But there is a two-track approach to counter-narcotics in Plan Colombia. For the first time in Colombian history, a voluntary eradication program is being offered to all farmers who grow coca on small individual plots. If they agree to eradicate their coca crop, the government will provide them with cash recompensation and the tools they need to move into legitimate farming—such as seed, equipment and technical support.

At the same time the Colombian National Police is spraying large industrial coca plantations. In reality, the so-called "military" part of Plan Colombia, is really no more than an escort service for the Colombian National Police's activities of spraying industrial coca plantations and destroying cocaine laboratories. The only reason why this is needed is because both guerrillas and paramilitaries will fire from the ground at the spraying aircraft, and fire at the Police when they enter these areas in order to destroy a drug laboratory. So 14 Black Hawks and 45 Huey transport helicopters will provide the necessary protection and transportation requirements for three battalions of 900 men each. That is all the U.S. trained and funded counter-narcotics units are and will be doing. Counter-guerrilla or counter-paramilitary operations are forbidden.

But most importantly, Plan Colombia is a massive government strategy to bring social development and create a social safety net for Colombia's population. The Government of Colombia is investing $900 million dollars in four distinctive social strategies:

Employment in Action, which consists of hiring unqualified workers to boost employment levels in local infrastructure projects throughout the country. More than 1.502 projects, fully funded, are under way, in 237 municipalities.

Families in Action, subsidies to poor families in exchange for a commitment to keep their children in school.

Youth in Action, a national program to train young unemployed men and women in private sector companies with government subsidies. It will reach a total of 104.000 youths.

Roads for Peace, which includes 14 major roads, local roads, river infrastructure and bridges, 4 times more roads than all those built in the last 20 years.

[. . .]

What does Plan Colombia aim to achieve?

Build and strengthen public institutions throughout Colombia. This includes reforming the judicial system and combating corruption, as well as the restructuring and modernizing Colombia's Armed Forces and National Police. It also includes training local government officials and strengthening the Government's ability to protect and defend the human rights of all its citizens. Significant social investments are being made in areas that have been traditionally neglected by the Government, especially in the Putumayo region in southern Colombia, where half the country's coca is grown. Plan Colombia will make investments in alternative economic development for the farmers who grow coca. It will also fund the development of infrastructure, education and health care.

Reduce the illegal drug trade. The Government is committed to reducing narco-trafficking and illegal drugs by 50% over the next five years. This will be achieved by destroying illegal coca crops through aerial spraying and providing alternative development for farmers and peasants currently engaged in growing small amounts of coca. It also means seizing a greater number of illegal drugs and destroying the infrastructure of the drug traffickers, including their coca laboratories, and transportation, communications and distribution networks.

Revitalize the economy. A strong, growing economy with opportunity for all Colombians is the key to building peace and making progress in the war against illegal drugs. This means creating new employment, expanding international trade and increasing foreign investment in the country. The Government cannot ask poor farmers in coca growing areas to destroy their illegal crops without providing them with assistance—in the form of cash payments, equipment and technical support—to grow legal crops. Plan Colombia also aims to fund a "social safety net" for the poorest members of Colombian society.

Advance peace talks between the Government and guerrilla organizations, to negotiate a comprehensive peace agreement with armed insurgents. Success in reducing Colombia's drug trade will cut off funds used by all violent actors in the country, thereby making a peace agreement more possible.

Source: Embassy of Colombia in Washington. Available online. URL: http://www.colombiaemb.org/opencms/opencms/plancolombia/.

Kingpin Act Applied to Colombian Narco-Terrorists (2004)

One of the most effective strategies against terrorism and the illegal drug trade is to cut access to sources of financing. The U.S. Treasury took the additional step of applying antiterrorist fund-raising provisions to the Colombian narcotics trade.

Treasury takes action against FARC/AUC Narco-Terrorist Leaders in continued effort to Halt Narcotics Trafficking

February 19, 2004

In another important effort in the battle against narcotics trafficking, the Treasury Department took action today against leaders and key figures of the Colombian narco-terrorist organizations, the Revolutionary Armed Forces of Colombia (Fuerzas Armadas Revolucionarias de Colombia, "FARC") and the United Self-Defense Forces of Colombia (Autodefensas Unidas de Colombia, "AUC").

The Treasury's Office of Foreign Assets Control (OFAC) has added the names of FARC leaders, including Pedro Antonio Marin and Jorge Briceno Suarez, key AUC figures, including Carlos Castano Gil and Salvatore Mancuso Gomez and AUC front companies to the list of "Tier II" persons designated under the Foreign Narcotics Kingpin Designation Act (Kingpin Act). The 40 Colombian names added to the Kingpin Act list include 19 FARC individuals, 18 individuals associated with the AUC and three front companies connected to the AUC. These 40 persons are subject to the economic sanctions imposed against foreign drug cartels under the Kingpin Act.

The OFAC action prohibits U.S. individuals and companies from doing business with the 40 designated persons and blocks their assets found in U.S. jurisdiction. Today's designations comprise the first actions by Treasury against the operatives and fronts of the FARC and the AUC; and they are part of Treasury's plan to further identify, expose, isolate and incapacitate these Colombian narco-terrorists and their support networks.

These Kingpin Act designations reinforce the reality that the FARC and the AUC are not simply terrorist/guerrilla organizations fighting within Colombia to achieve political agendas. They are part and parcel of the narcotics production and export threat to the United States, as well as Europe and other countries of Latin America.

The FARC and the AUC organizations were designated by President Bush as Significant Foreign Narcotics Traffickers on May 29, 2003. As the White House announced at that time, "This action underscores the President's determination to pursue narco-terrorists. This action also underscores the President's determination to do everything possible to fight drug traffickers, undermine their operations and end the suffering that trade in illicit drugs inflicts on Americans and other people around the world." [. . .]

This action is part of the ongoing interagency effort to carry out the mandate of the Kingpin Act, which applies economic sanctions against foreign narcotics trafficking kingpins worldwide. It reflects the increasing cooperation, coordination and integration among these agencies in the battle against international narcotics trafficking and narco-terrorism.

A total of 104 organizations, individuals and businesses in 12 foreign countries are now designated under the Kingpin Act. In addition to the prohibitions on transactions and blocking of assets subject to U.S. jurisdiction, penalties under the Kingpin Act range from civil penalties of up to $1,075,000 per violation to more severe criminal penalties. Criminal penalties for corporate officers are up to 30 years in prison and fines up to $5,000,000. Criminal fines for corporations are up to $10,000,000. Other individuals face up to ten years in prison for criminal violations of the Kingpin Act.

Source: U.S. Department of the Treasury, Office of Public Affairs. Available online. URL: http://www.ustreas.gov/press/releases/js1181.htm.

PART III

Research Tools

6

How to Research Terrorism and Global Security

INTRODUCTION

Any research project requires a basic set of information. This set includes a topic, a research question, an argument, evidence, and a conclusion.

Topic. Teachers usually assign a broad topic to study, but you should be able to find a way to make it relevant and interesting to you. Any subject has multiple dimensions and can be developed in numerous directions. Terrorism can be described in terms of location (in the United States or in a foreign country), motive (religion, discrimination), or tactic (bombing, hijacking, poisoning). Find something among these many aspects that sparks your attention. Do you know someone who was killed on 9/11? Then consider studying al-Qaeda, hijackings, or the U.S. response to the tragedy. Have you visited a country or do you have family in a country that has experienced a terrorist attack? Consider studying one particular incident or one particular terrorist group active in that country. If you are considering a career in the military—or have family in the military now—perhaps study the U.S. response to terrorism or investigate incidents when U.S. military bases have been targeted. If espionage, diplomacy, or financing are more your interest, look into surveillance, wiretapping, treaties, or fund-raising activities related to terrorism.

Research Question. Next identify what you want to know. Consider your subject using the basic journalism questions: Who are these people? What do they want? Why are they acting in this manner? Where are they active? How do they distribute their message? What is their message? Another possibility is to explore a counterfactual, meaning what if history had been different? What if al-Qaeda had succeeded in pulling off an attack on New Year's Day 2000? Once you identify your question (and you can begin with more than one), it is time to start researching the topic. Your first goal is to establish the facts; you must know *what* happened before you can explain *why* it happened. For the Tokyo subway attack, for example, you need to establish the date, the type of poison used, the casualty figures, and the name of the group behind the attack.

Evidence. Your next step is to head to a library or log on to a research portal for terrorism and gather the information to back up your hypothesis. Articles in daily newspapers are likely too numerous to be a good starting point for your research, and an Internet search for *terrorism* will return more than 250 million hits. Books are also likely to provide more information than you need during this phase. Instead, try searching for your terrorist group or incident in weekly or monthly news magazines such as *Time, Newsweek, U.S. News and World Report,* or the *Economist,* a British news magazine. Encyclopedias such as the *World Book* and *Encyclopedia Britannica* are another good source for establishing the broad outlines of a group or incident. If your library has them, specialized encyclopedias such as the *Encyclopedia of Terrorism* and *The Black Book of Communism: Crimes, Terror, Repression, Terrorism in the 20th Century* can be invaluable. The U.S. Department of State publishes an annual report, *Country Reports on Terrorism* (formerly *Patterns of Global Terrorism*), that provides a breakdown of incidents by region and profiles of active groups, particularly groups classified as Foreign Terrorist Organizations by the U.S. government. Many of the other Web sites that offer incident and group profiles (listed below) reproduce the *Country Reports* information, so it is best to start at the actual source. Still, they tend to offer information beyond just the recycled profiles, so they are worth a look.

As you gather your evidence, put together a time line of key events. This will help you find gaps in your research and provide a quick reference when you begin to be overwhelmed by detail. A time line will also help keep data in chronological order, a critical detail because so many terrorist attacks are described as revenge for a previous attack. The time line can also be included as an appendix to the final research paper.

Try to locate and use primary sources whenever possible. Primary sources are statements that come from the actual people involved; secondary sources talk about what the people did. A research project needs to stay as close to actual events as possible to guarantee accuracy, and it is simply more interesting to, for example, read a statement by Osama bin Laden rather than read what the *New York Times* reports about the statement. Similarly, rather than just quoting an American Civil Liberties Union press release on the Patriot Act, take the time to find the actual text under discussion. While it is unlikely that you actually will interview a terrorist in person, numerous quotations and primary documents are available both online and in print. Terrorism is a form of violence, and you should not get too close to your topic.

Argument. This is the *why* portion of the project. Now that you have established the facts in your research you should analyze the information you have in order to explain *why* an event occurred or turned out the way it did. Why did the Japanese cult release poison into the Tokyo metro system? What did they want to accomplish? Why did they think this strategy would work? Other topics might raise questions; such as: Why do people become suicide bombers? Why did Timothy McVeigh decide to bomb an office building? What did he think would happen as a result? You began with a research question; now formulate your answer into a statement. "Puerto Rican nationalists attacked the U.S. Capitol because. . . ." "Osama bin Laden hates the United States because. . . ." Often your research will uncover an answer given by the terrorists themselves. Groups tend to issue statements explaining their actions—their own version of the *why* question—but their explanation is naturally biased, so it is good to find and consider other points of view. One man's "freedom fighter" is another man's "terrorist." Now you should consider whether or not they achieved their intended results. If they did not achieve their goal, then why not?

Try to cover the issue fairly. While you need to know the motives behind a terrorist attack, you also need to know and present the opinion of all involved parties. A paper on the Palestinian group Hamas, for example, would discuss why the group objects to the existence of the State of Israel. But complete coverage of Hamas should also explain the Israeli side—what is their justification for the existence of their state? Other Palestinian groups, such as Yasser Arafat's Palestine Liberation Organization have approached the Israeli question from a different perspective, an angle that should be discussed as well. Justification is different from legitimacy; a group may have a highly developed explanation (justification) for their position, but the argument may have no legal foundation (legitimacy). Typically, terrorists believe their cause is legitimate while the targets do not.

Conclusion. Finally, draw all of the information together and see if it makes sense. Does the research data support the original hypothesis? If the answer is yes, the project is complete. But if the answer is no, it is time to revisit the original research question. Can the question be refined in light of the data discovered? Must the argument be modified to show that a particular factor did *not* affect the event or group in question? If the paper does not make a convincing argument, more research is needed.

RESEARCHING THE TOPIC

Researchers must make sure to use reliable sources to support their argument. With an emotion-laden topic such as terrorism, it becomes even more important to scrutinize the accuracy of the data and make sure it is free of bias. Fortunately, many publishers of reference materials already have procedures in place to verify their information. Research tools can be divided into two categories: traditional and nontraditional.

Traditional Research Tools

Traditional research tools are printed-paper sources that predate the Internet. They may not be quite as convenient to use as a personal computer, but many have editorial boards and review panels that evaluate all data before it is published. Many long-established publishers have embraced electronic publishing and produce online versions of their products. Your library may subscribe to one of these electronic sources. Talk to the reference librarians where you are working; these are the people who best know what the resources are in their collections and can help you to connect to other interesting materials you might discover as your project unfolds. Examples in each category are given below:

ENCYCLOPEDIAS AND ALMANACS

Encyclopedia sets are a staple of public and school libraries, and the two best-known general encyclopedias are the *Encyclopedia Britannica* and the *World Book Encyclopedia.* Almanacs are also valuable for basic country information and time lines. More specialized publications include the CIA *World Fact*

Book (also available online) and the *Statesman's Yearbook,* which provide exhaustive data on every country in the world, from trade levels to birth rates. The *Oxford Companion: Politics of the World* features concise histories of countries and pared-down explanations for ongoing international conflicts. There are several encyclopedias of terrorism available, including Harvey W. Kushner's *Encyclopedia of Terrorism* (Sage), the three-volume *Encyclopedia of World Terrorism,* edited by Martha Crenshaw (M. E. Sharpe), and the companion *Encyclopedia of World Terrorism: Documents.* Be aware that there may be multiple books with similar titles, so be sure to note the editor and the publisher. Other potentially useful reference works include the Congressional Quarterly's *World Encyclopedia of Parliaments and Legislatures* and its *Encyclopedia of Politics and Religion.* Once you locate a useful volume on the reference shelf, keeping looking to see what else is shelved in the same area; you may find more useful materials.

MAGAZINES

Weekly news magazines are a great reference tool as they provide more detailed and considered coverage of events. U.S. news magazines include *Newsweek, Time,* and *U.S. News and World Report.* The British *Economist* is highly regarded as well. All four have search engines available on their Internet sites.

NEWSPAPERS

National newspapers are preferable to local newspapers. Often articles from the national papers are reprinted in local papers with at least one day's delay. Look for the *New York Times, Wall Street Journal, Washington Post,* and the *Los Angeles Times.* Paper indexes to the newspapers may be available at local libraries, and most newspapers' Web sites also allow searching of their archives—but they charge if you want to print the full article.

JOURNALS

Scholarly journals, with established review policies, are not always available in public or high school libraries. However, online research tools for these publications, such as *Social Sciences Index* are likely available, and the librarian could order you a copy of a promising article. Among the best are *Foreign Affairs* and *Foreign Policy.* More specialized journals include *Studies in Conflict and Terrorism* and *Terrorism and Political Violence.*

BOOKS

A library catalog search of *terrorism* provides almost as many hits as a Google search on the term. However, there are annotated bibliographies that may help locate appropriate books. These include: Librarians' Internet Index (www.lii.org/pub/subtopic/154), Western Washington University (www.library.wwu.edu/ref/subjguides/polsci/terror.htm), the Memorial Institute for the Prevention of Terrorism (www.mipt.org/terrorismbibliography.asp), LLRX (www.llrx.com/features/terrorbiblio.htm), and the University of Michigan (www.isr.umich.edu/cps/har/TerrorismBibliography.doc).

TRANSCRIPTS

Networks have long made transcripts of their news reports available, but it often took days, if not weeks, to receive them. Now reports from the British Broadcasting Company (BBC: www.bbc.co.uk) and Cable News Network (CNN: www.cnn.com) are posted online immediately. Both BBC and CNN online also provide links to additional articles on a topic. Other cable networks are also making their reports available online, often with additional background materials and teacher guides. Among the best are the *Wide Angle* and *Frontline* shows from PBS. Court TV's Crime Library (www.crimelibrary.com) also has an extensive section on terrorism.

Electronic Research Tools

The Internet has brought thousands of reference sources into homes, libraries, coffee houses, anyplace with a modem or WiFi access. Many long-standing publications have chosen to make their products available on the Web. The Internet is strongest when covering current events. It can provide information and photos of terrorist attacks and counterterrorism milestones within hours, in contrast to the next day for newspapers, next week for news magazines, next year for scholarly journals, and next couple of years for books and print encyclopedia entries. At the same time, by posting anything that becomes available, without consideration or evaluation, errors naturally occur.

False information is a particular problem with electronic sources. Anyone with Internet access can upload their own research studies, blogs, rumors, and gossip. Many terrorist groups have their own Web sites—4,000 according to one estimate—and users must be aware of the inherent bias in such sites. Terrorists use such sites for propaganda, recruitment, training, and fund-raising; some terrorist groups now take PayPal.[1] There have been cases of terrorist groups creating a fake Web site that appears to belong to an enemy or small cells creating multiple sites under multiple names to try to appear larger than they really are. The Internet is filled with treasures and trash—the challenge is to differentiate between the two.

WIKIPEDIA: A WORD OF CAUTION

Wikipedia (www.en.wikipedia.org) is an online encyclopedia that has become a first stop for research on almost any topic. It is an open-source, user-run project that features more than 1 million articles in English and hundreds of thousands of articles in more than 200 other languages (even Klingon). While it is a good tool to orient researchers and provide a broad overview of a topic, it should not be considered a definitive source. Librarians dislike the site for its lack of quality control, and increasingly teachers and college professors are refusing to accept it as a valid source in research projects.[2]

The problem stems from its open-source structure. Because so many people can create and alter entries, intellectual vandalism has begun to occur. Put simply, many Wikipedia entries are written by experts in their field, but the entries can be altered by pranksters or people with their own motives or axes to grind. In addition, some authors are not as expert as they believe and factual errors may appear; it is quite possible inadvertently to replace facts with mistakes. Wikipedia has no editorial review board in place, but there is a team of 800 or so volunteers who check the accuracy of posts *after* they appear online; there is no screening before posting. This makes the process somewhat like shooting first and asking questions later.

Often the vandals are moving faster than the volunteers. In early 2006 Wikipedia's sponsors temporarily blocked postings from the U.S. Congress after discovering that staffers had polished the entries on their members of congress while making unflattering alterations in rivals' entries.[3] Staff from the Central Intelligence Agency, marine corps, navy, and even the Department of Justice have also been caught rewriting history, in one case to say that President Bill Clinton was "dumber" than Republican presidents.[4] The most infamous case of Wikipedia vandalism to date concerned John Seigenthaler, Sr., a retired newspaper editor who had once been an assistant to Robert F. Kennedy. A prankster anonymously altered Seigenthaler's entry to say erroneously that he had been a suspect in the assassinations of both Robert Kennedy and his brother, President John F. Kennedy. Seigenthaler published a severe criticism of Wikipedia in *USA Today* that provoked more attacks on his Wikipedia entry, this time obscenity-laced accusations and near libelous statements against Seigenthaler and his family.

The Seigenthaler case illustrates academia's basic problem with Wikipedia: You cannot fully trust the information. What if a student was researching a topic, such as the Kennedy assassinations, and happened to find and quote the erroneous Seigenthaler allegation before it had been corrected? The disinformation was online for nearly four months before it was discovered.[5] At minimum, the student might fail the assignment; if the allegation was repeated, Siegenthaler's reputation might be ruined and lawsuits might ensue. Most in-print publications and reputable online sources will have procedures in place to catch most errors of this type before they ever reach term papers.

WEB PORTALS

Since popular search engines such as Google and Ask.com produce millions of hits on a term such as *terrorism,* they are not a good place to begin your research. Instead of trying to wade through those results, use a Web portal to filter and organize the information. There are a variety of high-quality Internet sites for terrorism.

National Counterterrorism Center
URL: http://www.nctc.gov/
Created in 2004 as a central collecting point for U.S. intelligence on terrorism, the National Counterterrorism Center works with the Department of State to produce annual reports on terrorist groups and activities. The NCTC Web site has a counterterrorism calendar (not documenting events but highlighting terrorists) and an extensive database, the Worldwide Incidents Tracking System.

U.S. Department of State, Counterterrorism Office
URL: http://www.state.gov/s/ct/rls/crt/
Federal law requires the Department of State to submit annual reports to Congress detailing the activities and threats linked to terrorism. The result, *Country Reports on Terrorism,* is available online. Previously known as *Patterns of Global Terrorism,* the report was renamed following the creation of the National Counterterrorism Center in 2004. These State Department publications are the primary source for many terrorist profiles on other Web sites.

Terrorism Knowledge Base
URL: http://www.tkb.org
The Memorial Institute for the Prevention of Terrorism, located in Oklahoma City, hosts the Terrorism Knowledge Base, a comprehensive databank of global terrorist incidents and organizations. The site contains a complete set of all issues of *Patterns of Global Terrorism* (1976–2004) and *Terrorism in the United States* (1982), its FBI counterpart. The Knowledge Base is searchable by terrorist group, incident, and region.

Federation of American Scientists Intelligence Resource Program
URL: http://fas.org/irp/index.html
Contains extensive information on intelligence and governmental secrecy. Includes information on intelligence and security agencies around the world

and complete texts of speeches, laws, and other relevant documents. Much of the data on terrorist groups is taken from the U.S. Department of State's annual *Patterns of Global Terrorism* reports (made available at this site), so those pages tend to duplicate other sources, but the site does well collecting U.S. government reports on terrorist events.

ON-LINE REFERENCE SOURCES

While the web portals are central collecting points for information gathered elsewhere, the following sources provide original reports and analysis of current issues related to terrorism.

Anti-Defamation League
URL: http://www.adl.org
The Anti-Defamation League Web site contains a wealth of information about civil rights, hate crimes, anti-Semitism, and terrorism. The site provides news digests, updates on relevant court cases, group profiles, and a time line of recent attacks. This is a particularly good source for information on U.S. domestic terrorist organizations and white supremacist militias. It also contains a unique database of terrorist symbols.

Center for Defense Information
URL: http://www.cdi.org.
From the site's home page, select "terrorism" from the drop-down menu on the upper left. CDI provides insights, in-depth analysis, and facts on the military, security, and foreign policy challenges as the United States and the world face terrorism. Their site contains brief analytical examinations not only of events but also of the issues related to best practices in responding to terrorism.

Constitutional Rights Foundation
URL: http://www.crf-usa.org/terror/terrorism_links.
An enormous Web site of links to other sources. Although there is little original content, it has a broader scope than many sites. Among the unique information are classroom materials, urban myths about terrorism, and links to numerous foreign newspapers.

Council on Foreign Relations
URL: http://www.cfr.org/issue/135/terrorism.html
The Council on Foreign Relations is the premier U.S. think tank on international affairs. It publishes the highly regarded journal, *Foreign Affairs.* The council's Web site is divided into "Regions" and "Issues." The Issues section provides

links to a variety of highly readable articles on terrorism. Materials range from speeches to profiles, published articles, and question-and-answer documents.

CQ Press
URL: http://www.cqpress.com/incontext/terrorism//
Sponsored by Congressional Quarterly, the site has links to relevant CQ publications. It is particularly strong in its coverage of religion and religious concepts.

Global Security
URL: http://www.globalsecurity.org
Global Security is a private organization that focuses on military aspects of terrorism. The Web site contains digests of relevant newspaper and wire-service reports on current U.S. military operations, weapons of mass destruction, intelligence gathering, and homeland security.

Jamestown Foundation
URL: http://www.Jamestown.org
The Jamestown Foundation is a nongovernmental organization that seeks to inform and educate policymakers about events and trends in societies that are strategically or tactically important to the United States but which frequently restrict access to such information. Jamestown publishes a variety of e-newsletters, including *Terrorism Monitor, Terrorism Focus,* and *Spotlight on Terror.* The Web site has searchable archives for all Jamestown publications.

Knox Dudley Library, Naval Postgraduate School, U.S. Navy
URL: http://library.nps.navy.mil/home/terrorism.htm
In addition to profiles of terrorist groups, largely based on State Department reports, the navy site offers online bibliographies of terrorist-related materials and provides links to key U.S. government documents. The site is particularly strong in its coverage of the 9/11 attack and the U.S. military operations in Afghanistan and Iraq.

Library of Congress
September 11, 2001, Documentary Project
http://memory.loc.gov/ammem/collections/911_archive/index.html
Following a precedent set after the Japanese attack on Pearl Harbor in 1941, the September 11, 2001, Documentary Project captures how Americans reacted to the 9/11 attacks. Instead of political or scientific studies of 9/11, this collection captures interviews, drawings, and other private memorial activities by the American public. The collection includes video interviews, photographs, drawings, and written narratives.

RAND Corporation
URL: http://www.rand.org/publications/electronic/terrorism.html.
RAND is a nongovernmental think tank that researches "important and complicated problems," ranging from national security to aging and child development. RAND research reports are downloadable from their Web site free of charge. The reports are written for experts and may be dense reading, but they often provide detailed information on aspects of terrorism not available elsewhere, such as cyberterrorism.

Rick A. Ross Institute for the Study of Destructive Cults, Controversial Groups, and Movements
URL: http://www.rickross.com
The Rick Ross Institute has an extensive database containing information about cults, destructive cults, controversial groups and movements, including religious, hate-based, political, commercial, and even Sci-Fi/UFO groups. Online files include news stories, research papers, reports, court documents, book excerpts, personal testimonies, and hundreds of links to additional relevant resources. The institute focuses on cult operations and efforts to "deprogram" former cult members, and its identification of some groups as cults may be controversial, but it is an unusual source of considerable information about rather obscure groups.

September 11 News
URL: http://www.september11news.com
September 11 News is a private archive created by A. D. Williams of Calgary, Alberta, Canada. It is a massive collection of news reports, magazine covers, time lines, photographs, and more about the events of September 11, 2001. While there are full-text articles available, the archive's richest feature is its collection of photographic images.

Southern Poverty Law Center
URL: http://www.splcenter.org/intel/intpro.jsp
Another excellent source for information on U.S. domestic terrorist organizations and white supremacist militias.

Terrorism Files
URL: http://www.terrorismfiles.org
This site provides one-page profiles of about two dozen terrorist organizations and a brief "encyclopedia" section on the history of terrorism and drug trafficking. The site's home page provides a regularly updated digest of newspaper and wire-service articles. However, there seems to be no filtering process, and

many articles are not directly related to terrorism, such as reviews of movies with terrorism plot lines. Terrorism Files is sponsored by Nabou.com Services, which seeks to be a comprehensive Web resource offering news, reviews, information, and media on a variety of subjects.

Terrorism Research Center
URL: http://www.terrorism.com
Founded in 1996, the Terrorism Research Center is an independent institute dedicated to the research of terrorism, information warfare and security, critical infrastructure protection, homeland security, and other issues including low-intensity political violence and gray-area phenomena. The Web site includes a continuously updated list of terrorist incidents. It also contains profiles of terrorist groups, incidents, and countries, but most of it is on a subscription-only basis, and individual student subscriptions are not available.

United States Institute of Peace
URL: http://www.usip.org/library/topics/terrorism.html#docs
Site contains reports produced by leading scholars from around the world, plus links to a broad selection of resources from governments, libraries, terrorist groups, and international organizations.

---

[1] Council on Foreign Relations. "Q&A: Terrorists and the Internet" (March 6, 2006). Available online. URL: http://www.cfr.org/publication/10005/terrorists_and_the_internet.html; Steve Coll and Susan B. Glasser. "Terrorists Turn to the Web as Base of Operations." *Washington Post*, August 7, 2005, p. A1.

[2] David Meghan. "Bias, Sabotage Haunt Wikipedia's Free World." *Boston Globe*, February 12, 2006, p. A1; Kathy Ishizuka. "The Wikipedia Wars." *School Library Journal* 50, no. 11, November 2004, p. 24–25.

[3] Ibid.

[4] "Look Who's Using Wiki to Rewrite History." *Business Week*, March 13, 2006, p. 49.

[5] Mary Ellen Bates. "Truth and Fiction on the Web." *Online* 30, no. 2 (March/April 2006), p. 64.

7

Facts and Figures

1. International Terrorist Attacks, 1982–2003

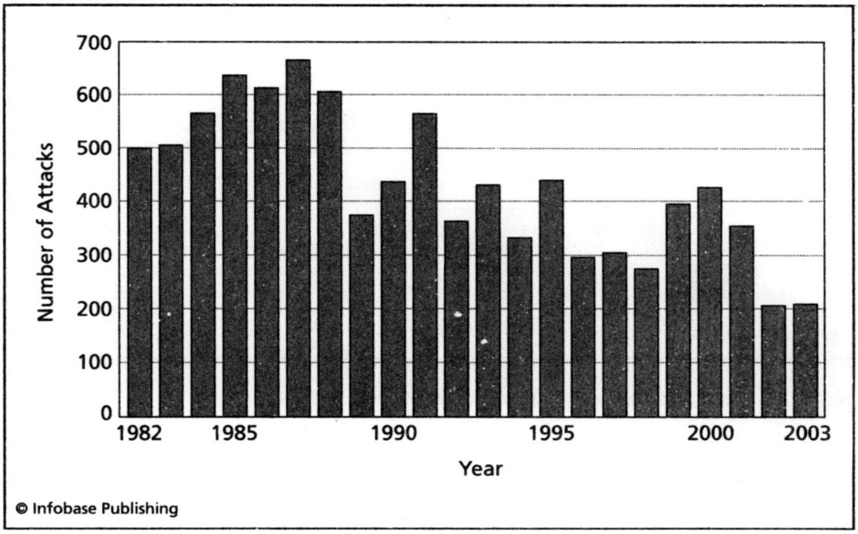

Source: U.S. Department of State, *Patterns of Global Terrorism 2003.*

2. Total Facilities Struck by International Attacks, 1998–2003

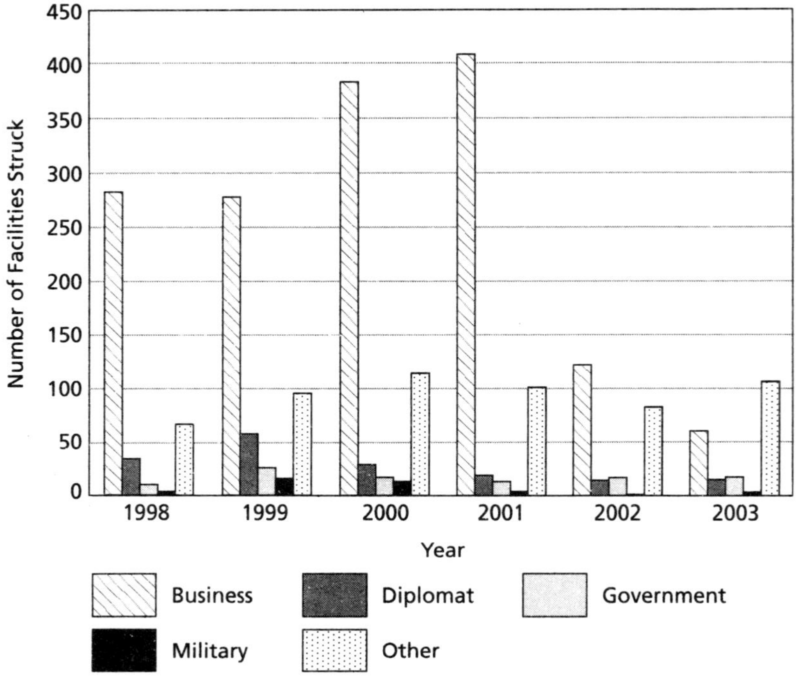

Source: U.S. Department of State, *Patterns of Global Terrorism 2003.*

3. Incidents by Tactic, 1968–2006

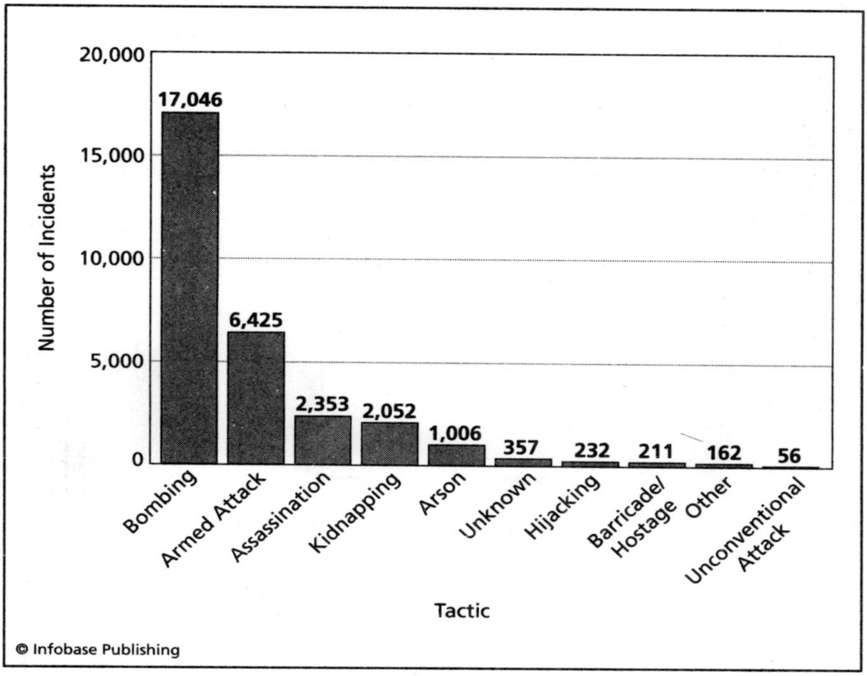

Source: MIPT Terrorism Knowledge Base. A Comprehensive Database of Global Terrorist Incidents and Organizations. Available online. URL: http//www.tkb.org/IncidentTacticModule.jsp. Accessed on August 31, 2006.

4. Motives of Female Suicide Bombers, 1985–2005

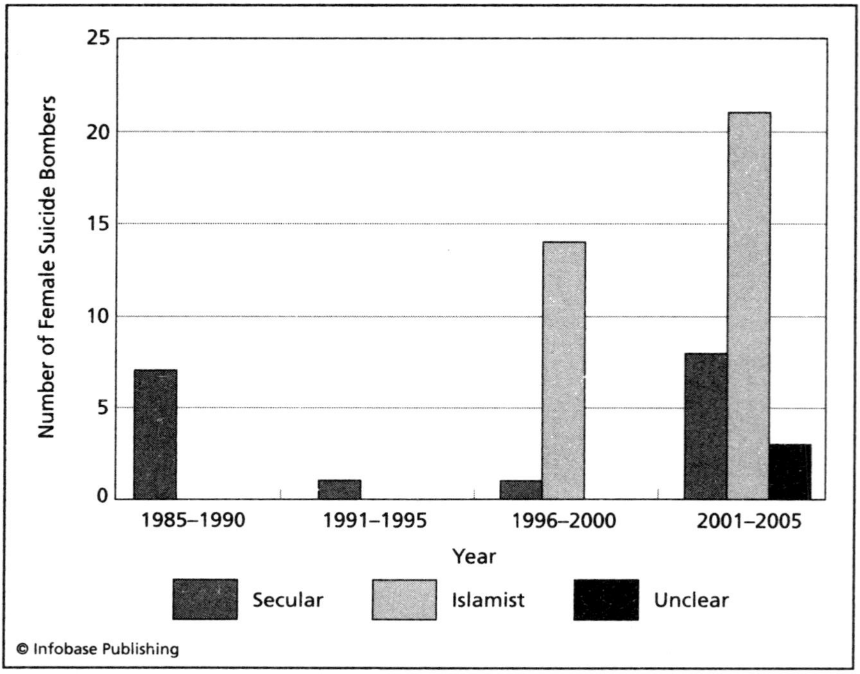

Source: "Female Killers," *Newsweek,* December 12, 2005, 34.

5. Incidents by Group Classification, 1968–2006

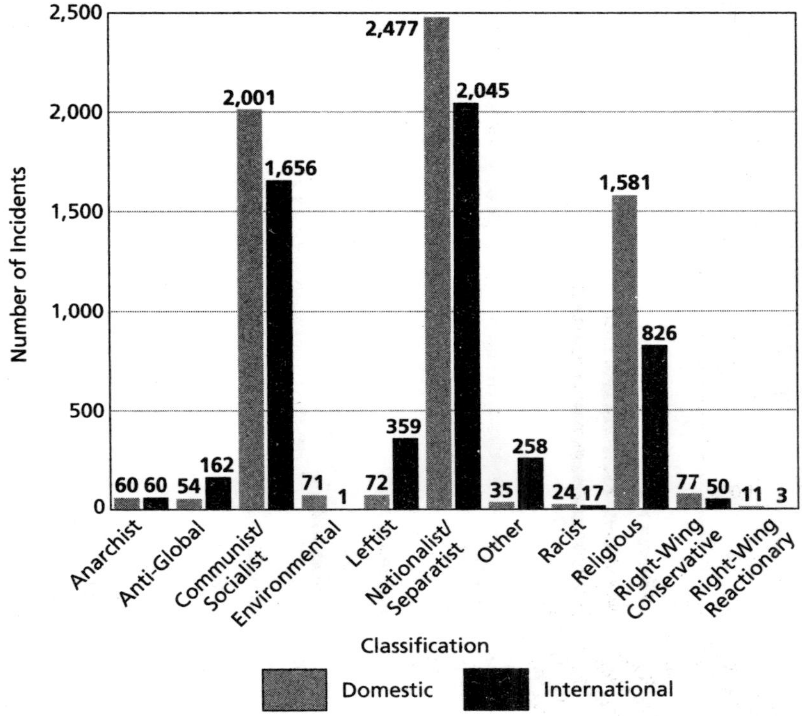

Note: International incidents includes data for 1968–2006.
Domestic incidents includes data for 1998–2006.

Source: MIPT Terrorism Knowledge Base. A Comprehensive Database of Global Terrorist Incidents and Organizations. Available online. URL: http//www.tkb.org/IncidentTacticModule.jsp. Accessed on August 31, 2006.

6. Incidents by Target, 1968–2006

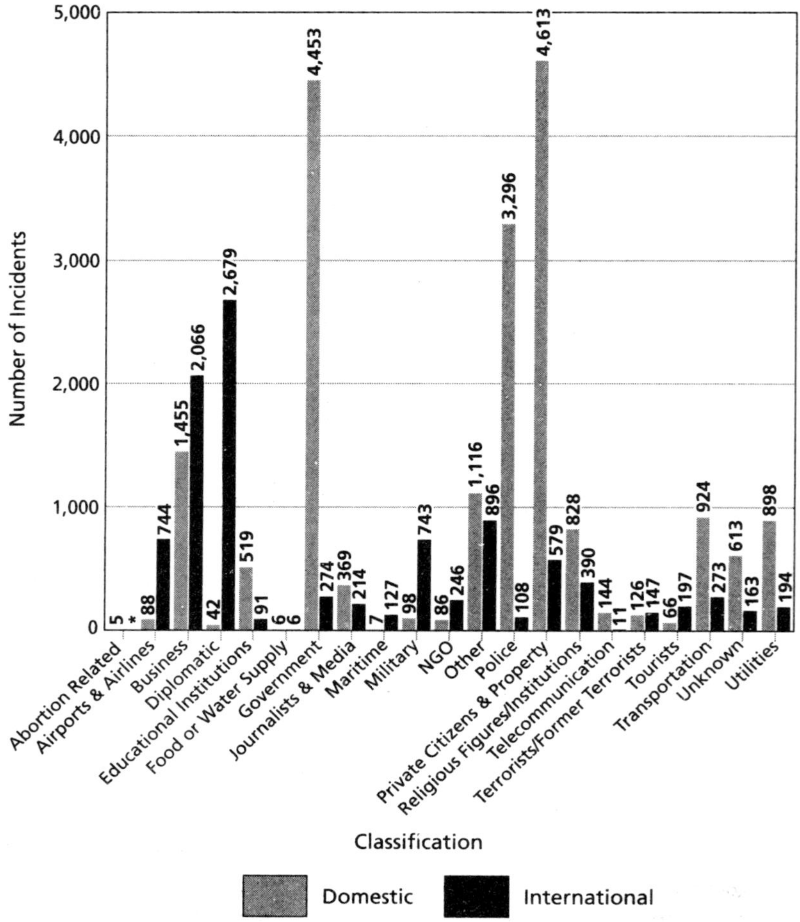

*Only domestic data is available for "abortion related" classification.

Source: MIPT Terrorism Knowledge Base. A Comprehensive Database of Global Terrorist Incidents and Organizations. Available online. URL: http//www.tkb.org/IncidentTacticModule.jsp. Accessed on August 31, 2006.

7. Total International Attacks by Region, 1998–2006

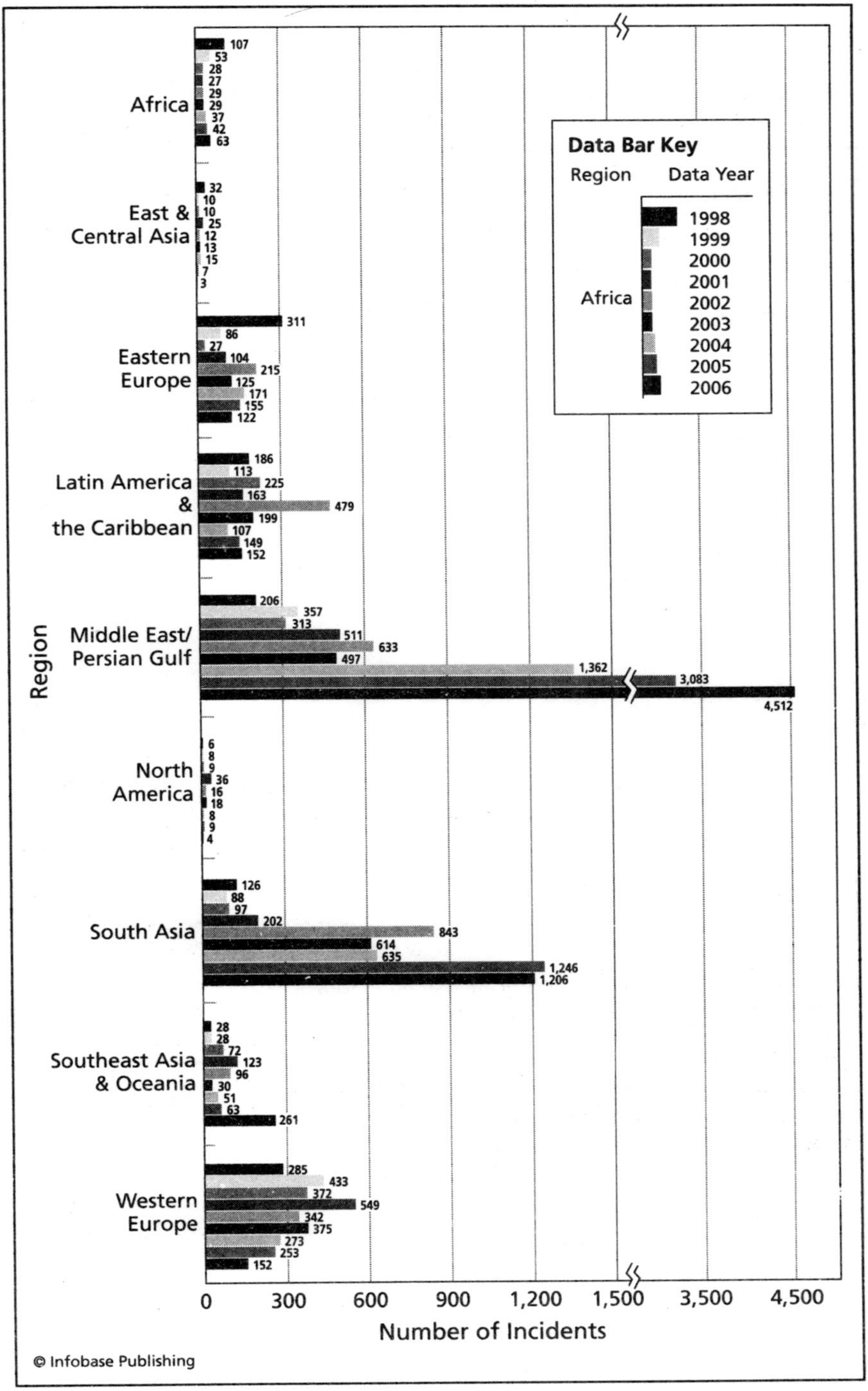

Source: MIPT Terrorism Knowledge Base. A Comprehensive Database of Global Terrorist Incidents and Organizations. Available online. URL: http//www.tkb.org/IncidentTacticModule.jsp. Accessed on August 31, 2006.

8. International Attacks, Injuries, and Fatalities, 1968–2006

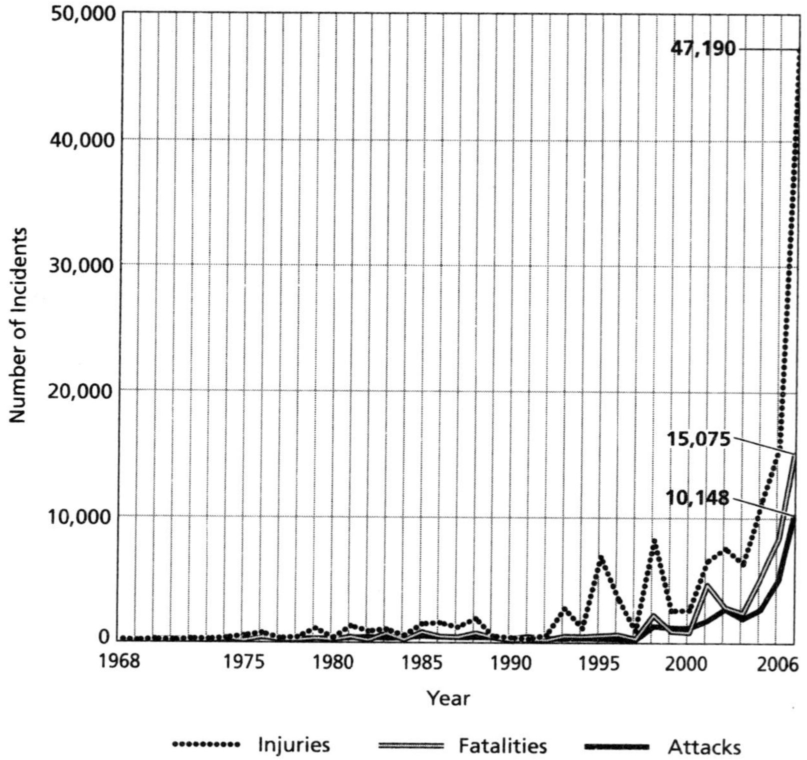

Note: Data for 1968–1997 covers only international incidents. Data for 1998–2006 covers both domestic and international incidents. Data for 2006 is through August 31.

Source: Data based on MIPT Terrorism Knowledge Base. A Comprehensive Database of Global Terrorist Incidents and Organizations. Available online. URL: http//www.tkb.org/IncidentTactic-Module.jsp. Accessed on August 31, 2006.

8

Key Players

INDIVIDUALS

MAHMOUD ABBAS (1935–) chairman of Palestine Liberation Organization (PLO) since 2004. Also known as Abu Mazen, a term of respect. Mahmoud Abbas received a doctorate in history from Moscow's Oriental College. While his scholarly work has been accused of denying the Holocaust, his political career with Palestinian organizations earned him a reputation for pragmatism and moderation. Abbas was a cofounder of Fatah in 1957 and worked closely with PLO chairman Yasser Arafat for at least three decades. He was named prime minister of the Palestinian Authority in 2003 but resigned after four months, after clashes with Arafat over policy. Following Arafat's death in 2004, Abbas became chairman of the PLO and was subsequently elected president of the Palestinian Authority in January 2005.

SHEIKH OMAR ABD AL-RAHMAN (1938–) Muslim spiritual leader of Egypt-based Gama'a al-Islamiyya ("The Islamic Group"). Accused of encouraging the 1981 assassination of Egyptian president Anwar Sadat and the 1993 World Trade Center bombing. In 1995 a U.S. court sentenced Abd al-Rahman to life in prison for a conspiracy to blow up landmarks in New York City, including the UN headquarters and the Lincoln Tunnel.

ABU NIDAL (1937–2002) Palestinian activist, staunch opponent of the PLO, and founder of the Abu Nidal Organization. Born Sabri al-Banna, Nidal died in Baghdad in 2002.

YASSER ARAFAT (1929–2004) chairman of Palestine Liberation Organization (PLO) from 1969 until his death in 2004. Arafat advocated guerrilla warfare to defeat Israel but in 1993 signed the Oslo Accords with Israel recognizing the state's right to exist. As a result, Arafat shared the 1994 Nobel

Peace Prize with Israeli prime minister Yitzhak Rabin. He subsequently became the first president of the Palestinian National Authority. Arafat was born Mohammed Abdel-Raouf Arafat al Qudwa al-Hussein in 1929 and trained as a civil engineer at Cairo University. Arafat remains a controversial figure in history, heralded as a national hero by some, condemned as a brutal terrorist by others. In either case, he became the international face of the Palestinian independence movement and always wore a kaffiyeh, the traditional Palestinian checkerboard-patterned headdress.

SHOKO ASAHARA (1955–) charismatic leader of AUM SHINRIKYO. Born Chizuo Matsumoto, he changed his name to Shoko Asahara in 1986 and founded the Aum Shinrikyo doomsday cult one year later. Partially blind, Asahara was a highly regarded yoga instructor, but began preaching that he was destined to save the world from destruction, which would begin with a U.S. attack on Japan. Asahara was arrested in May 1995 on multiple charges of murder and illegal drug and weapons possession. He eventually confessed to the Tokyo subway attack and was sentenced to death.

YAHYA AYYASH (1966–1996) Hamas member who reportedly suggested suicide bombings as a tactic against Israel. Dubbed "The Engineer" by Israeli prime minister Yitzhak Rabin for his prowess at bomb-making, Ayyash was assassinated in January 1996.

ANDREAS BAADER (1943–1977) coleader of the Baader-Meinhof Gang, a West German terrorist group known for bombings and bank robberies in the 1970s. Baader committed suicide while in prison.

SHAMIL BASAYEV (1965–2006) military leader of the Chechen insurgency. In 1998 he and Arab mercenary Ibn al-Khattab established the Islamic International Peacekeeping Brigade to create an Islamic state spanning the North Caucasus. Basayev was killed in July 2006 by an accidental explosion.

LAURIE BERENSON (1969–) U.S. citizen who dropped out of the Massachusetts Institute of Technology and moved to El Salvador and then Peru in the early 1990s, where she became acquainted with members of the Tupac Amaru Revolutionary Movement (MRTA). She was arrested following a raid on a MRTA safe house on November 30, 1995, and sentenced to life in prison by a military tribunal. When military tribunals were declared unconstitutional, Berenson was retried in a civilian court in 2001 and sentenced to 20 years in jail in Peru.

OSAMA BIN LADEN (1957–) the head of the al-Qaeda terrorist network that carried out the terrorist attacks against the United States on September 11, 2001. Born to a wealthy family in Saudi Arabia in 1957, he founded al-Qaeda in 1988 in order to establish a global Islamic state (caliphate). To this end, al-Qaeda declared in 1998 that it is the "duty of all Muslims to kill U.S. citizens, civilian and military, and their allies everywhere." Al-Qaeda was based in Afghanistan until the U.S.-led coalition overthrew the extreme Muslim Taliban regime at the end of 2001; it now is organized into a number of smaller units dispersed throughout Asia. Bin Laden is believed to be hiding along the Afghanistan-Pakistan border, and the FBI has offered a $25 million reward for his arrest.

CARLOS THE JACKAL (1949–) infamous terrorist of the 1970s, born Illich Ramírez Sánchez in Venezuela. Carlos led the 1976 Red Army Faction hijacking of an Air France jet to Entebbe, Uganda.

NESTOR CERPA CARTOLINI (1953–1997) leader of Peru's Tupac Amaru Revolutionary Movement. Cerpa led the insurgent group that attached the residence of the Japanese ambassador to Peru in December 1996. He died when government forces stormed the residence in April 1997.

PABLO ESCOBAR (1949–1993) head of the Medellin cocaine cartel that dominated Colombia in the 1980s. Escobar terrorized government officials into ignoring his operations while cultivating a "Robin Hood" image among Colombia's poor. Fearing assassination by rivals or extradition to the United States, Escobar surrendered to Colombian officials in 1991. He spent the next two years in a luxurious prison he built himself but escaped during a transfer on July 22, 1992. He died in a shoot-out on December 2, 1993.

SHEIKH MUHAMMAD HUSSEIN FADLALLAH (1935–) spiritual leader of Hezbollah, Shiite cleric.

ABIMAEL GUZMÁN (1934–) a university professor who founded Peru's Shining Path (Sendero Luminoso) movement in the 1960s. Guzmán was arrested in 1992, but his conviction a year later was overturned in 2003 because it was handed down by a secret military court, and technically Guzmán is a civilian. He was retried in a civilian court and convicted and sentenced to life in October 2006.

GEORGE HABBASH (1926–) founder of the Arab National Movement in 1952 while a medical student at the American University of Beirut. The ANM evolved into the Popular Front for the Liberation of Palestine (PFLP).

THEODORE (TED) KACZYNSKI (1942–) also known as the Unabomber, sent 16 letter bombs between 1978 and 1996, mainly targeting university professors. Kaczynski lived as a recluse in a primitive cabin in Montana until his arrest in 1996. The previous year, the *New York Times* and the *Washington Post* agreed to publish a "Manifesto" in which the Unabomber explained his motives. Kaczynski's brother recognized portions of the document and notified authorities. Serving life sentence in prison since 1998.

MEIR KAHANE (1932–1990) a Jewish rabbi from New York City. His writings and teachings encouraged Jews to defend Israel against Arabs and the "Palestinian problem." His preferred solution was not compromise with the Palestinians but expulsion and even extermination. Kahane moved to Israel in 1971 and founded Kahane Chai (Kach). Kahane was assassinated in 1990, and his son, Binyamin, became leader of the group.

LEILA KHALED (1944–) famous female Palestinian hijacker. Khaled was born in Haifa, Palestine, in 1944, but four years later her family fled to Lebanon following the violence surrounding the establishment of Israel. Her father worked in the Palestinian national movement, and she became active at age 15, joining the Arab National Movement and later the Popular Front for the Liberation of Palestine. She was best known for a successful hijacking in 1969 and, following plastic surgery to disguise her face, an unsuccessful one in 1970 that landed her in a London jail for 45 days. As one of the few well-known female Palestinian activists, Khaled became a media sensation. Numerous articles described her as the "glamour girl of international terrorism" and focused on her "deadly beauty" and a ring she often wore, made from a bullet and a hand-grenade pin. She currently lives in Jordan and is a member of the Palestinian National Council.

ASLAN MASKHADOV (1951–2005) elected president of Chechnya in 1997. When his official term of office was set to expire, he unilaterally extended it. Moscow refused to acknowledge the extension and staged an election that made Akhmad Kadyrov president. Maskhadov went into hiding and continued to serve as the political leader of the Chechen independent movement. He was killed in a shoot-out with Russian forces on March 8, 2005.

TIMOTHY McVEIGH (1968–2001) bomber of the Alfred P. Murrah Federal Building in Oklahoma City on April 19, 1995, to protest government activities. Executed June 11, 2001.

ULRIKE MEINHOF (1934–1976) coleader of the Baader-Meinhof Gang, a West German terrorist group known for bombings and bank robberies in the 1970s. Meinhof was a well-known journalist who helped Andreas Baader escape from police custody in 1970s and then joined his organization. She was found hanging in her jail cell in 1976.

Key Players

KHALID SHEIKH MOHAMMED (1964 or 1965–) uncle of 1993 World Trade Center bomber Ramzi Yusef and the principal architect of the September 11, 2001, attacks. Mohammed has also taken credit for other al-Qaeda attacks, including that on the USS *Cole* in 2000 and the Bali nightclub bombing in 2002. He was captured in Pakistan on March 1, 2003.

TERRY NICHOLS (1955–) an accomplice to TIMOTHY MCVEIGH in bombing the Alfred P. Murrah Federal Building in Oklahoma City. Serving life sentence in prison since 1998.

MOHAMMED SADDIQ ODEH (1965–) leader of al-Qaeda in Kenya. Blamed for 1998 embassy bombings in Kenya and Tanzania.

VELUPILLAI PRABAKHARAN (1954–) the charismatic leader of the Liberation Tigers of Tamil Eelam.

MUAMMAR QADDAFI (1940–) leader of Libya and confessed sponsor of terrorism. Qaddafi led the military coup that toppled Libya's monarchy in 1969. Although he holds no official title, he has been the supreme leader of the country ever since. Qaddafi created his own ideology, "Islamic socialism," that blends state control over the economy with Islamic values. Backed with Soviet money, Libya supported the Palestine Liberation Organization and a variety of terrorist activities. In 1988 Qaddafi ordered the bombing of Pan Am Flight 103 over Lockerbie, Scotland, in which 270 people were killed. After enduring a decade of international sanctions and isolation, Qaddafi apologized for the Pan Am bombing and agreed to pay cash settlements to the victims' families.

RICHARD REID (1973–) the infamous "shoe bomber." On December 22, 2001, Reid attempted to ignite explosives hidden in his shoes while aboard an American Airlines flight from Paris to Miami. Reid, a British Muslim, was overpowered by other passengers, arrested, and convicted of terrorism. Reid was linked with al-Qaeda and was sentenced to 110 years in a maximum-security U.S. prison.

AHMED RESSAM (1967–) arrested while trying to enter the United States from Canada on December 14, 1999. Suspected of preparing for a major terrorist attack to coincide with millennium (year 2000) celebrations.

FUSAKO SHIGENOBU (1945–) the leader of the Japanese Red Army. Often considered the most feared female terrorist, Shigenobu operated out of Lebanon after being expelled from Japan. With help from the Popular Front for the Liberation of Palestine, the JRA carried out multiple bombings in the

1970s. Shigenobu was arrested in Osaka in November 2000 and is currently serving a 20-year prison term in Japan.

UNABOMBER FBI code name for THEODORE (TED) KACZYNSKI.

SHEIKH AHMAD IBRAHIM YASSIN (c. late 1930s–2004) founder and spiritual leader of Hamas. Yassin was killed by an Israeli rocket in March 2004.

RAMZI AHMED YUSEF (1967–) organizer of the 1993 bombing of World Trade Center. Arrested in Pakistan at safe house connected to Osama bin Laden.

ABU MUSAB AL-ZARQAWI (1966–2006) leader of the main Islamic militant faction in Iraq, Tawhid wal Jihad (Unification and Jihad). A Jordanian by birth, al-Zarqawi trained with Osama bin Laden and al-Qaeda, but he also operated independently, favoring guerrilla attacks and bombings. Al-Zarqawi was believed to be behind the kidnapping and beheading of Western relief workers in Iraq in 2005. Al-Zarqawi spent seven years (1992–99) in prison in Jordan and was sentenced to death twice in absentia by Jordanian courts. His real name is believed to be Ahmad Fadeel al-Nazal al-Khalayleh. Al-Zarqawi was killed in a U.S. air raid in 2006.

AYMAN AL-ZAWAHIRI (1953–) a top-ranking al-Qaeda leader, second only to Osama bin Laden. Al-Zawahiri often makes public statements on behalf of bin Laden, and many believe he is bin Laden's personal physician as well. Al-Zawahiri founded Egyptian Islamic Jihad and was a key organizer of the 1998 U.S. Embassy bombings in Kenya and Tanzania.

ORGANIZATIONS

ABU NIDAL ORGANIZATION founded in 1974 by Abu Nidal and disgruntled members of the Palestine Liberation Organization. ANO carried out a number of well-known attacks, including explosions at airports in Rome and Vienna in 1985. ANO claimed credit for assassinating PLO deputy chair Abu Iyad and PLO security chief Abu Hul in 1991 and of murdering a Jordanian diplomat in Lebanon in 1994. The group's activities declined in the late 1990s, and its status is unclear since Nidal's death in 2002.

ABU SAYYAF a militant Islamic group based in the southern Philippines and seeking an independent Islamic state in Muslim-populated areas of the southern Philippines, namely Mindanao and the Sulu Archipelago. The group, founded in 1991, is an offshoot of the Moro National Liberation Front. Abu Sayyaf is most notorious for its frequent kidnappings of Western tourists and subsequent ransom demands. Many hostages have been held for months and ultimately rescued, while others have been executed. The group is thought to be self-financed through its ransom payoffs. Khadafi Janjalani became leader of the group when his brother, Abdurajak Abubakar Janjalani, died in December 1998. Abu Sayyaf is believed to work with Jemaah Islamiah and al-Qaeda.

ALEPH current name of AUM SHINRIKYO.

ALEX BONCAYAO BRIGADE an urban terrorist squad linked to the Communist Party of the Philippines. The group likely dates to the 1980s, as its first major operation was the 1989 assassination of U.S. Army Colonel James Rowe, who was based in the Philippines. ABB signed a truce with the Filipino military in December 2000.

ALLIANCE OF PALESTINIAN FORCES consists of Palestinian organizations that opposed the 1993 Oslo Peace Agreement between Israel and the PLO.

ANSAR AL-ISLAM seeks an Islamic state in Iraq. The group's membership is comprised of both Iraqi Arabs and Kurds. Founded in December 2001, the group is variously known as Ansar al-Sunnah, Helpers of Islam, and the Kurdish Taliban, and it is one of the fiercest opponents of the U.S.-led Coalition forces in Iraq. Ansar al-Islam has claimed responsibility for the suicide attacks on Kurdish groups in February 2004 and a U.S. military dining hall in Mosul in December 2004.

ANTI-IMPERIALIST TERRITORIAL NUCLEI (NTA) based in Italy's Friuli region. The NTA is a Marxist-Leninist organization advocating class struggle against Italian business elites and resistance to U.S. imperialism and NATO. The group emerged in 1995 and positions itself as the successor to the Red Brigades, an Italian leftist group active in the 1970s and 1980s. NTA activity largely ceased after the January 2004 arrest of its leader. Experts estimate NTA's membership at no more than 20 people.

AL-AQSA MARTYRS' BRIGADES militant youth wing of Fatah. Founded at the start of the Second Palestinian Intifada in 2004, al-Aqsa targets Israelis in the Gaza Strip, West Bank, and Israel as well as Palestinians who allegedly collaborate with the Israeli authorities. The group's primary weapons are suicide bombers and rockets. The first known female suicide bomber in Palestine, who attacked in January 2002, was a member of al-Aqsa. Hamas and al-Aqsa have jointly claimed credit for a series of terrorist incidents since 2003.

ARMED FORCES OF NATIONAL LIBERATION (Fuerzas Armadas de Liberación Nacional) sought independence for Puerto Rico. The FALN carried out a series of bombings during the 1970s, including attacks in New York City and Chicago. The group faded as members were arrested. It has largely been inactive since 1977.

ARMED ISLAMIC GROUP known by its French acronym, GIA, emerged in Algeria following the cancellation of the 1992 parliamentary elections. GIA seeks a fundamentalist Islamic regime in Algeria. GIA is unusually violent and has been known to wipe out entire villages of Algerians. Estimates put GIA's victims at some 10,000 Algerians and 100 European expatriates living in Algeria. GIA is becoming increasingly overshadowed by the Salafist Group.

ARMENIAN ARMY FOR THE SECRET LIBERATION OF ARMENIA emerged in Lebanon in 1975, founded by Hagop Hagopian, with links to Popular Front for the Liberation of Palestine. Sought Turkish recognition of 1915 genocide and reparations. Marxist-Leninist ideology. In 1983 detonated bombs at the Turkish airline counter at Orly airport, inside the Istanbul airport, and at the Grand Bazaar in Istanbul.

ARYAN NATIONS a white supremacist group operating in the United States. Based in Coeur d'Alene, Idaho, the Aryan Nations was founded in 1974 by Rev. Richard Girnt Butler. It acts as an umbrella group, sharing information among like-minded organizations and has produced several splinter groups. The group went bankrupt in 2000 when it lost a civil suit related to attacks on Victoria and Jason Keenan. The court assigned all of AN's property to the Keenans, but members have tried to form a new network.

ASBAT AL-ANSAR an extremist Sunni Islamic group in Lebanon with alleged ties to al-Qaeda. Sometimes referred to as the Islamic Resistance Movement, the group's Arabic name translates as "League of Followers." Members are mostly Palestinian and seek to eliminate Western influence and to overthrow the Lebanese government. Asbat al-Ansar has targeted international facilities, such as the Russian and Italian embassies in Beirut, the Ukrainian consulate, and McDonald's franchises in Beirut. It is a vocal opponent of U.S. involvement in Iraq and openly advocates killing U.S. hostages. Members unsuccessfully tried to assassinate U.S. ambassador David Satterfield in 2000.

AUM SHINRIKYO a doomsday cult founded in Japan in 1987 by Shoko Asahara. At its height Aum Shinrikyo ("supreme truth") had more than 40 branches across Asia, Russia, and the United States and claimed to have 40,000 followers. Members were noted for their austere lifestyle—they surrendered all their possessions upon joining and were known to starve themselves and commit acts of violence to prove their loyalty to Asahara. The group was suspected of murdering judges and family members who tried to interfere in their activities. On March 20, 1995, Aum Shinrikyo members released packets of sarin nerve gas on several Tokyo subway lines, killing 12 people. Tokyo police soon swarmed the Aum Shinrikyo compound, arresting members. In 2000 four planners of the subway attack were sentenced to death; a fifth received a life term. The group is now known as Aleph.

BAADER-MEINHOF GANG *See* RED ARMY FACTION.

AL-BADHR MUJAHIDEEN operates in the mountains of Pakistan and Afghanistan, targeting the Indian army. Al-Badhr dates to a 1971 attack on Bengalis in Eastern Bengal. Since then it has rarely acted alone, preferring to team up with like-minded groups such as Hizbul-Mujahedin and Hizb-I Islam.

BASQUE FATHERLAND AND LIBERTY since 1959 known by its Basque acronym ETA; has primarily targeted Spanish government officials in its quest for a Basque homeland, governed according to Marxism. ETA claims territory in northern Spain and southwestern France.

BLACK SEPTEMBER founded in 1970. Black September was a branch of Fatah, a component of the Palestine Liberation Organization. The group took its name from the bloody conflict of September 1970 when Jordan expelled the PLO from its territory in an operation that left more than 4,000 Palestinian operatives dead. Black September was organized with a cell structure—small groups of four or five members that operated independently—and specialized in terrorist operations in Western Europe. The group is best known for kidnapping and assassinating 11 members of the Israeli Olympic team in Munich in 1972. Following the Munich massacre, Israeli intelligence began a worldwide campaign to hunt down and kill the remaining members of Black September. The PLO shut down the group in 1973 or 1974.

CAMBODIAN FREEDOM FIGHTERS (CFF) composed largely of exiles and expatriates and based in Long Beach, California. The CFF seeks to overthrow the government led by the Cambodian People's Party, which employs a communist ideology. CFF emerged after the communists seized power in 1998, and many prominent Cambodians fled the country. The CFF took credit for a November 2000 attack on government facilities, but the government has prosecuted members on many other charges. CFF scaled back its activities when the U.S. government threatened to deport its leader, Chhun Yasith.

CHRISTIAN PATRIOTS white supremacist group that seeks to "cleanse" the United States of Jews and other "inferior" groups.

COMMUNIST PARTY OF INDIA formed in 2001 when two leftist Indian groups merged. The two predecessors, the Maoist Communist Center of India (founded in the early 1970s) and People's War (1975), are commonly referred to as the "Naxalties." CPI insurgents control several remote areas of India and seek to establish a Maoist government based on the elimination of socioeconomic classes.

COMMUNIST PARTY OF NEPAL-MAOISTS/PEOPLE'S LIBERATION ARMY turned to insurgency when it failed to win many seats in Nepal's 1991 general election. Since 1996 seeks to overthrow Nepal's monarchy, to establish a communist regime, including collective agriculture and state-owned industries, and to eliminate caste system. Led by Pushpa Kamal Dahal ("Prachanda"), the rebels signed a peace agreement in November 2006.

COMMUNIST PARTY OF THE PHILIPPINES/NEW PEOPLE'S ARMY (NPA) the military wing of the Communist Party of the Philippines (CPP). The group was founded in 1969 and its top leaders operate out of the Netherlands. CPP embraces Maoism and seeks to overthrow the government in Manila and opposed the U.S. military presence in the Philippines. The NPA uses guerrilla tactics to assassinate members of the Philippine government and security forces and U.S. embassy personnel.

CONTINUITY IRISH REPUBLICAN ARMY (CIRA) the military arm of Republican Sinn Féin, which broke away from the larger Sinn Féin in 1986. With only about 50 members CIRA claims to continue the IRA fight to make Northern Ireland independent of Great Britain, and it refuses to observe IRA cease-fires. CIRA tactics include bombing, kidnapping, extortion, and robbery.

COVENANT, THE SWORD, AND THE ARM OF THE LORD a violent Arkansas-based white supremacist group. Founded around 1970 by James Ellison, its camp was raided by federal law-enforcement officials who shut down the movement in 1985. The officers discovered an enormous cache of weapons, including grenades, rockets, and 30 gallons of cyanide.

DEMOCRATIC FORCES FOR THE LIBERATION OF RWANDA the latest incarnation of the Army for the Liberation of Rwanda. Along with the Interhamwe civilian militia, ALRW members, linked to the Hutu government, carried out the anti-Tutsi genocide of 1994, killing a half-million Tutsis or more. When the Tutsi-dominated Rwandan Patriotic Front invaded

Rwanda and took control of the government, the two Hutu groups fled to neighboring Zaire (now Democratic Republic of Congo) and joined forces to make cross-border attacks on Tutsi forces.

DEMOCRATIC FRONT FOR THE LIBERATION OF PALESTINE (DFLP) was created in 1969 by Niaf Hawatmeh and Yasser Abd Rabbo, members of the Popular Front for the Liberation of Palestine. The DFLP embraced a Maoist orientation, emphasizing the role of the peasantry and the military in any revolutionary change. The DFLP sought to find a compromise solution to the Palestine-Israel issue, causing a rift with more hard-line PLO members. At one time it was the third-largest PLO member, but its numbers have declined since a group split off to form the Palestine Democratic Union in 1991. The DFLP tried to limit its terrorist attacks to the disputed Palestinian lands.

DIRECT ACTION French left-wing group, joined with Red Army Faction in 1985 for pan-European terrorist movement.

EAST TURKISTAN ISLAMIC MOVEMENT (ETIM) seeks to unite the Turkic peoples of Turkey, Kazakhstan, Kyrgyzstan, Uzbekistan, Pakistan, Afghanistan, and western China into one Islamic state. ETIM is based in China's Xinjiang Province and has ties with al-Qaeda. Members fought on the Taliban side in Operation Enduring Freedom. The group's leader, Hassan Makhsum, was killed in a Pakistani government raid on suspected al-Qaeda camps in western Pakistan.

EXTRADITABLES a paramilitary group formed by Colombia's Medellin cartel in 1987. At that time, the United States was pressuring Colombia to extradite cartel members on drug trafficking charges and the group was formed to prevent such a move. Pablo Escobar was a major figure in the group.

AL-FARAN militant group based in Kashmir. Kidnapped and executed five Western tourists in July 1995. Exact goals and origins remain murky. Some experts believe it consists of Harakut-ul-Ansar and Jaish-e-Mohammed members wanting to trade hostages for their comrades jailed in India. Others believe al-Faran was created by the Indian military to discredit the Kashmiri militant groups.

FATAH the dominant branch of the Palestinian Liberation Organization, founded in 1959 by Yasser Arafat to work for the creation of a Palestinian state and the destruction of Israel. There are several explanations for the origins of Fatah's name, which loosely translated as *victory* in Arabic. It is also an anagram of the Arabic words *Harahkat al-Tahrir al Filistini,* meaning

Palestine Liberation Movement. Fatah is a secular, nationalist organization, unlike other Muslim-based Palestinian groups.

FIRST OF OCTOBER ANTI-FASCIST RESISTANCE GROUP (GRAPO) opposes the United States and the current government structure in Spain. Founded in 1975, the militia is closely related to the Spanish Communist Party and seeks to overthrow the constitutional monarchy and replace it with a Marxist-Leninist government. It also wants the United States to withdraw all of its military forces from Spanish soil and publicly gloated over the September 11, 2001, terrorist attacks. GRAPO's activities have waned in recent years as more and more members are arrested. There are perhaps 20–25 active members left.

FREE SOUTH MOLUCCAN ORGANIZATION ethnic group from Indonesia that had settled in the Netherlands in 1951 when their homeland (South Moluccas) was incorporated by Indonesia. In 1977 briefly seized a Dutch train and school to bring attention to their cause.

GUSH EMUNIUM or "Bloc of the Faithful," was a hard-line Jewish movement based in the West Bank. Followers of Rabbi Meir Kahane, in 1983, decided to avenge the deaths of Jews in Israel by destroying the Dome of the Rock, a Muslim shrine in Jerusalem. Members were arrested before they could carry out their plan.

HAMAS an Arabic acronym for Islamic Resistance Movement and also translates as *zeal.* Hamas seeks the total destruction of Israel and the establishment of a Palestinian Islamic state in its place. This Palestinian organization dates to the 1970s and is known for its multiple suicide attacks against Israeli civilian targets in Israel, Gaza, and the West Bank. Hamas provides social services to many Palestinians, contributing to its wide popularity. Hamas leader Sheikh Ahmad Ibrahim Yassin died in an Israeli air strike in 2004. Hamas and the al-Aqsa Martyrs' Brigade have jointly claimed credit for a series of terrorist incidents since 2003. Hamas won the January 2006 elections for the Palestinian Legislative Council.

HARAKAT UL-JIHAD-I-ISLAMI (HUJI) the Movement of Islamic Holy War seeks to wrest control of the Jammu and Kashmir region from India and annex it to Pakistan. Founded in 1985 HUJI members are mainly Pakistanis who follow the Sunni form of Islam, and many received their military training fighting on the Afghan side against the USSR in the 1980s. Led by Fazlur Rehman Khalil until 2000, when Khalil resigned in favor of Faruq Kashmiri.

HARAKAT UL-JIHAD-I-ISLAMI/BANGLADESH (HUJI-B) which seeks to turn secular Bangladesh into an Islamic state. HUJI-B members have been accused of several attacks against Bangladeshi political leaders and cultural events. The group maintains links with Harakat ul-Jihad-I-Islami, Harakat ul-Mujahideen, and al-Qaeda.

HARAKAT UL-MUJAHIDEEN (HUM) a Pakistani Islamic group that targets Indian and civilian targets in the disputed Kashmir region. Known from 1993 until recently as Harakat ul-Ansar, HUM trained terrorists in Afghanistan under Taliban rule. The group is believed to have ties with Osama bin Laden, and its leaders signed bin Laden's fatwa against the West and the United States in 1998.

HEZBOLLAH a Shia Islamic radical group based in Lebanon. Also known as "Party of God" or "Islamic Jihad for the Liberation of Palestine," the group seeks to return Jerusalem to Palestinian control and to destroy Israel. Founded in 1982, Hezbollah has allies in Iran and Syria and has been known to train and fund other radical Palestinian groups. Hezbollah's trademark is the suicide truck bomber, and its operatives attacked the U.S. Marine barracks and embassy in Beirut in the 1980s and the Israeli embassy and a Jewish cultural center in Argentina. Hezbollah also took credit for the 1985 hijacking of TWA flight 847 and the kidnappings of 18 Americans in Lebanon in the 1980s. By 1992 Hezbollah had become a legitimate political party in Lebanon, even winning seats in parliament.

HIZB E-TAHRIR (Party of Liberation). Founded in the 1950s in Jerusalem, Hizb e-Tahrir advocates the creation of an Islamic caliphate and stresses its peaceful nature. The group has members across the globe, but it is most active in Central Asia.

HIZB-I ISLAMI GULBUDDIN Gulbuddin Hekmatyar's faction within the Hizb-I Islami party. Hekmatyar is a warlord who served as prime minister during the Afghan civil war of the early 1990s. Hekmatyar reportedly ran terrorist training camps in Afghanistan and offered asylum to Osama bin Laden after he was ejected from Sudan.

HIZBUL-MUJAHEDIN (HM) is the military wing of Pakistan's Jamaat-i-Islami political party, the largest Islamic party in the country. HM seeks not only to remove Jammu and Kashmir from Indian sovereignty, but some members seek outright independence for that region. Unlike other Kashmir-oriented groups, HM draws its membership primarily from Kashmiris themselves. The group focuses on Indian targets inside Kashmir.

IRGUN Zionist organization operating in Middle East in 1930s and 1940s. Also known as Irgun Tsvai Leumi. Led by future Israeli prime minister Menachem Begin, Irgun opposed the 1947 UN partition plan and bombed the British headquarters in Palestine in 1947.

IRISH NATIONAL LIBERATION ARMY (IRLA) not only seeks to end British rule over Northern Ireland and to create a unified Irish state but also to make united Ireland a Marxist-Leninist state. IRLA dates to 1975 and began as a wing of the Irish Republican Socialist Party. It is best known for bombing a Ballykelly pub in 1982, an attack that caused 17 deaths. IRLA announced a cease-fire in 1998 that has largely held.

IRISH REPUBLICAN ARMY (IRA) the military complement to the Sinn Féin political party. Founded in 1969, it sought to expel Great Britain from Northern Ireland through a series of bombings, murders, and kidnappings. It staged attacks in Northern Ireland and Britain itself. After IRA leaders signed the Belfast Agreement of 1998, two factions broke away to continue armed struggle: Continuity IRA and Real IRA. The IRA completed the process of decommissioning its considerable arsenal in September 2005.

ISLAMIC ARMY OF ADEN (IAA) based in Yemen, backs Osama bin Laden's campaign against U.S. and Western targets. Since its establishment in 1998, IAA has also called for the overthrow of the Yemeni government. It claimed responsibility for the attack in 2000 on the USS *Cole.*

ISLAMIC GREAT EAST RAIDERS-FRONT (IBDA-C) seeks to establish an Islamic state in Turkey that will not associate with the Western world. It will work with other non-Islamic opposition movements in Turkey in order to destabilize the secular government. IBDA-C prefers civilian targets and has attacked banks, newspapers, television towers, even tobacco shops. However, officials believe it is trying to take credit for other groups' attacks in order to generate publicity.

ISLAMIC GROUP (in Arabic, Al-Gama'a al-Islamiyya) is a militant group established in the early 1970s to overthrow the Egyptian government and install an Islamic regime. The group claimed responsibility for the June 1995 attempt to assassinate Egyptian President Hosni Mubarak and the 1997 attacks on tourists in Luxor. The group began in the 1970s as a loose affiliation of militant students, then split into at least two factions following cease-fire agreements in 1997 and March 1999. Mustafa Hamza leads the pro-cease-fire faction, while Rifa'i Taha Musa seeks to continue militant activities.

ISLAMIC INTERNATIONAL PEACEKEEPING BRIGADE (IIPB) Chechen warlord Shamil Basayev and Arab mercenary Ibn al-Khattab established the IIPB in 1998. The group seeks to establish an Islamic regime across the North Caucasus region of Russia. The IIPB participated in the 2002 seizure of a Moscow theater packed with 700 hostages. The group is believed to have ties with al-Qaeda, perhaps training operatives.

ISLAMIC JIHAD GROUP (IJG) is based in Uzbekistan and may be a splinter group that broke away from the Islamic Movement of Uzbekistan. IJG opposes the government of Uzbekistan in addition to the United States and Israel. It has targeted representatives of all three states, including three July 2004 suicide bombings of the U.S. embassy, the Israeli embassy, and the Uzbek prosecutor's office, all in Tashkent. IJG is the first Central Asian group to use female suicide bombers.

ISLAMIC MOVEMENT OF UZBEKISTAN (IMU) throughout Central Asia and linked to al-QAEDA. The movement's original goal was to overthrow the government of Uzbekistan and establish an Islamic state, but now its goals have expanded to broader anti-American issues. IMU has been blamed for bombings in Kyrgyzstan and Tashkent, Uzbekistan. Members of the group have been known to kidnap American and Japanese hikers and geologists.

AL-ITTIHAD AL-ISLAMI (AIAI) seeks to establish Islamic rule in Somalia. AIAI emerged in the 1990s when the Somali government disintegrated. AIAI is described more accurately as an umbrella group for a number of factions formed around local sheiks. While all advocate Islamic rule, they differ on how closely the Koran should be followed.

IZZ AL-DIN AL-QASAM BRIGADE, military wing of Hamas.

JAISH-E-MOHAMMED (JEM) seeks to annex Kashmir Province to Pakistan. The Islamic militant group broke away from Harakat ul-Mujahideen in 2000 and is also known as the Army of Mohammed. Led by Masood Azhar, JEM has been linked to the kidnapping of U.S. journalist Daniel Pearl in 2002.

JAPANESE RED ARMY (JRA) one of the few international terrorist groups led by a woman, Fusako Shigenobu. Founded in 1970–71, the JRA sought to overthrow Japan's constitutional monarchy and launch a global communist revolution. During the 1970s and 1980s the group specialized in hijackings and bombings, including a bombing at Tel Aviv's Lod Airport in 1972 (24 fatalities). Shigenobu maintained ties with the Palestinian Front for the Liberation of Palestine and based her operations in Lebanon. In 1988 a JRA operative was arrested and accused of planning to bomb sites in New York City, possibly at the request of Libyan leader Muammar Qaddafi. Shigenobu was arrested in November 2000 and announced that the group would cease activities.

JEMAAH ISLAMIAH ORGANIZATION an umbrella group for militant Islamic cells operating in Southeast Asia. The group is blamed for suicide bombings in Jakarta (2003, 2004), Bali (2003, 2005), and Manila (2000). Jemaah Islamiah was founded around 1969 by Abu Bakar Bashir and Abdullah Sungkar; Riduan Isamuddin ("Hambali") became the group's military leader in the early 1990s. The group follows the Darul Islamic movement and seeks to establish an Islamic regime uniting Southeast Asia. The targets of its bombing attacks tend to be Australian embassies or areas popular with Australian tourists.

AL-JIHAD began in the 1970s as an Egyptian Islamist movement that targeted senior Egyptian government officials. Members were responsible for the 1981 assassination of President Anwar Sadat. In 2001 the group merged with al-Qaeda and its leader, Ayman al-Zawahiri, became a top deputy to Osama bin Laden. Since the merger, al-Jihad's focus has been outside Egypt.

JUSTICE COMMANDOS OF THE ARMENIAN GENOCIDE emerged in Lebanon in 1974. Sought Turkish recognition of 1915 genocide and reparations.

KAHANE CHAI (KACH) a militant Israeli group seeking to make Israel an Arab-free state ruled according to Jewish law. The group evolved from Kach, an Israeli political party founded by Rabbi Meir Kahane in 1971 and banned by the Israeli parliament in 1988. When Kahane was assassinated two years later, Kach split, forming Kahane Chai ("Kahane Lives on"). His son Binyamin became leader of Kahane Chai, only to be assassinated along with his wife by Palestinian militants in December 2000. Kahane Chai member Baruch Goldstein led an attack on the Tomb of the Patriarchs in 1994.

KONGRA-GEL seeks to establish an independent state for the Kurds, an ethnic group distributed in Iraq, Turkey, and Syria. Founded in 1974 by Abdullah Ocalan, the group embraced a Marxist-Leninist ideology. The group has renamed itself multiple times and has been known as the Kurdistan Workers Party (1978–2002) and the Kurdistan Freedom and Democracy Congress (2002–03). Kongra-Gel members predominantly live in Iraq and carry out attacks on urban sites and tourist areas in Turkey. Ocalan renounced terrorism in 1999, but not all members have obeyed his "peace initiative."

KU KLUX KLAN organization of white supremacists predominantly located in the southern United States. Dating to 1865, the KKK intimidated, attacked, and lynched blacks. In the early 20th century, the KKK also targeted Catholics, Jews, and recent immigrants.

KUMPULAN MUJAHIDEEN MALAYSIA seeks to establish an Islamic state that would encompass Malaysia, Indonesia, and part of the Philippines. The group primarily operates out of Malaysia, and the Malaysian government has detained numerous members, which may account for the relatively low level of activity. The group has ties to Jemaah Islamiah.

KURDISTAN FREEDOM AND DEMOCRACY CONGRESS former name of KONGRA-GEL.

KURDISTAN WORKERS PARTY former name of Kongra-Gel, often abbreviated PKK.

LASHKAR E-TAYYIBA (LT) translates as "Army of the Righteous." LT is a Sunni Islamic militia based in Pakistan that fights Indians in Kashmir. The group has been implicated in numerous anti-India incidents, including an attack on the Indian parliamentary building in late 2001. Pakistan banned LT in 2002.

LASHKAR I JHANVI (LJ) banned by the Pakistani government in 2001. As the militant wing of the Sunni Sipha-i-Sahaba Pakistan Islamic group, LJ initially focused its attacks on Shia Muslims and tried to assassinate Pakistani prime minister Nawaz Sharif in January 1999. The group has claimed responsibility for a number of car bombings as well as the 2002 murder of American journalist Daniel Pearl.

LASHKAR JIHAD Indonesian terrorist group founded in 2000. Targets Christians and likely in contact with al-Qaeda.

LEHI also known as the Stern Gang, was a Zionist nationalist organization in the 1940s. The group was led by future Israeli prime minister Yitzhak Shamir, and it opposed the 1947 UN Partition Plan.

LIBERATION TIGERS OF TAMIL EELAM (LTTE) an ethnic-based insurgency seeking an independent Tamil state (Tamil Eelam) in northeastern Sri Lanka. Founded in 1976 by Velupillai Prabakharan, the Tamil Tigers have conducted a secular guerrilla movement against the government of Sri Lanka. The LTTE movement is renowned for its Black Tigers, a division of suicide bombers founded in 1987 that has carried out hundreds of attacks (including the assassination of Indian Prime Minister Rajiv Gandhi) before a cease-fire agreement was reached in 2001. The LTTE also operated as a de facto government, creating police, schools, and courts. The group has been internationally condemned for using child soldiers in its campaigns. Under the cease-fire, LTTE renounced demands for independence in favor of political and economic autonomy, but attacks still continue.

LIBYAN ISLAMIC FIGHTING GROUP opposes the secular government of Muammar Qaddafi and wants to establish a Muslim state. The group traces its origins to the Afghanistan-USSR war and emerged after that war ended in 1989.

LORD'S RESISTANCE ARMY (LRA) led by Joseph Kony, seeks to overthrow the Ugandan government in favor of a regime that strictly would follow the Ten Commandments. Despite claims to be a Christian force, the LRA engages in rape, murder, torture, child soldier conscription, and sex trafficking of children. Sudan has allowed LRA to operate near its border with Uganda. The group was formed in the early 1990s.

LOYALIST VOLUNTEER FORCE (LVF) an extremist paramilitary group opposed to the 1998 Good Friday Peace Agreement. Unlike the Irish Republican Army, the LVF consists of Protestants who want Northern Ireland to remain part of the United Kingdom. The group targets Catholics and Protestant backers of the peace process. It sometimes operates under the name *Red Hand Defenders.*

MAY 19 COMMUNIST ORDER (M-19) also known as the Resistance Conspiracy, robbed a series of banks in the United States in the 1980s and used the money to stage at least eight bombings. On November 7, 1983, M-19 bombed the U.S. Capitol building to protest U.S. military action in Grenada and Lebanon. Since the explosion occurred at 10:58 P.M., no injuries were reported. The group was a fund-raising arm—or at least a front operation—for a coalition of neo-communist groups, including the Weather Underground, the Black Liberation Army, and the Palestine Liberation Organization. The name was derived from the birth date of Vietnam's Ho Chi Minh and Malcolm X. The group never had more than about 20 members, and most had been arrested by the mid 1980s.

MEDELLIN CARTEL cocaine smuggling ring in Colombia, headed by Pablo Escobar. Most active in the 1980s, at its peak the cartel controlled 80 percent of the global cocaine market.

MICHIGAN MILITIA believed to be the largest paramilitary group in the United States, with 12,000 members. Founders Ray Southwell and Norman E. Olson believe they are in a race to "defend freedom" and are preparing their members for the coming battle by stockpiling weapons and conducting survival and firearms training.

MILITIA OF MONTANA/FREEMEN (MOM) led by John Trochmann. MOM is a violent white supremacist group that refuses to acknowledge the sovereignty of U.S. law. In 1996 16 residents of a MOM compound held FBI agents at bay for 81 days over a dispute involving firearms and fraud.

MINNESOTA CHRISTIAN MILITIA a right-wing terrorist group operating in the United States. In 1995 four members were convicted of possessing ricin, a deadly poison.

MOROCCAN ISLAMIC COMBATANT GROUP (GICM) a relatively new movement that wants an Islamic regime to govern Morocco. Members have trained in Afghanistan, and many are veterans of the Afghan-Soviet war. GICM devotes more attention to international Islamic causes than domestic endeavors. It is an ardent supporters of al-Qaeda and is suspected of carrying out terrorist operations in western Europe as well as North Africa.

MOUNTAINEER MILITIA a right-wing paramilitary group based in West Virginia. A 1996 FBI raid found an extensive, illegal arsenal of weapons acquired by group members.

MUSLIM BROTHERHOOD a Muslim political organization founded in Egypt in 1928. Similar organizations were later founded in Syria and Jordan. The Brotherhoods advocate a nonviolent form of Islam and open, democratic political systems.

NATIONAL LIBERATION ARMY (ELN) the smaller of Colombia's two left-wing insurgent movements. Fabio Vasquez Castano, after training in Cuba, founded ELN in 1964. The movement seeks to end Colombia's uneven distribution of wealth with a blend of Castro-style guerrilla combat and liberation theology. ELN targets infrastructure and earns income by kidnapping oil company personnel.

NATIONAL LIBERATION FRONT (FLN) led Algeria's effort to secure independence from France. Founded in 1954, the FLN directed the 1954–62 war of independence and then evolved into a ruling party that controlled Algerian politics for decades.

NEW RED BRIGADES opposes Italian economic policies and involvement in NATO. The group claims to be the successor to the Red Brigades terrorist group of the 1970s and 1980s. Officials believe the New Red Brigades were linked to the assassinations of two Italian labor ministers, but they have not confirmed the connection. The government has arrested a large portion of the group's leadership, significantly curtailing its activities.

"THE ORDER" a militant white-supremacist group that broke away from Aryan Nations. The Order was renown for its armed-car robberies and penchant for murder. Founder Robert Matthews died in a confrontation with the U.S. government in 1984 and the members migrated to similarly minded groups.

PALESTINE AUTHORITY institution created by the 1993 Oslo Accords for Palestinian self-government in the West Bank and Gaza Strip. Formally separate from PLO, but PLO Chairman Yasser Arafat was the Authority's first president.

PALESTINE DEMOCRATIC UNION (PDU) was created in 1991 by Yasser Abd Rabbo. Also known as FIDA, the PDU broke away from the hard-line Maoist Popular Front for the Liberation of Palestine, preferring to embrace a softer, more socialist stance. The group has accepted the Palestine Authority arrangement and works as a political party within that framework. Unlike other PLO members, PDU does not have a military branch. Rabbo has served in the PA government.

PALESTINE LIBERATION ARMY technically the military arm of the PLO, but the PLO does not exercise control over its forces. Established in 1964, the PLA actually consists of elite military battalions based in Arab host countries. Palestinians living in these countries could opt to fulfill their mandatory military service in the local PLA battalion rather than in their national army.

PALESTINE LIBERATION FRONT (PLF) was founded in the late 1970s by Abu Abbas. The group is a successor to the Popular Front for the Liberation of Palestine and backs the PLO. In 1985 the PLF hijacked the *Achille Lauro* cruise ship and shot an elderly wheelchair-bound passenger, Leon Klinghoffer, who was still alive when the terrorists threw him and his wheelchair overboard. After 1985 the PLF operated out of Iraq until the U.S.-led invasion when Abbas was captured by U.S. special forces in April 2003. He died in U.S. custody in April 2004.

PALESTINE LIBERATION ORGANIZATION (PLO) was founded in 1964 by the Arab League as an umbrella organization bringing together eight separate organizations working to establish a Palestinian state. Member groups include Fatah, the Popular Front for the Liberation of Palestine, and the Democratic Front for the Liberation of Palestine, the Palestinian People's Party, the Palestine Liberation Front, the Arab Liberation Front, the Popular Struggle Front, and As-Sa'qua. The PLO has had three chairmen: Ahmad Shuqeiri (1964–69), Yasser Arafat (1969–2004), and Mahmoud Abbas (2004–). The PLO was organized into two administrative bodies: the Palestinian National Council and the PLO Executive Committee. Its headquarters have moved from Jordan (1964–70) to Lebanon (1970–82), Tunisia (1982–93), and Ramallah, West Bank (1993–).

PALESTINIAN ISLAMIC JIHAD emerged from the Muslim Brotherhood inspired by the 1979 Iranian Revolution. PIJ's leader, Ramadan Abdullah Shallah, once taught at the University of South Florida. The group seeks the destruction of Israel and subsequent creation of a Palestinian state.

PALESTINIAN REVOLUTIONARY FORCES the military commando units of the PLO, distinct from the larger Palestine Liberation Army. Yasser Arafat became commander in chief on September 16, 1970, as Jordan launched the Black September military campaign against the PLO. The Palestinian Revolutionary Forces concentrated on actions in the Middle East, while the related Black September Organization specialized in European attacks.

PALESTINE LIBERATION FRONT, which merged with Arab National Movement and Youth for Revenge to form the Popular Front for the Liberation of Palestine in 1967. The PLF emerged in 1976 from a breakaway faction of the Popular Front for the Liberation of Palestine—General Command.

PATRIOT COUNCIL members were arrested in 1995 on charges of attempting to manufacture ricin in order to poison local law-enforcement officials in Minnesota.

PEOPLE AGAINST GANGSTERISM AND DRUGS (PAGAD) seeks to protect Muslims in South Africa. Founded in 1995, the group has carried out an active bombing campaign, targeting synagogues, tourist facilities, and gay clubs. It has also targeted Western-connected restaurants, such as the Cape Town Planet Hollywood restaurant, which was bombed in August 1998. Between 1996 and 2000 PAGAD reportedly carried out 189 bombings.

PEOPLE'S MUJAHIDEEN ORGANIZATION OF IRAN (PMOI) opposed Ayatollah Khomeini's 1979 Islamic revolution in Iran and seeks to overthrow the current Iranian government. Although embracing Islamic ideas itself, PMOI's theology is less radical than Khomeini's and combined with Marxism. PMOI was founded in the 1960s by middle-class university students. The group also is anti-Western and attacked several U.S. targets in the 1970s. In the 1980s, during the Iran-Iraq war, Iraqi leader Saddam Hussein funded the PMOI, and the group helped suppress Kurdish uprisings in Iraq. Following Saddam's fall from power, PMOI signed a ceasefire with Western forces in May 2003. PMOI is led by an Iranian woman, Maryam Rajavi.

PHINEAS PRIESTHOOD a white supremacist group that bombed a newspaper office and twice robbed a branch of the U.S. Bank in Spokane, Washington, in 1996. The robbers said they were protesting the treatment of members of the Montana Militia/Freemen Movement.

POPULAR FRONT FOR THE LIBERATION OF PALESTINE (PFLP) the second-largest faction in the Palestine Liberation Organization. The PFLP was founded in 1967 by George Habash, a Christian, and members emphasized the need to create a new type of revolutionary individual to achieve Palestinian aspirations. The secular group is credited with a number of violent incidents, particularly hijackings in the 1960s and 1970s. Perhaps its most famous member was Leila Khaled, one of the few documented female terrorists. Khaled was a highly visible member of the various hijacking teams. Habash retired in 2000, but his successor, Abu Ali Mustafa, was killed August 27, 2001. Ahmad Sadat was subsequently elected PFLP general secretary in October 2001.

POPULAR FRONT FOR THE LIBERATION OF PALESTINE—GENERAL COMMAND a PFLP splinter group formed by Ahmad Jabril in 1968. The group focused more on armed resistance than politics and opposed Yasser Arafat and any attempts at accommodation with Israel. The group has long been linked to Syria and Iran. In 1976 an anti-Jabril faction split away to form the Palestine Liberation Front.

POPULAR PUERTO RICAN ARMY active in the United States since the late 1970s. Also known as "Los Macheteros," the group seeks independence for Puerto Rico, now a U.S. territory. Most of their activity takes place on the island of Puerto Rico, mainly against U.S. military facilities and personnel.

POSSE COMITATUS a right-wing extremist group in the United States that denies the legitimacy of the federal government. Since the group's creation in the late 1960s, members have not recognized any authority higher than the sheriff; its name is taken from the Wild West notion of using an ad hoc volunteer force to enforce local laws. The group loathes Jews and tax collectors.

AL-QAEDA is the militant Islamic group that carried out the terrorist attacks against the United States on September 11, 2001. The group is also responsible for multiple attacks on U.S. facilities, citizens, and allies, including the bombing of the USS *Cole* (2000) and the U.S. embassies in Kenya and Tanzania (1998). Founded by Osama bin Laden in 1988, al-Qaeda ("the Base") seeks to establish a global Islamic state (caliphate). Mechanisms to attain this goal include defeating the United States (in the belief that Israel exists only due to U.S. support), deporting non-Muslims and Westerners from Islamic countries, and overthrowing governments that it believes do not conform to Islamic governance. To this end, al-Qaeda declared in 1998 that it is the "duty of all Muslims to kill U.S. citizens, civilian and military, and their allies everywhere." Al-Qaeda's core membership consists of Arab veterans of the USSR-Afghanistan war of the 1980s. Al-Qaeda was based in Afghanistan until the U.S.-led coalition overthrew the extreme Muslim Taliban regime at the end of 2001. It now is organized into a number of smaller units dispersed throughout Asia.

AL-QASSAM military wing of HAMAS, claims to sponsor Palestinian suicide bombers.

REAL IRISH REPUBLICAN ARMY consists of former Irish Republican Army operatives who objected to the Northern Ireland peace process and 1997 cease-fire agreement. The Real IRA functions as the military wing of the 32-county Sovereignty Movement. The group formed after the cease-fire and is led by Michael McKevitt. A large part of its membership, including McKevitt, remains in jail. The group targets security personnel in Northern Ireland. The Real IRA is responsible for the Omagh car bombing (August 15, 1998) that left 29 dead and hundreds injured.

RED ARMY FACTION (BAADER-MEINHOF GANG) founded by Andreas Baader and Ulrike Meinhof, radical, left-wing West Germans; opposed American bases in West Germany and Vietnam War. Active the 1970s; robbed banks for funding; attacked U.S. officers' mess in Frankfurt.

RED BRIGADES a left-wing group that sought to remove Italy from NATO and other Western organizations. Founded in 1970 by Renato Curcio, Margherita Cagol, and Alberto Franceschini, the Red Brigades broke into factories and kidnapped Italian businessmen and government leaders. In 1978 the group kidnapped and executed former Italian prime minister Aldo Moro. Members had demanded that an ongoing criminal trial of Curcio and 14 others be suspended before Moro would be released. Moro's murder horrified the Italian public and removed what marginal support the Red Brigades had enjoyed. Although the group kidnapped and murdered several more prominent leaders, internal divisions and arrests have reduced the Red Brigades to probably fewer than 50 active members.

RED HAND DEFENDERS (RHD) formed in 1998 to keep Northern Ireland a part of the United Kingdom. Largely Protestant in membership, the group concentrates on Catholic targets, including parochial school staffs and Catholic postal workers. RHD and the Ulster Defense Association often take credit for the same attack, making their relationship difficult to untangle.

REVOLUTIONARY ARMED FORCES OF COLOMBIA (FARC) with more than 12,000 soldiers, is the leading Latin American guerrilla group. Founded in 1964 to be the military branch of the Colombian Communist Party, FARC has now diversified into bombing, kidnapping, and drug running. FARC members frequently kidnap foreign nationals and raise most of their funds through ransom demands, local "tax" levies, and the drug trade. Although FARC has strayed from its Marxist roots, it continues to receive aid from Cuba. It also easily moves in and out of neighboring Venezuela and considers the Venezuelan government of Hugo Chavez to be an ally.

REVOLUTIONARY NUCLEI (RN) a small Greek terrorist organization that opposes Greek business leaders, the European Union, NATO, and U.S. operations in Greece. The group was primarily active between 1995 and 1998 and is believed to be linked to the Greek Revolutionary People's Struggle. RN has detonated several primitive bombs but tends to take steps to minimize casualties, such as telephone warnings and off-hour attacks. The last confirmed RN attack was in November 2000 when two bombs were planted at the Athens branch of Citigroup.

REVOLUTIONARY ORGANIZATION "NOVEMBER 17" Greek terrorist group named for a 1973 student uprising. Established in 1975, members target Western governments that supported the military regime that ruled Greece from 1967 to 1974. Specifically, it opposes the United States, Turkey, and NATO and wants no military contacts with these entities. It also wants Greece to withdraw from the European Union. November 17 claims responsibility for more than 100 attacks and is suspected of planning to attack the 2004 Olympic Games in Athens.

REVOLUTIONARY PEOPLE'S LIBERATION FRONT/PARTY an offshoot of the Turkish Revolutionary Youth. The group dates to 1978 and varies its name depending on its activities: "Front" for military actions and "Party" for political issues. Known by its Turkish abbreviation, DHKP/C, the group describes itself as Marxist-Leninist and seeks to establish a socialist regime and to improve conditions in Turkish prisons. It has targeted the United States, NATO, Turkish businessmen, and Turkish security and military personnel.

REVOLUTIONARY PROLETARIAN INITIATIVE NUCLEI (NIPR) also claims to be continuing the work of Italy's Red Brigades. NIPR emerged in 2000 and opposes Italy's economic and international policies, particularly related to labor relations and foreign companies.

REVOLUTIONARY STRUGGLE links itself to the Greek 17 November terrorist organization. Only active since 2003, the group raises particular concern because its two main attacks to date targeted "first responders," that is, police officers and rescue personnel. It is the first Greek terrorist group to target this particular sector.

RIYADUS-SALIKHIN RECONNAISSANCE AND SABOTAGE BATTALION OF CHECHEN MARTYRS is another group linked to Chechen warlord Shamil Basayev (see p. 279). *Riyadus-Salikhin* means "requirements for getting into paradise," and the group seeks an Islamic state uniting the North Caucasus region of Russia. Riyadus-Salikhin claimed responsibility for the Beslan school hostage crisis (2004), simultaneous Russian airline bombings (2004), Moscow subway bombings (2004), and the Moscow theater hostage crisis (2002).

SALAFIST GROUP FOR CALL AND COMBAT (GSPC) the leading terrorist group in Algeria. Founded in 1996 by a faction that broke away from the Armed Islamic Group (GIA), GSPC has since surpassed GIA in size and influence. While both GSPC and GIA seek to overthrow the current regime in Algeria and found an Islamic state, the organizations differ on two key topics. GSPC observes a stricter, more fundamentalist interpretation of the Koran (*salafi* means "fundamentalist"), and it refuses to target civilians deliberately in its armed struggle. Instead it targets Algerian governmental and military installations, mainly outside urban areas.

SHINING PATH or Sendero Luminoso, a militant communist movement in Peru. Dating to the 1960s, Shining Path was founded by Abimael Guzmán, a university professor who recruited students to his cause. The group seeks to rid Peru of foreign influence and establish a communist regime led by Peruvian peasants. It has used a bloody campaign of bombing, assassination, kidnapping, and drug-running in pursuit of this goal, killing some 30,000 Peruvians. For a time the group controlled a considerable amount of rural Peru, but eventually the peasants became fed up with the group and formed their own militias. Guzmán was arrested in 1992 and subsequently called for a cease-fire, which has significantly weakened the group.

SINN FÉIN political branch of the Irish Republican Army.

SIPAH-I-SAHABA (SSP) is a Sunni Islam group operating from Pakistan. The group emerged following the Shia Islamic revolution in Iran and bitterly opposes that branch of Islam. SSP has called for killing Shia clerics and for denouncing Shia as non-Muslim. SSP won seats in the Pakistani parliament.

SPECIAL PURPOSE ISLAMIC REGIMENT a Chechen guerrilla group best known for the siege of a Moscow theater in 2002. It particularly targets Russian soldiers and police operating in Chechnya.

SYMBIONESE LIBERATION ARMY (SLA) consisted of about a dozen people in their 20s who sought to mobilize students and African-American prisoners to improve the lives of African-Americans impoverished by capitalism in the United States and to promote racial harmony. In the mid-1970s they robbed at least two banks, planted a few small bombs, murdered a public school superintendent, and mainly spent their time plotting and honing their firearms skills. They are best known for kidnapping newspaper heiress Patricia Hearst to attract publicity to their cause and to swap for her two jailed SLA members. While they did attract enormous publicity, particularly from audiotapes of Hearst explaining their ideology, they changed their demands to a $6 million ransom. The ransom was ultimately paid in food donated to the poor, but Hearst was not released. She remained with the group until she was arrested by police in September 1975 and at trial claimed she had been brainwashed.

TAWHID WAL JIHAD better known as the al-Zarqawi Network or al-Qaeda in Iraq, is the leading Sunni terrorist group in Iraq. Abu Musab al-Zarqawi founded the network in April 2004 as an umbrella group for Iraqi rebels opposed to the U.S.-led coalition forces then occupying Iraq. Tawhid wal Jihad (Unification and Jihad) seeks to expel the U.S. and Western forces and to establish an Islamic state in Iraq. However, Shia Muslims were not only excluded from membership, but they were also designated as targets. The group has carried out a number attacks, including the 2002 assassination of Laurence Foley, a U.S. Agency for International Development employee in 2002, the murder of the head of the Iraqi Governing Council, and in March 2004 the killing of some 180 Shiites celebrating a religious holiday. Zarqawi's followers have aiso claimed credit for kidnapping and beheading several U.S. citizens working in Iraq.

TUNISIAN COMBATANT GROUP draws its members from Tunisians living outside Tunisia. Founded in 2000, the group works to advance the international Islamic jihad and to establish an Islamic regime to govern Tunisia. One of the group's founders, Tarek Maaroufi, was jailed for killing Ahmad Shah Massoud, an anti-Taliban operative, on September 9, 2001.

TUPAC AMARU REVOLUTIONARY MOVEMENT (MRTA) founded in 1983. MRTA seeks to establish a Marxist-Leninist regime in Peru and to eliminate U.S. and Japanese economic influence in the country. Fourteen members seized the Japanese ambassador's residence in Lima in December 1996, holding 72 people hostage until police stormed compound in April 1997. The 14 militants, including leader Nestor Cerpa, were killed in the raid.

TURKISH HEZBOLLAH the Islamic wing of the Kurdish sovereignty movement. Since its establishment in the early 1980s, Turkish Hezbollah has progressed from fighting the Kurdistan Workers' Party to attacking non-Islamic facilities such as liquor stores and bordellos and to targeting Turkish interests, such as businesspeople and journalists.

ULSTER DEFENSE ASSOCIATION/ULSTER FREEDOM FIGHTERS (UDA) founded in 1971, UDA was the largest Protestant paramilitary group in Northern Ireland, and it initially supported the Good Friday Peace Agreement. However, the UDA soon abandoned the peace process and resumed a campaign against Catholics and Protestant paramilitaries that still support the peace process. It is also suspected to have deep involvement in illegal drug trafficking.

ULSTER VOLUNTEER FORCE founded in 1966 to oppose Northern Ireland's unification with Ireland. It historically was regarded as the most violent, most bloody of the Ulster loyalist paramilitary forces, killing some 550 people during its history. The group actively supported the Good Friday peace process but engaged in violence with groups that did not support peace.

UNITED LIBERATION FRONT OF ASSAM established in 1979 to seek self-determination for Assam, a region in northeastern India. The group was initially popular, but its increasingly bloody campaign led to a government crackdown in 1990. The group also lost support in Assam when it began to focus on civilian targets. The Front operated camps across the border in Bhutan, but that government raided the camps in 2003, significantly damaging the Front's capabilities.

UNITED SELF-DEFENSE FORCES OF COLOMBIA (AUC) a right-wing group formed in April 1997 to coordinate the activities and demobilization of nationalist paramilitary forces in Colombia. AUC forces are made up of groups frequently targeted by Marxist guerrillas: economic leaders, narcotics traffickers, and rural communities. The group claims to earn 70 percent of its income from cocaine.

WASHINGTON STATE MILITIA planned to attack communications or railroad facilities using pipe bombs before a 1996 FBI raid.

WEATHERMEN a U.S.-based group of the 1960s opposing the Vietnam War. Only a few hundred strong, members tended to be 20-something college students or recent graduates. In an effort to destroy "American imperialism," the Weathermen bombed banks, university departments, and military facilities. In 1970 the name of the organization was changed to the gender-neutral *Weather Underground.*

9

Organizations and Agencies

Amnesty International
URL: http://www.amnestyusa.org
5 Penn Plaza, 14th floor
New York, NY 10001
Phone: (212) 807-8400
Amnesty International is a worldwide movement of people who campaign for internationally recognized human rights. AI conducts research and activities focused on preventing and ending grave abuses of the rights to physical and mental integrity, freedom of conscience and expression, and freedom from discrimination. AI is independent of any government, political ideology, economic interest, or religion.

American Civil Liberties Union
URL: http://www.aclu.org
125 Broad Street, 18th floor
New York, NY 10004
Phone: (212) 549-2500
The American Civil Liberties Union works to defend the rights outlined in the Constitution of the United States, including freedom of speech, association, and assembly; freedom of the press; freedom of religion; and the strict separation of church and state. It also seeks to preserve an individual's right to equal protection under the law, right to due process, and right to privacy. The ACLU also works to extend rights to segments of the U.S. population that have traditionally been denied their rights, including Native Americans and other people of color, women, prisoners, people with disabilities, and the poor.

Anti-Defamation League
URL: http://www.adl.org

823 United Nations Plaza
New York, NY 10017
Phone: (212) 885-7700
Founded in 1913, the Anti-Defamation League seeks to end anti-Semitism and bigotry. It maintains an extensive database on U.S. terrorist organizations and white supremacist militias.

Association of Southeast Asian Nations (ASEAN)
URL: http://www.aseansec.org
ASEAN Secretariat
70A, Jalan Sisingamangaraja
Jakarta 12110 Indonesia
The Association of Southeast Asian Nations was begun in 1967 by Indonesia, Malaysia, the Philippines, Singapore, and Thailand. Five other countries have since joined: Brunei, Vietnam, Laos, Myanmar, and Cambodia. ASEAN seeks to accelerate economic growth, social progress, and cultural development in the region through joint endeavors and to promote regional peace and stability through abiding respect for justice and the rule of law. Transnational crime and terrorism are key areas of ASEAN cooperation.

Bureau of Alcohol, Tobacco, Firearms, and Explosives
URL: http://www.atf.gov
650 Massachusetts Avenue NW
Washington, DC 20226
Phone: (202) 927-7777
This branch of the U.S. Department of Justice conducts criminal investigations, regulates the U.S. firearms and explosives industries, and assists other law-enforcement agencies. This work is part of the U.S. government's broader strategy to prevent terrorism, reduce violent crime, and protect the public in a manner that is faithful to the Constitution and the laws of the United States. ATF's expertise in explosives and arson is vital for interagency efforts to protect Americans from terrorism, while enforcement of alcohol and tobacco regulations reduces a major form of fund-raising for terrorists.

Central Intelligence Agency
URL: http://www.cia.gov
Office of Public Affairs
Washington, DC 20505
Phone: (703) 482-8062
The Central Intelligence Agency's primary mission is to collect, evaluate, and disseminate foreign intelligence to assist the president and senior U.S.

government policymakers in making decisions relating to the national security. The Central Intelligence Agency does not make policy; it is an independent source of foreign intelligence information for those who do. The Central Intelligence Agency may also engage in covert action at the president's direction in accordance with applicable law.

Council of Europe
URL: http://www.coe.int
Avenue de l'Europe
67075 Strasbourg, France
The Council of Europe is Europe's oldest political organization. Founded in 1949, the Council of Europe has 46 member states. The Council seeks to promote the common fundamental values of human rights, the rule of law, and democracy; to strengthen the security of European citizens, in particular by combating terrorism, organized crime, and trafficking in human beings; and to foster cooperation with other international and European organizations.

Council on American-Islamic Relations
URL: http://www.cair-net.org
453 New Jersey Avenue SE
Washington, DC 20003-4034
Phone: (202) 488-8787
CAIR's mission is to enhance understanding of Islam, encourage dialogue, protect civil liberties, empower American Muslims, and build coalitions that promote justice and mutual understanding.

Department of Homeland Security
URL: http://www.dhs.gov
Washington, DC 20528
Phone: (202) 282-8000
The Department of Homeland Security was established in 2002 in the wake of the September 11, 2001, terrorist attacks in the United States. DHS will combine a broad range of agencies involved in protecting the U.S. homeland into one centralized agency. Agencies under the DHS include Citizenship and Immigration, Coast Guard, Border Protection, Federal Emergency Management, Secret Service, and Transportation Security.

Department of State
URL: http://www.state.gov
2201 C Street NW
Washington, DC 20520
Phone: (202) 647-4000

The State Department leads the United States in its relationships with foreign governments, international organizations, and the people of other countries. It aims to provide a more free, prosperous, and secure world. The State Department represents the U.S. overseas and conveys U.S. policies to foreign governments and international organizations through American embassies and consulates in foreign countries and diplomatic missions; negotiates and concludes agreements and treaties on issues ranging from trade to nuclear weapons; coordinates and supports international activities of other U.S. agencies, hosts official visits, and performs other diplomatic missions; and leads interagency coordination and manages the allocation of resources for foreign relations.

Department of the Treasury
URL: http://www.treasury.gov
1500 Pennsylvania Avenue NW
Washington, DC 20220
Phone: (202) 622-2000
Through its Office of Terrorism and Financial Intelligence, the Treasury Department deploys its intelligence and enforcement functions with the twin aims of safeguarding the financial system against illicit use and combating rogue nations, terrorist facilitators, money launderers, drug kingpins, and other national security threats. Treasury's Office of Foreign Assets Control applies and enforces economic trade sanctions against suspected foreign terrorists.

Drug Enforcement Administration
URL: http://www.dea.gov
Mailstop: AES
2401 Jefferson Davis Highway
Alexandria, VA 22301
Phone: (202) 307-1000
A branch of the Justice Department, the Drug Enforcement Administration (DEA) works to stem the illegal drug trade within the United States and abroad. The agency has field offices worldwide and reports on illegal drug production and distribution in Afghanistan, Colombia, and other regions known to have links with terrorist organizations.

European Union (EU)
URL: http://europa.eu.int/index_en.htm
The European Union (EU) is a family of democratic European countries, committed to working together for peace and prosperity. It is not a state

intended to replace existing states, nor is it just an organization for international cooperation. The EU is a series of common institutions that allow for joint approaches toward promoting democracy, freedom, and social justice while preserving diversity. Founded in the aftermath of World War II, the EU has grown from six members to embrace 25 countries and 450 million people. The European Union has no central headquarters. Its key institutions are distributed among Belgium, France, Germany, and Luxembourg, while its institutional presidency rotates among member states every six months.

Federal Bureau of Investigation
URL: http://www.fbi.gov
J. Edgar Hoover Building
935 Pennsylvania Avenue NW
Washington, DC 20535-0001
Phone: (202) 324-3000
Founded in 1908, the FBI is the principal investigative arm of the U.S. Department of Justice. The mission of the FBI is to uphold the law through the investigation of violations of federal criminal law; to protect the United States from foreign intelligence and terrorist activities; to provide leadership and law-enforcement assistance to federal, state, local, and international agencies; and to perform these responsibilities in a manner that is responsive to the needs of the public and is faithful to the Constitution of the United States. Regarding terrorism, the FBI's role is to protect the United States and U.S. persons and interests throughout the world from terrorist attack. This is accomplished through professional investigation, intelligence activities, and coordinated efforts with local, state, federal, and foreign entities as appropriate.

Federal Emergency Management Agency
URL: http://www.fema.gov
500 C Street SW
Washington, DC 20482
Phone: (800) 621-3362
FEMA was an independent agency before it was incorporated into the new Department of Homeland Security in 2003. FEMA's mission is to respond to, plan for, recover from, and mitigate against disasters. Historically primarily concerned with natural disasters, such as hurricanes and flooding, it is now part of the U.S. government efforts to increase national preparedness for terrorist attacks.

Internal Revenue Service
URL: http://www.irs.gov

The IRS has a dual role in the U.S. federal government's terrorism policies. First, it has granted special tax liability exemptions for individuals who have been the victims of terrorism and conferred tax-exempt status on new charities created to aid those victims. Second, the IRS Criminal Investigation division uses its financial expertise to analyze unusual financial transactions and detailed financial information to expose money laundering, fund-raising, and tax fraud related to terrorist activities.

International Criminal Police Organization (Interpol)
URL: http://www.interpol.int
General Secretariat
200 quai Charles de Gaulle
69006 Lyon, France

Interpol is the world's largest international police organization, with 184 member countries. Created in 1923, it facilitates cross-border police cooperation and supports and assists all organizations, authorities, and services whose mission is to prevent or combat international crime. Interpol operates secure global police communications systems, maintains databases, and provides law-enforcement officials with emergency support and operational activities, especially in its priority crime areas of fugitives, public safety and terrorism, drugs and organized crime, trafficking in human beings, and financial and high-tech crime.

Institute for Counter-Terrorism
URL: http://www.ict.org.il
Interdisciplinary Center Herzlia
P.O. Box 167
Herzlia, 46150, Israel

The Institute for Counter-Terrorism is a research institute and think tank dedicated to developing innovative public policy solutions to international terrorism. The institute aims to affect policy at the highest levels, in joint cooperation with the world community.

Jamestown Foundation
URL: http://www.jamestown.org
1111 16th Street NW, Suite 320
Washington, DC 20036
Phone: (202) 483-8888

Established in 1984, the Jamestown Foundation is a private, nonprofit organization that seeks to inform and educate policymakers and the broader policy community about events and trends in societies that are strategically or tactically important to the United States and that frequently restrict access to such information. Utilizing indigenous and primary sources, Jamestown's material is delivered without political bias, filter, or agenda. It is often the only source of information that should be, but is not always, available through official or intelligence channels, especially in regard to Eurasia and terrorism. Jamestown publishes three separate e-newsletters on terrorism: *Terrorism Monitor, Terrorism Focus,* and *Spotlight on Terrorism.*

Memorial Institute for the Prevention of Terrorism
URL: http://www.mipt.org
P.O. Box 889
621 North Robinson, 4th floor
Oklahoma City, OK 73101
Phone: (405) 278-6300
The Memorial Institute for the Prevention of Terrorism located in Oklahoma City is dedicated to preventing terrorism or mitigating its effects. Founded in 1999 as a nonprofit corporation in Oklahoma, MIPT grew out of the desire of the survivors and families of the Murrah Federal Building bombing of April 19, 1995, to have a living memorial. MIPT intends to honor that desire by trying to prevent other cities from living through what Oklahoma City had to live through. MIPT feels a special obligation to first responders—police officers, firefighters, emergency medical technicians, and all of the others who are first on the scene in the aftermath of terrorist activity. It sponsors research to discover equipment, training, and procedures that might assist them in preventing terrorism and responding to it.

Middle East Research and Information Project
URL: http://www.merip.org
1500 Massachusetts Avenue NW, Suite 119
Washington, DC 20005
Phone: (202) 223-3677
For more than 30 years, the Middle East Research and Information Project (MERIP) has worked to provide information and analysis on the Middle East that would be used by the existing media. MERIP is a nonprofit, nongovernmental organization based in Washington, D.C. A completely independent organization, it has no links to any religious, educational, or

political organizations in the United States or elsewhere. Its flagship publication is the *Middle East Report.*

National Institute of Justice
URL: http://www.ojp.usdoj.gov/nij/about.htm
810 Seventh Street NW
Washington, DC 20531
Phone: (202) 307-2942
The National Institute of Justice is the research, development, and evaluation agency of the U.S. Department of Justice and is dedicated to researching crime control and justice issues. NIJ provides objective, independent, evidence-based knowledge and tools to meet the challenges of crime and justice, particularly at the state and local levels. Select publications focus on local terrorism-prevention efforts.

National Security Agency/Central Security Service
URL: http://www.nsa.gov
9800 Savage Road, Suite 6248
Fort George G. Meade, MD 20755-6248
Phone: (301) 688-6311
The National Security Agency/Central Security Service (NSA/CSS) is the federal cryptologic organization. Its twofold mission is the protection of U.S. information systems and the production of foreign signals intelligence information. It is the agency authorized to conduct wiretap operations outside of U.S. soil, although a controversial White House policy allowed the NSA to eavesdrop on international communications from within the United States in 2002–04. NSA/CSS is on the high-tech frontier of communications and data processing and is a major center of foreign language analysis and research within the U.S. government. In 2004 the NSA opened a business center in Annapolis, Maryland, to work with private homeland security companies in the war on global terrorism.

North Atlantic Treaty Organization (NATO)
URL: http://www.nato.int
NATO Headquarters
Boulevard Leopold III
1110 Brussels, Belgium
The North Atlantic Treaty Organization (NATO) is an alliance of 26 countries from North America and Europe committed to fulfilling the goals of the North Atlantic Treaty signed on April 4, 1949. In accordance with the treaty,

the fundamental role of NATO is to safeguard the freedom and security of its member countries by political and military means. NATO is playing an increasingly important role in crisis management and peacekeeping. NATO is contributing to the fight against terrorism through military operations in Afghanistan, the Balkans, and the Mediterranean and by taking steps to protect its populations and territory against terrorist attacks.

Oklahoma City National Memorial
URL: http://www.oklahomacitynationalmemorial.org
620 North Harvey
Oklahoma City, OK 73102
Phone: (405) 235-3313
The Oklahoma City National Memorial museum sits atop the site of the Alfred P. Murrah federal building, which was destroyed by a truck bomb on April 19, 1995. The museum is a memorial to the 168 victims as well as an educational institution working to promote conflict resolution and violence prevention. It is also a repository of data on the tragedy, including firsthand accounts by survivors and rescue personnel.

Organization for Security and Cooperation in Europe (OSCE)
URL: http://www.osce.org
Kaerntner Ring 5-7
1010 Vienna, Austria
The OSCE is the world's largest regional security organization whose 55 participating states span the geographical area from Vancouver to Vladivostok. With its expertise in conflict prevention, crisis management, and early warning, the OSCE contributes to worldwide efforts in combating terrorism. Many effective counterterrorism measures fall into areas in which the OSCE is already active, such as police training and border monitoring.

Terrorism Research Center
URL: http://www.terrorism.com
Founded in 1996, the Terrorism Research Center is an independent institute dedicated to the research of terrorism, information warfare and security, critical infrastructure protection, homeland security, and other issues of low-intensity political violence and gray-area phenomena. The Center's Web site includes a continuously updated list of terrorist incidents, as well as profiles of terrorist groups, incidents, and countries, but most of it is on a subscription-only basis and individual student subscriptions are not available.

Organizations and Agencies

United Nations
URL: http://www.un.org
First Avenue at 46th Street
New York, NY 10017

Founded in 1945, the United Nations is central to global efforts to solve problems that challenge humanity. The purposes of the United Nations are to maintain international peace and security; to develop friendly relations among nations; to cooperate in solving international economic, social, cultural, and humanitarian problems and in promoting respect for human rights and fundamental freedoms; and to be a center for harmonizing the actions of nations in attaining these ends. Cooperating in this effort are more than 30 affiliated organizations, known together as the UN system. The United Nations leads the international campaigns against drug trafficking and terrorism. As of 2005, 191 countries are members of the United Nations.

10

Annotated Bibliography

This chapter provides an overview of the current literature on terrorism, including definitions, tactics, responses, and individual terrorist groups. Print sources range from books to magazine and newspaper articles, while electronic sources include digital archives, magazines, and television and radio transcripts. The bibliography is divided into the following categories:

- I. General
    - A. What Is Terrorism?
    - B. Who Are the Terrorists?
    - C. What Do Terrorists Want?
        1. Media Coverage: General
        2. Media Coverage: TWA Flight 847, 1985 hijacking
        3. Religion
    - D. How Do Terrorists Operate?
        1. Cyberterrorism
        2. Finance
        3. Hijacking
        4. Kidnapping
        5. Narcoterrorism
        6. Suicide Attacks
        7. Weapons of Mass Destruction
- II. United States
    - A. Domestic Terrorist Groups and Incidents
        1. Anti-Federalist/Right-Wing/Militia
        2. Atlanta Olympics
        3. Islamic Terrorist Groups
        4. 9/11
        5. 1993 Attack on World Trade Center

Materials were selected for this bibliography based on their currency, comprehensiveness, and accessibility. Most of the materials here should be available in public or school libraries or easily through interlibrary loans. Periodicals, including magazines and newspapers, may not be available in hard copy but usually can be downloaded through Internet research portals available at public and research libraries.

I. GENERAL

What Is Terrorism?

Since the 9/11 terrorist attacks against the United States, hundreds if not thousands of books have been published about specific incidents, groups, or causes of terrorism. Such works generally have an introductory chapter discussing "What Is Terrorism?" but for a thorough introduction to the subject several older works are more appropriate.

Clutterbuck, Richard L. *Terrorism in an Unstable World.* New York: Routledge, 1994. Terrorism scholar Clutterbuck provides a broad overview of the terrorism threats faced by the world at the end of the cold war.

Hoffman, Bruce. *Inside Terrorism,* 2d ed. New York: Columbia University Press, 2006. Bruce Hoffman is perhaps the most often quoted expert on terrorism today and heads the RAND think tank's program on terrorism. Before RAND, Hoffman headed the Center for the Study of Terrorism and Political Violence, based in Scotland. The original 1998 version of this book was a standard text for students of terrorism because of its clear writing, thorough history of the causes of terrorism, and vivid descriptions of groups and incidents. The new edition has been updated to include the 9/11 attacks.

Laqueur, Walter. *No End to War: Terrorism in the 21st Century.* New York: Continuum, 2004. The preeminent U.S. historian of terrorism, Laqueur updates his previous work to address the latest breed of terrorists, and he warns that the escalating violence of terrorism in the 21st century will continue to produce higher and higher body counts.

———. "We Can't Define 'Terrorism,' but We Can Fight It." *Wall Street Journal,* July 15, 2002, p. A12. Laqueur says there are two problems related to defining the meaning of *terrorism:* not only the problem of finding a legal definition acceptable to all countries, but the newer problem of political correctness and media outlets that do not want to use the pejorative label *terrorist.*

Nicholson, Marc E. "An Essay on Terrorism," *American Diplomacy* 8, no. 3 (2003). According to Nicholson, a former U.S. Foreign Service officer, terrorism succeeds by wearing down public sentiment. Eventually scared voters will insist that their government address the terrorists' demands.

Reich, Walter, ed. *Origins of Terrorism: Psychologies, Ideologies, Theologies, States of Mind.* Washington, D.C.: Woodrow Wilson Center Press, 1998. A collection of individual articles on the logic of terrorism and specific case studies, this classic study provides an excellent overview of the various motivations behind terrorist activity.

Saul, Ben. "Definition of 'Terrorism' in the UN Security Council: 1985–2004." *Chinese Journal of International Law* 4, no. 1 (2005): 141–166. Even if the United Nations formally has not agreed on a definition of terrorism, they have not ignored the issue over the years. Saul examines UN resolutions that describe terrorist acts and discusses efforts to find common ground.

Who Are the Terrorists? Demographic Characteristics

Ali, Farhana. "Muslim Female Fighters: An Emerging Trend," *Terrorism Monitor*, (November 3, 2005), 245A. Available online. URL: http://www.jamestown.org/terrorism/news/article.php?articleid=2369824. Last accessed January 3, 2006. Asks not only why are more Islamic groups using female terrorists, but why has the phenomenon suddenly begun? Ali finds that one answer is that women are often invisible to society—and expendable.

Bloom, Mia. *Dying to Kill: The Allure of Suicide Terror.* New York: Columbia University Press, 2005. Bloom examines the history of suicide terrorism and argues that the tactic often backfires because it inevitably generates a harsh response from the target population. The book includes a section on the increasing role of women as suicide bombers.

Dickey, Christopher. "Women of Al Qaeda." *Newsweek,* December 12, 2005, pp. 27–36. Lengthy feature traces evolution of female suicide bombers, with emphasis on al-Qaeda and Iraq, includes graphs on the location and frequency of female suicide attacks.

Hacker, Frederick J. *Crusaders, Criminals, Crazies: Terror and Terrorism in Our Time.* New York: W. W. Norton, 1976. A noted psychologist examines the motive behind terrorism and finds that most terrorists are quite sane; their actions are designed to accomplish a specific goal. Dr. Hacker advised the Hearst family when Patricia Hearst was kidnapped.

Krueger, Alan B., and Jitka Maleckova. "Does Poverty Cause Terrorism? The Economics and Education of Suicide Bombers." *New Republic,* June 24, 2002, pp. 27–33. This often-cited study indicates that poverty is rarely the root cause of terrorism; in fact, terrorists actually tend to come from wealthier families.

Nacos, Brigitte L. "The Portrayal of Female Terrorists in the Media: Similar Framing Patterns in the News Coverage of Women in Politics and in Terrorism." *Studies in Conflict and Terrorism* 28, no. 5 (2005). pp. 435–451. A broad study focusing on the romanticized image of female terrorists in the media, categorizing the stereotypes.

Sageman, Marc. *Understanding Terror Networks.* Philadelphia: University of Pennsylvania Press, 2004. Who becomes a terrorist? Sageman, a professor of psychiatry and former CIA operative along Afghanistan's border with Pakistan, provides a sociopsychological profile of terrorists, specifically members of al-Qaeda. He shows that with Islamic fundamentalists, terror networks often begin with ordinary friendships among alienated individuals. As friends discuss their grievances, their anger increases, eventually fueling them to action.

Victor, Barbara. *Army of Roses: Inside the World of Palestinian Women Suicide Bombers.* New York: Rodale, 2003. Argues that social and political forces are coercing Palestinian women into becoming suicide bombers. In profiling five female suicide bombers, Victor blames cynicism and hopelessness as creating a climate that pushes women toward martyrdom.

What Do Terrorists Want?

MEDIA COVERAGE: GENERAL

Alexander, Yonah, and Richard Latter, eds. *Terrorism and the Media: Dilemmas for Government, Journalists, and the Public.* McLean, Va.: Brassey's, 1990. When does the media cross the line between reporting and advocacy on behalf of terrorists? Uses case studies from the United States, Great Britain, and Europe.

Cohen-Almagor, Raphael. "Media Coverage of Acts of Terrorism: Troubling Episodes and Suggested Guidelines." *Canadian Journal of Communications* 30 (2005), pp. 383–409. Using case studies from the United States, Great Britain, Germany, Israel, and Canada, the author suggests a code of ethics for journalists covering terrorism.

Foley, Michael. "Dubbing SF Voices Becomes the Stuff of History." *Irish Times,* September 17 1994, p. 5. Foley describes London's effort to keep Sinn Féin from presenting its case to the British public. Specifically, British television and radio were banned from broadcasting the voice of Sinn Féin president Gerry Adams.

Giuffo, John. "*Nightline* Is Spawned Out of the Hostage Crisis." *Columbia Journalism Review* 40, no. 4 (November/December 2001): 86–87. Regular nightly coverage of the Iranian hostage crisis kept the story alive in the public mind and changed how networks covered ongoing terrorist events.

Goltz, Thomas. *Chechnya Diary: A War Correspondent's Story of Surviving the War in Chechnya.* New York: St. Martin's, 2003. Case study of one incident in one village during the first Chechen war, the Samashki Massacre. Discusses the moral aspects of how a journalist covers a war.

Jenkins, Brian Michael. "The Psychological Implications of Media-Covered Terrorism." RAND Paper No. 6627, 1981. Available online. URL: http://www.rand.org/pubs/papers/P6627/. November 16, 2005. Media and terrorists have a symbiotic relationship, but the media tend to report only the most sensational attacks, distorting public opinion.

Moore, Jensen, Samantha Kemming, Betsy Neibergall, and David P. Fan. "Effects of the September 11, 2001 Terrorist Attack on U.S. Press Coverage." Association for Education in Journalism and Mass Communications Annual Convention Research Paper. Miami Beach, Fla., 2002. Available online. URL: list.msu.edu/cgi-bin/wa?A2=ind0209b&L=aejmc&D=0&P=9376&F=P. Last accessed November 16, 2005. Study of U.S. press coverage of Osama bin Laden's October 7, 2001, television statement and how it changed Americans' views of Islam.

Nacos, Brigitte L. *Terrorism and the Media: From the Iran Hostage Crisis to the World Trade Center Bombing.* New York: Columbia University Press, 1994. Explores how terrorist acts are carefully staged to convey a specific message.

———. "Media 'Crucial' to Terrorists, Author Finds." *Columbia University Record,* February 24, 1995. An expert in communications and media stories discusses why terrorists crave publicity, good or bad.

Oliverio, Annamarie. *The State of Terror.* SUNY Series in Deviance and Social Control. Albany: State University of New York Press, 1998. Case study of *Achille Lauro* and TWA Flight 847 regarding the interaction among the media, terrorists, and governments.

Rubin, Jeffrey Z., and Nehemia Friedland. "Theater of Terror." *Psychology Today,* March 1986, p. 24. The authors explore terrorism as theater, examining how terrorists chose targets and actions that will resonate with the audience.

Schmid, Alex P. "Terrorism and the Media: The Ethics of Publicity." *Terrorism and Political Violence* 1, no. 4 (1989): 564. Asks how best to balance open coverage of terrorism without taking sides.

MEDIA COVERAGE: TWA FLIGHT 847, 1985 HIJACKING

When Hezbollah terrorists hijacked TWA Flight 847 in June 1985, the media swarmed to cover the saga. While the hijackers dragged frightened hostages before the cameras, television crews dragged out frightened family members. Together, the media circus put extreme pressure on the White House to find some solution—any solution—to the crisis. The incident provoked a wide-ranging debate on the relationship between the media and terrorists. Some of the best articles are listed below:

Carlson, Kurt. *One American Must Die: A Hostage's Personal Account of the Hijacking of Flight 847.* New York: Congdon & Weed, 1986. An eyewitness account of the 1985 hijacking by Hezbollah and the subsequent media circus.

Fromm, Joseph. "TV: Does It Box in [the] President in a Crisis?" *U.S. News and World Report,* July 5, 1985, pp. 23–24.

Hamilton, Garry. "Under the Gun." *Ryerson Review of Journalism* (1986). Available online. URL: http://www.rjj.ca/print/575. Accessed 1/11/06. Compares Canadian and U.S. coverage of the hijacking of TWA flight 847.

Oliverio, Annamarie. *The State of Terror.* SUNY Series in Deviance and Social Control. Albany: State University of New York Press, 1998. Case study of *Achille Lauro* and TWA Flight 847 regarding the interaction among the media, terrorists, and governments.

Randolph, Eleanor. "Networks Turn Eye on Themselves." *Washington Post,* June 30, 1985, p. A25.

Shales, Tom. "America's Ordeal by Television: With the Beirut Hostages Free, Videoland Forgets Oh So Quickly." *Washington Post,* July 2, 1985, p. C1.

———. "Unanswered Questions: Television's Excesses, on Screen and Off." *Washington Post,* July 1, 1985, p. D1.

Yoder, Edwin M., Jr. "The Press Shouldn't Play Censor." *Washington Post,* 30 June 1985, p. C8.

RELIGION

Jurgensmeyer, Mark. *Terror in the Mind of God: The Global Rise of Religious Violence.* 3d ed. Los Angeles: University of California Press, 2003. Drawing upon the history of religion, Jurgensmeyer argues that all religions have an element of violence and make martyrdom attractive. Includes section on Aum Shinrikyo.

Kepel, Gilles. *Jihad: The Trail of Political Islam.* New York: Belknap, 2003. Traces the 20th-century spread of Islam through Asia and beyond, with a particular focus on how militant strains emerged.

Lincoln, Bruce. *Holy Terrors: Thinking About Religion after September 11.* Chicago: University of Chicago Press, 2003. An expert in Russian history compares four texts to unravel the religious beliefs behind each: (1) the final instructions to the 9/11 hijackers; (2) a September 13, 2001, interview with Jerry Falwell; (3) President Bush's declaration of war from October 7, 2001; and (4) an October 2001 speech by Osama bin Laden.

Rapoport, David C. "Fear and Trembling: Terrorism in Three Religious Traditions," *American Political Science Review* 78, no. 3 (September 1984): 658–677. Rapoport examines the origins of terrorism, beginning with the three earliest known groups: the Thugs, Assassins, and Zealots. He also debunks the popular view that the rise of terrorism is connected with technological innovations.

Stern, Jessica. *Terror in the Name of God: Why Religious Militants Kill.* New York: HarperCollins, 2003. Using firsthand interviews with terrorists, Stern explains how they reconcile murder and God. Unlike most studies of religion and terrorism, Stern moves beyond Islamic fundamentalism to include hard-line Israeli attacks and right-wing American movements.

How Do Terrorists Operate?

CYBERTERRORISM

Arquilla, John, and David Ronfelt. *Networks and Networks: The Future of Terror, Crime, and Militancy.* Santa Monica, Calif.: RAND, 2002. These authors coined the term *netwar* in the 1980s to discuss two brands of terrorism: terrorist/criminal and militant social activists. Also discusses how the information revolution is facilitating the work of these groups.

Clarke, Richard A. *Against All Enemies: Inside America's War on Terror.* New York: Free Press, 2004. The first White House counterterrorism chief discusses the efforts to protect national infrastructure under Presidents Clinton and Bush.

Coll, Steve, and Susan B. Glasser. "Terrorists Turn to the Web as Base of Operations." *Washington Post,* August 7, 2005, p. A1. This lengthy feature article discusses how al-Qaeda turned to cyberspace after being driven out of Afghanistan, making it the first "virtual" terrorist organization, one with no physical headquarters but instead a collection of Web sites and Internet links.

Green, Joshua. "The Myth of Cyberterrorism." *Washington Monthly,* November 2002, pp. 8–13. Green dismisses the hysteria over potential terrorist attacks in cyberspace, providing numerous examples of existing precautions to protect data.

Kristof, Nicholas D. "Terrorists in Cyberspace." *New York Times,* December 20, 2005, p. A31. Editorial examines how terrorists create events, such as the Iraqi "beheading videos," to create images to post on militant Islamic websites.

Labi, Nadya. "Jihad 2.0." *Atlantic Monthly,* July/August 2006, pp. 102–108. This extensive article examines the case and tactics of "Irhabi 007," who created a massive online encyclopedia for terrorists.

FINANCE

Adams, James. *The Financing of Terror: The PLO, IRA, Red Brigades, and M-19, and Their Money Supply.* New York: Simon and Schuster, 1986. How do terrorists finance their activities? While the conventional wisdom is that crime pays for crime (kidnapping, drug running, bank robbery) several terrorist groups, namely the Palestine Liberation Organization, is largely self-financing, thanks to shrewd investments.

Napoleoni, Loretta. *Terror Incorporated: Tracing the Dollars behind the Terror Networks.* New York: Seven Stories Press, 2005. Napoleoni examines the economic roots of terrorism, including U.S. financial aid to authoritarian regimes during the cold war, the contemporary illegal drug trade, and the links among terror networks. The book includes numerous firsthand accounts from terrorists interviewed by the author and has been praised as "perhaps the most systematic treatment in print of how terror is financed."

HIJACKING

Ashwood, Thomas M. *Terror in the Skies.* New York: Stein and Day, 1987. Written before 9/11 and increased security measures, Ashwood describes hijacking events and discusses appropriate responses and precautions for passengers.

Baum, Philip. "Leila Khaled: In Her Own Words," *Aviation Safety International,* October 2000. Available online. URL: http://www.asi-mag.com/editorials/leila_khaled.htm. Accessed 11/23/05. Transcript of a lengthy interview with Khaled; she not only discusses the goals of her hijacking plan, but also the training technique and preparations behind them.

Bohn, Michael K. *The Achille Lauro Hijacking: Lessons in the Politics and Prejudice of Terrorism.* Washington, D.C.: Brassey's, 2004. A detailed case study of the 1985 hijacking of an Italian cruise ship and the efforts to locate and convict the responsible members of the Palestine Liberation Front. Particularly focuses on the one fatality, Leon Klinghoffer, and his family's complicated search for justice for a U.S. citizen murdered in international waters.

Breadun, Deaglan de. "Plane Hijacker Turned Politician Disapproves of Today's 'Terrorism.'" *Irish Times,* August 4, 2005, p. 255A. Available online. URL: http://www.ireland.com/newpaper/world/2005/0804/2293435572FR04KHALED.html. Last accessed November 28, 2005. Khaled criticizes both the 9/11 and 7/7 terrorist attacks, saying they were pointless and indiscriminant in their targets.

Carlson, Kurt. *One American Must Die: A Hostage's Personal Account of the Hijacking of Flight 847.* New York: Congdon & Weed, 1986. An eyewitness account of the 1985 hijacking by Hezbollah and the subsequent media circus.

Cassese, Antonio. *Terrorism, Politics and Law: The Achille Lauro Affair.* Princeton, N.J.: Princeton University Press, 1989. Another case study of the 1985 cruise ship hijacking, this time from the perspective of an expert in international law.

Davies, Barry. *Fire Magic: Hijack at Mogadishu.* London: Bloomsbury Publishing, 1994. A member of the GSG-9 unit that rescued passengers aboard a Lufthansa flight hijacked in 1977 by Palestinian terrorists and taken to Somalia.

Khaled, Leila. *My People Shall Live: The Autobiography of a Revolutionary.* London: Hodder and Stoughton, 1973. A firsthand account by the world's "most famous" female hijacker.

Longman, Jere. *Among the Heroes: United Flight 93 and the Passengers and Crew Who Fought Back.* New York: HarperCollins, 2002. Using interviews with families and emergency personnel to recreate the final moments of the fourth plane in the 9/11 attack.

Moon, Timur. "Leila Khaled: Hijacked by Destiny," Al-Jazeera, October 17, 2002. Available online. URL: http://www.aljazeerah.info/Opinion%20editorials/2002%20Opinion%editorials/Oct%202002%20op%20eds/Oct%2017,%202002%20op%20eds.htm. Last accessed November 28, 2005. Another profile of Khaled, focusing on her posthijacking activities for the Palestinian movement.

Oliverio, Annamarie. *The State of Terror.* SUNY Series in Deviance and Social Control. Albany: State University of New York Press, 1998. Case study of *Achille Lauro* and TWA Flight 847 regarding the interaction among the media, terrorists, and governments.

Snow, Peter, and David Phillips. *Leila's Hijack War: The True Story of 23 Days in September.* London: Pan Books, 1970. Describes the four simultaneous Palestinian hijackings in 1970 and the efforts to release Leila Khaled from British custody.

Der Spiegel magazine, *Inside 9-11: What Really Happened.* New York: St. Martin's Press, 2002. A German newspaper interviews people who knew the 9/11 terrorists and tries to provide a glimpse into their activities in Hamburg.

St. John, Peter. *Air Piracy, Airport Security, and International Terrorism: Winning the War against Hijackers.* New York: Quorum Books, 1991. Profiles types of hijackers, types of hijackings, and provides specific techniques passengers can use to avoid and survive a hijacking. Includes statistics and recommendations for improved security.

KIDNAPPING

Kidnapping is the primary form of terrorism in Latin America. These selected articles all provide overviews of the problem, statistics, and illustrative examples and demonstrate the profitability of ransom demands.

Brooke, James. "Kidnappings Soar in Latin America, Threatening Region's Stability." *New York Times,* April 7, 1995, p. A8.

International Crisis Group, "Hostages for Prisoners: A Way to Peace in Colombia?" ICG Latin American Briefing No. 4 (March 8, 2004). Available online. URL: http://www.crisisgroup.org/home/index.cfm?id=2535&=1. Last accessed December 20, 2006.

"Kidnapping: Not Just for Kids." *Insurance Buyers' News* 15, no. 4 (July/August 2004). p. 1, 3. Macko, Steve. "Kidnapping: A Latin American Growth Industry." *ENN Daily Intelligence Report* 3, no. 120 (1997). Available online. URL: http://www.emergency.com/latnkdnp.htm. Last accessed December 19, 2006.

Mydans, Seth. "How to Succeed in the Kidnapping Business." *New York Times,* October 8, 2000, p. D4.

Price, Niko. "A New Type of Kidnapper Terrorizes Latin America." *Washington Post,* August 29, 2004, p. A20.

NARCOTERRORISM

Bowden, Mark. *Killing Pablo.* New York: Penguin, 2002. Describes U.S. efforts to hunt down Pablo Escobar, kingpin of the deadly Colombian Medellín cocaine cartel.

Chalk, Peter. *Non-Military Security and Global Order: The Impact of Extremism, Violence and Chaos on National and International Security.* New York: St. Martin's Press, 2000. Focuses on six emerging issues in global security, including drug trafficking.

Clutterbuck, Richard. *Terrorism and Guerrilla Warfare: Forecasts and Remedies.* New York: Routledge, 1990. An early study of the linkage between terrorism, drug running, and illegal arms sales.

Davids, Douglas J. *Narco-Terrorism: A Unified Strategy to Fight a Growing Terrorist Menace.* Ardsley, N.Y.: Transnational Publishers, 2002. Army Major Davids argues that treating illegal drug production and terrorism as distinct problems will solve neither and probably make it worse. He offers a new, unified approach that addresses the extensive linkages between the two phenomena.

García Márquez, Gabriel. *News of a Kidnapping.* New York: Knopf, 1997. Describes kidnapping of 10 prominent Colombians by the Medellín cocaine cartel and the efforts to rescue the hostages.

McCoy, Alfred W. *The Politics of Heroin: CIA Complicity in the Global Drug Trade.* 2d ed. Chicago: Lawrence Hill Books, 2002. The first edition of McCoy's controversial book in 1972 accused the CIA of promoting the narcotics trade in Vietnam. The revised version takes a much broader view, traveling from Asia to Latin America in search of corruption.

Mitchell, Charles. *All Terrorists are Not Equal: The Drug War in Colombia after September 11th.* Carlisle Barracks, Pa.: U.S. Army War College, 2002. Available for purchase online. URL: http://www.stormingmedia.us/95/9594/A959404.html. Accessed July 15, 2006. Examines the changing U.S. strategy in Colombia as the War on Terror begins to eclipse the war on drugs.

Tarazona-Sevellano, Gabriela. *Sendero Luminoso and the Threat of Narcoterrorism.* New York: Praeger, 1990. Colombia is not the only Latin American country with drug and terrorist problems. While Tarazona-Sevellano's work predates the Fujimori crackdown on Sendero Luminoso, the group is reviving thanks to drug trafficking and his insights may be even more valuable than they were in 1990s.

SUICIDE ATTACKS

Bloom, Mia. *Dying to Kill: The Allure of Suicide Terror.* New York: Columbia University Press, 2005. Bloom examines the history of suicide terrorism and argues that the tactic often backfires because it inevitably generates a harsh response from the target population. The book includes a section on the increasing role of women as suicide bombers.

Gambetta, Diego, ed. *Making Sense of Suicide Missions.* New York: Oxford University Press, 2005. This collection of conference papers traces the history of suicide bombing, from kamikazes through al-Qaeda, showing that the bombers are unusual but not psychologically disturbed. Rather, individuals see clear advantages from their choice.

Hassan, Nasra. "An Arsenal of Believers: Talking to the 'Human Bombs.'" *New Yorker,* November 19, 2001. Based on interviews with dozens of potential and failed suicide terrorists, Hassan reveals the diverse motives propelling people to make this choice and also details the training process.

Kassman, Laurie. "Women Terrorists Force Changed Thinking by Security Officials." *Voice of America,* September 2, 2004. Available online. URL: www.iwar.org.uk/news-archive/2004/09-02.htm. Accessed November 16, 2005. Terrorist groups are turning to female suicide bombers because they are better able to blend into crowds and appear inconspicuous, allowing them to get nearer to their targets and cause greater damage.

Khosrokhavar, Farhard. *Suicide Bombers: Allah's New Martyrs.* Translated by David Macey. New York: Pluto, 2005. Takes a theological approach to suicide bombers, examining the role of martyrdom in fundamentalist Islam. In particular, the book examines the varying social contexts specific to different countries, contrasting them with each other as well as with transnational groups such as al-Qaeda. Khosrokhavar divides terrorists into those from the developing world and those from the Western world.

Margalit, Avishai. "The Suicide Bombers." *New York Review of Books,* January 16, 2003. Available online: URL: http://www.nybooks.com/articles/15979. Accessed December 31, 2005. Margalit focuses especially on the Hamas suicide campaign against Israel, not only the motivations of the bombers but also the political consequences of their attacks as well.

Oliver, Anne Marie, and Paul Steinberg. *The Road to Martyrs' Square: A Journey into the World of the Suicide Bomber.* New York: Oxford University Press, 2005. A case study in the Palestinian terrorist group Hamas, the study draws upon the six years the authors spent living in Gaza. Includes a unique photographic collection of Hamas graffiti and martyr propaganda as well as a profile of Hamas leader Sheikh Yasin.

Pape, Robert A. *Dying to Win: The Strategic Logic of Suicide Terrorism.* New York: Random House, 2005. Discusses the logic behind suicide terrorism: It wins. Terrorists do not choose to die out of desperation or intense religious devotion; more often, they make this final decision because experience shows that it will attract the attention they believe their cause deserves. Pape's research is based on a unique database of all suicide bombers since 1980.

Pedazhur, Ami. *Suicide Terrorism.* New York: Polity, 2005. Examines the phenomenon of suicide bombing in a variety of cultures, including the Middle East, Chechnya, and Sri Lanka.

Reuter, Christoph. *My Life Is a Weapon: A Modern History of Suicide Bombing.* Princeton, N.J.: Princeton University Press, 2004. Through interviews with the trainers and families of successful suicide bombers, the martyrs' clear-headed thinking emerges. Reuter argues that suicide bombers are not impulsive fanatics but a "cost-effective" form of warfare. They want to make a difference and to be remembered as heroes.

Shay, Shaul, and Shaul Shai. *The Shahids: Islam and Suicide Attacks.* New Brunswick, N.J.: Transaction, 2004. Tries to put Islamic suicide terrorism into context by comparing it to other forms of suicide terrorism. Draws upon recommendations of international organizations such as Amnesty International to offer potential avenues for preventing individuals from embracing suicide attacks.

Victor, Barbara. *Army of Roses: Inside the World of Palestinian Women Suicide Bombers.* New York: Rodale, 2003. Argues that social and political forces are coercing Palestinian women into becoming suicide bombers. In profiling five female suicide bombers, Victor blames cynicism and hopelessness for creating a climate that pushes women toward martyrdom.

WEAPONS OF MASS DESTRUCTION

Anti-Defamation League. "Beyond Anthrax: Extremism and the Bioterrorism Threat." New York: Anti-Defamation League, 2001. The fear of anthrax has caused more public panic than actual outbreaks of the disease.

Falkenrath, Richard, Robert Newman, and Bradley Thayer. *America's Achilles' Heel: Nuclear, Biological, and Chemical Terrorism and Covert Attack.* Cambridge, Mass.: MIT Press, 2000. Presents scenarios of terrorist attacks against the United States using weapons of mass destruction.

Johnson, Loch K. *Bombs, Bugs, Drugs, and Thugs: Intelligence and America's Quest for Security.* New York: New York University Press: 2000. Outlines the overlaps and gaps in America's antiterrorist network. Written prior to Department of Homeland Security reorganization.

Mates, Michael. "Report: Technology and Terrorism." NATO Parliamentary Assembly, 2001. Available online. URL: http://www.naa.be/archivedpub/comrep/2001/au-221-e.asp. Last accessed December 14, 2005. Discusses scientific and technological aspects of terrorism in the 21st century.

Miller, Judith, Stephen Engelberg, and William Broad. *Germs: Biological Weapons and America's Secret War.* New York: Simon and Schuster, 2001. What is germ warfare and is the United States prepared to defend itself against this kind of attack?

Reaves, Jessica. "The Nunn-Lugar Act: Old Fears, New Era." *Time,* October 1, 2001, p. 263B. Online edition. URL: http://www/time.com/time/nation/article/0,8599,177183,00.html. Last accessed December 20, 2006. Discusses fears of stolen nuclear weapons from unguarded Soviet arsenals.

Stern, Jessica. "Taking the Terror out of Bioterrorism." *New York Times,* April 8, 1998, p. 263B. Available online. URL: http://www.mtholyoke.edu/acad/intrel/stern.htm. Last accessed January 1, 2006. A short version of Stern's argument in *The Ultimate Terrorists.*

———. *The Ultimate Terrorists.* Cambridge, Mass.: Harvard University Press, 2000. Traces the evolution of terrorist tactics, predicting that terrorists will eventually use biological, chemical, and, possibly even nuclear technology to execute their attacks.

Tucker, Jonathan B. *Toxic Terror: Assessing Terrorist Use of Chemical and Biological Weapons.* Cambridge, Mass.: MIT Press, 2000. Profiles 12 terrorist groups or individuals that carried out—or came close to—chemical and biological weapons attacks from 1946 to 1998.

Warrick, Joby. "Soviet Germ Factories Pose New Threat; Once Mined for Pathogens in Bioweapons Program, Labs Lack Security." *Washington Post,* August 20, 2005, p. A1. An alarming report on how poorly guarded Soviet-era laboratories are, making it very easy for anyone to steal samples of deadly diseases.

II. UNITED STATES

Domestic Terrorist Groups and Incidents

ANTI-FEDERALIST/RIGHT-WING/MILITIA

Andryszweski, Tricia. *The Militia Movement in America: Before and after Oklahoma City.* Brookfield, Conn.: Millbrook Press, 1997. Survey of U.S. militia movement with particular emphasis on links with Oklahoma City bombing.

Giordano, Geraldine. *The Oklahoma City Bombing, Terrorist Attacks.* New York: Rosen, 2003. Detailed account of how McVeigh, Michael Fortier, and Terry Nichols planned and built their bomb . . . and how they were caught.

Levitas, Daniel. *The Terrorist Next Door: The Militia Movement and the Radical Right.* New York: St. Martin's Press, 2002. Traces the emergence of the U.S. militia movement, a combination of right-wing ideals and white-supremacist propaganda. Contains significant never-before-published materials from both government and private sources.

Pitcavage, Mark. "Every Man a King: The Rise and Fall of the Montana Freeman." *ADL Militia Watchdog* (1996). Available online. URL: http://www.adl.org/mwd/freemen.asp. Accessed January 12, 2006. History of the right-wing movement in the United States, including the Posse Comitatus.

Serrano, Richard A. *One of Ours: Timothy McVeigh and the Oklahoma City Bombing.* New York: Norton, 1998. *Los Angeles Times* reporter Serrano tries to explain how Timothy McVeigh changed from honor student to terrorist.

Southern Poverty Law Center. "The Rise and Decline of the 'Patriots.'" *Intelligence Report,* Summer 2001. Available online. URL: http://www.splcenter.org/intel/intelreport/article.jsp?aid=195. Accessed December 19, 2006. A detailed report on the decline of the patriot movement in the United States, suggesting that many members simply grew tired of waiting for the end of the world.

Stern, Jessica Eve. *Terror in the Name of God: Why Religious Militants Kill.* New York: HarperCollins, 2003. Using firsthand interviews with terrorists, Stern explains how they reconcile murder and God. Unlike most studies of religion and terrorism, Stern moves beyond Islamic fundamentalism to include hard-line Israeli attacks and right-wing U.S. movements.

Stickney, Brandon M. *All-American Monster: The Unauthorized Biography of Timothy McVeigh.* New York: Prometheus, 1996. An extensive investigation of McVeigh's formative years, showing his increasing alienation from society.

Tabor, James D., and Eugene V. Gallagher. *Why Waco? Cults and the Battle for Religious Freedom in America.* Los Angeles: University of California Press, 1995. Analysis of the federal standoff and how it could have been avoided. Tabor advised the Branch Davidians' lawyer during the incident. Also examines the theology embraced by the group and includes an appendix with writings by leader David Koresh.

Walter, Jess. *Ruby Ridge: The Truth and the Tragedy of the Randy Weaver Family.* New York: Regan Books, 2002. Acclaimed study of the Ruby Ridge incident by Pulitzer Prize–nominated journalist.

Wright, Stuart A. *Armageddon in Waco: Critical Perspectives on the Branch Davidian Conflict.* Chicago: University of Chicago Press, 1995. Surveys the rise and fall of the Branch Davidian movement, including media coverage of the standoff.

ATLANTA OLYMPICS

Coverage of the bombing at the 1996 Atlantic Olympic games falls into three categories: 1) news reports at the time of the attack; 2) studies of Richard Jewell, the security guard initially suspected of the bombing; and 3) reports about the eventual capture of the real bomber, Eric Robert Rudolph. Because of the considerable length between bombing and arrest, it is difficult to find comprehensive accounts and easy to find articles that are misleading, especially regarding Jewell.

Applebome, Peter. "A Story Where the Telling Itself Has Raised Many Questions." *New York Times*, October 28 1996, p. B7.

"Backgrounder: Eric Robert Rudolph," Anti-Defamation League, June 5, 2003.

Barringer, Felicity. "Once Accused, Now the Accuser." *New York Times,* February 8, 1999, p. C1.

Lopresti, Mike. "Eight Years after Atlanta, Closure Difficult for Jewell." *USA Today,* August 17, 2004.

Sack, Kevin. "A Man's Life Turned inside out by Government and the Media." *New York Times,* October 28, 1996, p. A1.

Schuster, Henry. *Hunting Eric Rudolph.* New York: Berkley Books, 2005. Details the five-year search to identify and locate the real Atlanta Olympics bomber.

ISLAMIC TERRORIST GROUPS

Emerson, Steven. *American Jihad: The Terrorists Living among Us.* New York: Free Press, 2003. Beginning with the 1993 attack on the World Trade Center, Emerson tracks the growth of Islamic fundamentalism within the United States itself. Includes appendixes detailing terrorist cells currently active in the United States and their sources of funding.

Frontline, PBS. "Terrorists among Us: Jihad in America." United States: Ventura, 2001. Controversial 1994 episode of *Frontline* on 1993 World Trade Center bombing updated to include 9/11. Based on work of Steve Emerson.

9/11 ATTACK

Clarke, Richard A. *Against All Enemies: Inside America's War on Terror.* New York: Free Press, 2004, including the threads that link together the 1993 and 2001 attacks on the World Trade Center. The White House terrorism chief under Clinton and Bush discusses America's war on terror from 1993 to 2004. Contains a first-hand account of what it was like to be in the White House on 9/11.

Longman, Jere. *Among the Heroes: United Flight 93 and the Passengers and Crew Who Fought Back.* New York: HarperCollins, 2002. Using interviews with families and emergency personnel to recreate the final moments of the fourth plane in the 9/11 attack.

McDermott, Terry. *Perfect Soldiers: The 9/11 Hijackers: Who They Were, Why They Did It.* New York: HarperCollins, 2005. Profiles the hijackers who carried out the 9/11 terrorist attacks. Argues that they were not fanatics but rather ordinary men and that many, many people with similar beliefs exist. McDermott, a *Los Angeles Times* reporter, conducted extensive interviews with relatives and friends of the hijackers and provides considerable new insight into the psychology of these men.

National Commission on Terrorist Attacks upon the United States. *The 9/11 Commission Report: Final Report of the National Commission on Terrorist Attacks upon the United States.* Authorized ed. New York: W. W. Norton, 2004. The official U.S. government report on the terrorist attacks of September 11, 2001. Examines the failures in U.S. intelligence operations and provides details of how the attacks were planned and carried out. Criticizes the U.S. intelligence-gathering establishment and calls for a massive overhaul of how the United States protects its citizens.

Der Spiegel magazine, *Inside 9–11: What Really Happened.* New York: St. Martin's Press, 2002. A German newspaper interviews people who knew the 9/11 terrorists and tries to provide a portrait of each man.

1993 ATTACK ON WORLD TRADE CENTER

Clarke, Richard A. *Against All Enemies: Inside America's War on Terror* (New York: Free Press, 2004). The White House terrorism chief under Clinton and Bush discusses America's war on terror from 1993 to 2004, including the threads that link together the 1993 and 2001 attacks on the World Trade Center.

Cooley, John K. *Unholy Wars: Afghanistan, America, and International Terrorism.* 3d ed. Sterling, Va.: Pluto Press, 2002. ABC correspondent Cooley traces the increasing unrest in the Muslim world from the 1993 World Trade Center attacks through the U.S. embassy attacks and 9/11 and then examines the war in Afghanistan and its effect on U.S. relations with the Islamic world.

Emerson, Steven. *American Jihad: The Terrorists Living among Us.* New York: Free Press, 2003. Beginning with the 1993 attack on the World Trade Center Emerson tracks the growth of Islamic fundamentalism within the United States itself. Includes appendixes detailing terrorist cells currently active in the United States and their sources of funding.

Frontline, PBS. "Terrorists among Us: Jihad in America." United States: Ventura, 2001. Controversial 1994 episode of *Frontline* on 1993 World Trade Center bombing updated to include 9/11. Based on work of Steve Emerson.

National Commission on Terrorist Attacks upon the United States. *The 9/11 Commission Report: Final Report of the National Commission on Terrorist Attacks upon the United States.* Authorized ed. New York: W. W. Norton, 2004. The official U.S. government report on the terrorist attacks of September 11, 2001, contains a section on the 1993 attack and the intelligence gained—and missed.

Reeve, Simon. *The New Jackals: Ramzi Yusef, Osama Bin Laden, and the Future of Terrorism.* Boston: Northeastern University Press, 1999. A biography of the mastermind behind the 1993 bombing of the World Trade Center and the man who successfully would destroy the towers two years after the book's publication.

PUERTO RICAN NATIONALISM

Hunter, Stephen, and J. S. Bainbridge, *American Gunfight: The Plot to Kill Harry Truman—and the Shoot-out That Stopped It.* New York: Simon and Schuster, 2005. In 1950 Puerto Rican nationalists stormed Blair House and came close to assassinating President Harry S. Truman.

SYMBIONESE LIBERATION ARMY

Hacker, Frederick J. *Crusaders, Criminals, Crazies: Terror and Terrorism in Our Time.* New York: W. W. Norton, 1976. A noted psychologist examines the motives behind terrorism and finds that most terrorists are quite sane; their actions are designed to accomplish a specific goal. Dr. Hacker advised the Hearst family when Patricia Hearst was kidnapped.

Hearst, Patty, and Alvin Moscow. *Patty Hearst: Her Own Story.* New York: Avon, 1982. Newspaper heiress Patricia Hearst details her 1974 kidnapping by the Symbionese Liberation Army and explains her role in subsequent SLA activities, including two infamous bank robberies. The book was the basis for the 1988 movie *Patty Hearst.*

PBS, "Guerrilla: The Taking of Patty Hearst," *American Experience* 2004. Transcript and background materials available online. URL: www.pbs.org/wgbh/amex/guerrilla/index.html. Accessed October 15, 2005.

WEATHER UNDERGROUND

Ayres, William. *Fugitive Days: A Memoir.* New York: Penguin, 2003. Firsthand account by one of the Weather Underground founders, including his difficult reintegration into U.S. society.

Jacobs, Ron. *The Way the Wind Blew: A History of the Weather Underground.* New York: Verso, 1997. A history of the Weather Underground, including the group's evolution and policy statements.

Varon, Jeremy. *Bringing the War Home: The Weather Underground, the Red Army Faction, and Revolutionary Violence in the Sixties and Seventies.* Berkeley: University of California Press, 2004. Using primary materials, Varon reconstructs the social atmosphere of the Vietnam era to show why middle-class, well-educated youth turned to violence to protest their government's activities.

Counterterrorism

LEGAL APPROACHES

Alexander, Yonah, ed. *Combating Terrorism: Strategies of Ten Countries.* Ann Arbor: University of Michigan Press, 2002. This collection of papers compares counterterrorism strategies in the United States, Argentina, Peru, Colombia, Spain, the United Kingdom, Israel, Turkey, India, and Japan, focusing on how each political system defines terrorism and the internal and external factors that influence their approaches. The book was compiled before 9/11, but each author added a brief update to cover that major development.

Doyle, Charles. "The USA Patriot Act: A Sketch." In *CRS Report for Congress*: Congressional Research Service, 2002. Available online. URL: http://www.fas.org/irp/crs/RS21203.pdf. Accessed July 16, 2006. Succinct, unbiased summary of the Patriot Act.

———. "The USA Patriot Act Sunset: A Sketch." In *CRS Report for Congress*: Congressional Research Service, 2004. Available online. URL: http://www.fas.org/irp/crs/RS21704.pdf. Accessed July 16, 2006. Updates Doyle's 2002 report with amendments and criticisms of the legislation.

Risen, James, and Eric Lichtblau. "Bush Lets U.S. Spy on Callers without Courts." *New York Times,* December 16, 2005, p. A1. This article exposed the controversial White House policy allowing the National Security Agency to eavesdrop on Americans without court-issued warrants.

MILITARY APPROACHES

Alexander, Yonah, ed. *Combating Terrorism: Strategies of Ten Countries.* Ann Arbor: University of Michigan Press, 2002. This collection of papers compares counterterrorism strategies in the United States, Argentina, Peru, Colombia, Spain, the United Kingdom, Israel, Turkey, India, and Japan, focusing on how each political system defines terrorism and the internal and external factors that influence their approaches. The book was compiled before 9/11, but each author added a brief update to cover that major development.

Bacevich, Andrew. *The New American Militarism: How Americans Are Seduced by War.* New York: Oxford University Press, 2005. Criticizes U.S. tendency to use military force to spread ideologies, specifically democracy.

Benjamin, Daniel, and Steven Simon. *The Next Attack: The Failure of the War on Terror and a Strategy for Getting It Right.* New York: Times Books, 2005. Argues that the Bush administration War on Terror has actually made the United States more vulnerable to a terrorist attack because it has spawned new militant Islamic groups.

Annotated Bibliography

Bensahel, Nora. *The Counterterror Coalitions: Cooperation with Europe, NATO, and the European Union.* Santa Monica, Calif.: RAND, 2003. Who are America's West European partners in the War on Terror? This book looks at foreign-relations approaches to fighting terrorism, with particular attention to Operation Enduring Freedom.

Brake, Jeffrey D. "Terrorism and the Military's Role in Domestic Crisis Management: Background and Issues for Congress." In *CRS Report for Congress*: Congressional Research Service, 2001. Written prior to 9/11, the report calls for a reorganization of U.S. counterterrorist procedures to create an integrated, rational program. Foreshadows creation of Department of Homeland Security.

Clarke, Richard A. *Against All Enemies: Inside America's War on Terror.* New York: Free Press, 2004. The White House terrorism chief under Clinton and Bush discusses America's war on terror from 1993 to 2004. Contains a firsthand account of what it was like to be in the White House on 9/11.

Cooley, John K. *Unholy Wars: Afghanistan, America, and International Terrorism.* 3d ed. Sterling, Va.: Pluto Press, 2002. ABC correspondent Cooley trace the increasing unrest in the Muslim world from the 1993 World Trade Center attacks through the U.S. Embassy attacks and 9/11 and then examines the war in Afghanistan and its effect on U.S. relations with the Islamic world.

Fair, C. Christine. *The Counterterror Coalitions: Cooperation with Pakistan and India.* Santa Monica, Calif.: Rand Corp, 2004. This book looks at foreign-relations approaches to fighting terrorism, with particular attention to U.S. contacts with Afghanistan, India, and Pakistan and Operation Enduring Freedom.

Hammes, Thomas X. *The Sling and the Stone: On War in the 21st Century.* St. Paul, Minn.: Zenith Press, 2004. Argues that warfare has evolved into a new form in the 21st century, one based on low-tech weapons and insurgency tactics. Efforts to fight the Taliban and al-Qaeda are prime examples. However, U.S. military strategy continues to emphasize high-tech solutions rather than addressing the basic causes.

Heymann, Philip B. *Terrorism and America: A Commonsense Strategy for a Democratic Society.* Cambridge, Mass.: MIT Press, 1998. Writing prior to 9/11, a leading American legal scholar debates how best to balance vigilance and democracy.

Johnson, Loch. *Bombs, Bugs, Drugs, and Thugs: Intelligence and America's Quest for Security.* New York: New York University Press, 2000. Outlines the overlaps and gaps in America's antiterrorist network. Written prior to Department of Homeland Security reorganization

Kepel, Gilles. *The War for Muslim Minds: Islam and the West.* New York: Belknap Press, 2004. Examines how the United States has failed to change its Middle East policy in recent years, continuing to see the region in the cold-war framework of Us versus Them.

Long, David E. "Coming to Grips with Terrorism after 11 September." *Brown Journal of World Affairs* 8, no. 2 (2002): 37–42. A former deputy director of the State Department Counterterrorism division argues that the United States must develop a comprehensive strategy to address terrorism. More soberingly, Long argues that the "war on terror" will be one fought for years, even decades, to come.

Mackey, Chris. *The Interrogators: Inside the Secret War Against Al Qaeda.* New York: Little, Brown, 2004. Mackey, a pseudonym, served as a U.S. interrogator of captured Taliban and al-Qaeda forces in the early weeks of Operation Enduring Freedom. His account provides an alternative to the numerous reports of abuse of U.S. prisoners in Afghanistan.

National Commission on Terrorist Attacks Upon the United States. *The 9/11 Commission Report: Final Report of the National Commission on Terrorist Attacks upon the United States.* Authorized ed. New York: W. W. Norton, 2004. The official U.S. government report on the terrorist attacks of September 11, 2001. Examines the failures in U.S. intelligence operations and provides details of how the attacks were planned and carried out. Criticizes the U.S. intelligence gathering establishment and calls for a massive overhaul of how the United States protects its citizens.

Pillar, Paul R. *Terrorism and U.S. Foreign Policy.* Washington, D.C.: Brookings Institution Press, 2001. An overview of U.S. terrorism and, particularly, counterterrorism policy, the book was originally written prior to 9/11. The paperback edition includes a new introduction dealing with that tragedy.

Rolfe, Pamela. "A Year after Madrid Attacks, Europe Stalled in Terror Fight." *Washington Post,* March 11, 2005, p. A12.

Scheuer, Michael. *Imperial Hubris: Why the West Is Losing the War on Terror.* Dulles, Va.: Brassey's, 2004. Argues that the U.S. "war on terror" is misplaced. Muslims do not hate the United States itself but rather the consequences of the military, political, and economic policies pursued by Washington.

Simon, Jeffrey D. *The Terrorist Trap: America's Experience with Terrorism.* 2d ed. Bloomington: Indiana University Press, 2001. An overview of U.S. policy toward terrorism from Thomas Jefferson to George Bush.

III. INTERNATIONAL

International Groups

AL-QAEDA

Bergen, Peter. *Holy War, Inc.: Inside the Secret World of Osama Bin Laden.* New York: Free Press, 2002. A quick look at al-Qaeda and bin Laden published soon after the 9/11 attacks. Bergen, a CNN reporter, interviewed bin Laden in 1997 and draws upon that experience to provide insight into how the al-Qaeda leader's hatred of the United States originated.

Bin Laden, Osama. *Messages to the World: The Statements of Osama Bin Laden.* Edited by Bruce Lawrence. New York: Verso, 2005. Contains translations and analysis of 24 statements by Osama bin Laden, including writing, interviews, and transcripts of radio and television messages. Also includes references to sections of the Koran cited by bin Laden.

Bodansky, Yossef. *Bin Laden: The Man Who Declared War on America.* New York: Prima, 2001. Written before 9/11, but still considered an excellent, comprehensive biography of the elusive al-Qaeda leader.

Annotated Bibliography

Clarke, Richard A. *Against All Enemies: Inside America's War on Terror.* New York: Free Press, 2004. The White House terrorism chief under Clinton and Bush discusses America's war on terror from 1993 to 2004. Describes how al-Qaeda and Osama bin Laden gradually came to the attention of the U.S. intelligence community.

Cooley, John K. *Unholy Wars: Afghanistan, America, and International Terrorism.* 3d ed. Sterling, Va.: Pluto Press, 2002. ABC correspondent Cooley traces the increasing unrest in the Muslim world from the 1993 World Trade Center attacks through the U.S. embassy attacks and 9/11 and then examines the war in Afghanistan and its effect on U.S. relations with the Islamic world.

Gohari, M. J. *Taliban: Ascent to Power.* Karachi, Pakistan: Oxford University Press, 2000. An extensive academic survey of life under the Taliban in Afghanistan and how Osama bin Laden found a refuge under that regime.

Gunaratna, Rohan. *Inside Al Qaeda: Global Network of Terror.* New York: Berkley/Penguin, 2003. Considered "the definitive study" of al-Qaeda, this book traces the group's origins in the 1980s, its recruiting and training methods, and its plans for a much larger assault on 9/11. Guanaratna also examines how al-Qaeda is expanding its network in Asia, including Malaysia and Indonesia. The 2003 edition also covers the kidnapping and murder of *Wall Street Journal* writer Daniel Pearl in Pakistan.

Kohlmann, Evan F. *Al-Qaida's Jihad in Europe: The Afghan-Bosnian Network.* New York: Berg, 2004. Argues that al-Qaeda began its attack on the West not on 9/11 but in the wars of Bosnia and Kosovo in the early 1990s. Specifically, al-Qaeda used the Balkans as a forward base to lay a groundwork for future activities in Germany, Britain, and throughout western Europe.

Mackey, Chris. *The Interrogators: Inside the Secret War Against Al Qaeda.* New York: Little, Brown, 2004. Mackey, a pseudonym, served as a U.S. interrogator of captured Taliban and al-Qaeda forces in the early weeks of Operation Enduring Freedom. His account provides an alternative to the numerous reports of abuse of U.S. prisoners in Afghanistan.

Sageman, Marc. *Understanding Terror Networks.* Philadelphia: University of Pennsylvania Press, 2004. Who becomes a terrorist? Sageman, a professor of psychiatry and former CIA operative along Afghanistan's border with Pakistan, provides a sociopsychological profile of terrorists, specifically members of al-Qaeda. He shows that with Islamic fundamentalists, terror networks often begin with ordinary friendships among alienated individuals. As friends discuss their grievances, their anger increases, eventually fueling them to action.

Schanzer, Jonathan. *Al-Qaeda's Armies: Middle East Affiliate Groups and the Next Generation of Terror.* Washington, D.C.: Washington Institute for Near East Policy, 2004. While al-Qaeda has been thrown out of Afghanistan, it still has active branches in Egypt, Lebanon, Algeria, Yemen, and Iraq. Includes interviews with al-Qaeda members in Iraq and Saddam Hussein's former intelligence officers.

Sifaoui, Mohamed. *Inside Al Qaeda: How I Infiltrated the World's Deadliest Terrorist Organization.* Translated by George Miller. New York: Thunder's Mouth, 2003. An Algerian journalist goes undercover as a member of an Islamic militant cell in the 1990s. Despite the sensational title, the book's "revelations" are not that shocking, and Sifaoui has been criticized as having his own axe to grind as an Algerian exile.

Weiner, Tim, and Steven Lee Myers. "Flaws in U.S. Account Raise Questions on Strike in Sudan." *New York Times,* August 29, 1998, p. A1.

Zahab, Mariam Abou, and Oliver Roy. *Islamist Networks: The Afghan-Pakistan Connection.* New York: Columbia University Press, 2004. Examines the gravitation of Muslims toward Pakistan following the Soviet-Afghan war, resulting in an alliance between al-Qaeda and the Pakistani military and security services. Also examines the issues surrounding Kashmir and how Islamic terrorists may be drawn into that conflict.

Country Cases

AFGHANISTAN (ALSO SEE AL-QAEDA SECTION)

Adamec, Ludwig W. *Historical Dictionary of Afghanistan.* 3d ed. Lanham, Md.: Scarecrow Press, 2003. Afghanistan from A to Z, including events, history, political parties, ethnic groups, and a thorough chronology.

Bradsher, Henry S. *Afghan Communism and Soviet Intervention.* New York: Oxford University Press, 2005. A well-regarded 1980s study of Afghanistan prior to the 1979 Soviet invasion has been rewritten and revised to include the rise and fall of the Taliban regime.

Cooley, John K. *Unholy Wars: Afghanistan, America, and International Terrorism.* 3d ed. Sterling, Va.: Pluto Press, 2002. ABC correspondent Cooley traces the increasing unrest in the Muslim world from the 1993 World Trade Center attacks through the U.S. embassy attacks and 9/11 and then examines the war in Afghanistan and its effect on U.S. relations with the Islamic world.

Fair, C. Christine. *The Counterterror Coalitions: Cooperation with Pakistan and India.* Santa Monica, Calif.: Rand Corp, 2004. This book looks at foreign-relations approaches to fighting terrorism, with particular attention to U.S. contacts with Afghanistan, India, and Pakistan and Operation Enduring Freedom.

Gohari, M. J. *Taliban: Ascent to Power.* Karachi, Pakistan: Oxford University Press, 2000. An extensive academic survey of life under the Taliban in Afghanistan and how Osama bin Laden found a refuge under that regime.

Goodson, Larry P. *Afghanistan's Endless War: State Failure, Regional Politics, and the Rise of the Taliban.* Seattle: University of Washington Press, 2001. Describes the rise and rule of the Taliban, with an emphasis on Pakistan's support.

Mackey, Chris. *The Interrogators: Inside the Secret War Against Al Qaeda.* New York: Little, Brown, 2004. Mackey, a pseudonym, served as a U.S. interrogator of captured Taliban and Al-Qaeda forces in the early weeks of Operation Enduring Freedom. His account provides an alternative to the numerous reports of abuse of U.S. prisoners in Afghanistan.

McCoy, Alfred W. *The Politics of Heroin: CIA Complicity in the Global Drug Trade.* 2d ed. Chicago: Lawrence Hill Books, 2002. The first edition of McCoy's controversial book in 1972 accused the CIA of promoting the narcotics trade in Vietnam. The revised version takes a much broader view, traveling from Asia to Latin America in search of corruption.

Rubin, Barnett R. *The Fragmentation of Afghanistan.* 2d ed. New Haven, Conn.: Yale University Press, 2002. A political history from the 1978 communist coup to that regime's collapse in 1992.

———. *The Search for Peace in Afghanistan: From Buffer State to Failed State.* New Haven, Conn.: Yale University Press, 1995. A sequel to Rubin's *Fragmentation of Afghanistan,* this volume has not been revised since the fall of the Taliban regime.

ALGERIA

Ciment, James. *Algeria: The Fundamentalist Challenge.* New York: Facts On File, 1997. Ciment begins with the 1992 outbreak of civil war in Algeria and examines the various Muslim and paramilitary insurgencies as well as the government crackdown.

Crenshaw, Martha. *Revolutionary Terrorism: The FLN in Algeria, 1954–1962.* Stanford, Calif.: Hoover Institution Press, 1978. Algeria's current civil war with Islamic terrorism is a direct result of its protracted war of independence. Crenshaw's work provides a vital background to help understand the current situation.

Horne, Alistair. *A Savage War of Peace: Algeria 1954–1962.* New York: NYRB Classics, 2006. A classic when published in 1977, Horne's work has been updated to take readers from the trials and jubilation of independence to the horrors of the bloody civil war of the 1990s.

COLOMBIA

Alexander, Yonah. *Combating Terrorism: Strategies of Ten Countries.* Ann Arbor: University of Michigan Press, 2002. This edited volume compares counterterrorism strategies in the United States, Argentina, Peru, Colombia, Spain, the United Kingdom, Israel, Turkey, India, and Japan, focusing on how each political system defines terrorism and the internal and external factors that influence their approaches. The book was compiled before 9/11, but each author added a brief update to cover that major development.

Bowden, Mark. *Killing Pablo.* New York: Penguin, 2002. Describes U.S. efforts to hunt down Pablo Escobar, kingpin of the deadly Colombian Medellín cocaine cartel.

García Márquez, Gabriel. *News of a Kidnapping.* New York: Knopf, 1997. Describes kidnapping of 10 prominent Colombians by Medellín cocaine cartel and the efforts to rescue the hostages.

McCoy, Alfred W. *The Politics of Heroin: CIA Complicity in the Global Drug Trade.* 2d ed. Chicago: Lawrence Hill Books, 2002. The first edition of McCoy's controversial book in 1972 accused the CIA of promoting the narcotics trade in Vietnam. The revised version takes a much broader view, traveling from Asia to Latin America in search of corruption.

Mitchell, Charles. *All Terrorists Are Not Equal: The Drug War in Colombia After September 11th.* Carlisle Barracks, Pa.: U.S. Army War College, 2002. Available for purchase online. URL: http://www.stormingmedia.us/95/9594/A959404.html.

Accessed July 15, 2006. Examines the changing U.S. strategy in Colombia as the War on Terror begins to eclipse the war on drugs.

GERMANY

Red Army Faction/Baader-Meinhof

Alexander, Yonah, and Dennis Pluchinsky. *Europe's Red Terrorists: The Fighting Communist Organizations.* London: Frank Cass, 1992. Survey of West European communist groups, their emergence in the 1970s and their subsequent decline in the 1980s.

Aust, Stefan. *The Baader-Meinhof Group: The Inside Story of a Phenomenon.* London: Bodley Head, 1987.

Becker, Jillian. *Hitler's Children: The Story of the Baader-Meinhof Terrorist Gang.* London: Michael Joseph, 1977. Argues that the post–World War II generation carried shame because many of their parents had collaborated with—or at least not fought—the Nazi regime. Many people who sympathized with the Baader-Meinhof Gang might have unconsciously wanted to prove that they would have fought the Nazis.

Varon, Jeremy. *Bringing the War Home: The Weather Underground, the Red Army Faction, and Revolutionary Violence in the Sixties and Seventies.* Berkeley: University of California Press, 2004. Using primary materials, Varon reconstructs the social atmosphere of the Vietnam era to show why middle-class, well-educated youth turned to violence to protest their government's activities.

Munich Olympics

Dobson, Christopher. *Black September: Its Short, Violent History.* London: Robert Hale, 1974. Written shortly after Black September ceased operations, the book chronicles its formation and operations.

Hirst, David. *The Gun and the Olive Branch: The Roots of Violence in the Middle East.* 3d ed. New York: Avalon, 2003. Now in its third edition, Hirst's book chronicles the emergence of the Palestinian-Israeli conflict from the 1880s to the present day. A former Middle East reporter for Britain's *Guardian* newspaper, Hirst is a veteran of the region and has survived two kidnappings.

Hunter, Thomas B. "Wrath of God: The Israeli Response to the 1972 Munich Olympic Massacre," *Journal of Counterterrorism and Security International* 7, no. 4 (Summer 2001), p. 287A. Available online. URL: http://www.specialoperations/com/Counterterrorism/operation_wrath_of_god.html. Last accessed January 16, 2006. Following the Munich Olympic massacre, Israeli special forces created a special commando to unit to locate and execute the surviving members of Black September.

McKay, Jim. *The Real McKay: My Wide World of Sports.* New York: Dutton, 1998. McKay covered the 1972 Munich Olympics massacre live for ABC television. He recounts that day in chapter 1, providing one of the most vivid accounts available.

Reeve, Simon. *One Day in September: The Story of the 1972 Munich Olympics Massacre.* New York: Arcade, revised 2006. Written as a companion to the documentary of the same name, *One Day in September* provides comprehensive coverage of Black September and its assault in Munich. It also contains a detailed look at the materials collected in connection with the German investigation in the failed rescue attempt.

Sonnenborn, Liz. *Murder at the 1972 Olympics in Munich.* Terrorist Attacks. New York: Rosen, 2003. A small, picture-filled book that provides an excellent introduction to the issues behind the Black September assault.

Wolff, Alexander. "Munich 1972: When the Terror Began." *Time,* August 25, 2002, p. 288. Online edition. URL: http://www.time.com/time/europe/magazine/printout/0,13155,901020902-340700,00.html. Accessed November 15, 2005. A lengthy study of the lessons of the Munich crisis 30 years later.

Hamburg Cell/al-Qaeda

McDermott, Terry. *Perfect Soldiers: The 9/11 Hijackers: Who They Were, Why They Did It.* New York: HarperCollins, 2005. Profiles the hijackers who carried out the 9/11 terrorist attacks. Argues that they were not fanatics but rather ordinary men and that many, many people with similar beliefs exist. McDermott, a *Los Angeles Times* reporter, conducted extensive interviews with relatives and friends of the hijackers and provides considerable new insight into the psychology of these men.

Miko, Francis T., and Christian Froehlich. "Germany's Role in Fighting Terrorism: Implications for U.S. Policy." Congressional Research Service Report RL-32710 (December 27, 2004). The 9/11 attack shook Berlin's belief that it was safe from terrorism, prompting the government to tighten asylum laws and increase its capacity for surveillance.

Der Spiegel magazine, *Inside 9-11: What Really Happened.* New York: St. Martin's Press, 2002. A German newspaper interviews people who knew the 9/11 terrorists and tries to provide an account of their life in Hamburg.

Whitlock, Craig. "Encounter on a Train Led Hamburg Cell to Bin Laden." *Washington Post,* August 10, 2004, p. A15 Buried in the 9/11 investigation is a story of the "Hamburg cell" and its original interest in pursuing Islamic fundamentalism in Chechnya, until a stranger on a train suggested introducing them to Osama bin Laden.

Counterterrorism

Davies, Barry. *Fire Magic: Hijack at Mogadishu.* London: Bloomsbury Publishing, 1994. A member of the GSG-9 unit that rescued passengers aboard a Lufthansa flight hijacked in 1977 by Palestinian terrorists and taken to Somalia.

German Embassy. "Counter-Terrorism Laws Take Effect." Fact Sheet available online. URL: http:// www.germany.info.relaunch/politics/new/pol_anti-terror.html. Accessed July 15, 2006.

Katzenstein, Peter J. "Same War, Different Views: Germany, Japan, and the War on Terrorism," *Current History* 57, no. 4 (Fall 2003): 731–760. After World War II both Germany and Japan adopted constitutions that promoted pacifism and resisted international military operations; both states also faced left-wing terrorist movements in the 1970s. But these two experiences left them unprepared for new forms of terrorism in the 1990s and beyond.

Miko, Francis T., and Christian Froehlich, "Germany's Role in Fighting Terrorism: Implications for U.S. Policy," Congressional Research Service Report RL-32710 (December 27, 2004). The 9/11 attack shook Berlin's belief that it was safe from terrorism, prompting the government to tighten asylum laws and increase its capacity for surveillance.

ITALY

Red Brigades

Alexander, Yonah, and Dennis Pluchinsky. *Europe's Red Terrorists: The Fighting Communist Organizations.* London: Frank Cass, 1992. Survey of West European communist groups, their emergence in the 1970s, and their subsequent decline in the 1980s.

Drake, Richard. *The Aldo Moro Murder Case.* Cambridge, Mass.: Harvard University Press, 1996. A detailed investigation into the Red Brigades' murder of the former Italian prime minister, using new documentary evidence.

———. *Apostles and Agitators: Italy's Marxist Revolutionary Tradition.* Cambridge Mass.: Harvard University Press, 2003. Examines the emergence, philosophy, and tactics of the Red Brigades, placing the group in the broader context of Italian politics in the 20th century.

JAPAN

Aum Shinrikyo

Bracket, D. W. *Holy Terror: Armageddon in Tokyo.* New York: Weatherhill, 1996. Provides a biography of Aum Shinrikyo's enigmatic founder, Shoko Asahara.

Court TV Crime Library. "False Prophet: The Aum Cult of Terror." Available online. URL: www.crimelibrary.com/terrorists_spies/terrorists/prophet1.html. Accessed December 22, 2006.

Falkenrath, Richard, Robert Newman, and Bradley Thayer. *America's Achilles' Heel: Nuclear, Biological, and Chemical Terrorism and Covert Attack.* Cambridge, Mass.: MIT Press, 1998. Presents scenarios of terrorist attacks against the United States using weapons of mass destruction, such as releasing sarin in a U.S. subway system.

Jurgensmeyer, Mark. *Terror in the Mind of God: The Global Rise of Religious Violence.* 3d ed. Los Angeles: University of California Press, 2003. Drawing on the history of religion, Jurgensmeyer argues that all religions have an element of violence and make martyrdom attractive. Includes section on Aum Shinrikyo.

Kaplan, David E., and Alan Marshall. *The Cult at the End of the World.* New York: Crown, 1996. The rise and demise of the popular Japanese millennial cult.

Kristof, Nicholas D. "At Trial in Tokyo, Guru Says Aim Was to Give 'Ultimate Joy.'" *New York Times,* April 25, 1996, p. A11. Reports testimony and evidence presented in trial of Shoko Asahara, leader of Aum Shinrikyo.

Lifton, Robert Jay. *Destroying the World to Save It: Aum Shinrikyo, Apocalyptic Violence, and the New Global Terrorism.* New York: Henry Holt, 1999. Describes

Aum Shinrikyo members and operations, while warning that similar apocalyptic groups remain

Metraux, Daniel A. *Aum Shinrikyo and Japanese Youth.* Lanham, Md.: University Press of America, 1999. Why were well-educated, middle-class Japanese youth so attracted to this bizarre cult?

Poolos, J. *The Nerve Gas Attack on the Tokyo Subway.* Terrorist Attacks. New York: Rosen, 2003. A well-illustrated account of the March 20, 1995, sarin attack in Tokyo, including a history of the Aum Shinrikyo group and its leader, Shoko Asahara.

Reader, Ian. *Religious Violence in Contemporary Japan: The Case of Aum Shinrikyo.* Surrey, England: Curzon, 2000.

Tucker, Jonathan B. *Toxic Terror: Assessing Terrorist Use of Chemical and Biological Weapons.* Cambridge, Mass.: MIT Press, 2000. Profiles 12 terrorist groups or individuals that carried out—or came close to—chemical and biological weapons attacks from 1946 to 1998.

Van Biema, David. "Prophet of Poison." *Time,* April 3, 1995, pp. 27–32. Describes the government raid on the Aum Shinrikyo compound, the huge stockpile of chemical weapons, and what attracted youth to the movement.

Walsh, James. "Shoko Asahara: The Making of a Messiah." *Time,* April 3, 1995, pp. 30–31. Extensive profile of the man who created Aum Shinrikyo.

Japanese Red Army

Farrell, William. *Blood and Rage: The Story of the Japanese Red Army.* Lexington, Mass.: Lexington Books, 1990. Details the violent history of the JRA, including its association with Palestinian terrorists and relocation to Lebanon.

Varon, Jeremy. *Bringing the War Home: The Weather Underground, the Red Army Faction, and Revolutionary Violence in the Sixties and Seventies.* Berkeley: University of California Press, 2004. Using primary materials, Varon reconstructs the social atmosphere of the Vietnam era to show why middle-class, well-educated youth turned to violence to protest their government's activities.

Counterterrorism

Alexander, Yonah, ed. *Combating Terrorism: Strategies of Ten Countries.* Ann Arbor: University of Michigan Press, 2002. This collection of papers compares counterterrorism strategies in the United States, Argentina, Peru, Colombia, Spain, the United Kingdom, Israel, Turkey, India, and Japan, focusing on how each political system defines terrorism and the internal and external factors that influence their approaches. The book was compiled before 9/11, but each author added a brief update to cover that major development.

Katzenstein, Peter J. "Same War, Different Views: Germany, Japan, and the War on Terrorism." *Current History* 57, no. 4 (Fall 2003): 731–760. After World War II both Germany and Japan adopted constitutions that promoted pacifism and resisted international military operations; both states also faced left-wing terrorist movements in the 1970s. But these two experiences left them unprepared for new forms of terrorism in the 1990s and beyond.

Pangi, Robyn. "Consequence Management in the 1995 Sarin Attacks on the Japanese Subway System." BCSIA Discussion Paper 2002-4, ESDP Discussion Paper ESDP-2002-01, John F. Kennedy School of Government, Harvard University, February 2002. A highly detailed study of the Aum Shinrikyo sarin attack as a failure of crisis management. Pangi describes how no officials linked the multiple reports coming from the subway system, no one could identify the poison, and hospitals could not handle the influx of wounded.

THE MIDDLE EAST

Black September

Dobson, Christopher. *Black September: Its Short, Violent History.* London: Robert Hale, 1974. Written shortly after Black September ceased operations, the book chronicles its formation and operations.

Hirst, David. *The Gun and the Olive Branch: The Roots of Violence in the Middle East.* 3d ed. New York: Avalon, 2003. Now in its third edition, Hirst's book chronicles the emergence of the Palestinian-Israeli conflict, from the 1880s to the present day. A former Middle East reporter for Britain's *Guardian* newspaper, Hirst is a veteran of the region and has survived two kidnappings.

Reeve, Simon. *One Day in September: The Story of the 1972 Munich Olympics Massacre*: London: Faber & Faber, 2000. Written as a companion to the documentary of the same name, *One Day in September* provides comprehensive coverage of Black September and its assault in Munich. It also contains a detailed look at the materials collected in connection with the German investigation in the failed rescue attempt.

Sonnenborn, Liz. *Murder at the 1972 Olympics in Munich.* Terrorist Attacks. New York: Rosen, 2003. A small, picture-filled book that provides an excellent introduction to the issues behind the Black September assault.

Hamas

Alexander, Yonah. *Palestinian Religious Terrorism: Hamas and Islamic Jihad.* New York: Transnational, 2002. An extensive (425-page) survey and comparison of the two movements.

Anti-Defamation League, "Hamas, Islamic Jihad and the Muslim Brotherhood: Islamic Extremists and the Terrorist Threat to America." New York: Anti-Defamation League, 1993.

Laqueur, Walter, ed. *Voices of Terror: Manifestos, Writings and Manuals of Al Qaeda, Hamas, and Other Terrorists from around the World and throughout the Ages.* New York: Reed Press, 2004.

Mishal, Shaul, and Avraham Sela, *The Palestinian Hamas: Vision, Violence, and Coexistence.* New York: Columbia University Press, 2000. Discusses the rise of Hamas and its constant need to adapt to developments in other Palestinian groups. Also emphasizes the social and economic programs sponsored by Hamas.

Nusse, Andrea. *Muslim Palestine: The Ideology of Hamas.* Amsterdam: Harwood Academic Publishers, 1998. Hamas writings on a variety of topics, particularly the Israeli peace process.

Oliver, Anne Marie, and Paul Steinberg. *The Road to Martyrs' Square: A Journey into the World of the Suicide Bomber.* New York: Oxford University Press, 2005. A case study in the Palestinian terrorist group Hamas, the study draws upon the six years the authors spent living in Gaza. Includes a unique photographic collection of Hamas graffiti and martyr propaganda as well as a profile of Hamas leader Sheikh Yasin.

Hezbollah

Alexander, Yonah. *Palestinian Religious Terrorism: Hamas and Islamic Jihad.* New York: Transnational, 2002. An extensive (425-page) survey and comparison of the two movements.

Jaber, Hala. *Hezbollah: Born with a Vengeance.* New York: Columbia University Press, 1997. A smaller reference guide, focusing on terminology, tactics, goals, and events.

Irgun

Begin, Menachem. *The Revolt: Story of the Irgun.* Jerusalem: Steimatzky, 1977. The founder of Irgun discusses the group's campaign to establish a Jewish state. Begin later became Israel's prime minister and signed the Camp David accords with Egyptian president Anwar Sadat.

Palestine Liberation Organization

Alexander, Yonah. *Palestinian Secular Terrorism: Profiles of Fatah, Popular Front for the Liberation of Palestine, Popular Front for the Liberation of Palestine-General Command, and Democratic Front for the Liberation of Palestine.* New York: Transnational, 2003. Compares the PLO with its rivals and offshoots.

———. *Terrorism: The PLO Connection.* New York: Taylor and Francis, 1989. In addition to work in its own name, the PLO has collaborated with numerous organizations and state sponsors of terrorism. Includes an appendix of documents and a chronology.

Hart, Alan. *Arafat: A Political Biography: The Definitive Biography Written in Cooperation with Yasser Arafat.* London: Sidgwick and Jackson, 1994. A controversial book about an even more controversial man, not updated since Arafat's death.

Schoenberg, Harris O. *A Mandate for Terror: The United Nations and the PLO.* New York: Shapolsky Books, 1989. Traces the connection between the birth of Israel and the birth of the PLO.

Unification and Jihad (Iraq, Abu Mussab al Zarquawi)

Gettleman, Jeffrey. "Zarqawi's Journey: From Dropout to Prisoner to Insurgent Leader." *New York Times,* July 13, 2004, p. A8.

Isikoff, Michael, and Mark Hosenball. "The World's Most Dangerous Man." *Newsweek,* June 23, 2004. Online edition. URL: http://nl.newsbank.com/nl-search/we/Archives?p_action=doc&p_docid=107BFC5B1 915FFA0&p_docnum=2&s_dlid=DL0106122215071302121&s_ecproduct=SUB-FREE&s_subterm=Subscription%20until%3A%2012%2F14%22015%2011%3A59%2 OPM&s_subexpires=12%2F14%2015%2011%3A59%20PM&s_username=nwsub&s_upgradeable=no. Last accessed December 22, 2006.

Napoleoni, Loretta. "Profile of a Killer." *Foreign Policy* (2005). November/December, 15–17.

Thomas, Evan, and Rod Nordland. "Death of a Terrorist." *Newsweek,* June 19, 2006, pp. 24–39. A series of articles reporting on Zarqawi's death and the likely impact.

Weaver, Mary Anne. "Inventing Zarqawi." *Atlantic Monthly,* July/August 2006, pp. 87ff. One of the longest, most in-depth profiles of Zarqawi, published days before his assassination.

Whitlock, Craig. "Amman Bombings Reflect Zarqawi's Growing Reach." *Washington Post,* November 13, 2005, p. A1.

NEPAL

Brooke, James. "Nepal's Maoist Guerrillas Let the Revolution Rest, for Now." *New York Times,* June 2, 2003, p. A2.

Lakshmanan, Indira A. R. "In Nepal, a New Red Army Emerges: Maoist Guerrillas Fight for an Empire." *Boston Globe,* June 24, 2001, p. A1.

Lancaster, John. "Concern Grows over Nepal's Child Fighters; 'Untouchables' Used by Rebels in Brutal War." *Washington Post,* June 14, 2005, p. A18. As caste hierarchy remains fundamental to Nepalese society, members of the lowest castes are finding that their best prospects for improving their life lie with the classless Maoist movement.

Rohde, David. "Youth Ensnared in Nepal's War with Maoists." *New York Times,* December 9, 2004, p. A1. Human rights groups condemn the rebels' increasing use of child soldiers and suggest it may be an indication that the group is losing popular support.

Sengupta, Somini. "Where Maoists Still Matter." *New York Times Magazine,* October 30, 2005, pp. 54ff. Sengupta provides a detailed account of the hardships Nepalese face daily and how the insurgency has stepped in to provide the social, educational, and financial programs.

PERU

Alexander, Yonah, ed. *Combating Terrorism: Strategies of Ten Countries.* Ann Arbor: University of Michigan Press, 2002. This collection of papers compares counterterrorism strategies in the United States, Argentina, Peru, Colombia, Spain, the United Kingdom, Israel, Turkey, India, and Japan, focusing on how each political system defines terrorism and the internal and external factors that influence their approaches. The book was compiled before 9/11, but each author added a brief update to cover that major development.

Gorriti, Gustavo. *The Shining Path: A History of the Millenarian War in Peru.* Chapel Hill: University of North Carolina Press, 1999. Detailed look at the largest communist movement in Peru.

Stern, Steve J., ed. *Shining and Other Paths: War and Society in Peru, 1980–1995.* Durham, N.C.: Duke University Press, 1998. U.S. and Peruvian scholars examine the causes and consequences of the Peruvian civil war.

Tarazona-Sevellano, Gabriela. *Sendero Luminoso and the Threat of Narcoterrorism.* New York: Praeger, 1990. Colombia is not the only Latin American country with drug and terrorist problems. While Tarazona-Sevellano's work predates the Fujimori crackdown on Sendero Luminoso, the group is reviving, thanks to drug trafficking, and her insights may be even more valuable than they were in 1990s.

RUSSIA: CHECHNYA

Chivers, C. J., and Steven Lee Myers. "Chechen Rebels Driven Mainly by Nationalism." *New York Times,* September 12, 2004, p. A1. Explains why terrorism in Chechnya is driven by nationalism, not Islamic fundamentalism.

Cornell, Svante E. "The War against Terrorism and the Conflict in Chechnya: A Case for Distinction." *Fletcher Forum of World Affairs* 27, no. 2 (2003): 167–184. Russian president Vladimir Putin wants the world to regard the civil war in Chechnya as an example of terrorism.

Cuny, Frederick C. "Killing Chechnya." *New York Review of Books,* April 15, 1995, pp. 15–20. A noted humanitarian aid worker describes the devastation caused by the Russian invasion of Chechnya in December 1994. Cuny disappeared in Chechnya in March 1995 and is presumed dead.

de Waal, Thomas. "The Chechen Conflict and the Outside World." *Crimes of War Project: The Magazine,* April 18, 2003. Available online. URL: www.crimesofwar.org. Available online. URL: http://www.crimesofwar.org/print/Chechnya/chech-waal-print.html. Accessed December 29, 2005. Traces rising influence of Islam in Chechen war.

———. "Fighting for Chechnya: Is Islam a Factor." *Wide Angle: Greetings from Grozny* (2002). Available online. URL: http://www.pbs.org/wnet/wideangle/printable/chechnya_briefing_print.html. Accessed January 12, 2006. Contrary to the conventional wisdom, de Waal argues that the Chechen rebels adopted Islamic fundamentalism only when they needed funding.

Dunlop, John B. *Russia Confronts Chechnya: Roots of a Separatist Conflict.* New York: Cambridge University Press, 1998. Covers centuries of Chechen history, including the uneasy relationship with Russia. Provides intriguing profile of Jokhar Dudayev, and describes the failed attempts to negotiate a compromise on independence.

Evangelista, Matthew. *The Chechen Wars: Will Russia Go the Way of the Soviet Union?* Washington, D.C.: Brookings Institution Press, 2002. Just as each of the 15 Soviet Socialist Republics became an independent state when the USSR broke apart in 1991, many of the Russian Federation's 89 units would like their own state as well.

Gall, Carlotta, and Thomas de Waal. *Chechnya: A Small Victorious War.* New York: New York University Press, 2000. Correspondents from the *Moscow Times* examine Yeltsin's poorly planned campaign in Chechnya.

———. *Chechnya: Calamity in the Caucasus.* New York: New York University Press, 1998.

Goltz, Thomas. *Chechnya Diary: A War Correspondent's Story of Surviving the War in Chechnya.* New York: St. Martin's Press, 2003. Case study of one incident in one village during the first Chechen war, the Samashki Massacre. Discusses the moral aspects of how a journalist covers a war.

Lieven, Anatol. *Chechnya: Tombstone of Russian Power.* New Haven, Conn.: Yale University Press, 1999. Lieven covered the first Chechen war (1994–96) for the *Financial Times* and provides an eyewitness account of Chechen society and politics. Shows the historical and cultural grievances Chechens bear against Russia, and reveals the confusion and corruption within the Russian troops sent to the region.

Politkovskaya, Anna. *A Small Corner of Hell: Dispatches from the Caucasus.* Chicago: University of Chicago Press, 2003. Despised by the Kremlin, Politikovskaya is renowned for her balanced reporting on the Chechen conflict. Politikovskaya was the only reporter allowed inside the 2002 Moscow theater siege. Two years later she was mysteriously poisoned en route to investigate the Beslan school hostage crisis. She was assassinated in 2006.

Tishkov, Valery. *Chechnya: Life in a War-Torn Society.* Los Angeles: University of California Press, 2004. Russian president Boris Yeltsin's adviser on nationalities takes an anthropological look at Chechen society and its mix of violence and nationalism. Includes extensive coverage of the 1944 deportation and its consequences.

SPAIN

Alexander, Yonah, ed. *Combating Terrorism: Strategies of Ten Countries.* Ann Arbor: University of Michigan Press, 2002. This collection of papers compares counterterrorism strategies in the United States, Argentina, Peru, Colombia, Spain, the United Kingdom, Israel, Turkey, India, and Japan, focusing on how each political system defines terrorism and the internal and external factors that influence their approaches. The book was compiled before 9/11, but each author added a brief update to cover that major development.

Idoiaga, Gorka Espiau. "The Basque Conflict: New Ideas and Prospects for Peace." United States Institute of Peace Special Report no. 161, April 2006. Available online. URL: http://www.usip.org/pubs/specialreports/sr161.pdf. Accessed July 16, 2006. An excellent overview of the history of the Basque movement that brings the analysis up to the 2004 Madrid bombing and the subsequent cease-fire negotiations.

Kurlansky, Mark. *The Basque History of the World: The Story of a Nation.* New York: Penguin, 1999. A highly readable survey of the Basque people, culture, history, and politics.

UNITED KINGDOM

Irish Republican Army

The number of books on the Irish conflict is enormous. These represent a selection of some newer works.

Bel, J. Bowyer. *The IRA 1968–2000: Analysis of a Secret Army.* New York: Frank Cass, 2000.

Donohue, Laura. *Counter-terrorist Law and Emergency Powers in the United Kingdom, 1922–2000.* Portland, Ore.: Irish Academic Press, 2001.

English, Richard. *Armed Struggle: The History of the IRA.* New York: Oxford University Press, 2003.

O'Callaghan, Sean. *Informer: The Real Life Story of One Man's War against Terrorism.* New York: Bantam Books, 1998.

Londonistan

Caldwell, Christopher. "After Londonistan." *New York Times Magazine,* June 25, 2006, pp. 40ff. An extensive analysis of the policy and social consequences of the 7/7 terrorist attacks in London, released on the first anniversary of the bombings.

House of Commons, Intelligence and Security Committee, "Report into the London Terrorist Attacks on 7 July 2005," May 2006, p. 11. Official report into the 7/7 attacks and the performance of the British intelligence services.

Ignatius, David. "Revolt of Privilege, Muslim Style." *Washington Post,* July 27, 2005, p. A21. This thought-provoking editorial describes the alienation felt by the children of Muslim immigrants in England.

Ulph, Stephen. "Londonistan." *Terrorism Monitor* (February 26, 2004). Available online. URL: http://www.Jamestown.org/terrorism/news/article.php issue_id=2914. Last accessed December 22, 2006. Explains why London is popular with Islamic dissidents, and profiles each group active there.

Counterterrorism

Alexander, Yonah, ed. *Combating Terrorism: Strategies of Ten Countries.* Ann Arbor: University of Michigan Press, 2002. This collection of papers compares counterterrorism strategies in the United States, Argentina, Peru, Colombia, Spain, the United Kingdom, Israel, Turkey, India, and Japan, focusing on how each political system defines terrorism and the internal and external factors that influence their approaches. The book was compiled before 9/11, but each author added a brief update to cover that major development.

House of Commons, Intelligence and Security Committee, "Report into the London Terrorist Attacks on 7 July 2005," May 2006, p. 11. Official report into the 7/7 attacks and the performance of the British intelligence services.

Chronology

1920

- ***September 16:*** Bomb explodes on Wall Street, killing 35 New Yorkers. "Communists" are blamed for the attack.

1922

- ***June:*** League of Nations instructs Great Britain to establish a "Jewish national home" in Palestine.

1946

- ***July 22:*** Irgun, a Jewish extremist group led by future Israeli prime minister Menachem Begin, bombs King David Hotel in Jerusalem, headquarters of British administration, Ninety-one people die in the explosion.

1947

- ***April 9:*** Members of Irgun and the Stern Gang kill entire population of Dayr Yasin, a Palestinian town of 254 people.
- ***July:*** Irgun hangs two British sergeants in Palestine.
- ***November 29:*** United Nations accepts Partition Plan for Palestine, dividing the British Mandate of Palestine into three sections: a Jewish state, an Arab state, and an internationally administered region incorporating Jerusalem and Bethlehem. Palestinian groups opposed the plan as it gave 55 percent of the land to the Jews, who made up only 33 percent of the population.

1948

- ***May 15:*** Britain leaves Palestine; Israeli prime minister David Ben-Gurion announces creation of Israel.
- ***May 16:*** Egypt and Jordan invade Israel.

- ***September 17:*** Members of the Stern Gang murder Count Folke Bernadotte of Sweden, who had been a UN mediator between the Israeli, Arab, and Palestinian groups.
- ***December 28:*** Muslim Brotherhood assassinates Egyptian prime minister Mahmoud Fahmey el-Nokrashy Pasha, blaming him for allowing the creation of Israel.

1949

- Israel signs Armistice Agreements with Egypt, Jordan, Lebanon, and Syria.

1950

- ***November 1:*** Puerto Rican nationalists Oscar Collaza and Griselio Torresola storm Blair House, trying to kill President Harry S. Truman. White House guards kill Torresola.

1951

- ***July 20:*** Palestinian gunman kills Jordan's King Abdullah I.

1952

- George Habbash founds Arab National Movement at American University of Beirut.

1954

- ***March 1:*** Puerto Rican nationalists open fire at the U.S. Capitol, wounding five congressmen.

1955

- ***August 20:*** Philippeville massacre in Algeria: members of the National Liberation Front (FLN) kill 37 Europeans, including women and children.

1956

- ***October 21–22:*** FLN murders 49 people in Algeria.

1959

- ***August 31:*** Basque Fatherland and Liberty Movement (ETA) founded to create independent Basque country from portions of Spain and France.

1961

- ***May 1:*** First hijacking of U.S. commercial airplane. Antulio Ramirez Ortiz demanded to be flown to Havana, Cuba.

1963

- ***September 15:*** KKK militants bomb Sixteenth Street Baptist Church in Birminghama, Alabama. Four young girls die in explosion.

1964

- ***June 2:*** Palestine Liberation Organization founded to represent interests of Palestinian people and defeat the state of Israel.

1967

- Israel defeats Syria, Jordan, and Egypt in Six-Day War, gaining new territories from each: the Golan Heights (from Syria), the West Bank (Jordan), the Gaza Strip and Sinai Peninsula (Egypt).

1968

- ***July 22:*** PFLP hijacks El Al plane en route from Rome to Tel Aviv, diverting plane to Algeria. Hijackers offer to trade passengers for 16 prisoners held in Israel. The crew and passengers are held for 39 days and ultimately released on August 31.
- ***August 28:*** U.S. ambassador to Guatemala assassinated by rebels.
- ***December 26:*** PFLP gunmen attack El Al plane as it departs Athens for New York City, killing one passenger.

1969

- ***February 18:*** PFLP gunmen attack El Al plane at Zurich airport, killing copilot.
- ***February 20:*** PFLP gunmen bomb a supermarket in Jerusalem, killing two people.
- ***July 18:*** Palestinian terrorists bomb Marks and Spencer, a Jewish-owned department store in London.
- ***July 29:*** PFLP hijackers seize El Al jet, taking it to Damascus. Once in Syria, they destroy the plane and release the hostages, although Syria decides to detain the six Israeli citizens aboard to trade for Egyptians held by Tel Aviv.
- ***July 30:*** U.S. ambassador to Japan stabbed by Japanese citizen.
- ***August 12:*** Rioting breaks out between Unionist and Nationalist groups in Northern Ireland, triggering the 30 years of conflict known as "The Troubles."
- ***August 14:*** London dispatches British troops to Northern Ireland, beginning military rule.
- ***August 29:*** Two PFLP gunmen, including Leila Khaled, hijack TWA flight departing Rome for Athens, force pilot to land in Damascus.

- ***September 3:*** U.S. ambassador to Brazil kidnapped by MR-8, a Marxist insurgency.
- ***September 19:*** PFLP operatives lob grenades at Israeli embassies in the Netherlands and Germany. The Brussels El Al office is also targeted.

1970

- ***February 10:*** Palestinian commandos attack busload of El Al passengers in Munich; one passenger killed.
- ***February 21:*** PFLP bomb a Swissair passenger jet en route to Israel, killing 47 people.
- ***March 6:*** Two members of Weather Underground accidentally killed while making bombs in Greenwich Village townhouse in New York City.
- ***March 31:*** Eight Japanese Red Army members hijack Japanese Airlines flight, forcing it to fly from Tokyo to Fukuoka, Seoul, and on to North Korea. The passengers were released in Seoul while the hijackers took refuge in North Korea.
- ***June 24:*** French-Canadian nationalists detonate bomb outside Canadian Ministry of Defense in Ottawa.
- ***July 3:*** Falls Road Curfew; for two days British Army troops searched homes in Belfast for IRA members and weapons. The brutality and destructiveness of the search widened the rift between Unionists and Nationalists.
- ***July 31:*** U.S. Agency for International Development adviser Dan Mitrione kidnapped and murdered in Uruguay by members of Tupamaros terrorist group.
- ***August 9:*** Northern Ireland introduces internment without trial.
- ***September 6:*** Members of the Popular Front for the Liberation of Palestine hijack four aircraft flying from Europe to New York City, forcing one TWA and one Swissair plane to land at Dawson's Field in Jordan. A Pan American flight was diverted to Cairo. Aboard the fourth aircraft, an El Al flight, security guards kill hijacker Patrick Arguello and arrest Leila Khalid, the second hijacker. That plane lands at London's Heathrow airport and Khalid is jailed.
- ***September 9:*** PFLP sympathizer hijacks British Overseas Airways Corporation flight from Bombay to Rome, demanding release of Leila Khaled. The plane later lands at Dawson's Field.
- ***September 12:*** PFLP operatives destroy the three aircraft on the ground at Dawson's Field, and the flaming wreckage is shown on international television. PFLP releases 255 passengers, keeps remaining 56 as hostages.
- ***September 13:*** British government agrees to release Leila Khalid in exchange for the 56 passengers still held by PFLP.

- ***September 16:*** King Hussein declares martial law, Jordanian army attacks PLO facilities in Jordan; in 10-day campaign, between 5,000 and 10,000 Palestinians are killed while PLO relocates to Lebanon. The episode is known as "Black September" and soon a PLO paramilitary group with that name is formed.
- ***September 30:*** Formal exchange of remaining hijacking hostages for Leila Khalid and six other PFLP operatives held in Germany and Switzerland.
- ***October 5:*** French-Canadian nationalists (Liberation Front of Quebec) kidnap British trade official James Cross and Quebec's labor minister, Pierre LaPorte. Cross is released, but LaPorte is killed.

1971

- ***January 30:*** Kashmiri Liberation Front hijacks Indian Air flight, destroys plane when India refuses to release prisoners as demanded.
- ***March 1:*** Weather Underground bombs U.S. Senate building.
- ***October 31:*** IRA bombs restaurant atop London's Post Office Tower.
- ***November 21:*** Jordan's prime minister, Wasfi Tel, assassinated by Black September.
- ***December 4:*** Ulster Volunteer Force bombs Belfast pub, killing 15 people.

1972

- ***January 30:*** British paratroopers kill 13 unarmed civilians in Derry, Northern Ireland. Event dubbed "Black Sunday."
- ***February 22:*** Palestinian hijackers seize Lufthansa flight en route from Delhi to Greece. They agree to release passengers in South Yemen in return for a $5 million ransom paid by West Germany.
- ***March 30:*** London dissolves Northern Ireland parliament and introduces direct rule.
- ***May 8:*** Black September hijacks Sabena Flight 572 from Vienna to Tel Aviv. Israeli commandos later rush plane, killing two hijackers and one passenger.
- ***May 11:*** Red Army Faction bombs U.S. Army base in Frankfurt, Germany, killing one U.S. soldier and injuring 13.
- ***May 12:*** Red Army Faction bombs police facilities in Augsburg and Munich, Germany.
- ***May 15:*** Red Army Faction plants bomb in car belonging to Judge Wolfgang Buddenberg, whose wife is injured when she starts the engine.
- ***May 19:*** Red Army Faction bombs offices of Springer, a German publisher.
- ***May 20:*** West German police discover three more Red Army Faction bombs at Springer offices.

- ***May 25:*** Red Army Faction detonates a pipe bomb at U.S. Army base in Heidelberg, killing three U.S. soldiers.
- ***May 30:*** Members of the Japanese Red Army and PFLP mount grenade-and-rifle attack on Lod (Ben Gurion) airport in Tel Aviv, Israel, killing at least 20 people.
- ***July 21:*** 22 IRA bombs kill 11 people in Belfast. Attack remembered as "Bloody Friday."
- ***September 5:*** Black September Organization (part of PLO) takes Israeli Olympic team hostage in Munich, Germany, and plans to trade athletes for 234 Palestinians held in Israel. Two athletes were killed in the initial assault; the other nine were loaded onto two helicopters for a flight to Egypt. The terrorists killed all nine when German police ambushed the helicopters during a stopover at a German airbase.
- ***December 6:*** IRA kidnaps Jean McConville, a widow and mother of 10 children, who had gone to help a wounded British soldier. Her body is not found until 2003.

1973

- ***March 1:*** Black September attacks Saudi embassy in Khartoum, killing American ambassador to Sudan, chargé d'affaires, and Belgian chargé d'affaires.
- ***May 4:*** Members of People's Revolutionary Armed Forces kidnap U.S. consul Terence Leonhardy, Guadalajara, Mexico.
- ***July 20:*** Japanese Red Army and Popular Front for the Liberation of Palestine hijack Japan Airlines plane over the Netherlands, diverting the flight to Libya.
- ***August 5:*** Palestinian terrorists attack passengers as they leave TWA flight in Greece, killing five.
- ***December 17:*** Palestinian terrorists pull weapons from luggage at Rome airport. They take hostages; bomb one plane on the tarmac; hijack a second plane to Greece, then to Syria, Kuwait, and to an unknown final destination.

1974

- ***January 31:*** Simultaneous attacks by Japanese Red Army (Shell Oil in Singapore) and Popular Front for the Liberation of Palestine (Japanese embassy in Kuwait). Hostages used as bargaining chips.
- ***February 3:*** IRA detonates bomb aboard bus carrying British military personnel, including family members. Twelve people killed.
- ***February 4:*** Symbionese Liberation Army kidnaps newspaper heiress Patricia Hearst from her apartment in San Francisco.
- ***April 11:*** Popular Front for the Liberation of Palestine members attack apartment building in Kiryat Shemona, Israel, killing 18, including nine children.

- ***April 13:*** Members of New People's Army kill three U.S. sailors outside Subic Bay naval station, Philippines.
- ***May 15:*** Members of the Democratic Front for the Liberation of Palestine seize school in Maalot, Israel; 26 students and adults killed.
- ***May 15:*** Nationalists and paramilitary groups stage strike in Northern Ireland.
- ***May 17:*** Symbionese Liberation Army headquarters in Los Angeles is attacked by police and burns to ground.
- ***June 17:*** Provisional Irish Republican Army bombs Tower of London; one tourist killed, more than 40 injured.
- ***August 6:*** Bomb explodes at Los Angeles International Airport, killing two people.
- ***August 19:*** U.S. ambassador to Cyprus assassinated.
- ***September 13:*** Members of Japanese Red Army seize French embassy in the Netherlands. Hostages later exchanged for jailed JRA operative; Basque ETA bombs café in Madrid, killing 12 and wounding 80; Puerto Rican separatists (FALN) bomb five New York City banks.
- ***November 17:*** Red Army Faction members murder Gunter von Drenkmann, president of the West German Supreme Court.
- ***November 21:*** Provisional IRA bombs two pubs in Birmingham, England, killing 21 and wounding 200.
- ***November 22:*** Palestine Liberation Organization granted observer status at United Nations.

1975

- ***January 27:*** Puerto Rican nationalists bomb bar on Wall Street, killing four patrons.
- ***January 29:*** Bomb explodes in State Department bathroom; Weather Underground claims responsibility.
- ***February 27:*** Red Army Faction kidnaps Peter Lorenz, head of the German Christian Democratic party. Lorenz is released six days later.
- ***March 1:*** Kurdish terrorists hijack Iraqi airplane and land in Iran. Officials in Iran arrest the terrorists and execute them on April 7.
- ***April 7:*** Moro Islamic Liberation Front hijacks Philippine Airlines jet, taking passengers and crew hostage. Group takes crew onward to Libya, where front members are granted asylum.
- ***April 24:*** Red Army Faction members seize West German embassy in Stockholm. Two of the 11 hostages are executed before the terrorists accidentally set off their own bomb.

- ***June 27:*** Baader-Meinhof and PFLP team hijack Air France flight, diverting it to Entebbe, Uganda. Israeli commandos storm the plane on July 3.
- ***August 4:*** Japanese Red Army takes 50 hostages at U.S. consulate and Swedish embassy in Kuala Lumpur, Malaysia. Hostages later exchanged for five jailed JRA operatives.
- ***September 15:*** Members of Black September seize Egyptian embassy in Madrid. Six diplomatic hostages later released in Algeria.
- ***December 21:*** PFLP operatives seize 81 hostages at OPEC meeting in Vienna. They later surrender for $50 million and passage to Algeria.
- ***December 23:*** Revolutionary Organization November 17 kill Richard Welch, CIA station chief in Athens.

1976

- ***January 4–5:*** Protestants kill five Catholics in Northern Ireland; one day later IRA reciprocates by executing 10 Protestants taken from a bus.
- ***January 12:*** United Nations Security Council grants Palestine Liberation Organization right to participate in debates but not the right to vote on issues.
- ***May 23:*** Members of Free South Moluccan Organization seize passenger train (51 hostages) and school in the Netherlands. Two hostages die when Royal Dutch Marine Commandos board the train.
- ***June 27:*** Red Army Faction members, PFLP members, and "Carlos the Jackal" hijack Air France flight, diverting it to Entebbe, Uganda, and demanding the release of jailed RAF leaders. Israeli commandos rescue the 53 hostages.
- ***July 21:*** IRA kills Christopher Ewart-Biggs, British ambassador to Ireland.
- ***August 11:*** Four passengers killed when PFLP attack El Al terminal at Istanbul airport.
- ***September 21:*** Former Chilean foreign minister Orlando Letelier killed by car bomb in Washington, D.C.

1977

- ***March 9:*** Hanafi Muslims take over three buildings in Washington, D.C., holding 134 hostages and wounding future mayor Marion Barry.
- ***August 3:*** FALN detonates two bombs in New York City in campaign for Puerto Rican independence.
- ***September 5:*** Red Army Faction kidnaps Hanns-Martin Schleyer, president of the West German Employers Association. Kidnappers offer to exchange Schleyer for imprisoned RAF members.
- ***September 28:*** Japanese Red Army hijacks Japan Airlines flight, diverting it to Bangladesh. To free passengers, Tokyo releases six JRA members from jail and pays $6 million ransom.

- ***October 17:*** Palestinians hijack Lufthansa plane, demand release of Red Army Faction leaders. Hijackers kill pilot, force copilot to fly to Mogadishu, Somalia. Commandos storm the plane at Mogadishu airport, killing three of the four hijackers.
- ***October 18:*** Despondent over failure of October 17 hijacking, RAF leaders Andreas Baader, Jan-Carl Raspe, and Gudrun Ensslin commit suicide in prison. RAF militants execute Hanns-Martin Schleyer.
- ***November:*** Egyptian president Anwar Sadat secretly visits Israel, becoming first Arab leader to recognize the Jewish state.
- ***December:*** Single Japanese Red Army operative hijacks Malaysia Airlines Flight 653. Hijacker shoots the pilot and the plane crashes, killing all aboard.

1978

- ***March 16:*** Red Brigades kidnap former Italian prime minister Aldo Moro.
- ***April 11:*** Commandos from Fatah (PLO) land near Haifa, Israel, and hijack bus. Firefight breaks out when Israeli security forces intervene, killing 25 passengers and nine terrorists.
- ***May 9:*** Red Brigades murder former Italian prime minister Aldo Moro.
- ***September 17:*** Egyptian president Anwar Sadat and Israeli prime minister Menachem Begin sign the Camp David accords. Under the agreement, Israel would demilitarize and return the Sinai Peninsula to Egyptian control in exchange for Egypt formally extending diplomatic recognition to Israel, a move no other Arab state had made.

1979

- ***February 14:*** Adolph Dubs, U.S. ambassador to Afghanistan kidnapped by Muslim insurgents, later killed in botched rescue attempt.
- ***March 22:*** IRA assassinates Richard Sykes, British ambassador to the Netherlands.
- ***May 26:*** KKK attacks civil rights march in Decatur, Alabama, killing two people.
- ***August 27:*** IRA bomb kills Earl Mountbatten of Burma, cousin of Queen Elizabeth II, and three others boating in Ireland. In separate bombing, IRA kills 18 British soldiers at Narrow Water, County Down.
- ***November 3:*** KKK kills five members of U.S. Communist Party in Greensboro, N.C.
- ***November 4:*** Mob seizes U.S. embassy in Tehran, Iran, and 66 Americans; 53 hostages held for 444 days, being released on January 20, 1981.
- ***November 20:*** Sunni Muslim terrorists take hostages at Grand Mosque in Mecca; 158 people are killed before siege ends on December 4.

Chronology

1980

- ***April 30:*** Six Iraq-sponsored terrorists take 26 people hostage at Iranian embassy in London; British Special Forces retake embassy on May 5. All hostages and one terrorist survive.
- ***May 17:*** Sendero Luminosa stages its first attack, burning ballot boxes in the village of Chuschi, Peru.
- ***December 2:*** Members of El Salvador national guard assassinate three nuns and a missionary, all U.S. citizens.
- ***December 31:*** Hotel bombed in Nairobi, Kenya, killing 16. PFLP takes credit.

1981

- ***January 20:*** Iran releases last 53 hostages held at U.S. embassy in Tehran.
- ***May 11:*** Red Army Faction assassinates Heinz Herbert Karry, minister of economics for Hesse, a West German state.
- ***August 31:*** Red Army Faction bombs U.S. air base in Ramstein, West Germany, injuring 18.
- ***October 6:*** Egyptian president Anwar Sadat assassinated by members of Egyptian military.
- ***October 10:*** IRA bomb explodes at Ebury Bridge Road in London, killing two people.
- ***October 20:*** Weather Underground members rob Brinks armored car in Nyack, New York, killing three security officers and netting $1.6 million.
- ***October 26:*** IRA bomb explodes at restaurant on Oxford Street, London's main shopping district.
- ***November 28:*** Muslim Brotherhood bombs Damascus, Syria, as part of plan to remove Syrian president Hafez Assad.
- ***December 7:*** Bandits hijack three Venezuelan aircraft and demand $10 million. They later flee to Cuba without receiving the ransom. Terrorists had claimed to be Puerto Rican nationalists, but officials blamed Red Flag (Venezuela) or M-19 (Colombia).
- ***December 17:*** Red Brigades of Italy kidnap U.S. Army general James Lee Dozier, NATO commander for southern Europe. Italian commandos rescue him after 42 days.

1982

- ***February 2:*** Syria attacks Muslim Brotherhood camp in Hamah; 20,000 people die in resulting battle.

- ***March 2:*** Sendero Luminosa attacks Huamanga prison in Peru, liberating captured comrades and signaling a major increase in aggressive activity.
- ***June 3:*** Palestinian Abu Nidal Organization dispatches assassin to kill Israeli ambassador Shlomo Argov. The plan fails and Israel responds by invading Lebanon days later to clear out PLO camps.
- ***July 20:*** IRA bomb explodes at Hyde Park, London, killing two soldiers and seven military horses. Another bomb explodes at Regents' Park, North London, killing seven military musicians.
- ***September 14:*** Lebanese president Bachir Gemayel assassinated by member of Syrian Social Nationalist Party.
- ***September 15:*** Israel dispatches troops to occupy West Beirut and seal off Palestinian refugee camp.
- ***September 16:*** Militia composed of Phalangists (Lebanese Christians) enters Sabra and Shatilla refugee camps and kills the residents, perhaps 2,000 Palestinians. Israeli army does not intervene.
- ***December 6:*** Irish National Liberation Army, a radical IRA faction, bombs dance club in Ballykelly, Northern Ireland, killing 17 people.

1983

- ***April 8:*** U.S. citizen kidnapped by Revolutionary Armed Forces of Colombia.
- ***April 18:*** Islamic Jihad/Hezbollah bombs U.S. embassy in Beirut, Lebanon, killing 63.
- ***September 16:*** Puerto Rican nationalist group FALN robs armored car in West Hartford, Connecticut, taking $7.2 million.
- ***October 3:*** South Korean political delegation killed by North Korean terrorists while in Rangoon, Burma. Twenty-one people die in attack.
- ***October 23:*** U.S. Marine barracks in Beirut, Lebanon, attacked by Hezbollah suicide bomber, killing 241 soldiers. French paratrooper barracks in Beirut also hit by suicide bomber, killing 58 soldiers.
- ***November 15:*** Greek November 17 group kills U.S. Navy officer George Tsantes and his driver while they were stopped at a traffic light in Athens.
- ***December 17:*** IRA bomb explodes at Harrods department store in London, killing six.
- ***December 31:*** FALN bombs police stations, FBI offices, and federal courts in New York City.

1984

- ***March 16:*** Islamic Jihad kidnaps Beirut CIA station chief William Buckley, who is later executed.

- ***June 5:*** Sikh group seizes Golden Temple in Amritsar, India; 100 people killed in rescue operation.
- ***June 18:*** Members of white supremacist group "The Order" murder Alan Berg, a Jewish talk show host in Denver.
- ***August/September:*** Members of Rajneesh cult poison food at restaurants in The Dalles, Oregon, hoping to secure victory in local elections.
- ***September 20:*** Islamic Jihad/Hezbollah deploys truck bomb at U.S. embassy facility in East Beirut, Lebanon, killing 23 people.
- ***October 12:*** IRA bombs hotel in Brighton, England, ahead of Conservative Party conference. Five people die, Prime Minister Margaret Thatcher escapes unharmed.
- ***October 31:*** Indian Prime Minister Indira Gandhi assassinated by her security detail in retaliation for Amritsar incident.
- ***December 3:*** Members of Hezbollah/Islamic Jihad hijack Kuwait airliner, killing two employees of U.S. Agency for International Development.
- ***December 11:*** Red Army Faction and other European left-wing terrorist groups bomb NATO pipeline in Belgium.

1985

- ***February 7:*** Narco-terrorist Rafael Quintero seizes, tortures, and kills U.S. Drug Enforcement agent Enrique Salazar and a DEA pilot.
- ***March 16:*** Hezbollah kidnaps AP reporter Terry Anderson, a U.S. citizen, in Beirut. Anderson was ultimately released in December 1991.
- ***April:*** Nineteen-year-old Loula Abboud, a Christian Lebanese woman, executes a suicide bombing attack in Lebanon's Bekaa Valley.
- ***October 1:*** Israeli fighter jets bomb PLO headquarters in Tunisia, killing at least 60 people.
- ***June 9:*** Hezbollah kidnaps American University in Beirut dean Thomas Sutherland, a U.S. citizen. He was released on November 18, 1991.
- ***June 14:*** Members of Hezbollah hijack TWA flight 847, killing U.S. Navy diver Robert Stetham. Passengers and crew are held hostage for 17 days.
- ***June 19:*** Four U.S. marines and nine civilians killed by Farabundo Marti National Liberation Front in El Salvador.
- ***June 23:*** Air India flight explodes in flight, killing 329 people. Attack blamed on Sikhs and Kashmir rebels.
- ***August 8:*** Red Army Faction detonates car bomb at U.S. Air Force base in Rhein-Main, West Germany.
- ***September 30:*** Four Soviet diplomats kidnapped in Beirut.

- ***October 7:*** Palestine Liberation Front operatives hijack *Achille Lauro* cruise ship. One elderly, wheelchair-bound passenger, Leon Klinghoffer, is murdered, and his body is dumped overboard.
- ***November 6:*** M-19 raids Colombian Supreme Court. Soldiers attack to rescue the 500 hostages, but 20 terrorists, 11 soldiers, 11 Supreme Court justices, and 50 other hostages die.
- ***November 23:*** Members of Abu Nidal hijack EgyptAir flight 648 en route from Greece to Cairo; 58 passengers die during rescue attempt.
- ***December 27:*** Abu Nidal Organization stages attacks at airports in Vienna and Rome, killing 18 and injuring 111 people.

1986

- ***April 5:*** Explosion at West Berlin disco kills three people and wounds 300, including many U.S. soldiers. U.S. blames Libya.
- ***April 15:*** U.S. bombs Libya in retaliation for Berlin disco attack.
- ***May 3:*** In Sri Lanka, the Liberation Tigers of Tamil Eelam (LTTE) detonate bomb aboard a Sri Lankan airplane, killing 21. The flight's takeoff had been delayed, likely preventing higher casualties had the explosion occurred in flight.
- ***May 7:*** LTTE blamed for bombing in Colombo, Sri Lanka, that killed 14 people.
- ***May 14:*** Japanese Red Army fires on Japanese, U.S., and Canadian embassies in Jakarta, Indonesia.
- ***June 18:*** Prison riot in Lima, Peru, sparked by Shining Path, a left-wing terrorist group.
- ***September 5:*** Members of Abu Nidal Organization, attempting to hijack Pan Am Flight 73 in Karachi, Pakistan, instead open fire in terminal, killing 20 people.
- ***September 6:*** Abu Nidal Organization attacks Neve Shalom synagogue in Istanbul, killing 22.
- ***October 25:*** Basque terrorists use car bomb to kill governor of Guiuzcoa Province and his family.

1987

- ***January 20:*** Church of England envoy Terry Waite kidnapped by Hezbollah in Lebanon. He is released November 17, 1991.
- ***April 24:*** November 17 group bombs Athens bus carrying 16 U.S. soldiers.
- ***June 9:*** Japanese Red Army fires on U.S. and U.K. embassies in Rome, Italy.

- ***November 8:*** IRA bomb explodes at Remembrance Day ceremony in Enniskillen, Northern Ireland, killing 11 people.
- ***November 29:*** North Koreans detonate a bomb aboard a South Korean passenger jet, killing 115.
- ***December 8:*** First Intifada begins as spontaneous popular uprising against Israeli occupation of Gaza, lasts until 1993.
- ***December 26:*** One U.S. soldier killed in Barcelona by Catalan separatists.

1988

- ***February 17:*** Hezbollah militants kidnap and execute U.S. Marine Corps lieutenant colonel William R. Higgins, member of truce detachment in Lebanon.
- ***April 12:*** Japanese Red Army member Yu Kikumura arrested for carrying three bombs on New Jersey Turnpike. He is convicted of planning to blow up targets in New York City, perhaps on behalf of Libyan leader Muammar Qaddafi.
- ***April 14:*** U.S. serviceman killed by bomb outside USO club in Naples; attack blamed on Japanese Red Army.
- ***July 11:*** Abu Nidal Organization bombs *City of Poros*, a Greek cruise ship, in Athens, killing nine people.
- ***September 7:*** Italian police arrest 21 Red Brigade members in Rome.
- ***December 21:*** Pan Am flight 103 explodes over Lockerbie, Scotland, killing 259 passengers and crew plus 11 people at the site of impact. Libyan operatives had placed bomb in baggage.

1989

- ***April 3:*** Animal Liberation Front frees 1,000 lab animals from research facility at University of Arizona, then burns another campus facility.
- ***April 21:*** New People's Army assassinates U.S. Army colonel James Rowe in Manila.
- ***August 18:*** Guerrilla fighters seize hospital in Colombo, Sri Lanka, and a neighboring army facility and kill 24 soldiers. Liberation Tigers of Tamil Eelam blamed for attack.
- ***August 18:*** Medellín cartel assassinates Luis Carlos Galan, the front-runner to become president of Colombia, and two other candidates. Government responds by invoking state of emergency.
- ***September 19:*** French UTA flight 772 bombed in flight by Libyans, killing 170.
- ***November 27:*** Aviana Flight 203 bombed. Pablo Escobar and Medellín cartel blamed; 111 dead.

- ***November 30:*** Red Army Faction car bomb kills Alfred Herrhausen, head of Deutsche Bank.

1990

- ***January 7:*** Medellín cartel kidnaps more than 20 Colombian businessmen.
- ***January 15:*** U.S. embassy in Peru bombed by Tupac Amaru Revolutionary Movement.
- ***April 6:*** Shining Path kills 24 villagers in Alto Parualli, Peru.
- ***April 13:*** Shining Path kills 50 villagers in Sonomoro, Peru.
- ***May 13:*** Two U.S. soldiers killed in Philippines by New People's Army.
- ***July 9:*** Forty-eight Tupac Amaru members dig 350-meter tunnel to escape from Canto Grante maximum security prison in Peru.
- ***July 14:*** LTTE fighters execute 35 Muslims on a bus in Kalmunai, Sri Lanka.
- ***July 20:*** IRA bombs London Stock Exchange, but warning allows for evacuation of building, preventing injuries.
- ***August 30:*** Medellín cartel kidnaps TV journalist Diana Turbay, daughter of former Colombian president Julio Cesar Turbay. She is killed in failed rescue attempt in 1991.

1991

- ***February 7:*** IRA fires shots into 10 Downing Street, London, during Cabinet meeting.
- ***February 13:*** Red Army Faction fires on U.S. embassy Chancery building in Bonn.
- ***February 18:*** Bomb kills one person at London's Victoria and Paddington Stations. IRA takes credit.
- ***May 21:*** Female Tamil Tiger suicide bomber presents former Indian prime minister Rajiv Gandhi with a garland of flowers, then detonates the bomb hidden under her clothing, killing them and 12 bystanders.
- ***April 1:*** Red Army Faction assassinates Detlev Karsten Rohwedder, head of East German privatization program.
- ***June 19:*** Medellín cartel leader Pablo Escobar surrenders to Colombian government.

1992

- ***January 11:*** Secular group prevents Islamic fundamentalist government from taking power in Algeria, triggering bloody campaign.
- ***February 28:*** IRA bomb explodes at London Bridge rail station, injuring 28 people.

- ***March 17:*** Hezbollah attacks Israeli embassy in Argentina, killing 29.
- ***April 10:*** IRA bombs 30 St. Mary Axe, a building in London's financial district, killing three people and destroying the Baltic Exchange building.
- ***June 29:*** Armed Islamic Group assassinates Algerian president Muhammad Boudiaf.
- ***July 16:*** Shining Path detonates two bombs in Lima, killing 18.
- ***August 21–22:*** U.S. federal agents kill Vicki Weaver and her teenage son Sam Weaver at Ruby Ridge, Idaho, in standoff sparked over subpoena on weapons charges. Incident fuels antigovernment hatred among U.S. militia movement.
- ***September 13:*** Peruvian government captures Shining Path leader Abimael Guzmán.
- ***December 29:*** Three bombs detonate outside hotels housing U.S. soldiers in Aden, Yemen; al-Qaeda suspected. Two civilians killed.

1993

- ***January 25:*** Pakistani national Mir Amal Kansi shoots into traffic outside CIA headquarters in Langley, Virginia. Two people killed. Kansi flees to Pakistan.
- ***January 31:*** Revolutionary Armed Forces of Colombia kidnap three U.S. missionaries.
- ***February 26:*** Truck explodes in underground parking garage at World Trade Center in New York City, killing six and wounding 1,000.
- ***March 12:*** More than 300 people die in 13 separate—but almost simultaneous—truck bombings at financial sites in Bombay, India.
- ***April 14:*** Iraqi intelligence agents attempt to kill former U.S. president George H. W. Bush in Kuwait.
- ***April 19:*** FBI and ATF agents end standoff at Branch Davidian complex outside Waco, Texas; 73 men, women, and children die when complex erupts in flames.
- ***April 24:*** IRA truck bomb explodes at Bishopsgate in London's financial district; two people killed, and damage is estimated at £350 million. Medieval church collapses. Liverpool Street station heavily damaged.
- ***May 1:*** Tamil Tigers assassinate Sri Lankan president Ranasinghe Premadasa.
- ***June 26:*** United States shells headquarters of Iraqi Intelligence Service over alleged attempt to assassinate former U.S. president George H. W. Bush.
- ***August 20:*** Oslo Accords between PLO and Israel signed, granting Palestinians right to self-rule in West Bank and Gaza strip under newly formed Palestinian Authority.
- ***September 9:*** Palestinian Liberation Organization press release "recognizes the right of the state of Israel to exist in peace and security."

- ***September 13:*** Formal White House signing of Oslo Accords by PLO chairman Yasser Arafat and Israeli prime minister Yitzhak Rabin.
- ***December 2:*** Pablo Escobar located and killed by Colombia security forces.
- ***December 15:*** Downing Street Declaration signed by prime ministers of Ireland and Great Britain, giving residents of Northern Ireland the right of political self-determination.

1994

- ***February 25:*** Jewish militant Baruch Goldstein opens fire in the Tomb of the Patriarchs on the West Bank during an Islamic prayer service. His barrage of gunfire kills 29 worshippers and wounds another 150. Angry worshippers then beat Goldstein to death.
- ***March 8:*** IRA fires four mortar shells at Heathrow Airport.
- ***March 10:*** IRA again fires four mortar shells at Heathrow Airport, causing evacuation of one terminal.
- ***March 12:*** IRA fires four mortar shells at Heathrow Airport yet again; no injuries reported.
- ***May 26:*** Chechen insurgents seize bus in Stavropol, Russia, taking 30 hostages.
- ***July 18:*** Bombs explode at Jewish cultural center in Buenos Aires, Argentina, killing 86 people. Hezbollah suspected.
- ***July 29:*** Chechen insurgents seize 19 hostages at airport in Mineralny Vody, Russia.
- ***August 1:*** Irish Republican Army declares cease-fire.
- ***September 23:*** FARC (Colombia) kidnaps U.S. citizen Thomas Hargrove.
- ***December 10:*** Russian troops invade Chechnya to reassert Moscow's authority.
- ***December 24:*** Algeria's Armed Islamic Group hijacks Air France jet en route to Paris. Three deaths result.

1995

- ***January 22:*** Bomb at Israeli military facility kills 19; Islamic Jihad claims responsibility.
- ***January 30:*** Car bomb explodes in Algiers shopping district, killing 42 and injuring more than 250.
- ***March 8:*** Two U.S. diplomats shot and killed in Karachi, Pakistan.
- ***March 20:*** Aum Shinrikyo members release sarin nerve gas in Tokyo subway system, killing 12 and injuring 5,000.

- ***April 19:*** Timothy McVeigh detonates truck bomb outside Alfred P. Murrah Federal Building in Oklahoma City, Oklahoma, killing 168 people.
- ***June 26:*** Members of Gama' a al-Islamiyya ("The Islamic Group") try to assassinate Egyptian president Hosni Mubarak during a visit to Addis Ababa, Ethiopia.
- ***August 21:*** Hamas bombs bus in Jerusalem, killing six people.
- ***November 4:*** Israeli prime minister Yitzhak Rabin assassinated by Yigal Amir, a militant Jew who believed Rabin had betrayed his people by agreeing to the Oslo Peace Accords with the PLO.
- ***November 13:*** Bombing at military facility in Riyadh, Saudi Arabia, by Islamic Movement of Change; one fatality.
- ***November 17:*** Members of the Islamic Group shoot and stab to death 58 foreign tourists and four Egyptians in Luxor, Egypt.
- ***November 19:*** Members of Gama' a al-Islamiyya ("The Islamic Group") detonate car bomb at Egyptian embassy in Pakistan, killing 16 people.

1996

- ***January 19:*** FARC rebels in Colombia kidnap U.S. citizen, demand $1 million ransom.
- ***January 31:*** Liberation Tigers of Tamil Eelam fighters attack Colombo Central Bank with truck bomb, killing 90 people and injuring some 1,400.
- ***February 9:*** IRA detonates bomb at South Quay light rail station in London's Docklands, causing two deaths.
- ***February 16:*** ELN rebels kidnap U.S. citizen in Colombia.
- ***February 26:*** Hamas suicide bomber blows up bus in Jerusalem, killing 26.
- ***March 4:*** Tel Aviv shopping center bombed; 20 deaths reported. Hamas and Palestinian Islamic Jihad claim credit.
- ***April 28:***Members of Gama' a al-Islamiyya ("The Islamic Group") attack international tourists at Europa Hotel in Cairo, killing 18.
- ***June 15:*** IRA truck bomb at Manchester, England, shopping center causes heavy property damage and personal injury, but no fatalities.
- ***June 25:*** Hezbollah truck bomb blows up Khobar Towers, a U.S. Air Force facility in Dhahran, Saudi Arabia, killing 20 and injuring 372 people.
- ***July 20:*** Basque terrorists bomb airport in Reus, Spain, popular with tourists, wounding 35.
- ***July 27:*** Pipe bomb explodes at the Olympic Games in Atlanta, causing two deaths.
- ***November 16:*** Apartment building in Kaspiysk, Dagestan (Russia), bombed, killing 69; Moscow blames Chechen insurgents.

- ***December 11:*** FARC kidnaps and executes U.S. citizen in Colombia.
- ***December 17:*** Members of Tupac Amaru Revolutionary Movement seize Japanese ambassador's residence in Lima, Peru, initially holding 700 hostages.

1997

- ***January 16:*** Two Atlanta abortion clinics bombed; incidents later connected to Olympic bomber Eric Robert Rudolph.
- ***February 23:*** Palestinian national opens fire at New York City's Empire State Building, killing one person before committing suicide.
- ***February 24:*** Colombian ELN operatives kidnap U.S. businessman, demand $2.5 million ransom.
- ***February 28:*** Gay/lesbian bar in Atlanta bombed; incident later connected to Olympic bomber Eric Robert Rudolph.
- ***March 7:*** Colombian FARC operatives kidnap two businessmen, demand $50,000.
- ***April 22:*** Peruvian police storm Japanese ambassador's residence, freeing hostages held since December. All terrorists killed in the raid.
- ***April 23:*** Bomb explodes in Armavir (Russia) railway station, killing three; Moscow blames Chechen insurgents.
- ***May 28:*** Bomb explodes in Pyatigorsk (Russia) railway station, killing two; Moscow blames Chechen insurgents.
- ***July 19:*** IRA declares cease-fire.
- ***September 4:*** Hamas bombing at Jerusalem mall kills 8 people.
- ***September 23:*** String of violent attacks by Islamic Salvation Front kill 85 people in Algeria.
- ***October 15:*** Liberation Tigers of Tamil Eelam detonate bomb at Colombo World Trade Center; 13 fatalities reported.
- ***October 23:*** ELN rebels kidnap two Organization of American States staff and Colombian human-rights worker.
- ***November 17:*** Islamic Group shoots tourists in Egypt's Valley of the Kings, killing 58.

1998

- ***January 5:*** A truck bomb enters the Temple of the Tooth (a Buddhist shrine) and detonates. Tamil Black Tigers blamed for the deaths of seven bystanders.
- ***January 29:*** Eric Robert Rudolph bombs abortion clinic in Birmingham, Alabama, killing a guard.

- ***March 5:*** Two bombs explode aboard bus in Maradana, Sri Lanka, killing 32 people. Liberation Tigers of Tamil Eelam blamed for attack.
- ***March 10:*** Real IRA bomb explodes at Royal Ulster Constabulary office in Armagh, Northern Ireland.
- ***March 21–23:*** Members of FARC kidnap 27 people, including Colombian election chief.
- ***April 10:*** Good Friday Agreement signed, ending conflict in Northern Ireland.
- ***April 20:*** Red Army Faction notifies Reuters that it is ending its struggle.
- ***May 14:*** Tamil Tiger ambushes Sri Lankan general Larry Wijeratne with a bomb, killing Wijeratne and two guards.
- ***June 24:*** Real IRA car bomb explodes in Newtownhamilton, Northern Ireland, injuring one person.
- ***August 7:*** U.S. embassies in Dar es Salaam, Tanzania, and Nairobi, Kenya, bombed, killing 224. Attack linked to al-Qaeda.
- ***August 15:*** Real IRA car bomb explodes in a shopping district of Omagh, Northern Ireland, killing 29 and injuring hundreds.
- ***August 20:*** U.S. forces bomb bin Laden training camp in Afghanistan and suspected chemical weapons lab in Sudan.
- ***October 18:*** Members of Colombia's National Liberation Army bomb oil pipeline, killing 71.
- ***October 19:*** Earth Liberation Front burns ski resort in Vail, Colorado.

1999

- ***February 14:*** Uganda's Allied Democratic Forces detonate pipe bomb at bar, killing five people.
- ***February 16:*** Five car bombs that detonate in Tashkent are attributed to the Islamic Movement of Uzbekistan.
- ***February 16:*** Greek embassy in Vienna seized by Kurds protesting arrest of Kurd leader Abdullah Ocalan.
- ***March 23:*** ELN kidnaps U.S. citizen in Boyaca, Colombia. Ransom demand is $400,000, but hostage released July 20 for $40,000.
- ***May 30:*** Colombia's ELN raids church in Ciudad Jardin, taking 160 hostages.
- ***June 27:*** Nigerian insurgents seize Shell oil platform, kidnap three foreign workers.
- ***July 29:*** Liberation Tigers of Tamil Eelam suicide bomber kills Neelan Thiruchelvam, a member of the Sri Lankan parliament and peace advocate, and two bystanders.

- ***August 23:*** Islamic Movement of Uzbekistan members kidnap eight Kyrgyz soldiers and four Japanese geologists while trying to establish a base in Kyrgyzstan.
- ***September 4:*** Bomb explodes at apartment building in Buniaksk, Dagestan (Russia), killing 62; Moscow blames Chechen insurgents.
- ***September 16:*** Bombs explode at apartment building in Moscow and Volgodonsk (Russia), killing 18; Moscow blames Chechen insurgents.
- ***September 23:*** Russian air force begins to bomb targets in Chechnya.
- ***December 14:*** "Millenium bomber" Ahmed Rassam arrested trying to bring carload of explosives across border from Canada to Washington state.
- ***December 18:*** Liberation Tigers of Tamil Eelam suicide bomber attempts to kill Sri Lankan president Chandrika Kumaratunga during a rally, but instead only wounds her. Ten bystanders were not so lucky and die in the attack.
- ***December 23:*** Colombia's People's Liberation Army kidnaps U.S. citizen.
- ***December 24:*** Indian airlines flight from Katmandu to New Delhi hijacked with 189 people aboard; all released unharmed on December 31.
- ***December 31:*** Earth Liberation Front burns research lab at Michigan State University, causing $400,000 in damages.

2000

- ***January 7:*** Liberation Tigers of Tamil Eelam bomb kills C. V. Gooneratne, Sri Lanka's industrial minister, and 20 others during veterans' parade.
- ***January 27:*** Basque ETA blamed for fire at Spanish car dealership.
- ***March 22:*** Second ("Al-Aqsa") Intifada begins in Palestinian territories.
- ***April 19:*** Abu Jihad, a top PLO member, assassinated in Tunis.
- ***May 18:*** Bomb explodes at Buddhist temple in Battilacoa, Sri Lanka, killing 23. Liberation Tigers of Tamil Eelam blamed.
- ***June 8:*** Greek November 17 organization assassinates British defense attaché in Athens.
- ***June 27:*** ELN militants in Colombia kidnap 5-year-old boy (a U.S. citizen) and his Colombian mother.
- ***August 12:*** Islamic Movement of Uzbekistan kidnaps four Americans in Kyrgyzstan; they soon escape.
- ***October 3:*** Liberation Tigers of Tamil Eelam bomb kills 21 in Muttur, Sri Lanka.
- ***October 12:*** Members of Colombia's Popular Liberation Army seize 10 employees of REPSOL, a Spanish energy company working in Ecuador. One

hostage, U.S. citizen Ronald Sander, is executed; others released February 23, 2001, for $13 million ransom.

- ***October 12:*** Al-Qaeda attacks USS *Cole,* moored outside Aden, Yemen. Two suicide bombers ram the ship with a small boat loaded with explosives. The resulting explosion killed 17 sailors.
- ***October 30:*** Basque ETA bomb kills Spanish judge and his driver and injures 60 bystanders.
- ***December 23:*** Bomb explodes near U.S. embassy in Manila; Moro Islamic Liberation Front suspected.
- ***December 24:*** Multiple Christian churches bombed in Indonesia, killing 15 and injuring 100; Jemaah Islamiah blamed.

2001

- ***January 14:*** Lashkar e-Tayyiba attacks Srinagar airport, killing five Indians.
- ***March 4:*** Real IRA car bomb explodes outside BBC TV offices in West London; one injury reported; Hamas bombs Netanya, Israel, killing three and wounding 65.
- ***March 15:*** Three Chechen insurgents hijack Russian flight from Istanbul to Moscow, divert plane to Saudi Arabia, where aircraft is stormed by security forces.
- ***March 30:*** Earth Liberation Front burns 30 sport utility vehicles at Eugene, Oregon, car dealership.
- ***May 21:*** Animal Liberation Front arson attack at University of Washington plant genetics research lab causes $5.6 million in damages.
- ***May 27:*** Abu Sayyaf members kidnap 20 people (17 Filipinos, 3 U.S. citizens) from resort in Palawan, Philippines.
- ***June 1:*** Hamas suicide bomber hits "Dolphinarium" dance club in Tel Aviv, killing 21 people and wounding 140.
- ***June 11:*** Oklahoma City bomber Timothy McVeigh executed by lethal injection.
- ***August 9:*** Hamas suicide bomber hits pizzeria in Jerusalem, leaving 15 people dead.
- ***August 27:*** PFLP general secretary Abu Ali Mustafa killed by Israeli rockets at his office. In a separate incident, PFLP gunmen shoot Meir Lixenberg, an Israeli driving in the West Bank.
- ***September 11:*** Al-Qaeda operatives hijack four airplanes, crashing two into the World Trade Center in New York and one into the Pentagon outside Washington, D.C. The fourth jet crashed in rural Pennsylvania when passengers try to overpower the terrorists.

- ***September 22:*** First anthrax-laced letter discovered in New York City.
- ***October 1:*** Suicide attack on legislatures in Kashmir and Jammu leaves 31 people dead. Jaish-e-Mohammed initially claims responsibility, but later recants.
- ***October 7:*** U.S. invades Afghanistan.
- ***November 17:*** PFLP kills Israeli tourism minister Rehavam Zeevi to avenge Mustafa's August 27 death.
- ***December 1–2:*** Hamas suicide bombers strike targets in Jerusalem and Haifa, killing two dozen people.
- ***December 13:*** Indian parliament attacked, leaving nine people dead. Government of India blames two militant Pakistani groups, Jaish-e-Mohammed and Lashkar e-Tayyiba.
- ***December 22:*** Richard Reid of Great Britain attempts to ignite explosives hidden in his shoes while aboard an American Airlines flight from Paris to Miami.

2002

- ***January 17:*** Al-Aqsa Martyrs' Brigade shooter kills six in Hadera, Israel.
- ***January 22:*** Five Indian security guards killed in drive-by shooting at U.S. consulate in Calcutta, India. Responsibility claimed by Lashkar-e-Tayyiba.
- ***January 23:*** *Wall Street Journal* reporter Daniel Pearl, a U.S. citizen, is kidnapped in Pakistan. Pakistani government blames Lashkar i Jhangvi, a militant Islamic group, while the "National Movement for the Restoration of Pakistani Sovereignty" claims credit. The National Movement is believed to be linked to the Jaish-e-Mohammed group. Pearl's body is found on May 16; he is believed to have been executed on January 29 or 30.
- ***January 27:*** Palestinian suicide terrorist Wafa Idriss attacks a shopping area in Jerusalem, killing herself and one bystander. Idriss is the first female Palestinian suicide bomber, and she quickly acquires heroic status within the Palestinian movement.
- ***February 16:*** PFLP suicide bomber kills four people at West Bank food court.
- ***February 20:*** FARC hijacks airplane. Members kidnap one passenger, Senator Jorge Gechen Turbay, and release everyone else.
- ***February 22:*** Sri Lankan government and Tamil LTTE announce cease-fire.
- ***March 7:*** PFLP suicide bomber wounds 10 people at West Bank supermarket.
- ***March 9:*** Al-Aqsa Martyrs' Brigade suicide bomber kills one person at Jerusalem restaurant.

- ***March 17:*** Islamabad, Pakistan, Protestant International Church damaged by grenades; five people, including two U.S. citizens, die in attack.
- ***March 20:*** Bomb explodes across from U.S. embassy in Lima, Peru, killing 10 people. Shining Path blamed for attack.
- ***March 27:*** Hamas suicide bomber attacks Passover worshippers at Park Hotel in Netanya, Israel, killing 22 people. Israel responds by launching Operation Defensive Shield.
- ***March 30:*** Hindu temple in Jamuu, Kashmir, bombed by Islamic Front; 10 fatalities.
- ***April 11:*** Nineteen tourists die when al-Qaeda detonates truck bomb outside a synagogue in Tunisia.
- ***April 12:*** Twenty-year-old Palestinian woman from al-Aqsa Martyrs' Brigade detonates explosives belt at a bus stop in Jerusalem, killing six people.
- ***May 8:*** Al-Qaeda blamed for truck bomb in Karachi, Pakistan, that killed 12 people, mostly French citizens.
- ***May 14:*** Indian army base in Kalchuk attacked, leaving 17 fatalities. Indian government blames Lashkar e-Tayyiba.
- ***June 7:*** Philippine military raids Abu Sayyaf camp to release hostages, but two die in the ensuing battle.
- ***June 14:*** Suicide car bombing outside U.S. consulate and Marriot Hotel in Karachi, Pakistan; 11 deaths.
- ***June 19:*** Hamas suicide bomber kills six people on bus in West Jerusalem.
- ***July 17:*** Two suicide bombers attack bus station in Tel Aviv, killing five persons.
- ***July 31:*** Hamas bomb detonates at Hebrew University in Jerusalem, killing nine.
- ***August 4:*** Hamas suicide bomber kills nine passengers on bus in Safed, Israel.
- ***August 6:*** Hindu pilgrims attacked by Lashkar-e-Tayyiba in Kashmir, killing nine.
- ***September 19:*** Hamas suicide bomber kills six people aboard bus in Tel Aviv.
- ***October 6:*** Suicide bomber attacks French tanker *Limburg* near Yemen. One person dies in this attack that is linked to al-Qaeda.
- ***October 12:*** Jemaah Islamiah bombs two nightclubs in Bali, Indonesia, killing 202 people, predominantly tourists. A third bomb explodes outside the U.S. consultate causing minor injuries.
- ***October 23:*** About 40 Chechen insurgents seize the Dubrovka Theatre in Moscow, taking the audience and performers (about 700 people in all) hostage

and demanding that Russian troops withdraw from Chechnya. After 58 hours police pump an anesthetic gas into the building and execute the unconscious terrorists. Most of the 130 victims died from the gas, not the terrorists.

- ***October 28:*** Al-Zarqawi Network assassinates U.S. diplomat Laurence Foley in Jordan.
- ***November 21:*** Hamas suicide bomber kills 11 persons on bus in Jerusalem.
- ***November 24:*** Lashkare-e-Tayyiba bombs two temples in Kashmir, killing 13.
- ***November 28:*** Al-Qaeda bombs hotel in Mombasa, Kenya; 15 people die.
- ***December 26:*** Moro Islamic Liberation Front attacks bus carrying Filipino workers for Canadian company, killing 13 people.
- ***December 27:*** Truck bomb destroys headquarters of Russia-backed government in Grozny, Chechnya, and kills 80 people.

2003

- ***January 5:*** Twenty-two people die from Al-Aqsa Martyrs' Brigade suicide-bomber attack on Tel Aviv bus.
- ***March 4:*** Moro Islamic Liberation Front blamed for bombing at Davao airport and killing 21 people.
- ***March 5:*** Suicide bomber attacks bus in Haifa, Israel, killing 15 people.
- ***March 20:*** U.S. launches war in Iraq.
- ***March 29:*** Dilnoza Holmuradova, a 19-year-old Uzbek female, launches suicide attack at Chorsu Market in Tashkent, Uzbekistan, killing 47.
- ***April 2:*** Moro Islamic Liberation Front blamed for bombing at Davao ferry terminal, killing 16 people.
- ***May 5:*** FARC executes 10 hostages in Colombia to prevent government rescue. Dead included former Colombian minister of defense Gilberto Echeverri Mejia.
- ***May 12:*** Al-Qaeda truck bombs blow up three housing blocs for foreigners in Riyadh, Saudi Arabia, killing 30 people; truck bomb rocks Chechen government facilities in Znamenskoye, killing 59 people; Chechen woman detonates explosive belt at a prayer meeting in Chechnya, killing 14 people, but intended target, Chechen president Akhmed Kadyrov, survives.
- ***May 16:*** Suicide bombings in Casablanca, Morocco, target hotel, nightclub, restaurant, and Jewish community center. Recorded casualties were 60 dead and 101 injured. Al-Qaeda suspected.
- ***May 20:*** Three people killed and 50 injured when female suicide bomber detonates her explosives at shopping mall in Afula, Israel. Both Al-Aqsa Martyrs' Brigade and Islamic Jihad claim responsibility.

- ***June 9:*** Shining Path rebels in Peru kidnap 68 employees of Argeninean firm Techint. All hostages freed within two days, reportedly because of ransom payment.
- ***June 11:*** Hamas suicide bombing on bus in Jerusalem kills 17.
- ***July 6:*** Two female Chechen suicide bombers attack a concert in Moscow, killing 14.
- ***July 10:*** Female Chechen suicide bomber detained at a restaurant on Tverskaya Street, a popular shopping district in Moscow. A bomb disposal expert is killed while trying to disarm the device; Sendero Luminosa kills two soldiers in Peru.
- ***August 1:*** Truck bomb kills 50 at military hospital in Mozdok, North Ossetia, near Chechnya; Earth Liberation Front claims credit for arson attack at San Diego housing complex under construction; damage estimated at $50 million.
- ***August 5:*** Jemaah Islamiah bombs J. W. Marriott hotel in Jakarta, Indonesia, killing 12 people.
- ***August 7:*** Tawhid wal Jihad detonates truck bomb outside Jordanian embassy in Iraq, killing 19.
- ***August 19:*** The Canal Hotel in Baghdad, used as UN headquarters in Iraq, is bombed, killing 23 people, including the UN special envoy for Iraq, Sergio Vieira de Mello; Hamas and Hezbollah claim responsibility for suicide bomber aboard Jerusalem bus that killed 20.
- ***September 9:*** Hamas suspected in suicide bombings in Tel Aviv and Jerusalem, 13 deaths.
- ***September 22:*** Second car bomb at UN headquarters in Baghdad; one person killed.
- ***October 4:*** Hezbollah suicide bomber attacks Haifa restaurant, leaving 19 dead.
- ***October 15:*** Insurgents attack U.S. diplomatic convoy in Gaza, killing three Americans.
- ***October 26:*** Iraqi irregular forces attack al-Rashid hotel in Baghdad where U.S. deputy secretary of defense Paul D. Wolfowitz is staying.
- ***October 27:*** Tawhid wal Jihad detonates bombs at five Baghdad police stations and the Red Cross headquarters, killing 35 people.
- ***November 8:*** Al-Qaeda bombs an additional housing complex in Riyadh, Saudi Arabia, killing 17 people.
- ***November 12:*** Suicide bomber kills more than 30 people at base used by Italian paramilitary police in Nasiriya, Iraq.

- ***November 15:*** Suicide bombers attack two synagogues in Istanbul, Turkey, killing 20; FARC suspected of launching grenades into two Bogotá bars popular with Americans. One person dead, 72 wounded.
- ***November 20:*** Suicide bombers attack British consulate and HSBC Bank in Istanbul, leaving 41 dead and 555 wounded.
- ***December 5:*** Russian train bombed near Stavropol, killing 42 people. Moscow blames Chechens.
- ***December 9:*** Suicide bombing outside Moscow's National Hotel kills six people.
- ***December 25:*** Two attempts to assassinate Pakistani president General Pervez Musharraf blamed on Jaish-e-Mohammed; Popular Front for the Liberation of Palestine suicide bomber kills four people at bus top in Petah Tikva, Israel.

2004

- ***January 18:*** Tawhid wal Jihad detonates car bomb outside Green Zone gate in Iraq, killing 31.
- ***January 28:*** Car bomb kills four people outside Shaheen Hotel, Baghdad.
- ***February 6:*** Chechen suicide bomber detonates her bomb at a Moscow subway station, killing herself and 41 commuters.
- ***February 10–11:*** Car bombs at Iraqi police and recruiting stations kill 100 people.
- ***February 27:*** Abu Sayyaf bombs ferry in Manila Bay, killing more than 130 passengers.
- ***March 2:*** Suicide bombers kill more than 500 Shia worshippers at mosques in Iraq; Suicide bombers kill 43 Shia worshippers at mosques in Pakistan.
- ***March 11:*** Al-Qaeda bombs four commuter trains in Madrid, Spain, killing 191 people.
- ***April 21:*** Seventy-four people killed by multiple bombings in Basra, Iraq.
- ***May 6:*** Suicide bomber explodes outside U.S. headquarters in Baghdad.
- ***May 9:*** Chechen president Akhmed Kadyrov assassinated.
- ***May 18:*** Abdel-Zahraa Othman, president of the Iraqi Governing Council, killed by car bomb.
- ***June 6:*** Dual car bombs kill nine people outside U.S. Army installation in Baghdad.
- ***June 13:*** Convoy of Western workers in Baghdad hit by car bomb, killing 13.

- ***June 21:*** Algeria's Salafist insurgents bomb power-generating facility, taking it off-line for months.
- ***June 24:*** Tawhid wal Jihad takes credit for multiple bombings at Iraqi government and police offices, killing 100 people.
- ***July 30:*** Suicide bombers attack U.S. embassy, Israeli embassy, and Uzbekistan's prosecutor-general's office, all in Tashkent. Islamic Jihad Group claims responsibility.
- ***August 21:*** Chechen insurgents raid Russian facility in Grozny, killing 22.
- ***August 24:*** Two Russian airliners simultaneously explode in flight, killing 90 passengers and crew. Two Chechen "black widows" reportedly had boarded the aircraft at the last moment.
- ***August 29:*** Moscow-backed candidate Alu Alkhanov wins presidential election in Chechnya.
- ***August 31:*** Chechen suicide bomber detonates her explosives outside Moscow's Rizhskaya metro station, killing 10 other people.
- ***September 1–3:*** Chechen terrorists seize a public school in Beslan, North Ossetia, holding 1,100 students, teachers, and parents hostage. When Russian troops storm the building on September 3, the operation goes horribly wrong and the school explodes into flames. At least 300 persons die in the assault, half of them children.
- ***September 9:*** Bomb explodes outside Australia's embassy in Jakarta, Indonesia, killing 11 people. Jemaah Islamiah is blamed for attack.
- ***October 7:*** Home-grown terrorists in Egypt kill 34 tourists in Taba and Nuweiba.
- ***November 11:*** PLO Chairman Yasser Arafat dies. He is succeeded by Mahmoud Abbas.
- ***December 21:*** Ansar al-Islam bombs U.S. military dining hall in Mosul, Iraq, killing 24.

2005

- ***January 13:*** Truck bomb kills two suicide bombers and six others at Karni Crossing Point, Israel. Hamas and al-Aqsa jointly claim credit.
- ***March 8:*** Former Chechen president Aslan Maskhadov dies during shoot-out with Russian forces.
- ***April 30:*** Two young Egyptian women open fire on a tourist bus in Cairo, then kill themselves.
- ***May:*** Tawhid wal Jihad kills more than 800 people in monthlong spree.
- ***July 7:*** Subway bombings in London Underground and aboard a city bus kill more than 50 commuters.

- ***July 10:*** Bomb explodes in Cesme, a popular tourist resort in Turkey. Kurdish separatist group suspected.
- ***July 12:*** Hezbollah suicide bomber kills five people shopping in Netanya, Israel.
- ***July 17:*** Tourist bus bombed on Turkish coast, killing five people. Kurdish separatist group suspected.
- ***July 21:*** Bombs explode in three more London Underground stations; no deaths, due to poorly constructed explosive devices.
- ***July 23:*** Car bombs kills 88 people around tourist sites in Egypt.
- ***July 28:*** Irish Republic Army formally announces end to armed struggle, orders members to relinquish their weapons.
- ***August 11:*** Israeli army deserter Eden Natan Zada opens fire on bus in northern Israel, killing six people before he was beaten to death by other passengers.
- ***September 12:*** Israel withdraws from Gaza Strip, handing control to the Palestinian Authority.
- ***September 28:*** Female suicide bomber detonates bomb at Iraqi miliary recruiting center.
- ***October 1:*** Suicide bombings in retail district of Bali, Indonesia, blamed on Jemaah Islamiah. Twenty-three deaths confirmed, including three bombers.
- ***October 16:*** Al-Aqsa Martyrs' Brigade kills three Israelis during a drive-by shooting at the Gush Etzion Crossing Point, Israel.
- ***November 9:*** Three hotels in Amman, Jordan, attacked by suicide bombers, killing 60 people. Abu Musab Zarqawi takes credit.

2006

- ***January 4:*** Insurgent attacks kill 50 people in Iraq, including 42 from a suicide bombing of a Shia funeral in Muqdadiyah.
- ***January 5:*** Maoist insurgents kill three police officers in Nepal.
- ***February 22:*** Al-Askari mosque in Samarra, Iraq, bombed. The mosque is one of Shia Islam's holiest sites and triggers Shia versus Sunni violence. No injuries are reported, but the building suffers major damage, including destruction of its golden dome. Al-Qaeda in Iraq leader Abu Musab al-Zarqawi, a Sunni Muslim, is blamed.
- ***April 17:*** Palestinian suicide bomber kills 11 people in Tel Aviv.
- ***June 7:*** Al-Qaeda in Iraq leader Abu Musab al-Zarqawi killed in U.S. airstrike.
- ***June 15:*** Tamil LTTE mine destroys passenger bus, killing 68.

- ***July 10:*** Chechen warlord Shamil Basayev killed while transporting bomb in Ingushetia.
- ***July 11:*** Commuter trains in Mumbai, India, bombed, killing 200.
- ***August 10:*** British government announces arrests in major al-Qaeda plot to bomb multiple airplanes leaving London for the United States.
- ***August 14:*** UN implements cease-fire between Hezbollah and Israel; 800 fatalities during conflict. UN dispatches 15,000 peacekeepers to southern Lebanon.
- ***August 31***: Thai insurgents simultaneously bomb 20 banks in Yala Province.
- ***September 8:*** Taliban car bomb explodes outside U.S. Embassy in Kabul, at least 10 deaths.
- ***September 13:*** Algeria's Salafist Group for Preaching and Combat (GSPC) and al-Qaeda merge, forming Qaedat al-Jihad in the Arab Maghreb Countries.
- ***October 12:*** Shining Path leader Abimael Guzmán sentenced to life in prison in Peru.
- ***October 16:*** Tamil Tiger truck bomb kills 102 Sri Lankan naval personnel.
- ***October 30:*** Pakistan destroys suspected al-Qaeda training facility near Afghan border, killing 80 people. In response, Taliban forces begin assassinating.
- ***November 23:*** Series of car bombs and explosions kills more than 200 people in Iraq; deadliest day since Iraq war began in 2003.
- ***December 31:*** Eight bombs detonate in Bangkok, Thailand.

2007

- ***January 2:*** Sri Lanka bombs suspected LTTE base in fishing village, killing 14.
- ***January 12:*** Rocket launched at U.S. Embassy in Athens. November 17 offshoot takes credit.
- ***January 16:*** Pakistani government carries out air strike on Islamist militant camp in South Waziristan, prompting wave of retaliatory suicide attacks.
- ***January 17:*** Philippine Army kills Abu Sayyaf leader Abu Sulaiman.
- ***January 23:*** Taliban suicide bomber attacks Camp Salerno, Afghanistan, killing 10 people.
- ***January 28:*** Some 50 fighters from the Movement for the Emancipation of the Niger Delta attack police station in Port Harcourt, releasing 125 prisoners.
- ***January 31:*** U.K. police disrupt plot to kidnap and behead a U.K. Muslim soldier.
- ***February 3:*** Truck bomb in Baghdad kills more than 135 people, injures another 225.

- ***February 12:*** Italy arrests 15 people accused of being active members of Red Brigades; German court orders release of Red Army Faction member Brigitte Mohnhaupt, after 24 years in jail.
- ***February 13:*** Seven car bombs detonate near Algerian police stations, killing six people.
- ***February 15:*** Trial begins for suspects in 2004 Madrid train bombing.
- ***February 18:*** Thai insurgents explode 28 bombs, burn two schools.
- ***February 26:*** Bomb explodes at Iraq's Ministry of Public Works, killing five and injuring Vice President Adil Abdul-Mahdi.
- ***February 27:*** Taliban suicide bomber attacks Bagram Air Base, Afghanistan, during visit by U.S. Vice-President Dick Cheney, killing 23 people.
- ***March 9:*** Nepalese Maoist rebels receive cabinet representation, agree to return seized property.
- ***March 10:*** More than 10,000 demonstrators take to the streets of Madrid to protest planned release of Basque separatist José Ignacio de Juana Chaos after serving 20 years for 25 murders.
- ***March 11:*** 30,000 people flee as fighting between Sri Lankan government troops and Tamil Tiger separatists escalates.

Glossary

air marshal A member of the U.S. Federal Air Marshal Service, founded in 1968. Air marshals are armed, undercover security guards who ride commercial aircraft to prevent hijackings or other in-flight crimes.

amnesty A government offer of forgiveness for criminals or terrorists who agree to surrender their weapons and provide intelligence; in return, no criminal charges will be filed.

anarchism A political philosophy advocating societies without rules or rulers because power inevitably corrupts; some anarchists believe violence is justified to remove a corrupt leader.

anarchy The complete lack of government and law.

anthrax A biological agent that is often fatal when inhaled. Envelopes laced with anthrax were mailed to U.S. senators and journalists in 2001. Two postal workers and three unrelated people died as a result. The perpetrator remains unknown.

antiterrorism Steps taken to cope with the aftermath of a terrorist attack, such as contingency plans, disaster preparedness, stockpiled medical supplies, and standard emergency communications procedures.

Apocalypse Ultimate, world-ending battle between good and evil.

Armageddon Ultimate, world-ending battle between good and evil.

assassination The premeditated murder of a political leader, such as President John F. Kennedy or President Abraham Lincoln, or public figure, such as John Lennon.

asymmetric warfare Battles waged between groups of unequal size, such as a national army versus a small guerrilla force. The strategies and weapons of large standing armies are usually overkill against small insurgencies.

ATF Bureau of Alcohol, Tobacco, and Firearms (now: Bureau of Alcohol, Tobacco, Firearms, and Explosives).

bioterrorism Attacks using biological agents, such as diseases (such as anthrax) or poisons (such as ricin).

Branch Davidians A religious cult based outside Waco, Texas. Led by David Koresh, members refused to surrender under federal laws on weapons. After a stand-off against agents from the Bureau of Alcohol, Tobacco, and Firearms, the group burned their compound and committed mass suicide on April 19, 1993.

caliphate An Islamic state ruled by Islamic law (sharia).

Camp David accords A 1978 peace agreement between Egyptian president Anwar Sadat and Israeli prime minister Menachem Begin. U.S. president Jimmy Carter sponsored the negotiations at the Camp David presidential retreat.

cartel Group of related companies or producers working together to regulate prices, such as the Organization of Petroleum Exporting Countries (OPEC).

cell Small, self-contained terrorist wing; if one cell is destroyed, the larger organization can continue its operations. Cells rarely have more than a dozen members.

chatter Overheard conversations between suspected terrorists; analysts watch for a sudden increase in chatter as a predictor of an imminent terrorist attack.

colonialism A political philosophy popular from the 18th to the early 20th century whereby European countries took control over lands and civilizations they believed to be less sophisticated. The colonial power believed it could better run the colony's politics, economics, and society than could the native people.

commandos Elite, special military forces used for dangerous tasks, such as hostage rescues or terrorist attacks. Can be applied to formal groups (such as the Green Berets or Navy Seals) or to terrorist groups themselves.

counterinsurgency Procedures to prevent organized groups from overthrowing a government.

counterterrorism Steps taken to prevent a terrorist attack, such as intelligence gathering, immigration controls, and preventive strikes on terrorist bases.

court martial A military court that judges military members based on military law, such as the U.S. Uniform Code of Military Justice.

cyberterrorism Terrorism involving computer systems, usually to coordinate activities and research potential targets. Also used to describe terrorist attacks that target computer systems, such as those that control airplane traffic or power grids.

disappeared People who have simply vanished after being taken into government custody; usually they are questioned, tortured, and executed and their bodies dumped in mass graves. Governments refuse to acknowledge the deaths.

Glossary

enemy combatant A member of the military of an enemy state during wartime.

Entebbe City in Uganda. Airport became famous in 1976 when five members of the Popular Front for Liberation of Palestine skyjacked an Air France flight departing Israel. Israeli commandos stormed the plane on the tarmac, killing all the terrorists. The raid became the plot of two movies.

Euroterrorism Blanket term for left-wing groups active in Western Europe, particularly in the 1970s and 1980s, such as the Red Army Faction (Germany), Red Brigades (Italy), and Action Direct (France).

extradition The legal transfer of a criminal suspect from the custody of one country, where they were apprehended, to the country where he or she faces charges.

fatwa A legal opinion based on Islamic law and endorsed by a Muslim cleric, such as Osama bin Laden's declaration of war on the United States.

fedayeen An Arab commando, willing to die for a cause.

fundamentalism The practice of closely following the sacred written texts.

Gaza Strip A sliver of land between Egypt and Israel. Israel won control over the area in the 1967 Six-Day War, but its largely Palestinian residents resisted Israeli rule. The area was handed over to the Palestine Authority in 1994.

Geneva Conventions A series of international agreements dating to 1859 listing the rights of prisoners of war and specifying humane treatment for POWs.

Good Friday Agreement The 1998 political settlement granting self-rule to Northern Ireland.

Guantánamo Bay A U.S. naval facility on Cuban soil. Prisoners captured during the U.S. war in Afghanistan were transferred to Guantánamo Bay to await trial.

guerrilla warfare Military actions conducted by irregular armed forces, usually against the established armies of a country. Guerrillas prefer quick, surreptitious actions rather than open warfare.

habeas corpus The right of a citizen to be charged with specific crimes as a guarantee against open-ended detention.

hate crimes Illegal actions targeting a specific group of people, such as African Americans, Jews, or homosexuals.

hijack To seize control of a commercial aircraft and use passengers as bargaining chips. Prior to September 11, 2001, hijackers rarely killed more than one or two passengers, preferring to trade their hostages for jailed comrades.

infrastructure The systems underpinning a society, such as electricity, water, health care, transportation, and communications.

insurgency A small, organized group actively working to overthrow a government.

intifada Arabic for *uprising.* Describes two waves of conflict between Palestinian youth and Israeli Defense Forces in the West Bank and Gaza Strip. The First Intifada ran from 1987 to 1993. The Second (Al-Aqsa) Intifada began in March 2000.

Islam Religion based on the teachings of the prophet Muhammad.

Islamism A movement that seeks to implement Islamic principles and law (Sharia) in politics as well as in religious life.

jihad Armed struggle to expand influence of Islam.

narcoterrorism Terrorism used to facilitate the illegal drug trade, such as forcing governments to tolerate heroin or cocaine trafficking.

nation A group of people with a shared past and common sense of destiny. Language, ethnicity, or religion may be one of the strands binding the people together. Nations may or may not have their own state.

nationalism A political philosophy arguing that nations (recognized groups of people with common characteristics) should have their own countries.

neo-Nazis Admirers of Adolf Hitler and his National Socialist (Nazi) party active in Germany in the 1930s and 1940s. Although the Nazi party has been banned in Germany, there are sympathizers in the United States who relate to the philosophy of white racial supremacy.

nihilism A Russian philosophy popular in the 1850s and 1860s. Nihilists believed in nothing (nil), a viewpoint that let them disregard conventional laws and social practices.

Occupied Territories Lands captured by Israel in the 1967 Six-Day War but claimed by neighboring Arab countries; includes the Gaza Strip, West Bank, and Golan Heights.

Operation Enduring Freedom The U.S.-led invasion of Afghanistan in October 2001 that removed the hard-line Islamic Taliban regime.

Operation Iraqi Freedom The U.S.-led invasion of Iraq in 2003 that removed Saddam Hussein from power.

Oslo Accords A 1993 agreement between the PLO and Israel that granted Palestinians the right to self-rule in the West Bank and Gaza Strip under the newly formed Palestinian Authority.

pacifism A political philosophy that opposes the use of war and violence to solve problems.

Palestine Territory between the Jordan River and the Mediterranean Sea, claimed simultaneously as a homeland by the Palestinians, an Arab people, and Jews. Great Britain controlled the area from 1917 to 1947, at which time the UN Special Committee on Palestine decided to divide the area into two separate states, one Arab and one Jewish.

Palestinian Authority The governing body used by Palestinians to control the West Bank and Gaza Strip. Created as a result of the 1993 Oslo Accords, the

PA has a president, prime minister, police force, and 88-member assembly, the Palestinian Legislative Council.

paramilitary Nonofficial but often well-trained military units, such as insurgents or death squads, that challenge official militaries or that governments use to repress the population secretly.

plastic explosives A moldable, claylike explosive that passes through metal detectors or other bomb-detection devices. Also known as Semtex or C4, plastic explosives were hidden in a tape recorder aboard Pan Am flight 103.

policy A plan of action to achieve a specific goal; usually refers to a government procedure.

populism A political movement that put the priorities of ordinary people ahead of the interests of the wealthy or influential. The philosophy has its origins in 19th-century Russia.

postcolonial The transition period from the end of colonial rule to independent statehood, usually considered to be 1945–75.

Protocols of the Elders of Zion A fraudulent book claiming that Jews have a secret plan to dominate the world. Since the book first appeared, numerous groups have used it to justify attacks on Jews and Jewish communities. The text first appeared in 1903 when it was serialized in a Russian newspaper. The text remains popular among anti-Jewish groups, right-wing extremists, and conspiracy theorists.

ricin Deadly poison made from castor beans.

sarin Deadly nerve gas that suffocates its victims by paralyzing their respiratory system; used in the 1995 Aum Shinrikyo attack in Tokyo.

secular Not related to religion. The secular world exists outside of churches, mosques, or synagogues.

separatist A person or group of people wanting to redraw state boundaries so they can rule themselves.

shahid Arabic term meaning *martyr* and used to describe suicide bombers.

shuhada plural of *shahid.*

Shia/Shiite One of the two major branches of Islam, popular with Iran and Hezbollah; Shia Islam split from Sunni Islam in the seventh century and takes a more fundamentalist approach to worship.

skinhead A U.S. and British movement that embraces neo-Nazi ideology. Members tend to be young, white males, who shave their heads and dress in blue jeans and boots.

skyjacking Hijacking aboard an aircraft.

sovereignty A legal concept meaning supreme authority; sovereign countries do not take orders from other countries or groups.

state A political organization with people, territory, government, and international recognition. States may have one dominant ethnic group (for instance, Japan) or a mix of many ethnic groups (as in the United States or Australia).

state-sponsored terrorism The practice of formal governments hiring informal, nonstate groups to carry out acts of terror to further specific foreign policy goals. The United States classifies five countries as state sponsors of terrorism: Cuba, Iran, North Korea, Sudan, and Syria. Iraq was listed as a state sponsor of terrorism prior to the removal of Saddam Hussein.

state terrorism A brutal control method that governments use to repress their own citizens, as practiced in the Soviet Union and Nazi Germany.

Stockholm syndrome A psychological condition whereby hostages begin to sympathize with their captors and may even join their cause.

suicide bombing Attacks in which individuals detonate explosives strapped to their bodies or crash trucks or other vehicles laden with explosives into a predetermined target. Some bombers appear to volunteer for the task, while others may be brainwashed.

Sunni The oldest and largest branch of Islam. Unlike Shia Islam, the Sunni branch offers a broader interpretation of religion and daily life.

threat matrix A daily summary of the current threats to national security prepared exclusively for the president of the United States. Other countries may have similar reports, but they probably are to be top secret.

tribunal A judicial body usually outside the normal civil court system.

Truth Commission A panel formed to investigate controversial, usually violent episodes in a country's past as a form of national healing and reconciliation.

The Turner Diaries Required reading for members of the U.S. militia/white supremacist movement. Written by William Pearce (using the pen name Andrew MacDonald) the book tells of Jewish efforts to take over the world and a resulting nuclear apocalypse. The characters use a truck bomb to blow up the FBI headquarters.

unlawful combatant A militant who does not follow the normal tactics of warfare, such as by attacking civilian targets.

weapons of mass destruction Armaments designed to destroy widespread targets, such as entire towns. Weapons may be biological, chemical, radiological, or nuclear. The United States invaded Iraq in 2003 to stop the alleged production of WMD.

West Bank Land between the west bank of the Jordan River and Israel; captured by Israel from Jordan in the 1967 Six-Day War. Palestinians claim it should be part of their future state.

white supremacy A philosophy proposing that Europeans, specifically Aryans, are a superior race and should dominate in politics, economics, and society in general. Followers include the Aryan nations and the Ku Klux Klan.

zero-sum game A political struggle where a gain for one side is a loss for the other. Zero-sum games have only winners and losers; compromise is considered impossible.

Zionism A political movement from the early 20th century seeking to establish a Jewish homeland in the Palestinian territories.

Index

Page numbers in **boldface** indicate major treatment of a subject. Page numbers followed by *f* indicate figures. Page numbers followed by *b* indicate biographical entries. Page numbers followed by *c* indicate chronology entries. Page numbers followed by *g* indicate glossary entries.

I